Developments in Learning and Assessment

edited by

Patricia Murphy and Bob Moon
at the Open University

Hodder & Stoughton
LONDON SYDNEY AUCKLAND TORONTO
in association with the Open University

This reader is one part of an Open University integrated teaching system and the selection is therefore related to other material available to students. It is designed to evoke the critical understanding of students. Opinions expressed in it are not necessarily those of the course team or of the University.

ISBN 0 340 51437 X

First published in Great Britain 1989

Selection and editorial material copyright © The Open University 1989

Typeset by Wearside Tradespools, Fulwell, Sunderland
Printed in Great Britain for Hodder and Stoughton Educational, a division of Hodder and Stoughton Ltd, Mill Road,
Dunton Green, Sevenoaks, Kent
by Richard Clay Ltd, Bungay, Suffolk

Contents

List of Contributors

ERNST von GLASERSFELD, University of Georgia.

ERIC LUNZER, School of Education, University of Nottingham.

JEROME BRUNER, George Herbert Mead University Professor at the New School for Social Research in New York.

PAULO FREIRE, Visiting Professor, Harvard University.

HERMAIN SINCLAIR, University of Geneva.

THOMAS ANDRE, Department of Psychology, Iowa State University.

DOUGLAS BARNES, Reader in Education, School of Education, University of Leeds.

ALAN BISHOP, Department of Education, University of Cambridge.

CLAIRE WOODS, Superintendent of Studies for the Education Department of South Australia.

SUSAN CAREY, Massachusetts Institute of Technology.

CELIA HOYLES, Professor of Mathematics Education, Institute of Education, London.

MADELEINE ATKINS, University of Newcastle-upon-Tyne.

PAM CZERNIEWSKA, School of Education, The Open University.

ROBERT STERNBERG, University of Yale.

GRAHAM RICHARDS, Dept. of Psychology, North-East London Polytechnic.

GEORGE TOLLEY, Manpower Services Commission.

GLENN FUTCHER, Forum Language Centre, Nicosia, Cyprus.

DESMOND NUTTALL, Inner London Education Authority, Research and Statistics Branch.

BRENDA DENVIR, Freelance writer.

PATRICIA BROADFOOT, Bristol University.

MARY JAMES, School of Education, The Open University.

SUSAN McMEEKING, The Open University.

BARRY STIERER, University of Bristol.

MARGARET BROWN, Kings College, London.

JANET WHITE, National Foundation for Education Research, Slough.

PATRICIA MURPHY, School of Education, The Open University.

MIKE WATTS, Roehampton Institute.

DI BENTLEY, Science Inspector for Inner London Education Authority.

EMANUEL MASON, University of Kentucky.

PATRICIA CEGELKA, San Diego State University.

RENA LEWIS, San Diego State University.

SUZANNE HENRY, International Business Machines, Inc., Lexington, Kentucky.

JILL LARKIN, Carnegie Mellan University, Pennsylvania.

FRED DANNER, University of Kentucky.

VALERIA WALKERDINE, Birmingham Polytechnic.

JAMES BRITTON, Emeritus Professor of Education, University of London.

ARTHUR APPLEBEE, Professor of Education, State University of New York.

NEVILLE BENNETT, Department of Education, University of Lancaster.

Acknowledgements

The publishers would like to thank the following for permission to reproduce material in this volume:

Ablex Publishing Corporation, New Jersey for 'Second Game: A School's-Eye View of Intelligence' by Sternberg, R. from Langer, J. A. (ed.) *Language Literacy and Culture; Issues of Society and Schooling* (1987); Academic Press Inc. for extracts from 'Problem Solving and Education' by André, T. and 'Cognitive Development: Learning and the Mechanisms of Change' by Lunzer, E. both from Phye, G. and André, T. (eds) *Cognitive Classroom Learning: Understanding, Thinking and Problem Solving* (1986); The American Psychological Association for 'Cognitive Science and Science Education' by Carey, S. from *American Psychologist* Vol. 41, No. 10, 1986; Bergin & Garvey Publishers Inc. and Macmillan London and Basingstoke for extracts from *The Politics of Education* by Freire, P. (1985); The British Psychological Society for 'Getting the Intelligence Controversy Knotted' by Richards, G. from *Bulletin of the British Psychological Society* Vol. 37, 1989; Carfax Publishing Company for 'Changing Perspectives on Teaching – Learning Processes in the Post-Era by Bennett, N. from *Oxford Review of Education* Vol. 13, No. 1, 1987 and 'Constructivism in the Classroom: Enabling Conceptual Change by Words and Deeds' by Watts, M. and Bentley, D. from *British Educational Research Journal* Vol. 13, No. 2, 1987; Elsevier Science Publishers for 'Three Approaches to Teaching and Learning in Education' by Mason, E. J., Cegelka, P., Lewis, R., Henry S., Larkin, J. H. and Donner, F. from *Instructional Science* Vol. 12, 1983; Harvard Educational Press for 'The Transactional Self' by Bruner, J. S. from *Actual Minds, Possible Worlds* (1986); Heinemann Educational Books for 'The Enterprise We Are Part Of' by Applebee, A., 'Knowledge as Action' by Barnes, D. and 'Places for Evolving Autobiography: English Classes at Work in the Curriculum' by Woods, C. all from Lightfoot, M. and Martin, M. (eds) *The Word for Teaching is Learning* (1988); Her Majesty's Stationery Office London for 'Records of Achievement: Report of the National Evaluation of Pilot Schemes' PRAISE, 1988; Instituto Superior de Psicologia Aplicada for 'The Validity of Assessments' by Nuttall, D. from *European Journal of Psychology of Education* Vol. 2, No. 2, 1987 (Special Issue ed. D. Satterly); Laurence Erlbaum Associates Inc. for Learning the Interactive Re-creation of Knowledge' in Stelle, L. (ed.) *Proceedings of the International Conference of Mathematical Education*, Hungary (1988) and for 'Learning As A Constructive Activity' by Von Glasersfeld, E. from Janner, C. (ed.) *Problems of Representation in Teaching & Learning of Mathematics* (1987); MCB University Press Ltd for 'Learning and Assessment' by G. Tolley, Vol. 35, No. 3, 1987 and 'Measurement or Assessment: A Fundamental Dichotomy and Its Educational Implications' by Futcher, G. Vol. 37, No. 2, 1987 both from *Education Today*; Methuen London and New York for 'Developmental Psychology and the Child-Centred Pedagogy' by Walkerdine, V. from Henriques, J., Holloway, W., Unwin, C., Venn, C. and Walkerdine, V. (eds) *Changing the Subject: Psychology, Social Regulation and Subjectivity* (1984); National Association for the Teaching of English (NATE Publications) for 'Vygotsky's Contribution to Pedagogical Theory' by Britton, J., 1987 and 'Reading – Caught or Taught? Some Issues Involved in Changed Approaches to the Teaching of Reading' by Whitehead, M. both from *English in Education* Vol. 21, No. 2, 1987; The Open University for 'Graded Assessment Projects' by Brown, M. (1989), 'National Writing Projects' by Czerniewska, P. (1989), 'Assessment Purposes and Learning' by Denvir, B. (1989), 'Gender and Assessment' by Murphy, P. (1989) and 'APU Language Assessment' by White and Gorman; D. Reidel Publishing Company for 'Mathematics Education in its Cultural Context' by Bishop, A. J. (Vol. 19) and 'What is the Point of Group Discussion in Mathematics?' by Hoyles, C. (Vol. 16, 1985) both from *Educational Studies in Mathematics*; Taylor and Francis Ltd for 'The Pre-Vocational Curriculum; A Review of the Issues Involved' by Atkins, M. J. from *The Journal of Curriculum Studies* Vol. 19, No. 1, 1986.

Every effort has been made to trace and acknowledge ownership of copyright. The publishers will be glad to make suitable arrangements with any copyright holders whom it has not been possible to contact.

Introduction

The 1960s and early 1970s was a period of intense curriculum activity. Ambitious projects and initiatives received widespread attention in many countries. In the short term the influence on schooling and teaching appeared disappointing and research and development suffered accordingly in the period of economic restraint that followed the 1973 OPEC oil crisis. Over the last decade there has been a further resurgence of interest in part fuelled by speculation about the quality of pupil learning or the 'standards debate'. Concerns about the curriculum are paralleled by an increased demand and interest in the assessment of pupil learning.

At the present moment, in the public, bureaucratic and education arenas the content, purposes and values of the school curriculum, is the subject of increasing attention and debate. In England and Wales since 1989, the curriculum has been prescribed and legislated for. Within this prescription is a selection of knowledge representing a particular cultural perspective and, value system and educational purpose. Furthermore, the organisation of this prescribed curriculum embodies a view of how children acquire knowledge and deploy it. The success of teachers at fulfilling the requirements of this curriculum, and pupils' ability to acquire the knowledge specified, is to be assessed by an externally developed, centrally controlled system of assessment. The intention is to make the results of the assessment part of the public domain. The model and instruments developed for the national assessment will define educational achievement for the school population. They will also determine how individual abilities are judged to develop within a subject based curriculum. For the most part the theories and values that shape the National Curriculum, and its assessment are implicit and in many instances contradictory. In such a climate of potential educational change and controversy there is an urgent need for critical reflection on curriculum and assessment practice.

Any attempt to analyse curriculum and assessment proposals or to evaluate practice must be conducted within a framework that takes account of the moral, social and political order adopted and the educational purposes defined. The selection of content and the definition of objectives for the curriculum and its assessment are also informed by epistemology and views of the learner and the learning process. This reader is concerned with these latter influences on the curriculum and assessment. The reader includes a collection of extracts and articles which look at aspects of the alliance between the learner, learning and what is learned. The intention is to raise issues within research which exert an influence, either actual or potential, on curriculum and assessment practice. The selection is necessarily constrained. The constraints reflect an educational perspective and an emphasis on domains within the curriculum. The focus is on research and development in the 1980s. The relevance of educational research and psychology to the curriculum is regarded by many with scepticism. However, there have been significant changes since the 1960s in particular the move from a behaviouristic to a cognitive orientation in psychology. This re-orientation coupled with a growing interest in learning in the field of cognitive psychology has resulted in research aimed at enriching understanding of how humans acquire new knowledge and new ways of doing things.

In the first section of the reader the child as a social being negotiating meaning within a cultural context and the child as an information processor and problem solver is explored. Finally, the section looks at the educational purposes and the cultural perspectives that influence the selection of knowledge. How learning is viewed within domains and how domain knowledge is construed is the subject of the next selection of chapters. The implications of the various theoretical positions adopted are then looked at from the teacher's perspective. Here the emphasis is on the changing nature of the teacher's role, and pedagogic knowledge. Finally, the circle is completed by reviewing issues in assessment. Assessment purpose and practice provides a further opportunity to review the ideas about pupils, subjects and educational purpose that have shaped recent proposals for educational reform.

Background note

This Reader has been prepared as part of a course Curriculum, Learning and Assessment from the Open University MA in Education. An accompanying volume, Policies for the Curriculum, provides a further source of readings. The two volumes together, along with other set texts, provide the background for a study guide focusing on the specific aspect of curriculum examined by the course. Further details are available from the Open University, Walton Hall, Milton Keynes, MK7 6AA.

SECTION 1
Ways of Knowing

Introduction

There is growing concern that the new developments in our understanding of the learning process should be integrated into established ideas about curriculum content and sequence, not the least to ensure that the current state of legislative activity can be critically evaluated. This first selection of readings represents evidence that points to an emerging consensus about learning based on an extensive and growing field of research. The way children construct knowledge and 'come to know' and the way their future actions are constructed out of this knowledge are at the core of the argument.

A model of 'knowing' rooted in Piaget is proposed by Glasersfeld in his constructivist epistemology. He sees the process of understanding in the context of communication as analogous to the process of coming to know in the context of experience. This process is typified as 'a matter of building up out of available elements conceptual structures that "fit"'. Glasersfeld defines knowledge as operative and not as a transferable commodity. The teacher has, therefore, to construct two models to determine the pathways that will guide the child's understanding towards the adult view of competence. One model is of the child's existing notions and operations, the other is an analytical model of the adult conceptualisation that is aimed for. He goes on to describe the type of mental effort and motivation that children need to come to know the abstract concepts and operations within domains like mathematics and science.

Lunzer reviews Piaget's contribution to developmental psychology and pinpoints areas of agreement and disagreement with present research understandings. Lunzer argues the case for distinct levels of abstraction among the constructs needed to solve problems or to derive explanations. However, Lunzer's view allows individuals to operate at different levels for different problems. In his critique of Piaget's logicism and discontinuity Lunzer highlights the exogenous nature of the origins of new constructs particularly in the sense that adult modelling, prompting and instruction play a greater role than Piaget allowed for. Other oversights he identifies include the role of analogy in thinking, and the continuity of development. Finally

Lunzer identifies mechanisms of cognitive change from an information-processing perspective which include, frame theory, metacognition, working memory and production systems. He establishes
links between aspects of these and Piaget's work. He concludes that
more than one theoretical approach is needed to advance understanding of cognitive development and that different theories inform different aspects of the learning process. In 'Transactional
Self' Bruner takes issue with aspects of Piagetian child development
in particular the perception of the child as 'lacking skills of
transaction'. Bruner considers children able to calibrate the working
of their minds against one another and to calibrate the worlds in
which they live through the principle of reference. He sees children
as driven to explore and overcome ambiguities in the meaning of
exchanges with others. He goes on to describe the way language is
used to create reality by the labelling of mental processes as
products and the search for correspondence. Learning to use
language, Bruner stresses, involves learning the culture and how 'to
express intentions in congruence with culture'. He warns of the
danger of separating cognition, affect and action and subsequently
losing sight of the role of culture in giving coherence and relevance
to our experiences. Freire looks at the learning process as an act of
knowing based on two interrelated contexts, one being the dialogue
between learners and educators and the other the social reality in
which people exist. Like Glasersfeld he typifies education as a
synthesis between the educator's systematised knowledge and the
learner's relatively unsystematised knowledge. He contrasts the
roles of educators as transmitters of knowledge or as knowing
subjects experiencing the act of knowing in dialogue with students.
He defines knowledge as 'a constant unity between action and
reflection upon reality'. He is concerned, like Bruner, to see people
as both in the world and with the world in that they express the
world's reality in language and thus 'gain objective distance' from it.

Sinclair embraces a Piagetian constructivist epistemology and
goes on to highlight the essential contribution of society and social
interaction in the construction of knowledge. Thus the way objects
are presented to children with their societal meanings is a significant
aspect of knowledge construction. It is in this way that children
learn the knowledge of their society and Sinclair suggests that the
growth of knowledge can be influenced positively or negatively by
socially determined meanings.

The next chapters move closer to curriculum issues in the
educational process. André looks at the increasingly popular objective in education to make people better problem-solvers. In this
context he explores the nature of thinking and problem solving and
the implications of alternative theoretical approaches to it (in
particular behavioural, Gestalt and information processing). Within

the information-processing perspective he describes a model of problem solving. The extract details the important role that domain-specific knowledge plays in problem solving with reference to how knowledge is stored and organised, the nature of concepts and the rules and skills that relate them. He distinguishes declarative and procedural knowledge as important issues for instruction and suggests that there is insufficient analysis within domains to this effect. Finally, André proposes a model to facilitate the learning of intellectual skills.

Barnes' article turns to the school curriculum and raises a general challenge to its academic base. He questions the nature of school knowledge and how it differs from the competencies required in everyday living. Like André he identifies the move towards problem solving in the curriculum as a response to this mismatch but suggests that the value loading of problems met in and out of the classroom may differ. In making problematic the traditional curriculum Barnes recognises the considerable divergency within it.

1.1

Learning as a Constructive Activity

Ernst von Glasersfeld

Ten or fifteen years ago, it would have been all but inconceivable to subject educators or educational researchers to a talk that purported to deal with a theory of knowledge. Educators were concerned with getting knowledge into the heads of their students, and educational researchers were concerned with finding better ways of doing it. There was, then, little if any uncertainty as to what the knowledge was that students should acquire, and there was no doubt at all that, in one way or another, knowledge could be transferred from a teacher to a student. The only question was, which might be the best way to implement that transfer – and educational researchers with their criterion-referenced tests and their sophisticated statistical methods were going to provide the definitive answer.

Something, apparently, went wrong. Things did not work out as expected.

If educational efforts are, indeed, failing, the presuppositions on which, implicitly or explicitly, these efforts have been founded must be questioned. [. . .] We begin therefore by inspecting the commodity that education claims to deal in, and that is 'knowledge'.

This chapter is an attempt to do three things. First, I consider the origin of the troubles we have had with the traditional conception of knowledge.

Second, I propose a conceptualisation of 'knowledge' that does not run into the same problem and that, moreover, provides another benefit in that it throws helpful light on the process of communication. In my experience, this is an area that has not been given much thought. Educators have spent and are rightly spending much time and effort on curriculum; that is, they do their best to work out what to teach and the sequence in which it should be taught. The underlying process of linguistic communication, however, the process on which their teaching relies, is usually simply taken for granted. There has been a naive confidence in language and its efficacy. Although it does not take a good teacher very long to discover that saying things is not enough to 'get them across', there is little if any theoretical insight into why linguistic communication does not do all it is supposed to do. The theory of knowledge that I am proposing, though it certainly does not solve all problems, makes this particular problem very clear.

Lastly, having provided what I call a *model* of 'knowing' that incorporates a specific view of the process of imparting knowledge, I briefly explore a way to apply that model.

The instrumentalist answer to the sceptic's attack

The nature of knowledge was a hotly debated problem as far back as the sixth century BC. The debate has been more or less continuous, and although in many ways it has been colourful, it has been remarkably monotonous in one respect. The central problem has remained unsolved throughout, and the arguments that created the major difficulty at the beginning are the very same that today still preclude any settlement of the question.

Towards the close of the fifth century BC the process of knowing had been conceptually framed in a relatively stable general scenario. By and large, the thinkers who concerned themselves with the cognizing activity tacitly accepted a scenario in which the knower and the things of which, or about which, he or she comes to know are, from the outset, separate and independent entities.

The problem arises from the 'iconic' conception of knowledge, a conception that requires a *match* or *correspondence* between the cognitive structures and what these structures are supposed to *represent*. Truth, in that conception, inevitably becomes the perfect match, the flawless representation. The moment we accept that scenario, we begin to feel the need to assess just how well our cognitive structures match what they are intended to represent. But that 'reality' lies forever on the other side of our experiential interface. To make any such assessment of truth we should have to be able, as Hilary Putnam put it, to adopt a 'God's eye view' (Putnam, 1982). Because we are not, and logically cannot be, in a position to have such a view of the 'real' world and its presumed representation, there is no way out of the dilemma. What we need is a different scenario, a different conception of what it is 'to know', a conception in which the goodness of knowledge is not predicated on likeness or representation.

The first explicit proposal of a different approach originated in those quarters that were most concerned with faith and its preservation. When, for the first time, the revolutionary notion that the Earth might not be the centre of the universe seriously threatened the picture of the world that the church held to be unquestionable and sacred, it was the defenders of the faith who proposed an alternative scenario for the pursuit of scientific knowledge. In his preface to Copernicus' treatise *De revolutionibus*. Osiander (1627) suggested: 'There is no need for these hypotheses to be true, or even to be at all like the truth; rather, one thing is sufficient for them – that they yield calculations which agree with the observations.'[1]

This introduces the notion of a second kind of knowledge, apart from faith and dogma, a knowledge that *fits* observations. It is knowledge that human reason derives from experience. It does not represent a picture of the 'real' world but provides structure and organisation to experience. As such it has an all-important function: It enables us to solve experiential problems.

In Descartes' time, this instrumentalist theory of knowledge was formulated and developed by Mersenne and Gassendi.[2]

From an explorer who is condemned to seek 'structural properties' of an inaccessible reality, the experiencing organism now turns into a builder of cognitive structures intended to solve such problems as the organism perceives or conceives. Fifty years ago, Piaget characterised this scenario as neatly as one could wish: 'Intelligence organises the world by organising itself' (Piaget, 1937). What determines the value of the conceptual structures is their experiential adequacy, their goodness of *fit* with experience, their *viability* as means for the solving of problems, among which is, of course, the never-ending problem of consistent organisation that we call *understanding*.

The world we live in, from the vantage point of this new perspective, is always and necessarily the world as we conceptualise it. 'Facts', as Vico saw long ago, are *made* by us and our way of experiencing, rather than *given* by an independently existing objective world. But that does not mean that we can make them as we like. They are viable facts as long as they do not clash with experience, as long as they remain tenable in the sense that they continue to do what we expect them to do.

This view of knowledge, clearly, has serious consequences for our conceptualisation of teaching and learning. Above all, it will shift the emphasis from the student's 'correct' replication of what the teacher does, to the student's successful organisation of his or her *own* experience. But before I expand on that I want to examine the widespread notion that knowledge is a commodity that can be communicated.

Communication and the subjectivity of meaning

The way we usually think of 'meaning' is conditioned by centuries of written language. We are inclined to think of the meaning of words in a text rather than of the meaning a speaker intends when he or she is uttering linguistic sounds. Written language and printed texts have a physical persistence. They lie on our desks or can be taken from shelves, they can be handled and read. When we *understand* what we read, we gain the impression that we have 'grasped' the meaning of the printed words, and we come to believe that this meaning was *in* the words and that we extracted it like kernels out of their shells. We may even say that a particular meaning is the 'content' of a word or of a text. This notion of words as containers in which the writer or speaker 'conveys' meaning to readers or listeners is extraordinarily strong and seems so natural that we are reluctant to question it. Yet, it is a misguided notion. To see this, we have to retrace our own steps and review how the meaning of words was acquired at the beginning of our linguistic career.

In order to attach any meaning to a word, a child must, first of all, learn to isolate that particular word as a recurrent sound pattern among the totality of available sensory signals. Next, she must isolate something else in her experiential field, something that recurs more or less regularly in conjunction with that sound pattern. Take an ordinary and relatively unproblematic word such as 'apple'. Let us assume that a child has come to recognise it as a recurrent item in her auditory experience. Let us further assume that the child already has a hunch that 'apple' is the kind of sound pattern that *should* be associated with some other experiential item. Adults interested in the child's linguistic progress can, of course, help in that process of association by specific actions and reactions, and they will consider their 'teaching' successful when the child has come to isolate in her experiential field something that enables her to respond in a way that they consider appropriate. When this has been achieved, when the appropriate association has been formed, there is yet another step the child must make before she can be said to have acquired the meaning of the word 'apple'. The child must learn to re-present to herself the designated compound of experiences whenever the word is uttered, even when none of the elements of that compound are actually present in her experiential field. That is to say, the child must acquire the ability to imagine or visualise, for instance, what she has associated with the word 'apple' whenever she hears the sound pattern of that word.[3]

This analysis, detailed though it may seem, is still nothing but a gross summary of certain indispensable steps in a long procedure of interactions. In the present context, however, it should suffice to justify the conclusion that the compound of experiential elements that constitutes the concept an individual has associated with a word cannot be anything but a compound of abstractions from that individual's own experience. For each one of us, then, the meaning of the word apple is an abstraction that he or she has made individually from whatever apple experiences he or she has had in the past. That is to say, it is subjective in origin and resides in a subject's head, not in the word that, because of an association, has the power to call up, in each of us, our own subjective representation.

If you grant this inherent subjectivity of concepts and, therefore, of meaning, you are immediately up against a serious problem. If the meanings of words are, indeed, our own subjective construction, how can we possibly communicate? How could anyone be confident that the representations called up in the mind of the listener are at all *like* the representations the speaker had in mind when he or she uttered the particular words? This question goes to the very heart of the problem of communication. Unfortunately the general conception of communication was derived from and shaped by the notion of words as containers of meaning. If that notion is inadequate, so must be the general conception of communication.

The trouble stems from the mistaken assumption that, in order to communicate, the representations associated with the words that are used must be the same for all communicators. For communication to be considered satisfactory and to lead to what we call 'understanding', it is quite sufficient that the communicators' representations be compatible in the sense that they do not manifestly clash with the situational context or the speaker's expectations.

A simple example may help to make this clear. Let us assume that, for the first time, Jimmy hears the word 'mermaid'. He asks what it means and is told that a mermaid is a creature with a woman's head and torso and the tail of a fish. Jimmy need not have met such a creature in actual experience to imagine her. He can construct a representation out of familiar elements, provided he is somewhat familiar with and has established associations to 'woman', 'fish', and the other words used in the explanation. However, if Jimmy is not told that in mermaids the fish's tail replaces the woman's legs, he may construct a composite that is a fish-tailed biped and, therefore, rather unlike the intended creature of the seas. Jimmy might then read stories about mermaids and take part in conversations about them for quite some time *without* having to adjust his image. In fact, his deviant notion of a mermaid's physique could be corrected only if he got into a situation where the image of a creature with legs as well as a fish's tail comes into explicit conflict with a picture or with what speakers of the language say about mermaids; that is, Jimmy would modify the concept that is his subjective meaning of the word *only* if some context forced him to do so.

How, you may now ask, can a context *force* one to modify one's concepts? The question must be answered not only in a theory of communication but also in a theory of knowledge. The answer I am proposing is essentially the same in both.

The basic assumption is one that is familiar to you. Organisms live in a world of constraints. In order to survive, they must be 'adapted' or, as I prefer to say, 'viable'. This means that they must be able to manage their living within the constraints of the world in which they live. This is commonplace in the context of biology and evolution. In my view, the principle applies also to cognition – with one important difference. On the biological level, we are concerned with species, i.e. with collections of organisms that, individually, cannot modify their biological makeup. But because they are not all the same, the species 'adapts' simply because all those individuals that are *not* viable are eliminated and do not reproduce. On the cognitive level, we are concerned with individuals and specifically with their 'knowledge', which, fortunately, is not immutable and only rarely fatal. The cognitive organism tries to make sense of experience in order better to avoid clashing with the world's constraints. It can actively modify ways and means to achieve greater viability.

'To make sense' is the same activity and involves the same presuppositions whether the stuff we want to make sense of is experience in general or the particular kind of experience we call communication. The procedure is the same but the motivation, the reason why we want to make sense, may be different.

Let me begin with ordinary experience. No matter how one characterises cognizing organisms, one of their salient features is that they are capable of learning. Basically, to have 'learned' means to have drawn conclusions from experience and to act accordingly. To act accordingly, of course, implies that there are certain experiences that one would like to repeat rather than others that one would like to avoid. The expectation that any such control over experience can be gained must be founded on the assumptions that (1) some regularities can be detected in the experiential sequence and (2) future experience will at least to some extent conform to these regularities. These assumptions, as David Hume showed, are prerequisites for the inductive process and the knowledge that results from it.

In order to find regularities, we must segment our experience into separate pieces so that, after certain operations of recall and comparison, we may say of some of them that they recur. The segmenting and recalling, the assessing of similarities, and the decisions as to what is to be considered different are all *our* doing. Yet, whenever some particular result of these activities turns out to be useful (in generating desirable or avoiding undesirable experiences), we quickly forget that we could have segmented, considered, and assessed otherwise. When a scheme has worked several times, we come to believe, as Piaget has remarked, that it could not be otherwise and that we have discovered something about the real world. Actually we have merely found *one* viable way of organising our experience. 'To make sense' of a given collection of experiences, then, means to have organised them in a way that permits us to make more or less reliable predictions. In fact, it is almost universally the case that we interpret experience either in view of expectations or with a view to making predictions about experiences that are to come.

In contrast, 'to make sense' of a piece of language does not usually involve the prediction of future non-linguistic experience. However, it does involve the forming of expectations concerning the remainder of the piece that we have not yet heard or read. These expectations concern words and concepts, not actions or other experiential events. The piece of language may, of course, be intended to express a prediction, e.g. 'tomorrow it will rain', but the way in which that prediction is derived from the piece of language differs from the way in which it might be derived from, say, the observation of particular clouds in the sky. The difference comes out clearly when it is pointed out that, in order to make sense of the utterance 'tomorrow it will rain' it is quite irrelevant whether or not there is any belief in the likelihood of rain. To 'understand' the utterance, it is sufficient that we come up with a conceptual structure that, given our past experience with words and the way they are combined, *fits* the piece of language in hand. The fact that, when tomorrow comes, it doesn't rain, in no way invalidates the interpretation of the utterance. On the other hand, if the prediction made from an observation of the sky is not confirmed by actual rain, we have to conclude that there was something wrong with our interpretation of the clouds.

In spite of this difference between the interpretation of experience and the interpretation of language, the two have one important feature in common. Both rely on the use of conceptual material that the interpreter must already have. 'Making sense', in both cases, means finding a way of fitting available conceptual elements into a pattern that is circumscribed by specific constraints. In the one case, the constraints are inherent in the way in which we have come to segment and organise experience; in the other, the constraints are inherent in the way in which we have learned to use language. In neither case is it a matter of matching an original. If our interpretation of experience allows us to achieve our purpose, we are quite satisfied that we 'know'; and if our interpretation of a communication is not countermanded by anything the communicator says or does, we are quite satisfied that we have 'understood'.

The process of understanding in the context of communication is analogous to the process of coming to know in the context of experience. In both cases, it is a matter of building up, out of available elements, conceptual structures that fit into such space as is left unencumbered by constraints. Though this is, of course, a spatial metaphor, it illuminates the essential character of the notion of viability and it brings out another aspect that differentiates that notion from the traditional one of 'truth': having constructed a viable path of action, a viable solution to an experiential problem, or a viable interpretation of a piece of language, there is never any reason to believe that this construction is the only one possible.

The construction of viable knowledge

When I began the section on communication by talking about the concept of meaning, it must have become apparent that I am not a behaviourist. For about half a century behaviourists have worked hard to do away with 'mentalistic' notions such as *meaning, representation, and thought.* It is up to future historians to assess just how much damage this mindless fashion has wrought. Where education is concerned, the damage was formidable. Because behaviourism is by no means extinct, damage continues to be done, and it is done in many ways. One common root, however, is the presumption that all that matters – perhaps even all there is – are observable stimuli and observable responses. This presumption has been appallingly successful in wiping out the distinction between training and education.

As I hope to have shown in the preceding section, a child must learn more than just to respond 'apple' to instantiations of actual apple experiences. If that were all she could do, her linguistic proficiency would remain equivalent to that of a well-trained parrot. For the bird and its trainer to have come so far is a remarkable achievement. For a human child it is a starting point in the development of self-regulation, awareness, and rational control.

[. . .]

Knowledge cannot be reduced to a stock of retrievable 'facts' but concerns (for example in mathematics) the ability to compute new results. To use Piaget's terms, it is *operative* rather than *figurative*. It is the product of reflection – and whereas reflection as such is not observable, its products *may* be inferred from observable responses.

I am using 'reflection' in the sense in which it was originally introduced by Locke, i.e. for the ability of the mind to observe its own operations. Operative knowledge, therefore, is not associative retrieval of a particular answer but rather knowledge of what to do in order to produce an answer. Operative knowledge is constructive and, consequently, is best demonstrated in situations where something new is generated, something that was not already available to the operator. The novelty that matters is, of course, novelty from the subject's point of view. A [. . .] teacher can infer this subjective novelty, not from the correctness of a response but from the struggle that led to it. It is not the particular response that matters but the way in which it was arrived at.

In the preceding pages, I have several times used the term *interpretation*. I have done it deliberately, because it focuses attention on an activity that requires awareness and deliberate choice. Although all the material that is used in the process of interpreting may have been shaped and prepared by prior interaction with experiential things and with people, and although the validation of any particular interpretation does, as we have seen, require further interaction, the process of interpreting itself requires reflection. If an organism does no more than act and react, it would be misusing the word to say that the organism is interpreting. Interpretation implies awareness of more than one possibility, deliberation, and rationally controlled choice.

A student's ability to carry out certain activities is never more than part of what we call 'competence'. The other part is the ability to monitor the activities. To do the right thing is not enough; to be competent, one must also know what one is doing and why it is right. That is perhaps the most stringent reason why longitudinal observation and Piaget's clinical method are indispensable if we want to find out anything about the reflective thought of children, about their operative knowledge, and about how to teach them to make progress towards competence. Consider, for example, the methods developed that make it possible for athletes to *see* what they are doing. Some of these methods involve stachistoscopy and are very sophisticated, others are as simple as the slow-motion replay of movies and videotapes. Their purpose is to give performers of intricate actions an opportunity to observe themselves act. This visual feedback is a far more powerful didactic tool than instructions that refer to details of the action that, normally, are dimly or not at all perceived by the actor himself.

The proficiency of good athletes springs to a large extent from the fact that they have, as it were, automated much of their action. As long as their way of acting is actually the most effective for the purpose, this automation is an advantage because it frees the conscious mind to focus on higher levels of control. When, however, something must be changed in the routine, this would be difficult, if not impossible, to achieve *without* awareness of the individual steps. Hence the efficacy of visual feedback.

What a teacher is striving to instil into the student is ultimately the awareness of a dynamic programme and its execution – and that awareness is in principle similar to what the athlete is able to glean from a slow-motion representation of his or her own performance. In the absence of any such technology to create self-reflection, the teacher must find other means to foster operative awareness.

A large part of educational research has been employing a

procedure that consists of setting tasks, recording solutions, and analysing these solutions as though they resulted from the child's fumbling efforts to carry out operations that constitute an adult's competence. The 'teaching experiment' (Steffe, 1977), on the other hand, starts from the premise that the child cannot conceive of the task, the way to solve it, and the solution in terms other than those that are available at the particular point in the child's conceptual development. The child, to put it another way, must interpret the task and try to construct a solution by using material she already has. That material cannot be anything but the conceptual building blocks and operations that the particular child has assembled in her own prior experience.

Children, we must never forget, are not repositories for adult 'knowledge' but organisms that, like all of us, are constantly trying to make sense of, to understand their experience.

It is not in the least facetious to say that the teacher's goal is to gain understanding of the child's understandings. The difference between the child interpreting (and trying to solve) a task in the given context, and the teacher interpreting the child's responses and behaviour in the context of the task, is that the teacher can test his interpretation by deliberately modifying certain elements in the child's experiential field. The teacher can also ask questions and see whether or not the responses are compatible with his or her conjectures about the child's conception of what is going on. Whenever an incompatibility crops up, the teacher's conjectures have to be changed and their replacements tested again, until at last they remain viable in whatever situations the teacher can think of and create.

In short, the teacher is constructing a *model* of the child's notions and operations. Inevitably, that model will be constructed, not out of the child's conceptual elements, but out of conceptual elements that are the teacher's own. It is in this context that the epistemological principle of *fit*, rather than *match*, is of crucial importance. Just as cognitive organisms can never compare their conceptual organisations of experience with the structure of an independent objective reality, so the teacher can never compare the model he or she has constructed of a child's conceptualisations with what actually goes on in the child's head. In the one case as in the other, the best that can be achieved is a model that remains viable within the range of available experience. [. . .]

Having generated a viable model of the child's present concepts and operations, the teacher hypothesises pathways to guide the child's conceptualisations towards adult competence. In order to formulate any such hypothetical path, let alone implement it, the teacher must not only have a model of the student's present conceptual structures but also an analytical model of the adult conceptualisations towards which his guidance is to lead.

Because the child necessarily interprets verbal instructions in terms of her own experience, the 'guidance' must take the form either of questions or of changes in the experiential field that leads the child into situations where her present way of operating runs into obstacles and contradiction. Analogous to the adult who organises general experience, the child is unlikely to modify a conceptual structure unless there is an experience of failure or, at least, surprise at something not working out in the expected fashion. Such failure or surprise, however, can be experienced only if there was an expectation – and that brings me to the last point I want to make.

If I have had any success at all in presenting the constructivist epistemology as a possible basis for education and educational research, this last point is easy to make and its importance should become obvious.

The more abstract the concepts and operations that are to be constituted, the more reflective activity will be needed. Reflection, however, does not happen without effort. The concepts and operations involved in, for example, mathematics are not merely abstractions, but most of them are the product of several levels of abstraction. Hence, it is not just one act of reflection that is needed, but a succession of reflective efforts – and any succession of efforts requires solid motivation.

The need for motivation is certainly no news to anyone who has been teaching. How to foster motivation has been discussed for a long time. But here again, I believe, the effect of behaviourism has been profoundly detrimental. The basic dogma of behaviourism merely says that behaviour is determined by the consequences it has produced in the past (which is just another way of saying that organisms operate inductively). There is every reason to agree with that. The trouble arises from the usual interpretation of 'reinforcement', i.e. of the consequence that is rewarding and thus strengthens specific behaviours and increases the probability of their recurrence.

There is the widespread misconception that reinforcement is the effect of certain well-known commodities such as biscuits, money, and social approval. It is a misconception, not because organisms will not work quite hard to obtain these commodities, but because it obscures the one thing that is often by far the most reinforcing for a cognitive organism: *to achieve a satisfactory organisation*, a viable way of dealing with some sector of experience. This fact adds a different dimension to the conception of reinforcement because whatever constitutes the rewarding consequence in these cases is generated wholly *within* the organism's own system.

Self-generated reinforcement has an enormous potential in cognitive, reflective organisms. (All of us, I am sure, have spent precious time and sweat on puzzles whose solution brought neither cookies, nor money, and negligible social approval.) But this potential has to be developed and realised.

When children begin to play with wooden blocks, they sooner or later place one upon another. Whatever satisfaction they derive from the resulting structure, it provides sufficient incentive for them to repeat the act and to improve on it. They may, for instance, implicitly or explicitly set themselves the goal of building a tower that comprises *all* the blocks. If they succeed, they are manifestly satisfied, irrespective of tangible rewards or an adult's comment, for they build towers also in the absence of observers. The reward springs from the achievement, from the successful deliberate imposition of an order that is inherent in their own way of organising. To repeat the feat, the tower has to be knocked down. That, too, turns out to be a source of satisfaction because it once more provides evidence of the experiencer's power over the structure of experience.

To some, these observations may seem trivial. To me, they exemplify a basic feature of the model of the cognitive organism, a feature that must be taken into account if we want to educate.

From the constructive point of view, it makes no sense to assume that any powerful cognitive satisfaction springs from simply being told that one has done something right, as long as 'rightness' is assessed by someone else. To become a source of real satisfaction, 'rightness' must be seen as the fit with an order one has established *oneself*. Teachers [. . .] tend to assume that there exists in every particular case an objective problem and an objectively 'true' solution. Children and students of any age are therefore expected somehow to come to 'see' the problem, its solution, and the *necessity* that links the two. But the necessity is conceptual and it can spring from nothing but the awareness of the structures and operations involved in the thinking subject's conceptualisation of the problem and its solution. [. . .]

Final remarks

Educators share the goal of generating knowledge in their students. However, from the epistemological perspective I have outlined, it appears that knowledge is not a transferable commodity and communication not a conveyance.

If, then, we come to see knowledge and competence as products of the individual's conceptual organisation of the individual's experience, the teacher's role will no longer be to dispense 'truth' but rather to help and guide the student in the conceptual organisation of certain areas of experience. Two things are required for the teacher to do this: on the one hand, an adequate idea of where the student is and, on the other, an adequate idea of the destination. Neither is accessible to direct observation. What the student says and does can be interpreted in terms of a hypothetical model – and this is one area of educational research that every *good* teacher since Socrates has done intuitively. Today, we are a good deal closer to providing the teacher with a set of relatively reliable diagnostic tools.

As for the helping and guiding, good teachers have always found ways and means of doing it because, consciously or unconsciously they realised that, although one can point the way with words and symbols, it is the student who has to do the conceptualising and the operating.

That leaves the destination, the way of operating that would be considered 'right' from the expert's point of view. [. . .] It is in this area that, in my view, research could make advances that would immediately benefit educational practice. If the goal of the teacher's guidance is to generate understanding, rather than train specific performance, his task will clearly be greatly facilitated if that goal can be represented by an explicit model of the concepts and operations that we assume to be the operative source of subject competence. More important still, if students are to taste something of the expert's satisfaction in a subject they cannot be expected to find it in whatever rewards they might be given for their performance but only through the becoming aware of the neatness of fit they have achieved in their own conceptual construction.

Notes

1 Translation from Popper, K. R. (1968) *Conjectures and Refutations*. New York: Harper Torchbooks, p. 98.
2 An excellent exposition can be found in Popkin, R. H. (1979) *The History of Scepticism from Erasmus to Spinoza*. Berkeley, CA: University of California Press.
3 If this isolating of the named thing or 'referent' is a demanding task with relatively simple perceptual compounds, such as apple, it is obviously much more difficult when the meaning of the word is a concept that requires further abstraction from sensory experience or from mental operations. But because we want to maintain that words such as 'all' and 'some', 'mine' and 'ours', 'cause' and 'effect', 'space' and 'time', and scores of others *have* meaning, we must assume that these meanings, though they cannot be directly perceived, are nevertheless somehow isolated and made retrievable by every learner of the language.

References

Piaget, J. (1937) *La Construction du Réel Chez l'Enfant*. Neuchâtel: Delachaux et Niestlé.

Popkin, R. H. (1979) *The History of Scepticism from Erasmus to Spinoza.* Berkeley, CA: University of California Press.
Popper, K. R. (1968) *Conjectures and Refutations.* New York: Harper Torchbooks.
Putnam, H. (1982) *Reason, Truth, and History.* Cambridge, MA: Harvard University Press.
Steffe, L. P. (1977) *Constructivist Models for Childrens' Learning in Arithmetic.* Paper presented at the Research Workshop on Learning Models, Durham, NH.

1.2

Cognitive Development: Learning and the Mechanisms of Change*

Eric Lunzer

Introduction

It could be said that during the first part of this century, developmental psychology was largely a matter of describing what children could reasonably be expected to do at successive ages or stages. Its orientation was normative, and its primary function was to provide adequate descriptions for the behaviours and aptitudes of ordinary children to act as standards against which one might evaluate the strengths and deficits of exceptional children. A secondary aim was to establish correlations and groupings of correlations among the various characteristics of children, and between such groupings of abilities and character traits on the one hand and possible antecedents on the other, especially parental abilities, parental circumstances, and parental treatment. Developmental psychology was therefore clinical or psychometric or both.

As to the mechanism governing progressive gains in cognition, it was assumed that this was simply a matter of learning in accordance with the principles established by behaviourist learning theories; the rate of such learning being modulated by more or less innate individual differences in a more or less general basic intelligence. Of course, adverse circumstances were seen as possible suppressors of learning, and it was the job of psychologists and educators to uncover these where they existed and to take appropriate remedial action.

Not all of these aims are unworthy, nor could it be gainsaid that at least part of the business of developmental psychology remains as it was. There is no substitute for a rich and representative data base,

---

* In this chapter Lunzer reviews the contribution of Piaget and details some alternative approaches. He provides numerous examples of research to exemplify the constructs he describes or critiques. Many examples and details have been omitted in the chapters selected for this reader.

to distinguish the exception from what is the rule. Also such a data base, although not sufficient, is one essential for the invention of explanatory theories. However, explanatory theory was lacking in this phase of developmental psychology – except in Europe, and especially in Geneva under the influence of Jean Piaget. At that time, this work was hailed by a few, criticised by a few more, but for the most part ignored.

It was a situation which changed radically following publication in English of a whole series of Piaget's work, mainly during the years 1950 to 1960. Particularly influential were the books on the general theory of intelligence (1950), on the child's conception of number (1952a), on the early development of intelligence (1952b), on moral development (1962), and on adolescent thinking (Inhelder and Piaget, 1958). Such was the persuasiveness of these and other works that from 1960 on, if not before, developmental psychology has been largely a matter of agreeing with Piaget or of disagreeing with him. One could be more precise by specifying two phases: agreement up to about 1968, and disagreement from then on.

A resume of Piaget's theory

Piaget's account of cognitive development consists of two sets of constructs: functional invariants and structural elements which evolve in a fixed progression.

Functional invariants

The central construct among the functional invariants is the notion of *scheme*. The scheme, for Piaget, is the psychological source of behavioural differentiation. When a scheme is evoked by environmental stimulation, that scheme determines the interpretation of the object: how it is perceived and how the individual will respond to it.

Schemes are the residue of previous experience, and the totality of schemes represents the child's world knowledge at any given time. But Piaget did not think of schemes as merely passive. Instead, they were rooted in action, inasmuch as even the categorisations derived from perceptual behaviour were arrived at because of their relevance to other forms of behaviour. Thus, the earliest schemes take the form of innate reflexes like sucking or grasping or visual focusing, while the earliest differentiations made among objects correspond to the different things a baby can do with them: movable or fixed, graspable, noisy, biteable, etc.

When the pattern of stimulation – itself the outcome of an activity which results from some scheme – results in the evocation of a new scheme, the process is termed *assimilation*. Piaget believes that every existing scheme seeks to assimilate to itself any object: for instance, a child of 9 months may be observed to try out all sorts of schemes on a new object, picking it up, rattling it, biting it, etc. Assimilation can, however, be distorting. Thus, there is distortion in treating a brick as if it were a car (or vice versa) as is quite typical in the play of nursery age children.

If Piagetian assimilation were to proceed unchecked, we might well end up in an extreme form of schizophrenia. But there is a corrective, and Piaget calls this *accommodation*. Accommodation of a scheme begins as the trial-and-error adaptation of a scheme to counter any element of novelty inherent in the current situation. Accommodation can also result in the differentiation of a scheme to form two new schemes. One of Piaget's favourite examples is the discovery that coveted objects can be obtained by acting on their support. There are different ways of doing this: you can pull a cloth, while something like a turntable has to be rotated. Accommodation is thought of as the mechanism of all learning, be it through trial-and-error or systematic inquiry or logical inference.

The last construct to note is the notion of *equilibration*. Suppose two schemes are to be activated by the same stimulus – there is conflict if they lead to contrary interpretations or to contrary behaviours or both, and such conflict must be resolved. The two schemes therefore tend to accommodate to one another, by differentiation or by fusion, and the outcome can be the birth of a third scheme more comprehensive than either – without actually destroying the original pair. Piaget maintained that the processes of mutual accommodation continued until all conflict was resolved by the formation of these more differentiated and all embracing schemes, and it is that tendency which he called *equilibration*.

The concept of equilibration has much in common with the theory of cognitive dissonance and its resolution (Festinger, 1957), and this may have contributed to the acceptability of Piagetian theory in the 1960s.

According to Piaget, the universal tendency to equilibration of schemes results in their structurisation. A set of schemes is relatively unstructured if each represents an alternative action sequence that results in a new state, i.e. one that cannot be predicted from the results of other schemes. Conversely, the set of schemes is structured in the measure that the outcome of any one scheme is precisely related to the effects of others because there are well-defined links between them. Imagine a toddler who knows his way to the park starting from home, and also the way to the local shops. Furthermore, although he also knows his way back home from the corner, he fails to notice that he has to pass this corner on the way to the shops or the park. What this child has is a set of unstructured schemes. They become more and more structured as he learns his way back and forth, the limit being an internalised map of the neighbourhood. [. . .]

It should be clear that wherever there are equivalent routes between two points, or equivalent action sequences between two states, there is structure. Also, there is structure whenever an action has an inverse. Piaget laid particular stress on the second of these, which he termed *reversibility*. Of course, not all schemes can be reversible, simply because not all of reality is reversible – for instance, many biological processes are irreversible. However, Piaget chose to concentrate on the development of mathematical and logical thinking, and these he thought do have structures which are potentially reversible. What is more, he considered that the kinds of reversibility that were observable at successive periods in development were distinct from each other and could therefore be used to identify each of three stages. They are the sensorimotor stage, the stage of concrete operations and the stage of formal operations, and they are held to be reached on average at 18 months, 7 or 8 years, and at some time between the ages of 11 and 15 years.

Structures in Piagetian theory

Piaget was strongly committed to the view that each of these stages is characterised by the emergence of new structures. The idea of structure is essential to an understanding of Piaget's view on equilibration and learning.

Piaget maintains that at each stage of development the child's understanding in any domain is associated with the structure of the equivalences that he can recognise. At the formal stage, the principal form of structure is the group. However, at the previous stage, the key structures are not groups, but a special form devised by Piaget himself, called *grouping*. A grouping is similar to the group in regard to most of its properties, but not all. Children of 7 or 8 years and older do show an ability to anticipate the effects of classificatory actions and their interrelations, and Piaget takes this to mean that they have constructed groupings and can apply them to problems when they are needed.

Both classification and ordering are interpreted by Piaget as arguing a more limited degree of structurisation than the group. Nevertheless, he maintains that even at the stage of concrete operations, children's understandings of equivalence relations exhibit a true group structure in two domains: number and spatial displacements. [. . .] (Piaget, 1952a; Piaget, Inhelder, and Szeminska, 1960). It is supposed that at the stage of formal operations, group structures are more ubiquitous. [. . .]

Learning and equilibration

We find little in Piaget's writings about learning in the sense of the acquisition of skills or learning as an accumulation of facts. His learning theory is concerned almost exclusively with the growth of understanding, which he takes to be synonymous with the changing structures of knowledge. These are seen as stable coordinations among mental actions. They are stable because they allow one to take cognisance of a network of related mental actions while avoiding contradictions.

Throughout his writings on the subject (e.g. especially, Piaget, 1959a, 1959b) Piaget insists that these structures are not learned in the conventional sense, through direct instruction and reinforcement; they are elaborated by a process of equilibration. In essence, this means that conflicting alternative schemes will coexist so long as they are not simultaneously active, but increasing familiarity makes their coexistence inevitable, and when this happens there is mutual accommodation resulting in the formation of a new overall scheme which is free from contradiction. The essential condition for this development seems to be the familiarity of the constituent schemes, which must be sufficient to allow them to be compared and integrated within a single act of attention.

This last point is one that is strongly urged by Pascual-Leone (Pascual-Leone and Smith, 1969) and by Case (1974, 1978a). In Piaget's own work, it is at best implicit. However, the notion of spontaneous equilibration and the role of conflict are explicit and central. They underlie the Genevan view of learning: that it must be spontaneous because it must arise out of schemes that are familiar; that it is produced by conflict; that intervention is effective only when introduced when the subject is on the brink of unaided discovery. Above all, the notion of powerful and stable structures underlies the most controversial tenets of Piagetian theory: that instruction in isolated competences (e.g. teaching conservation) is relatively useless and cannot create true understanding; and that the spontaneous development of structures results in distinct stages marked by different kinds of equilibrium, each ushered by a more limited phase of disequilibrium.

The positive legacy of Piaget: levels of construct

[. . .] Since about 1968 if not before, most of the literature on cognitive development has been critical of Piaget. Nevertheless, a large section of recent and current research continues to draw on his work, if only in that the same research paradigms are used, whether to urge some modification of his theories, or to expose them as invalid and substitute an alternative approach (Modgil and Modgil, 1982; Siegel and Brainerd, 1978). [. . .] Few would deny that the questions Piaget asked were important and remain so. Equally, there are certain aspects of his approach that were far in advance of his predecessors and more consonant with current psychological theory. There is no going back to the old-style learning theories so well described and analysed by Hilgard (1958). Finally, while many contemporary psychologists are critical of Piaget's interpretations, the data that he established remain valid within limits, and they continue to pose a challenge.

We begin with the 'functional invariants'. It is interesting to note what was revolutionary about Piaget's notion of schemes and why this made his approach so acceptable some 30 years after the ideas first evolved (during the 1920s and 1930s). In putting forward the concept of the scheme, Piaget was denying the stimulus–response approach of behaviourism and substituting a central cognitive initiator for the control of behaviour and learning. Perceptual stimulation, information pick-up, is dependent on ongoing be- haviour and hence on the activity of some ongoing scheme. Thereaf- ter, the interpretation of the stimulus is a function both of the original scheme and of the new schemes that it evokes. Such ideas might have seemed strange in the 1930s, but by the 1960s, they had become commonplace. The model for the brain had been, implicit- ly, the telephone exchange; now it was, explicitly, the computer. Much more needs to be established about the scheme than was said by Piaget, but in outline such a notion is basic to contemporary cognitive psychology. It should be added that the term *schema* has greater currency than Piaget's *scheme*. Again, while the terms *assimilation* and *accommodation* have not gained wide acceptance, this approach to perception and learning is in line with most current thinking in psychology.

However, despite the centrality of *functional invariants*, most of Piaget's writing and all of his research have been concerned with structural development. [. . .] In the next section, I argue that the central notion of structure is unacceptable. Nevertheless, the work on structural growth has produced a very considerable body of evidence on children's achievements at successive ages. Within limits, and the qualification is important, the experimental findings have been corroborated over the years. [. . .]

There remains the vexed issue of Piaget's developmental stages. The idea of relatively discontinuous stages has little support from research, nor is there much evidence for two phases of accelerated intellectual growth, one occurring at 6–8 years and the other at about 11–13 years, these being bounded by longer periods of equilibrium marked by a slower rate of development. What evi- dence there is would suggest the not very exciting view that the acquisition of cognitive schemes is a gradual business, whether or not it is assisted by instruction and example, and new competences always build on old. Nevertheless, if we look at the kind of content with which the individual must come to terms in the course of acculturation to the demands of our society, we are bound to recognise the need for the intervention of constructs. What is more, these constructs can readily be classified as belonging to one of three successive levels of abstraction.

First-order constructs

The lowest degree of abstraction belongs in the first instance to unanalysed objects (mother, dog, pencil, etc.) and to unanalysed properties of objects (red, large, long, hot, etc.). Psychologically, it would be incorrect to admit a distinction of level between these two categories because both correspond to discriminations that are acquired well before the meaningful use of words. To these we need to add perceptual judgements of relation, and in particular the notion 'greater than', and with it 'more'. Thus, Bryant (1972) has shown conclusively that very young children learn to discriminate in terms of relative rather than absolute size in making choices between two otherwise similar objects. Both *more* and *a lot* seem to belong to the same category as *greater*, and Donaldson and Balfour's (1968) finding that young children are apt to confuse the two words *more* and *less* should not be taken to imply that they have no conception of either but rather that they cannot decide, out of context, which is which. The phrase *out of context* is worth dwelling on, for the most general characteristic of unanalysed constructs is that they function only in context. [. . .]

The use of unanalysed constructs will get us a long way, for they are essential and quite adequate to interpret the familiar world of objects and events in terms of a commonsense one-directional set of expectations corresponding to rather simple laws of causality. Such a representation is developed in terms of behavioural expectations before the intervention of representation and language, which is partly why in his later writings, Piaget does not acknowledge an intuitive stage.

Second-order constructs

The second level of abstraction belongs to constructs that do not denote everyday objects, but properties and relations that are defined by these. [. . .]

An example is classificatory behaviour. In most simple classificatory tasks, the constructs do not need to be related to specific action sequences, but they do require the child to establish clear relations between the various properties of objects. It is thus no cause for surprise that the most effective tasks of classificatory adequacy involve the handling of two criterial dimensions, either simultaneously, as in matrix classification, or successively, as in classification and reclassification. In a very well thought out study, Halford (1980) demonstrated that 3 year-olds could learn to carry out one-way classifications but made no significant progress in two-way classifications. [. . .]

Third-order constructs

The third level of abstraction belongs to constructs that cannot be defined directly on objects and their properties because they entail a relationship between different constructs of that order. Weight can be defined by an action on objects, and so too can area, but pressure cannot, because it involves a relation between them. The number of a set of objects can be obtained directly by counting its members, but a proportion is a relation between the ratios of two numbers, not two objects. The price of a commodity is defined with reference to specific actions with an object, what you must pay for it, where inflation can only be defined by reference to changes in such things as prices, wages, etc.

Such constructs may denote new ideas. Thus, inflation is a concept for which there is no more primitive parallel. But this is not always the case. For instance we can experience a sense of pressure different from weight if another person's stiletto heel is brought to bear on our sandalled toe. It follows that third-order constructs (like second-order constructs before them) do not always denote new ideas. However, they do entail new ways of defining them and more precise relations between them.

Such considerations should help to introduce a further characterisation of levels of abstraction. How one arrives at one's constructs and how one combines them is the decisive factor influencing the way one conceives of the possible and its relation to the real. Inhelder and Piaget (1958) maintain that the critical distinction between the adolescent's way of thinking and that of the younger child is that while the latter thinks of the possible as a modification of the real, the former sees the real as an instantiation of the possible. This makes sense when taken to mean that, for certain purposes, whatever aspect of things is under investigation needs to be treated as if it were a construct rather than a primary datum.

All the foregoing can be taken as constituting a strong case for the recognition of distinct levels of abstraction among the constructs needed to solve particular problems or to arrive at certain kinds of explanations of things. It does not mean that individual subjects will invariably select the same level of construct for all problems.

Errors of Piagetian theory: logicism and discontinuity

In the last section, I have been at some pains to show that there is a good deal that is valuable underlying Piaget's theory of stages. Yet that theory has been the subject of severe criticism along two lines. The first is directed at the inherent logicism in Piagetian theory, while the second concerns the question of continuity.

Logicism is usually taken to denote a too-ready assumption by a psychologist that because a given line of inference is valid and important in logic, it is also a correct description of actual thought processes. [. . .]

Logical structures play a central part in Piaget's theory because they justify the notion of spontaneous equilibration. But that notion is plausible only when taken as a loose description. Thus, two of its subordinate principles are often helpful to understanding. These are the role of conflict in overcoming the resistance of well-established schemes, and what appears to be a built-in negative response to contradiction. The first theme has been recognised by many educators. The second may be a useful pointer for the study of the origins of logic. However, Piaget's detailed account of the mechanism of equilibration is far from convincing. In particular, Piaget supposes that conflict between existing schemes is resolved by the emergence of a new scheme that integrates them. The new scheme is endogenous in origin in the sense that the child's experience of conservation situations is all that he needs to make the jump, or rather, experience together with a kind of self-constructing logic – equilibration itself. What evidence we have suggests that new constructs are more often exogenous in origin. They tend to be exogenous both in the sense that the germ of the new scheme is to be found in a different context, and also in the sense that adult modelling, adult prompting, and adult instruction play a far greater role than Piaget would allow.

Another aspect of Piaget's excessive formalism is the failure to pay sufficient regard to the role of analogy in thinking at every level, and especially in children's conceptions concerning phenomena that cannot be directly observed. Recent research by science educators has shown the prevalence of a wide array of misconceptions about such things as the movement of light and heat, the distribution of molecules in a gas, what happens when we see, and the nature of an electrical circuit (Driver and Easley, 1978). These misconceptions cannot be explained in terms of the structure of children's reasoning. Some notions, such as the idea that light is concentrated in the vicinity of a candle, are fairly easy to shift (there being plenty of evidence of light rays travelling a very long way), but others, such as the idea that electric current is used up as it travels round a circuit, prove far more intractable. I believe this to be because electric current is an abstract third-order construct and a particularly difficult one at that, because it is related to several other constructs of the same order and has few relations with more elementary constructs. Be that as it may, it is clear that all such misconceptions arise because we interpret experience by analogy. And in trying to coordinate experience in a new area, we build up a model based on another that is more familiar. But these are dynamic content-models of what happens to what and how, rather than formal relations between arguments.

Piagetian theory lays particular stress on supposed discontinuities in development associated with the emergence of the concrete and formal stages. Yet there is now a considerable body of evidence pointing to a relatively unbroken continuity. Much of this has accumulated in the course of the 1970s.

To take one example, where the structuralist view argues for a more or less sharp break between the intuitive and the concrete levels at about the age of 7 years it is now clear that the relevant problems can be tackled with success at much younger ages, following on apparently modest alterations in procedure. Thus Rose and Blank (1974) showed that failure in conservation can be reduced by not repeating the question 'Are they the same?' thereby implying (apparently) that they are not. Likewise, Donaldson and her associates showed that if the transformation can be made to appear accidental rather than deliberately initiated by the adult, conservation appears much earlier (Light, Buckingham and Robbins, 1979; McGarrigle and Donaldson, 1974). [. . .]

Finally, there are the many studies of the effect of teaching on the acquisition of operational behaviour. Here again, there is a wealth of evidence against the traditional Piagetian view that operational thinking cannot readily be taught. Much of the work has been revised by Brainerd (1978), who comments: 'The four tutorial methods on which adequate evidence is available have produced improvements in the trained concepts that satisfy all the usual Genevan learning criteria' (p. 88). The criteria referred to are superior performance on pretest items, superior performance on at least one new type of item, an acceptable verbal justification of a correct response, evidence of transfer, and stability as shown by a late posttest (usually following an interval of 2–4 weeks).

From such evidence, one is led to conclude that there is no one turning point for the acquisition of concrete operational behaviour – or, as I would prefer to term it, the differentiation and stabilisation of second-order constructs. Well-adapted and successful solutions to relevant problems may be obtained as early as 4, or even 3 years, given optimal cueing and/or appropriate training. Consistent and flexible use of such constructs, including the search for relevant criteria in the face of some degree of miscueing by the situation or the adult is not something that comes suddenly, but only as a result of progressive transfer over a period of years.

Mechanisms of cognitive change

[. . .] The child's growing interpretation of the world is a function of the constructs at his disposal. These may be categorised by distinguishing three levels of abstraction, which are necessarily successive within any given domain. There is no necessary synchronicity for their attainment in different domains, and even within domains, the availability of the relevant constructs for the solution of particular problems is a gradual acquisition and not a sudden development.

There is no need to rehearse the debt to Piaget, and differences have been adequately set out in earlier sections. However, I have also argued that Piaget's theory of equilibration should be rejected, and because equilibration was the mechanism by which he sought to explain the process of cognitive changes, its rejection means that the modified statement I have just formulated is now purely descriptive. What are the processes which contribute to the emergence of new constructs, and especially of higher-order constructs? More generally, are there any fundamental developments, beyond the accumulation of innumerable bits of learning, which help to explain the fact that there are changes in cognitive attitude as well as accretions to knowledge and skill. Construct levels constitute one such change: the older and more sophisticated learner looks for different kinds of answers. There are others. For instance, we know from recent developments in metacognition that the individual becomes a more effective learner to the extent that he can plan his own activity once he has discovered just what he is doing in the course of learning and what it is that could make these things easy or difficult. [. . .]

Having rejected equilibration theory, one is thrown back on the assumption that what is learned is learned during episodes and not by a process of consolidation and restructuring which takes place in the periods between such episodes. [. . .]

Alternative approaches

Frame theory
The concept of cognitive frames and their role in the interpretation of experience is one which was first evolved within the context of artificial intelligence theory as a way of accounting for the fact that a finite system like the brain can recognise an infinite variety of situations by assigning each new complex to some familiar category,

which already incorporates a necessary structure and an equally necessary flexibility. The construct has been fruitfully applied to the interpretation of visual scenes, which change in lawful ways as a function of movements of the viewer and of the object (Minsky, 1968, 1975), and to the interpretation of spoken and written discourse (Rumelhart and Ortony, 1977; Schank and Abelson, 1977). A *frame* is a network of related elements (which can be thought of as ideas), which has the added characteristic that not only the elements but also the links among them are distinctive and defined. If you have a frame, you know what goes with what, and also how.

The notion of frame was introduced to help in accounting for the many inferences that are made in the interpretation of everyday experience, including the things that we hear and read. In order to do this satisfactorily, there have to be many of them, and they need to exist at many different levels.

Because experience is complex and many sided, frames have a parallel complexity. Because their function is explanatory, that complexity presents a challenge.

The notion of frame has much in common with Piaget's notion of a scheme, especially in its more general formulations and as used to describe the behaviour of babies. [. . .] But frames are better spelled out than Piagetian schemes, which is why they make one face questions like how and when frames are switched off, and what triggers the switching mechanism. One useful pointer is the suggestion that, at least in narrative contexts, subordinate frames activate their superordinates, but not vice versa (Abbot and Black, 1980, quoted by van Dijk and Kintsch, 1983). In other words, frames are used to locate the current contents of experience within some more general schema, but wherever possible, we operate with unanalysed chunks of information. We do not unpack parcels unless we have to.

[. . .]

Metacognition

[. . .] I can confine myself here to raising a single question, which is the role of metacognition in cognitive development as a whole. [. . .] Of particular interest is the late work of Piaget on growth of awareness (1977). His principal thesis is that performance generally precedes awareness. One learns to do something before one learns how one does it. The ability to walk on all fours may be taken as a particularly clear example. Although children manage this before they emerge from babyhood, it is a long while before they can rightly tell the order in which they must move their limbs when doing so. There are many other examples in the motor field, and it might be argued that the phenomenon is special to that field.

Verbalised insights are notoriously unhelpful for learning how to steer a bicycle or how to turn on skis.

[. . .]

There are studies in which it is apparent that performance precedes awareness. Perhaps the most striking is an inquiry by Brown and Smiley (1977). This involved four groups of subjects, respectively aged 8, 10, 12, and 18 years. The tasks dealt with comprehension and recall of a written passage. All subjects were asked to rate the idea units in a passage according to their importance and were also required to recall the passages. All four groups, including the youngest, were sensitive to differences in importance, in that the more important units, as judged by an independent group of advanced students, were better remembered by all. But the youngest subjects were unable to make deliberate ratings of importance. Their ratings did not agree with those of the independent judges, yet their relative recall reflected these judgements and not their own.

[. . .]

The metacognitive insight is a true act of reflection on an integral process performed by the child. Metacognition so defined, is not a matter of comparing the presence of something with its absence, but of establishing how something might be varied, how these variations are defined (including the variation actually chosen), and what would be the effect of doing things in a different way. [. . .] To quote Shatz (1978): 'Metacognitive ability depends on an objectivisation of process resulting from the release of consciousness from the major chores of selecting and controlling processing operations' (p. 25). Metacognition looks like a good candidate for a more general role in producing the second-order changes postulated at the beginning of this section. At the same time, it appears to be closely bound up with the availability of working memory space, to which we now turn.

Working memory

The thinking that takes place in response to a problem or a question entails a series of decision processes, many of which require conscious attention. These decisions depend on information to which we must attend, information which results from the selection and manipulation of items which need to be available in a short-term, rapid access store, but which derive ultimately from one of two origins, direct sensory information, or the residue of earlier processing retained in long-term memory – perhaps in the form of frame knowledge. Most psychologists are agreed that the decisions, the items that are manipulated and their resultants, as well as the overall plan which determines what happens next, all occupy space in some part of the brain which is functionally akin to the central processing unit in a computer. They would agree further that the items in short-term store also need space, and that the boundaries between these two spaces are not well defined, so that there is some interchange between them. A requirement to hold material in short-term memory may compete for space with the solution of a problem, with detriment to speed or accuracy or both (Baddeley and Hitch, 1974). When these ideas are applied to typical lines of reasoning shown by younger and older children, it is immediately apparent that arguments that are more mature are generally more demanding.

[. . .]

The idea of a link between cognitive development and processing demand is one which was first adumbrated by McLaughlin (1973), who compared the norms for recall of digit sequences of varying lengths with the ages given by Piaget for concrete and formal reasoning, speculating that a concrete reasoner would need to handle four chunks of information while a formal reasoner would need seven. A much more sophisticated version of the notion was given by Pascual-Leone in the late 1960s (see Pascual-Leone and Smith, 1969). When a person faces a problem, the visual display and the instructions he or she receives combined to evoke a number of schemes. Each of these schemes corresponds to some relevant understanding.

[. . .]

There are several issues which are either unsolved or unresolved. First, I do not believe there is any reliable way at present of giving an absolute quantification of processing requirement for any given task – although relative quantifications can be instructive. The magic number four (or three) within stages or levels is only thinly supported by the evidence, since decisions about what shall be counted as an item are generally made ad hoc if not post hoc for each new task. Secondly, when a person sets about the solution of a problem, there are two sorts of things he or she needs to access: propositions or facts and actions or transformations to be executed. Both of these make demands on working memory, yet attempts at quantification almost invariably ignore the latter. [. . .] Third, the problem of transfer cannot be solved either by taking it for granted or by insisting on domain specificity. [. . .]

However, despite the persistence of such problems, I have little doubt that both level of construct and processing requirement are necessary elements in any attempt to elucidate the mechanisms underlying changes in cognitive capacity.

Production systems

[. . .] A theory of cognitive development must incorporate some way of accounting for changes in the content which the child can handle, as well as changes in the complexity of the processing sequences that are brought to bear on that content. [. . .] The child has to learn new sequences which are flexible enough to be serviceable when applied to a range of related tasks, and while implementing such an executive, he or she needs to keep track of where she or he is at within the task as a whole while simultaneously observing the constraints involved in the current step. If we had a really good theory it would explain all these things. [. . .] Production systems are models which are very specific about the implementation of sequence. A production is a rule which specifies that one or more actions is to be performed if the conditions are as stated.

Production-system modelling helps to pinpoint differences in process as between more and less advanced solutions to specific tasks, as well as differences between related tasks of unequal difficulty, such as seriation of length and of weight (Baylor and Lemoyne, 1975). However, [. . .] few, if any, existing systems incorporate all of the features that would be necessary for a realistic model, i.e. one which not only does what the human processor does, but does it in a credible way, and fails under conditions where the human operator fails. [. . .] Because production systems are precise expressions, they are a salutary discipline for the theorist. The danger is the temptation to produce systems that are powerful and effective but lack credibility as models for the human processor, whether child or adult.

The logic of thinking

One of the central tenets of Gestalt psychology was the belief that the contents of the mind undergo a gradual process of restructuring while in store. It is a view which has few adherents today. There is physiological evidence of consolidation processes, the effects of which may be protracted over several hours or even days (Deutsch and Deutsch, 1973), the implications of which are by no means clear. Nevertheless, I assume that to all intents and purposes, cognitive changes occur during cognitive episodes or very shortly after. If children learn to learn, it is while learning.

As things stand at present, more than one theoretical approach is needed to advance our understanding of cognitive development and different contributions illuminate different facets of the problem. In Table 1, only the principal emphases are indicated. The penultimate insertions are given in brackets as a way of suggesting that there is a long way to go, and we are not sure where to look. [. . .]

I have to stress that all of the foregoing is no more than reasonable speculation in the light of the known. However, if it is at all near a correct picture, then much of the fundamental learning and relearning which might be responsible for far transfer takes

Table 1   *Learning to learn: a categorisation of problems and relevant theory*

Locus or processing	Relevant theories
Interpret	Frame theory
Access plan	Frame theory
	Production systems
Implement	Working memory theory
	Production systems
Review	
Constraints observed?	Metacognition
Form new plan	(Production systems)
	(Frame theory)
	(Levels of construct)
	(Metacognition)
FEEDBACK TO LTM	Traditional learning theory

place in and through the metacognitive episodes, either in the review phase of the original learning incident or through rehearsal after the event. The idea that the reconstructions so achieved may be more reasoned and reasonable than the original solution process would be entirely consistent with dual-process theory of problem solution, according to which there is a sharp distinction between the selection and execution of response which is characteristically unreflecting and the reasoned reconstructions offered by the solver as a rationalisation of his efforts (Evans, 1982; Wason and Johnson-Laird, 1972).

All this would imply that, in the end, the emergence of new forms of cognition and problem solution owe a great deal to an innate drive for consistency. I know of no alternative to the metatheory which accords to the infant right from the start certain innate logical functions, including the recognition of sameness (but not of equality), of negation, of variation and comparison, and of the rejection of contradiction (cf. Piaget, Grize, Szeminska and Bang, 1968). Out of these are born, more or less separately, the kind of logic, which is a slow-developing specialisation that relies heavily on teaching as a separate skill (e.g. Bourne and O'Banion, 1971; Lunzer, 1973; O'Brien, Shapiro and Reali, 1971, and, especially Osherson, 1974). The principal difference between these two is that whereas the former considers only relevant alternatives and their implications, formal logical systems are unable to accept such a limitation. This is mainly because *relevant* is a fuzzy category, and logic exists for the special purpose of eliminating fuzziness or circumventing it.

References

Abbott, V. and Black, J. B. (1980) *The Representation of Scripts in Memory* (Tech. Rep.). New Haven, CT: Yale University, Department of Psychology.

Baddeley, A. D. and Hitch, G. (1974) 'Working Memory', in G. H. Bower (ed.), *The Psychology of Learning and Motivation* (Vol. 8). New York: Academic Press, pp. 47–89.

Baylor, G. W. and Lemoyne, G. (1975) 'Experiments in seriation with children: Towards an information processing explanation of the horizontal dacalage', *Canadian Journal of Behavioural Science*, 7, pp. 4–29.

Bourne, L. E. and O'Banion, K. (1971) 'Conceptual Rule Learning and Chronological Age', *Developmental Psychology*, 5, pp. 525–34.

Brainerd, C. J. (1978) 'Learning Research and Piagetian Theory', in L. S. Siegel and C. J. Brainerd (eds), *Alternatives to Piaget: Critical essays on the theory*. New York: Academic Press, pp. 69–100.

Brown, A. L. and Smiley, S. S. (1977) 'Rating the Importance of Structural Units of Prose Passages: A Problem of Metacognitive Development', *Child Development*, 48, pp. 1–8.

Bryant, P. E. (1972) 'The Understanding of Invariance by Very Young Children', *Canadian Journal of Psychology*, 26, pp. 78–96.

Case, R. (1974) 'Structures and Strictures: Some Functional Limitations on the Course of Cognitive Growth', *Cognitive Psychology*, 6, pp. 544–73.

Case, R. (1978a) 'Intellectual Development from Birth to Adulthood: A Neo-Piagetian Interpretation', in R. S. Siegler (ed.), *Children's Thinking: What Develops?* Hillsdale, NJ: Erlbaum, pp. 37–71.

Deutsch, J. A. and Deutsch, D. (1973) *Physiological Psychology* (rev. edn). Homewood, IL: Dorsey Press.

Donaldson, M. and Balfour, G. (1968) 'Less is more: A Study of Early Language Comprehension', *British Journal of Psychology*, 59, pp. 461–71.

Driver, R. and Easley, J. (1978) 'Pupils and Paradigms: A Review of Literature Related to Concept Development in Adolescent Science Students', *Studies in Science Education*, 5, pp. 61–84.

Evans, J. St. B. T. (1982) *The Psychology of Deductive Reasoning*. London: Routledge.

Festinger, L. (1957) *A Theory of Cognitive Dissonance*. Stanford, CA: Stanford University Press.

Halford, G. S. (1980) 'A Learning Set Approach to Multiple Classification: Evidence for a Theory of Cognitive Levels', *International Journal of Behavioural Development*, 3, pp. 409–22.

Hilgard, E. R. (1958) *Theories of Learning* (2nd edn). New York: Appleton.

Inhelder, B. and Piaget, J. (1958) *The Growth of Logical Thinking From Childhood to Adolescence*. New York: Basic.

Light, P. H., Buckingham, N. and Robbins, A. (1979) 'The Conservation Task as an Interactional Setting', *British Journal of Educational Psychology*, 49, pp. 304–10.

Lunzer, E. A. (1973) 'The Development of Formal Reasoning: Some Recent Experiments and their Implications', in K. Frey and M. Lang (eds), *Cognitive Processes and Science Instruction*. Bern: Huber Verlap and Baltimore: Williams and Wilkins, pp. 212–45.

McGarrigle, J. and Donaldson, M. (1974) 'Conservation Accidents', *Cognition*, 3, pp. 341–50.

McLaughlin, G. H. (1973) 'Psycho-logic: A Possible Alternative to Piaget's Formulations', *British Journal of Educational Psychology*, 33, pp. 61–7.

Minsky, M. (ed.) (1968) *Semantic Information Processing*. Cambridge, MA: MIT Press.

Minsky, M. (1975) 'A Framework for Representing Knowledge', in P. Winston (ed.), *The Psychology of Computer Vision*. New York: McGraw-Hill.

Modgil, S. and Modgil, C. (eds) (1982) *Jean Piaget: Consensus and Controversy*. New York: Praeger.

O'Brien, T. C., Shapiro, B. J. and Reali, N. C. (1971) 'Logical Thinking – Language and Context', *Educational Studies in Mathematics*, 4, pp. 201–10.

Osherson, D. N. (1974) *Logical Abilities in Children: Vol. 1. Organization of Length and Class Concepts: Empirical Consequences of a Piagetian Formalism*. Hillsdale, NJ: Erlbaum.

Pascual-Leone, J. and Smith, J. (1969) 'The Encoding and Decoding of Symbols by Children: A New Experimental Paradigm and a neo-Piagetian Model', *Journal of Experimental Child Psychology*, 8, pp. 328–55.

Piaget, J. (1950) *The Psychology of Intelligence*. London: Routledge.

Piaget, J. (1952a) *The Child's Conception of Number*. New York: Humanities.

Piaget, J. (1952b) *The Origins of Intelligence in Children*. New York: International Universities.

Piaget, J. (1959a) 'Apprentissage et connaissance (premiere partie)', in P. Greco and J. Piaget, Apprentissage et connaissance. *Etudes d'epistemologie genetique* (Vol. 7, pp. 21–67). Paris: Presses Universitaires de France.

Piaget, J. (1959b) 'Apprentissage et connaissance (seconde partie)', in M. Goustard, P. Greco, J. B. Grize, B. Matalon et J. Piaget, 'La logique des apprentissages, *Etudes d'epistemologie genetique* (Vol. 8, pp. 159–88). Paris: Presses Universitaires de France.

Piaget, J. (1962) *The Moral Judgement of the Child* (M. Gabaith, trans). New York: Collier.

Piaget, J. (1977) *The Equilibration of Cognitive Structures*. Oxford: Blackwell.

Piaget, J., Grize, J. B., Szeminska, A. and Bang, V. (1968) 'Epistemologie et psychologie de la fonction', *Etudes d'epistemologie genetique* (Vol. 23). Paris: Presses Universitaires de France.

Piaget, J., Inhelder, B. and Szeminska, A. (1960) *The Child's Conception of Geometry*. New York: Basic.

Rose, S. A. and Blank, M. (1974) 'The Potency of Context in Children's Cognition: An illustration Through Conservation', *Child Development*, 45, pp. 499–502.

Rumelhart, D. E. and Ortony, A. (1977) 'The representation of knowledge in memory', in R. C. Anderson, R. J. Spiro and W. E. Montague (eds), *Schooling and the Acquisition of Knowledge*. Hillsdale, NJ: Erlbaum, pp. 99–135.

Schank, R. C. and Abelson, R. P. (1977) *Scripts, Plans, Goals and Understanding*. Hillsdale, NJ: Erlbaum.

Shatz, M. (1978) 'The relation between cognitive processes and the development of communication skills', in B. Keary (ed.), *Nebraska Symposium on Motivation*. Lincoln: University of Nebraska Press.

Siegel, L. S. and Brainerd, C. J. (eds) (1978) *Alternatives to Piaget: Critical Essays on the Theory*. New York: Academic Press.

van Dijk, T. A. and Kintsch, W. (1983) *Strategies of Discourse Comprehension*. New York: Academic Press.

Wason, P. C. and Johnson-Laird, P. N. (1972) *Psychology of Reasoning: Structure and Content*. London: Batsford.

1.3

The Transactional Self

Jerome Bruner

If you engage for long in the study of how human beings relate to one another, especially through the use of language, you are bound to be struck by the importance of 'transactions'. This is not an easy word to define. I want to signify those dealings which are premised on a mutual sharing of assumptions and beliefs about how the world is, how mind works, what we are up to, and how communication should proceed. It is an idea captured to some extent by Paul Grice's[1] maxims about how to proceed in conversation, by Deirdre Wilson and Dan Sperber's[2] notion that we always assume that what others have said must make *some* sense, by Hilary Putnam's[3] recognition that we usually assign the right level of ignorance or cleverness to our interlocutors. Beyond these specifics, there remains a shady but important area of sharing – Colwyn Trevarthen[4] calls it 'intersubjectivity' – that makes the philosopher's query about how we know Other Minds seem more practical than the philosopher ever intended it to be.

One knows intuitively as a psychologist (or simply as a human being) that the easy access we have into each other's minds, not so much in the particulars of what we are thinking but in general about what minds are like, cannot be explained away by invoking singular concepts like 'empathy'. Nor does it seem sufficient to perform a miracle of phenomenology, as did the German philosopher Max Scheler[5], and subdivide *Einfuhlung* into a half-dozen 'feelable' classes. Or to take the route of nineteenth-century psychologists and elevate 'sympathy' to the status of an instinct. More typically, the contemporary student of mind will try to unravel the mystery by exploring how we develop this sense of what other minds are about, or by examining its pathologies, as in autistic children and in young schizophrenics. Or he will try to unravel the details of interpersonal knowledge among adults by conducting experiments on facets of this knowledge, as have Fritz Heider and his students.[6] Or, yet another alternative, he will dismiss the issue of intersubjective knowledge as 'nothing but' projection, for whatever smug satisfaction that may give him. [. . .]

When I began a series of studies on growth in human infancy and

particularly on the development of human language and its precursors, I was struck with how quickly and easily a child, once having
mastered the manipulation of objects, could enter into 'handing
back and forth', handing objects around a circle, exchanging objects
for each other. The competence seemed there, as if *ab ovum*; the
performance was what needed some smoothing out. Very young
children had something clearly in mind about what others had in
mind, and organised their actions accordingly. I thought of it as the
child achieving mastery of one of the precursors of language use: a
sense of mutuality in action.

So too in a second study (which I shall tell about more fully later)
in which we were interested in how the child came to manage his
attention jointly with others – a prerequisite of linguistic reference.[7]
We found that by their first birthday children are already adept at
following another's line of regard to search for an object that is
engaging their partner's attention. That surely requires a sophisticated conception of a partner's mind.

Yet why should we have been surprised? The child has such
conceptions 'in mind' in approaching language. Children show
virtually no difficulty in mastering pronouns and certain demonstra-
tives, for example, even though these constitute that confusing class
of referring expressions called deictic shifters.[8] A deictic shifter is an
expression whose meaning one can grasp only through appreciating
the interpersonal context in which it is uttered and by whom it is
uttered. That is to say, when I use the pronoun *I*, it means me; when
my partner uses it, it refers to him. A spatial shifter pair like *here*
and *there* poses the same problem: *here* used by me is close to me;
here used by you is close to you. The shifter ought to be hard to
solve for the child, and yet it isn't.[9]

It *ought* to be, that is, if the child were as 'self-centered' as he is
initially made out to be by current theories of child development.
For our current theories (with notable exceptions carried over from
the past, like the views of George Herbert Mead)[10] picture the child
as starting his career in infancy and continuing it for some years
after, locked in his own perspective, unable to take the perspective
of another with whom he is in interaction. And, indeed, there are
even experimental 'demonstrations' to prove the point. But *what*
point? Surely not that we can take any perspective of anybody in
any plight at any time. We would not have been so slow in achieving
the Copernican revolution if that were the case, or in understanding
that to the Indians North America must have seemed like *their*
homeland. To show that a child (or an adult) cannot, for example,
figure out what three mountains he sees before him might look like
to somebody viewing them from their 'back' sides (to take as our
whipping boy one of the classic experiments demonstrating
egocentrism),[11] does not mean he cannot take another's perspective
into account *in general*.

It is curious, in view of the kinds of considerations I have raised, that psychological theories of development have pictured the young child as so lacking in the skills of transaction. The prevailing view of initial (and slowly waning) egocentrism is, in certain respects, so grossly, almost incongruously wrong and yet so durable, that it deserves to be looked at with care. Then we can get back to the main issue – what it is that readies the child so early for transacting his life with others on the basis of some workable intuitions about Other Minds and, perhaps, about Human Situations as well. The standard view seems to have four principal tenets:

1 *Egocentric perspective.* That initially young children are incapable of taking the perspective of others, have no conception of Other Minds, and must be brought to sociality or allocentrism through development and learning. In its baldest form, this is the doctrine of initial primary process in terms of which even the first perceptions of the child are said to be little more than hallucinatory wish-fulfilments.

2 *Privacy.* That there is some inherently individualistic Self that develops, determined by the universal nature of man, and that it is beyond culture. In some deep sense, this Self is assumed to be ineffable, private. It is socialised, finally, by such processes as identification and internalisation: the outer, public world becoming represented in the inner, private one.

3 *Unmediated conceptualism.* That the child's growing knowledge of the world is achieved principally by direct encounters with that world rather than mediated through vicarious encounters with it in interacting and negotiating with others. This is the doctrine of the child going it alone in mastering his knowledge of the world.

4 *Tripartism.* That cognition, affect, and action are represented by separate processes that, with time and socialisation, come to interact with one another. Or the opposite view: that the three stem from a common process and that, with growth, they differentiate into autonomous systems. In either case, cognition is the late bloomer, the weak vessel, and is socially blind.

I do not want to argue that these four premises are 'wrong', only that they are arbitrary, partial, and deeply rooted in the morality of our own culture. They are true under certain conditions, false under others, and their 'universalisation' reflects cultural bias. Their acceptance as universals, moreover, inhibits the development of a workable theory of the nature of social transaction and, indeed, even of the concept of Self. One could argue against the tenet of privacy, for example (inspired by anthropologists), that the distinction between 'private self' and 'public self' is a function of the culture's conventions about when one talks and negotiates the meanings of events and when one keeps silent, and of the ontological status given to that which is kept silent and that which is made

public. Cultures and subcultures differ in this regard; so even do
families.

But let us return now to the main point: to the nature of transaction
and the 'executive processes' necessary to effect it, to those transactional selves hinted at in the title of this chapter. Consider in more
detail now what the mastery of language entails with respect to these
ideas.

Take *syntax* first. We need not pause long over it. The main point
that needs making is that the possession of language gives us rules
for generating well-formed utterances, whether they depend on the
genome, upon experience, or upon some interaction of the two.
Syntax provides a highly abstract system for accomplishing communicative functions that are crucial for regulating joint attention
and joint action, for creating topics and commenting upon them in a
fashion that segments 'reality', for forefronting and imposing perspectives on events, for indicating our stance towards the world to
which we refer and towards our interlocutors, for triggering presuppositions, and so on. We may not 'know' all these things about our
language in any explicit way (unless we happen to have that special
form of consciousness which linguists develop), but what we do
know from the earliest entry into language is that others can be
counted upon to use the same rules of syntax for forming and for
comprehending utterances as we use. It is so pervasive a system of
calibration that we take it for granted. It entails not just the
formulas of Grice, or of Sperber and Wilson, or of Putnam to which
I referred, but the assurance that mind is being used by others as we
use it. Syntax indeed entails a particular use of mind, and however
much one may argue (as Joseph Greenberg[12] in his way and Noam
Chomsky[13] in his have argued) that we cannot even conceive of
alternative ways of using our minds, that language expresses our
natural 'organs of thought', it is still the case that the joint and
mutual use of language gives us a huge step in the direction of
understanding other minds. For it is not simply that we all *have*
forms of mental organisation that are akin, but that we *express* these
forms constantly in our transactions with one another. We can count
on constant transactional calibration in language, and we have ways
of calling for repairs in one another's utterances to assure such
calibration. And when we encounter those who do not share the
means for this mutual calibration (as with foreigners), we regress,
become suspicious, border on the paranoid, shout.

Language is also our principal means of *referring*. In doing so, it
uses cues to the context in which utterances are being made and
triggers presuppositions that situate the referent. [. . .] Indeed,
reference plays upon the shared presuppositions and shared con-

texts of speakers. It is to the credit of Gareth Evans[14] that he recognised the profound extent to which referring involves the mapping of speakers' subjective spheres on one another. He reminds us, for example, that even a failed effort to refer is not just a failure, but rather that it is an offer, an invitation to another to search possible contexts with us for a possible referent. In this sense, referring to something with the intent of directing another's attention to it requires even at its simplest some form of negotiation, some hermeneutic process. And it becomes the more so when the reference is not present or accessible to pointing or to some other ostensive manoeuvre. Achieving joint reference is achieving a kind of solidarity with somebody. The achievement by the child of such 'intersubjective' reference comes so easily, so naturally, that it raises puzzling questions.

The evidence from early pointing (usually achieved before the first birthday) and from the infant's early following of another's line of regard suggests that there must be something preadapted and prelinguistic that aids us in achieving initial linguistic reference. I do not doubt the importance of such a biological assist. But this early assist is so paltry in comparison to the finished achievement of reference that it cannot be the whole of the story. The capacity of the average speaker to handle the subtleties of ellipsis, of anaphora – to know that, in the locution 'Yesterday I saw *a* bird, *the* bird was singing', the shift from indefinite to definite article signals that the same bird is referred to in the second phrase as in the first – is too far removed from its prelinguistic beginnings to be accounted for by them. One has to conclude that the subtle and systematic basis upon which linguistic reference itself rests must reflect a natural organisation of mind, one into which we *grow* through experience rather than one we achieve by learning.

If this is the case – and I find it difficult to resist – then human beings must come equipped with the means not only to calibrate the workings of their minds against one another, but to calibrate the worlds in which they live through the subtle means of reference. In effect, then, this is the means whereby we know Other Minds and their possible worlds.

The relation of words or expressions to other words or expressions constitutes, along with reference, the sphere of *meaning*. Because reference rarely achieves the abstract punctiliousness of a 'singular, definite referring expression', is always subject to *polysemy*, and because there is no limit on the ways in which expressions can relate to one another, meaning is always underdetermined, ambiguous. To 'make sense' in language, as David Olson[15] argued persuasively some years ago, always requires an act of 'disambiguation'. Young children are not expert at such disambiguation, but procedures for effecting it are there from the earliest speech. They negotiate – even at two years of age – not only what is being referred to by an expression, but what other expressions the present one relates to. And children's early monologues, reported by Ruth Weir[16] a generation ago and more recently by Katherine Nelson and her colleagues in the New York Language Acquisition Group,[17] all point to a drive to explore and to overcome ambiguities in the meaning of utterances. The young child seems not only to negotiate sense in his exchanges with others but to carry the problems raised by such ambiguities back into the privacy of his own monologues. The realm of meaning, curiously, is not one in which we ever live with total comfort. Perhaps it is this discomfort that drives us finally to construct those larger-scale products of language – drama and science and the disciplines of understanding – where we can construct new forms in which to transact and negotiate this effort after meaning.

To create hypothetical entities and fictions, whether in science or in narrative, requires yet another power of language that, again, is early within reach of the language user. This is the capacity of language to create and stipulate realities of its own, its *constitutiveness*. We create realities by warning, by encouraging, by dubbing with titles, by naming, and by the manner in which words invite us to create 'realities' in the world to correspond with them. Constitutiveness gives an externality and an apparent ontological status to the concepts words embody: for example, the law, gross national product, antimatter, the Renaissance.[18] [...] At our most un-guarded, we are all Naive Realists who believe not only that *we* know what is 'out there', but also that it is out there for *others* as well. Carol Feldman[19] calls it 'ontic dumping', converting our mental processes into products and endowing them with a reality in some world. The private is rendered public. And thereby, once again, we locate ourselves in a world of shared reality. The constitutiveness of language, as more than one anthropologist has insisted, creates and transmits culture and locates our place in it – a matter to which I turn next.

Language, as we know, consists not only of a locution, of what is actually said, but of an illocutionary force – a conventional means of indicating what is intended by making that locution under those circumstances. These together constitute the speech acts of ordinary language, and they might be considered as much the business of the anthropologist as of the linguist. As a phenomenon, they imply that learning how to use language involves both learning the culture and learning how to express intentions in congruence with the culture. This brings us to the question of how we may conceive of 'culture' and in what way it provides means not only for transacting with others but for conceiving of ourselves in such transactions.

It would not be an exaggeration to say that in the last decade there has been a revolution in the definition of human culture. It takes the form of a move away from the strict structuralism that held that culture was a set of interconnected rules from which people derive particular behaviours to fit particular situations, to the idea of culture as implicit and only semiconnected knowledge of the world from which, through negotiation, people arrive at satisfactory ways of acting in given contexts. The anthropologist Clifford Geertz[20] likens the process of acting in a culture to that of interpreting an ambiguous text. Let me quote a paragraph written by one of his students, Michelle Rosaldo:[21]

In anthropology, I would suggest, the key development . . . is a view of culture . . . wherein meaning is proclaimed a public fact – or better yet, where culture and meaning are described as processes of interpretive apprehension by individuals of symbolic models. These models are both 'of' the world in which we live and 'for' the organisation of activities, responses, perceptions and experiences by the conscious self. For present purposes, what is important here is first of all the claim that meaning is a fact of public life, and secondly, that cultural patterns – social facts – provide the template for all human action, growth and understanding. Culture so construed is, furthermore, a matter less of artifacts and propositions, rules, schematic programmes, or beliefs, than of associative chains and images that tell what can be reasonably linked up with what; we come to know it through collective stories that suggest the nature of coherence, probability and sense within the actor's world. Culture is, then, always richer than the traits recorded in the ethnographer's accounts because its truth resides not in explicit formulations of the rituals of daily life but in the daily practices of persons who in acting take for granted an account of who they are and how to understand their fellows' moves.

I have already discussed the linguistics, so to speak, by which this is accomplished. What of the 'cultural' side of the picture? *How* we decide to enter into transaction with others linguistically and by what exchanges, how *much* we wish to do so (in contrast to remaining 'detached' or 'silent' or otherwise 'private'), will shape our sense of what constitutes culturally acceptable transactions and our definition of our own scope and possibility in doing so – our 'selfhood'. As Rosaldo reminds us (using the Ilongot people as contrast) our Western concern with 'individuals and with their inner hidden selves may well be features of *our* world of action and belief – itself to be explained and not assumed as the foundation of cross-cultural study'. Indeed, the images and stories that we provide for guidance to speakers with respect to when they may speak and what they may say in what situations may indeed be a first constraint on the nature of selfhood. It may be one of the many reasons why anthropologists (in contrast to psychologists) have always been attentive not only to the content but to the form of the myths and stories they encounter among their 'subjects'.

For stories define the range of canonical characters, the settings in which they operate, the actions that are permissible and comprehensible. And thereby they provide, so to speak, a map of possible roles and of possible worlds in which action, thought, and self-definition are permissible (or desirable). As we enter more actively into the life of a culture around us, as Victor Turner[22] remarks, we come increasingly to play parts defined by the 'dramas' of that culture. Indeed, in time the young entrant into the culture comes to define his own intentions and even his own history in terms of the characteristic cultural dramas in which he plays a part – at first family dramas, but later the ones that shape the expanding circle of his activities outside the family.

It can never be the case that there is a 'self' independent of one's cultural-historical existence. It is usually claimed, in classical philosophical texts at least, that Self rises out of our capacity to reflect upon our own acts, by the operation of 'metacognition'. But what is strikingly plain in the promising research on metacognition that has appeared in recent years – work by Ann Brown, by J. R. Hayes, by David Perkins,[23] and others – is that metacognitive activity (self-monitoring and self-correction) is very unevenly distributed, varies according to cultural background, and, perhaps most important, can be taught successfully as a skill. Indeed, the available research on 'linguistic repairs',[24] self-corrections in utterances either to bring one's utterances into line with one's intent or to make them comprehensible to an interlocutor, suggests that an *Anlage* of metacognition is present as early as the eighteenth month of life. How much and in what form it develops will, it seems reasonable to suppose, depend upon the demands of the culture in which one lives – represented by particular others one encounters and by some notion of a 'generalised other' that one forms (in the manner so brilliantly suggested by writers as various and as separated in time as St. Augustine in the *Confessions* and George Herbert Mead in *Mind, Self, and Society*).

It would seem a warranted conclusion, then, that our 'smooth' and easy transactions and the regulatory self that executes them, starting as a biological readiness based on a primitive appreciation of other minds, is then reinforced and enriched by the calibrational powers that language bestows, is given a larger-scale map on which to operate by the culture in which transactions take place, and ends by being a reflection of the history of that culture as that history is contained in the culture's images, narratives, and tool kit.

In the light of the foregoing, we would do well to reexamine the tenets of the classical position on egocentrism with which we began.

Egocentric perspective

Michael Scaife and I discovered, as I mentioned in passing, that by the end of the first year of life, normal children habitually follow another's line of regard to see what the other is looking at, and when they can find no target out there, they turn back to the looker to check gaze direction again. At that age the children can perform none of the classic Piagetian tasks indicating that they have passed beyond egocentrism. This finding led me to take very seriously the proposals of both Katherine Nelson[25] and Margaret Donaldson[26] that when the child understands the event structure in which he is operating he is not that different from an adult. He simply does not have as grand a collection of scripts and scenarios and event schemas as adults do. The child's mastery of deictic shifters suggests, moreover, that egocentrism per se is not the problem. It is when the child fails to grasp the structure of events that he adopts an egocentric framework. The problem is not with competence but with performance. It is not that the child does not have the capacity to take another's perspective, but rather that he cannot do so without understanding the situation in which he is operating.

Privacy

The notion of the 'private' Self free of cultural definition is part of the stance inherent in our Western conception of Self. The nature of the 'untold' and the 'untellable' and our attitudes towards them are deeply cultural in character. Private impulses are defined as such by the culture. Obviously, the divide between 'private' and 'public' meanings prescribed by a given culture makes a great difference in the way people in that culture view such meanings. In our culture, for example, a good deal of heavy emotional weather is made out of the distinction, and there is (at least among the educated) a push to get the private into the public domain – whether through confession or psychoanalysis. To revert to Rosaldo's Ilongot,[27] the pressures are quite different for them, and so is the divide. How a culture defines privacy plays an enormous part in what people feel private *about* and when and how. [. . .]

Unmediated conceptualism

In the main, we do not construct a reality solely on the basis of private encounters with exemplars of natural states. Most of our approaches to the world are mediated through negotiation with others. It is this truth that gives such extraordinary force to Vygotsky's theory of the zone of proximal development. [. . .] We know far too little about learning from vicarious experience, from interaction, from media, even from tutors.

Tripartism

I hope that all of the foregoing underlines the poverty that is bred by making too sharp a distinction between cognition, affect, and action, with cognition as the late-blooming stepsister. David Krech used to urge that people 'perfink' – perceive, feel, and think at once. They also *act* within the constraints of what they 'perfink'. We *can* abstract each of these functions from the unified whole, but if we do so too rigidly we lose sight of the fact that it is one of the functions of a culture to keep them related and together in those images, stories, and the like by which our experience is given coherence and cultural relevance. The scripts and stories and 'loose associative chains' that Rosaldo spoke of are templates for canonical ways of fusing the three into self-directing patterns – ways of being a Self in transaction. [. . .]

Insofar as we account for our own actions and for the human events that occur around us principally in terms of narrative, story, drama, it is conceivable that our sensitivity to narrative provides the major link between our own sense of self and our sense of others in the social world around us. The common coin may be provided by the forms of narrative that the culture offers us. Again, life could be said to imitate art.

Notes

1 H. P. Grice (1975) 'Logic and Conversation', in P. Cole and J. L. Morgan (eds), *Syntax and Semantics 3: Speech Acts*. New York: Academic Press.
2 Dan Sperber and Deirdre Wilson (1982) 'Mutual Knowledge and Relevance in Theories of Comprehension', in N. V. Smith (ed.), *Mutual Knowledge*. London: Academic Press.
3 Hilary Putnam (1975) *Mind, Language and Reality*, vol. 2. Cambridge: Cambridge University Press.
4 Colwyn Trevarthen (1979) 'Instincts for Human Understanding and for Cultural Cooperation: Their Development in Infancy', in M. von Cranach, K. Foppa, W. Lepenies, and D. Ploog (eds), *Human Ethology: Claims and Limits of a New Discipline*. Cambridge: Cambridge University Press.
5 Max Scheler (1954) *The Nature of Sympathy*. London: Routledge and Kegan Paul.
6 For a fuller discussion of the impact of Fritz Heider's work, see E. E. Jones (1975) 'Major Developments in Social Psychology during the Last Five Decades', in G. Lindzey and E. Aronson (eds), *Handbook of Social Psychology*, 3rd edn. New York: Random House, Vol. 1.
7 Jerome Bruner (1976) 'Learning How to Do Things with Words', in J. Bruner and A. Garton (eds), *Human Growth and Development*. Wolfson College Lectures. Oxford: Oxford University Press.
8 Michael Scaife and Jerome Bruner (1975) 'The Capacity for Joint Visual Attention in the Infant', *Nature*, 253, pp. 265–6.
9 The two classical discussions of 'shifters' are John Lyons (1977) *Semantics*, Vols. 1 and 2. Cambridge: Cambridge University Press; and Emile Benveniste (1971) *Problems in General Linguistics*. Coral Gables, Fla.: University of Miami Press, chs. 18–23. For a more psychological discussion see Eve Clark, 'From Gesture to Word: On the Natural History of Deixis in Language Acquisition', in Bruner and Garton (eds), *Human Growth and Development*.

10 For Mead's views see particularly George Herbert Mead (1934) *Mind, Self, and Society*. Chicago: University of Chicago Press.
11 The 'whipping boy' in this case is Jean Piaget's (1956) *The Child's Conception of Space*. London: Routledge and Kegan Paul.
12 Joseph Greenberg (ed.) (1963) *Universals of Language*. Cambridge, Mass.: MIT Press; see also Greenberg (1957) *Essays in Linguistics*. Chicago: University of Chicago Press.
13 Noam Chomsky (1976) *Reflections on Language*. London: Temple Smith.
14 Gareth Evans (1983) *The Varieties of Reference*, J. McDowell (ed.). Oxford: Oxford University Press; see also Charles Taylor's interesting review, 'Dwellers in Egocentric Space', *Times Literary Supplement*, 11 March 1983.
15 David Olson (1970) 'Language and Thought: Aspects of a Cognitive Theory of Semantics', *Psychological Review*, 77, pp. 257–73.
16 Ruth Weir (1962) *Language in the Crib*. The Hague: Mouton.
17 The work of the New York Language Acquisition Group was presented in preliminary reports at the New York Child Language Group, November 1983, in papers delivered by Jerome Bruner, John Dore, Carol Feldman, Katherine Nelson, Daniel Stern, and Rita Watson.
18 For a discussion of constitutiveness as a 'design feature' of language see Charles Hockett (1977) *The View from Language: Selected Essays*. Athens, Ga.: University of Georgia Press. But of course the principal source for the idea of constitutiveness is John Austin's (1962) discussion of performatives in *How to Do Things with Words*. Oxford: Oxford University Press.
19 Carol Feldman, 'Epistemology and Ontology in Current Psychological Theory' (American Psychological Association Address, Sept. 1983); see also her 'Thought from Language: The Linguistic Construction of Cognitive Representations', in Jerome Bruner and Helen Weinreich-Haste (eds), *Making Sense: The Child's Construction of the World*. London: Methuen, 1987.
20 Clifford Geertz (1973) *The Interpretation of Cultures*. New York: Basic Books.
21 Michelle Rosaldo (1984) 'Toward an Anthropology of Self and Feeling', in R. Schroeder and R. Le Vine (eds), *Culture Theory: Essays on Mind, Self and Emotion*. Cambridge: Cambridge University Press, pp. 137–58. Quotations from p. 140.
22 Victor Turner (1982) *From Ritual to Theatre*. New York: Performing Arts Journal Publications.
23 For an account of the work of Ann Brown, J. R. Hayes, and David Perkins on metacognition, see S. F. Chipman, J. W. Segal, and R. Glaser (1985) *Thinking and Learning Skills*, vol. 2. Hillsdale, N.J.: Erlbaum, esp. chs. 14, 15, and 17.
24 For a review of studies on 'repair' in child language, see Eve Clark, 'Awareness of Language: Some Evidence from What Children Say and Do', in A. Sinclair, R. J. Jarvella, and W. J. M. Levelt (eds) (1978) *The Child's Conception of Language*. Berlin and New York: Springer-Verlag. For a particularly striking example of early repair, see chapter by Mary Louise Kasermann and Klaus Foppa (1981), in Werner Deutsch (ed.), *The Child's Construction of Language*. London: Academic Press.
25 Katherine Nelson and J. Grundel (1977) 'At Morning It's Lunchtime: A Scriptal View of Children's Dialogue' (paper presented at the Conference on Dialogue, Language Development and Dialectical Research, University of Michigan, December).
26 Margaret Donaldson (1978) *Children's Minds*. New York: Norton.
27 Michelle Rosaldo (1980) *Knowing and Passion*. Stanford: Stanford University Press.

1.4

The Politics of Education*

Paulo Freire

To be an act of knowing, learning demands among teachers and students a relationship of authentic dialogue. True dialogue unites subjects together in the cognition of a knowable object, which mediates between them.

If learning to read and write is to constitute an act of knowing, the learners must assume from the beginning the role of creative subjects. It is not a matter of memorising and repeating given syllables, words, and phrases, but rather of reflecting critically on the process of reading and writing itself, and on the profound significance of language.

In so far as language is impossible without thought, and language and thought are impossible without the world to which they refer, the human word is more than mere vocabulary – it is word-and-action. The cognitive dimensions of the literacy process must include the relationships of people with their world. These relationships are the source of the dialectic between the products people achieve in transforming the world and the conditioning these products in turn exercise on people.

Action upon an object must be critically analysed in order to understand both the object itself and the understanding one has of it. The act of knowing involves a dialectical movement that goes from action to reflection and from reflection upon action to a new action. For the learner to know what he did not know before, he must engage in an authentic process of abstraction by means of which he can reflect on the action-object whole, or, more generally, on forms of orientation in the world. In this process of abstraction, situations representative of how the learner orients himself in the world are proposed to him as the objects of his critique.

We recognise the indisputable unity between subjectivity and objectivity in the act of knowing. Reality is never just simply the objective datum, the concrete fact, but is also people's perception of it. Once again, this is not a subjectivistic or idealistic affirmation, as

---

* The extracts presented here focus very briefly on Freire's view of the educational process generally, and the nature of people's knowledge.

it might seem. On the contrary, subjectivism and idealism come into play when the subjective-objective unity is broken.[1]

The learning process as an act of knowing implies the existence of two interrelated contexts. One is the context of authentic dialogue between learners and educators as equally knowing subjects. This is what schools should be – the theoretical context of dialogue. The second is the real, concrete context of facts, the social reality in which people exist.[2]

In the theoretical context of dialogue, the facts presented by the real or concrete context are critically analysed. This analysis involves the exercise of abstraction, through which, by means of representations of concrete reality, we seek knowledge of that reality.

It might seem as if some of our statements defend the principle that, whatever the level of the learners, they ought to reconstruct the process of human knowing in absolute terms. In fact, when we consider education in general as an act of knowing, we are advocating a synthesis between the educator's maximally systematised knowing and the learner's minimally systematised knowing – a synthesis achieved in dialogue. The educator's role is to propose problems about the codified existential situations in order to help the learners arrive at a more and more critical view of their reality. The educator's responsibility as conceived by this philosophy is thus greater in every way than that of his colleague whose duty is to transmit information that the learners memorise. Such an educator can simply repeat what he has read, and often misunderstood, since education for him does not mean an act of knowing.

The first type of educator, on the contrary, is a knowing subject, face to face with other knowing subjects. He can never be a mere memoriser, but a person constantly readjusting his knowledge who calls forth knowledge from his students. For him, education is a pedagogy of knowing. The educator whose approach is mere memorisation is antidialogical; his act of transmitting knowledge is inalterable. For the educator who experiences the act of knowing together with his students, in contrast, dialogue is the sign of the act of knowing. He is aware, however, that not all dialogue is in itself the mark of a relationship of true knowledge.

For dialogue to be a method of true knowledge, the knowing subjects must approach reality scientifically in order to seek the dialectical connections that explain the form of reality. Thus, to know is not to remember something previously known and now forgotten. It is as conscious beings that people are not only *in* the world but *with* the world, together with other men. Only people as 'open' beings, are able to achieve the complex operation of simultaneously transforming the world by their action and grasping and expressing the world's reality in their creative language.

People can fulfil the necessary condition of being *with* the world because they are able to gain objective distance from it. Without this objectification, whereby man also objectifies himself, man would be limited to being *in* the world, lacking both self-knowledge and knowledge of the world.

Unlike people animals are simply *in* the world, incapable of objectifying either themselves or the world. They live a life without time, properly speaking, submerged in life with no possibility of emerging from it, adjusted and adhering to reality. People, on the contrary, who can sever this adherence and transcend mere being in the world, add to the life they have the existence which they make. To exist is thus a mode of life that is proper to the being who is capable of transforming, of producing, of deciding, of creating, and of communicating himself.

Whereas the being that merely lives is not capable of reflecting upon itself and knowing itself living *in* the world, the existent subject reflects upon his life within the very domain of existence, and questions his relationship to the world. His domain of existence is the domain of work, of history, of culture, of values. 'Consciousness of' and 'action upon' reality are inseparable constituents of the transforming act by which people become beings of relations.[3] By their characteristic reflection, intentionality, temporality, and transcendence, people's consciousness and action are distinct from the mere *contacts* of animals with the world.[4] The animals' contacts are acritical; they do not go beyond the association of sensory images through experience. They are singular and not plural. Animals do not elaborate goals; they exist at the level of immersion and are thus atemporal.

Engagement and objective distance, understanding reality as object, understanding the significance of people's action upon objective reality, creative communication about the object by means of language, plurality of responses to a single challenge – these varied dimensions testify to the existence of critical reflection in people's relationships with the world. Consciousness is constituted in the dialectic of man's objectification of and action upon the world. Yet consciousness is never a mere reflection of but a reflection upon material reality.[5]

If it is true that consciousness is impossible without the world that constitutes it, it is equally true that this world is impossible if the world itself in constituting consciousness does not become an object of its critical reflection. Thus, mechanistic objectivism is just as incapable of explaining people and the world, since it negates people, as is solipsistic idealism, since it negates the world.

For mechanistic objectivism, consciousness is merely a 'copy' of objective reality. For solipsism, the world is reduced to a capricious creation of consciousness. In the first case, consciousness would be unable to transcend its conditioning by reality; in the second, in so far as it 'creates' reality, it is *a priori* to reality. In either case man is not engaged in transforming reality. That would be impossible in objectivistic terms, because for objectivism, consciousness, the replica or 'copy' of reality, is the object of reality, and reality would then be transformed by itself.[6] The solipsistic view is equally incompatible with the concept of transforming reality, since the transformation of an imaginary reality is an absurdity. Thus in both conceptions of consciousness there can be no true praxis. Praxis is only possible where the objective–subjective dialectic is maintained.[7]

Behaviourism also fails to comprehend the dialectic of man-world relationships. Under the form called mechanistic behaviourism, men are negated because they are seen as machines. The second form, logical behaviourism, also negates men, since it affirms that men's consciousness is 'merely an abstraction'.[8] The process of conscientisation cannot be founded upon any of these defective explanations of man-world relationships. Conscientisation is viable only because men's consciousness, although conditioned, can recognise that it is conditioned. This 'critical' dimension of consciousness accounts for the goals people assign to their transforming acts upon the world. Because they are able to have goals, people alone are capable of entertaining the result of their action even before initiating the proposed action.

For people, as beings of praxis, to transform the world is to humanise it, even if making the world human may not yet signify the humanisation of men. It may simply mean impregnating the world with man's curious and inventive presence, imprinting it with the trace of his works. The process of transforming the world, which reveals this presence of man, can lead to his humanisation as well as his dehumanisation, to his growth or diminution. These alternatives reveal to man his problematic nature and pose a problem for him, requiring that he choose one path or the other.

The reflectiveness and finality of people's relationships with the world would not be possible if these relationships did not occur in an historical as well as physical context. Without critical reflection there is no finality, nor does finality have meaning outside an uninterrupted temporal series of events. For people there is no 'here' relative to a 'there' that is not connected to a 'now', a 'before', and an 'after'. Thus people's relationships with the world are *per se* historical, as are people themselves. Not only do people make the history that makes them, but they can recount the history of this mutual making.

[. . .]

Like any act of study, reading is not just a pastime but a serious task in which readers attempt to clarify the opaque dimensions of their study. To read is to rewrite, not memorise, the contents of what is being read. We need to dispense with the naive idea of 'consuming' what we read.

Like Sartre, we might call this artificial notion the nutritionist concept of knowledge, according to which those who read and study do so to become 'fat intellectuals'.[9] This might justify such expressions as 'hungry for knowledge', 'thirst for knowledge', and to have or not to have an 'appetite for understanding'.

This same artificial concept currently informs educational practice in which knowledge is an act of transference. Educators are the posessors of knowledge, whereas learners are 'empty vessels' to be filled by the educators' deposits. Hence learners do not have to ask questions or offer any challenge, since their position cannot be other than to receive passively the knowledge their educators deposit.

If knowledge were static and consciousness empty, merely occupying a certain space in the body, this kind of educational practice would be valid. But this is not the case. Knowledge is not something that's made and finished. And consciousness is an 'intention' towards the world.

In humanistic terms, knowledge involves a constant unity between action and reflection upon reality. Like our presence in the world, our consciousness transforms knowledge, acting on and thinking about what enables us to reach the stage of reflection. This is precisely why we must take our presence in the world as the focus of our critical analysis. By returning to our previous experiences, we grasp the knowledge of those experiences.

The more we can uncover reasons to explain why we are as we are, the more we can also grasp the reason behind our reality and thus overcome our naive understanding. As passive individuals, learners are not invited to participate creatively in the process of their learning; instead they are 'filled' by the educators' words. Within the cultural framework of this practice, educators are presented to the learners as though the latter were separated from life, as though language-thought were possible without reality. In such educational practice, the social structures are never discussed as a problem that needs to be revealed.

Education of a liberating character is a process by which the educator invites learners to recognise and unveil reality critically. Education for domestication is an act of transferring 'knowledge', whereas education for freedom is an act of knowledge and a process of transforming action that should be exercised on reality. The passive learner, has a naive outlook on social reality, which for this one is a given, that is, social reality is a *fait accompli* rather than something that's still in the making.[10] Yet, it is impossible for us to escape the real world without critically assuming our presence in it. If we are in the sciences, for instance, we might try to 'hide' in what we regard as the neutrality of scientific pursuits, indifferent to how our findings are used, even uninterested in considering for whom or from what interests we are working. Usually when questioned about this, we respond vaguely that we work for the interest of humanity.

If we practice religion, we might establish an unfeasible separation between humanity and transcendence.

If we work in the social sciences, we might treat our society under study as though we are not participants in it. In our celebrated impartiality, we might approach this real world as if we were wearing 'gloves and masks' in order not to contaminate or be contaminated by it.

Our concept of history can be mechanistic and fatalistic. History is what took place not what is in the making or what will come. The present is something that should be normalised; whereas the future, as a repetition of the present, becomes the maintenance of the status quo.

In none of these cases can one appreciate people as a *presence* in the world, as beings of praxis, of action and thinking about the world.

The dichotomy between theory and practice, the universality of a knowledge stripped of its historical-sociological conditioning, the role of philosophy in explaining the world as merely an instrument for our acceptance of the world, education as a pure exposition of facts that transfer abstract values purported to be the inheritance of a pure knowledge – all of these reflect an ingenious perception of humanity in its relationships with the world.

As we become aware of the falseness of these beliefs we find it difficult to appreciate the very impossibility of theory without practice, the impossibility of thinking without a transforming action in the world, as well as the impossibility of knowledge for its own sake or the impossibility of a theory that only explicates reality and offers a neutral education. Once we verify our inquisitive nature as researchers and investigators of reflexive (and not merely reflective) consciousness, and once we make that knowledge accessible, we automatically ascertain our capacity to recognise or to remake existing knowledge. Moreover, we can identify and appreciate what is still unknown. If this were not so, that is, if the type of consciousness that recognises existing knowledge could not keep searching for new knowledge, there would be no way to explicate today's knowledge. Since knowing is a process, knowledge that exists today was once only a viability and it then became a new knowledge, relative and therefore successive to yesterday's existing knowledge.

Notes

1 'There are two ways to fall into idealism: the one consists of dissolving the real in subjectivity; the other in denying all real subjectivity in the interests of objectivity.' Jean Paul Sartre (1968) *Search for a Method*, trans. Hazel E. Barnes. New York: Vintage Books, p. 33.
2 See Karel Kosik (1967) *Dialéctica de lo Concreto*. Mexico: Grijalbo.
3 On the distinction between man's relationships and the contacts of animals, see Paulo Freire (1967) *Educação como práctica da liberdade*. Rio de Janeiro: Paz e Terra.
4 *Transcendence* in this context signifies the capacity of human consciousness to surpass the limitations of the objective configuration. Without this 'transcendental intentionality', consciousness of what exists beyond limitations would be impossible. For example, I am aware of how the table at which I write limits me only because I can transcend its limits, and focus my attention on them.
5 '"Man, a reasoning animal", said Aristotle.
   "Man, a reflective animal", let us say more exactly today, putting the accent on the evolutionary characteristics of a quality which signifies the passage from a still diffuse consciousness to one sufficiently well centred to be capable of coinciding with itself. Man not only "a being who knows" but "a being who knows he knows." Possessing *consciousness raised to the power of two* ... Do we sufficiently feel the radical nature of the difference?' Pierre Teilhard de Chardin (1965) *The Appearance of Man*, trans. J. M. Cohen. New York: Harper and Row p. 224.
6 Marx rejects the transformation of reality by itself in his third thesis' on Feuerbach, *Karl Marx: Selected Writings in Sociology and Social Philosophy*, trans. T. B. Bottomore. New York: McGraw-Hill, 1964, pp. 67–8.
7 In a discussion of men-world relationships during a *circulo de cultura*, a Chilean peasant affirmed 'I now see that there is no world without men.' When the educator asked, 'Suppose all men died, but there were still trees, animals, birds, rivers, and stars, wouldn't this be the world?' 'No,' replied the peasant, 'there would be no one to say, this is the world.'
8 We refer to behaviourism as studied in John Beloff's (1964) *The Existence of Mind*, New York: Citadel Press.
9 Jean Paul Sartre, (1959) *Situations I*, Paris: Librairie Gallimard.
10 In this sense, many illiterates and semi-illiterates are from a linguistic point of view actual political literates, much more so than certain erudite literates. This isn't surprising. The political practices of the former, their experiences through conflict (in essence, the midwife of real consciousness), teach them what the erudite do not or cannot learn from books.

1.5

Learning: The Interactive Re-Creation of Knowledge

Hermain Sinclair*

Knowledge

From a constructivist point of view, the essential way of knowing the real world is not directly through our senses, but first and foremost through out material and/or mental actions. In this context, action has to be understood in the following way: all activity by which we bring about a change in the world around us or by which we change our own situation in relation to the world. In other words, it is activity that changes the knower–known relationship. From the baby who laboriously pushes two objects together or who attracts his mother's attention by crying, to the scientist who invents new ways of making elementary particles react and the child or adult who tries to convince his friends of his opinions, new knowledge is constructed from the changes or transformations the subject introduces in the knower–known relationship.

At all levels the child constructs 'theories' (in action or thought) to make sense of his experience; as long as these theories work the child will abide by them. Since human beings tend to push their ideas as far as they will go and actively seek novel experiences, they will partly conserve and partly transform their ideas when experience widens, and new questions arise for which the theory is not adequate. This process has no predestined end: since the relation between knower and known is indissociable, there is no way to test acquired knowledge against an absolute reality.

As Piaget, who saw himself as a realist of a rather special kind, expresses it (1980, pp. 221–2): 'With every step forward in knowledge that brings the subject nearer to his object, the latter retreats . . . so that the successive models elaborated by the subject are no more than approximations that despite improvements can never reach . . . the object itself, which continues to possess unknown properties . . .' This does not mean that the knowing subjects are

---

* Sinclair's original chapter includes three parts: a constructivist conception of Knowledge; personal and social interaction in a constructivist framework and children's learning in mathematics. This chapter includes only aspects of the discussion from the first two parts.

forever living in a world of their own making; but it does mean that they can never get absolute knowledge of reality as it is.

The fundamental constructivist view thus postulates changes in the relation between subject and object; and the movement towards better – though never perfect – knowledge of the object has as its concomitant another movement whereby the subject obtains better knowledge of his own actions or thought processes. There may not be perfect synchronicity, but sooner or later every new conquest of the world of objects will lead the subject to restructure his action or thought operations system, just as new deductions and inferences derived from the internal system will lead to new interrogations of reality.

Social interaction, society, and learning

So far, the construction of knowledge would seem to be an almost totally endogenous process. [. . .] However, science is essentially a social enterprise, and society and social interaction in general are an essential factor in the constructivist view of knowledge.

In the first place, there is the epistemological necessity of having a way to judge the quality of the knowledge that is acquired. Since there is no direct way of checking the 'correctness' or the 'truth' of our knowledge against reality itself, but only of judging what von Glasersfeld (1983) calls its 'goodness of fit with experience, its viability as a means for the solving of problems', knowledge can only be considered 'objective' (in contrast with subjective belief) when 'it has been checked (and not simply accepted) by other scientists' (Piaget, 1965).

In the second place, there are psychological reasons for considering social interaction as essential for knowledge. Human beings do not only interact with objects and natural phenomena such as snow and flowers, but also, and in a sense primarily, with other human beings. Though Piaget refers only sporadically, and always only very theoretically, to the necessity and importance of this type of interaction, its contribution to the fundamental reflective processes is becoming clearer, especially through studies of peer-interaction among young children (Stambak et al., 1983; Sinclair, 1987). Even very simple reciprocal imitation (one child pushing a stick through a ball of cottonwool, another doing the same, and then going on to push the ball of cottonwool up and down the stick, and the first one imitating this further action) offers both partners an occasion to see their own actions from the outside and from the inside, as it were, and this may facilitate reflexion on the action as an object of thought.

In the third place, it is clear that society in general, with its accumulation of knowledge, intervenes in the individual processes of the construction of knowledge: if not, every generation would start all over again and we would still be at the level of cave-dwellers. Children do not interact with 'pure objects, only defined by their physical properties' (Piaget and Garcia, 1983, p. 274), but they interact with objects that have been made by their society (dolls, blocks, spoons . . .) and that are presented to them in a context where these objects (as well as natural objects such as flowers, pebbles, etc.) have certain meanings. As the children grow older, their direct experience with objects becomes more and more subordinated to 'the system of meanings the social milieu confers on the objects' (Piaget and Garcia, 1983, p. 295). Construction of knowledge therefore is on the one hand a result of very general processes, such as abstraction and equilibration, and on the other hand of the way objects are presented to the subject with their societal meanings. Society, conclude Piaget and Garcia, can modify the latter, but not the former. And, we may add, this is where 'learning' in the sense of children integrating the knowledge of their society in their time comes into the picture: adults in general, and teachers in particular, *present* children with real objects or with objects of thought in a certain way that makes it possible for them to rediscover or re-invent what it took their society a long time to elaborate. When Piaget, in his writings on education, asserts that 'to understand is to invent or to discover', the inventions or discoveries are new to the child, but seen from the adult's point of view, they are re-creations. Our children do not have to *invent* the wheel: they can begin to conceptualise the intricate properties of wheels as they exist in our society. Toddlers can, and do, compare the movement of a toy car with wheels to that of a toy car that has lost one or more of its wheels. Similarly, our written numerical system is presented to our children as an object of thought: they certainly have to reconstruct it (partly endogenously and partly socially) but that is not the same as having to invent it.

Some Piagetian studies have shown the influence of subtle changes in the way objects are presented. For example, when the transformation of a ball of modelling clay into a sausage-like roll is not done in a continuous rolling action, but by taking bits of clay from one side and sticking them onto the other, children who in the traditional situation give non-conservation answers now are convinced that the amount has not changed. Inhelder *et al.* (1975) explain this 'understanding' (which is stable in the sense that afterwards the traditional mode of transformation also leads to conservation answers) as follows: the taking away of bits of clay on one side centres the child's attention on the fact that first the amount becomes *less*, and then, when the bits are added to the other end, the amount becomes *more*, while the displaced bits remain the same. Compensation then becomes 'evident' whereas in the traditional mode the child focuses on what to him is a 'positive' aspect of the transformation: the clay is now 'longer'. The difficulty of taking into account both negative and positive effects of an action or thought process have often been stressed by Piaget and are particularly spectacular in numerical problems. There must be many different ways in which the presentation of objects of thought can foster even such endogenous processes as reflective abstraction. Not all of them have to do with conflict and compensation; in other cases, the child's cognitive system is trying to find new problems (just as all action schemes tend to be applied to more and more objects and situations) and society in the large sense, or the family, or the school, can present a hungry mind with new problems. On this point, constructivist theory rejoins Vygostky's ideas concerning a 'zone of proximal development' and the role of society and school. Constructivist psychology contributes to the study of learning mainly through the elucidation of the basic processes of knowledge acquisition. Except for the example just quoted, and Inhelder's *et al.* studies on learning (Inhelder, Sinclair and Bovet, 1974), Piagetian studies were not designed to discover in what kind of situations (either in or out of school) certain structures and procedures of action and thought are built up. The subtle, but powerful interaction between the societal presentation of objects which allows a great number of children nowadays to master scientific concepts only geniuses could construct in the past cries out for detailed study.

Fostering the growth of knowledge: teaching and learning

The study of learning in the sense discussed above (the interaction between societal presentation and endogenous processes of abstraction) seems to be particularly difficult in the field of logico-mathematical knowledge. Since there are no properties of real objects to be discovered, experimentation (suggested or demonstrated) which can lead to empirical abstraction is not adequate in most cases. Piaget's maxim of 'discovery' and 'invention' on the part of the child makes me think that he would have agreed with Bacon (surprisingly!) who has the following statements to make about what he calls 'the delivery of knowledges'.
 Bacon postulates (1965 edition, pp. 69–70):

> For as knowledges are now delivered, there is a kind of contract of error between the deliverer and the receiver. For he that delivereth knowledge, desireth to deliver it in such form as may be best believed, and not as may be best examined; and he that receiveth knowledge, desireth rather present satisfaction, than expectant inquiry; and so rather not to doubt, than not to err . . . But knowledge that is delivered as a thread to be spun on, ought to be delivered and intimated, if it were possible, in the same method wherein it was invented . . . But . . . no man

knoweth how he came to the knowledge which he hath obtained. But yet nevertheless ... a man may revisit and descend unto the foundation of his knowledge and consent; and so transplant it into another, as it grew in his own mind. For it is in knowledges as it is in plants: if you mean to use the plant, it is no matter for the roots; but if you mean to remove it to grow, then it is more assured to rest upon roots than slips: so the delivery of knowledges (as it is now used) is as of fair bodies of trees without the roots; good for the carpenter, but not for the planter. But if you will have sciences grow, it is less matter for the shaft of body of the tree, so you look well to the taking up of the roots. Of which the kind of delivery the method of the mathematics, in that subject, hath some shadow: but generally I see it neither put in use nor put in inquisition, and therefore note it for deficient.

Bacon may well have been too sanguine as regards the methods of mathematics teaching, but his view of the delivery of knowledge as fostering its growth certainly fits the constructivist framework. Yet it is difficult for adults to 'descend unto the foundations of their knowledge'.

As adults, we have absorbed, unconsciously in the main, the meanings our society and culture attaches to objects and actions; when presenting them to children we continue to be influenced by these meanings. Just as in science in general, such meanings and values (and even fashions) can both favour and hinder progress; the child's growth of knowledge is influenced in either a positive or a negative way by socially determined meanings. [. . .]

References

Bacon, F. (1965) Johnston, A. (ed.), New York: Shocken Books.

Glasersfeld von, E. (1983) 'Learning as a constructive activity'. *Proceedings of the 5th Annual Meeting of the North American Chapter of the International Group for the Psychology of Mathematics Education*, Montreal.

Inhelder, B., Sinclair, H. and Bovet, M. (1974) *Apprentissage et structures cognitives*. Paris: PUF.

Inhelder, B., Blanchet, A., Sinclair, A. and Piaget, J. (1975) 'Relations entre les Conservations d'Ensembles d'Éléments Discrets et Celles de Quantités Continues', *Année Psychologique*, 75, pp. 23–60.

Piaget, J. (1965) *Sagesse et Illusions de la Philosophie* Paris: PUF.

Piaget, J. (1970) *Psychologie et Épistémologie*. Paris: Editions Denoël.

Piaget, J. (1980) *Les Formes Élémentaires de la Dialectique*. Paris: Gallimard.

Piaget, J. and Garcia, R. (1983) *Psychogenèse et histoire des sciences*. Paris: Flammarion.

Sinclair, H. (1987) 'Symbolism and Interpersonal Interaction', *Cahiers de la Fondation Archives Piaget*, No. 8, Genève.

Stambak, M., Barrière, M., Bonica, L., Maisonnet, R., Musatti, T., Rayna, S. and Verba, M. (1983) *Les bébés entre eux*. Paris: PUF.

Steffe, L. P. and Cobb, P. (1988) *Construction of mathematical meanings and strategies*. New York, Berlin, Heidelberg: Springer Verlag.

1.6

Problem Solving and Education*

Thomas André

Context and introduction

Much of education is intended to make people better problem solvers. The justification for teaching children to read, write, or reckon is usually couched in some variant of: *These skills will be useful in solving problems later.* The arguments for a liberal college education usually have a future problem-solving component implicit within them. While problem solving is central to education, the study of problem solving has historically received only sporadic attention from educators and educational psychologists. An explicit theory of problem solving has not been available and educators interested in promoting problem solving have primarily been engaged in guesswork when designing programmes. Since the late 1960s or early 1970s, the study of thinking and problem solving has become respectable for psychologists, and the issues of promoting problem-solving skills has become an important one for educators. While a complete theory of problem solving does not yet exist, we have learned much about the kinds of thinking that goes on when individuals solve problems and about the kinds of factors that facilitate problem solving.

This chapter has two basic purposes: (1) to provide an overview of psychological research and theory in the area of problem solving, and (2) to discuss ways in which students can better be taught to become effective problem solvers. The general approach taken is to first provide a description of historically interesting theories of problem solving to provide background and then to focus the present chapter on a cognitive information-processing, schema-theoretic view of problem solving. A model for teaching of problem-

---

* André defines and describes problem solving and various areas for research within it. In his discussion of the problem-solving components he references a wide range of relevant research. Because of the focus of the reader the extract omits aspects of the research discussed and only highlights the component role of domain-specific knowledge in problem solving.

solving skills is proposed in which problem solving is assumed to be similar to the development of other intellectual skills. This model is used to analyse the instructionally important elements of intellectual skill acquisition and to provide a description of things teachers can do to promote the development of problem solving.

The nature of problem solving and approaches to studying problem solving

What is a problem?

While all of us know what a problem is at an intuitive level, a definition of what a problem is provides a place to start a discussion of problem solving. Most discussions of problem solving are usually consistent with this definition: *A problem is a situation in which the individual wants to do something but does not know the course of action needed to get what he or she wants* (Newell and Simon, 1972).

[. . .]

What is problem solving?

Problem solving consists of the mental and behavioural activities that are involved in dealing with problems. Problem solving may involve thinking (cognitive) components, emotional or motivational components, and behavioural components. Mentally transforming cents to dollars would be an example of a thinking component, a feeling of confidence in one's ability to solve the problem would represent an emotional component, and looking up something in a dictionary or library would be a behavioural component. This chapter focuses on the cognitive components of problem solving, but it is important to realise that motivational and behavioural components are involved in real-life problem solving. For example, a professional advertising photographer may take a series of trial Polaroid photographs to test the lighting and get an actual visual impression of a setup before the actual usable images are made. If someone gives you a puzzle, and you do not feel that solving it is worth your effort, you are unlikely to engage in problem solving. Psychological research has mostly been involved with cognitive approaches to problem solving, and a theory that integrates motivational and behavioural components into a comprehensive view of problem solving is still in the future.

Historical approaches to problem solving

The behavioural approach

The behavioural approach to psychology was the dominant force in American psychology during the first sixty years of the twentieth century, and problem solving was involved in some of the earliest studies of behavioural psychology. Thorndike (1898) studied the behaviour of cats placed in a box whose door could be opened if a lever was pressed. When first placed in the box, the cats would engage in a variety of behaviours such as trying to squeeze through an opening, biting at the wire, etc. Eventually, the cat would press the lever, open the door, and escape. When placed back in the box, the cat would engage in less random behaviour before escaping. Finally, the cat would come to be able to escape immediately upon entering the box. Thorndike explained the cat's problem solving by invoking the concepts that have come to be called reinforcement and extinction. Solution-irrelevant behaviour was gradually extinguished or eliminated because it did not lead to reinforcement, while the response of lever pressing was gradually strengthened by being reinforced by escape. In solving the problem, the cat did not show thought or planning of activities, so Thorndike called the process *trial-and-error learning* and used that basic model as a description of problem solving in general. With some quibbling among behaviourists as to the exact nature of such trial-and-error learning. Thorndike's view has provided the basic behavioural model of problem solving (Campbell, 1960; Davis, 1973; Mayer, 1983; Skinner, 1966; Staats, 1966).

According to behavioural views, trial-and-error learning occurs when a stimulus situation demands a response, but the correct response is not dominant in the response hierarchy for that situation. By *response hierarchy* is meant the set of responses a learner might make in that situation. A *dominant response* is the response that is most likely in a situation. The learner tries out responses in their order of dominance. Incorrect responses are extinguished, and the correct response reinforced until it becomes dominant in that situation. This behavioural view allows little room for thought and planning in problem solving. But it is clear that in many situations, humans do think about problems before engaging in behaviour. Human activity does not seem to be totally random. Behaviourists argue that such thinking consists of internal trial-and-error learning (Davis, 1973). Such trial-and-error learning can be mediated by discriminative stimuli produced by verbal responses (language) (Skinner, 1966; Staats, 1966).

The Gestalt approach to problem solving

Partly in reaction to American behaviourism and partly in reaction to other German schools of psychology, a group of German psychologists, called *Gestalt psychologists*, developed an approach to psychology that emphasised the role of mental structure and organisation in perception and thinking. With respect to problem solving, they emphasised the role of a sudden reorganisation of mental elements into a structure that provides a solution to a problem. This sudden reorganisation was called an *insight experience*.

The first Gestalt study of problem solving was provided by Kohler (1925), who studied problem solving in chimpanzees and other animals. Kohler presented chimpanzees with problems such as the two-stick problem. In this problem, the chimp needed to fit one stick into a second to make a stick long enough to reach a banana placed outside its cage. Kohler noted that the behaviour of the chimp did not seem to involve random trial and error, but rather it studied the problem, with a sudden solution emerging. Kohler called the sudden restructuring of the problem an *insight*. He argued that human problem solving also was based on thinking about a situation and rearranging the mental elements into a structure that provides a solution to the problem. Other Gestalt psychologists investigated the effects of mental habits in preventing problem restructuring and insight (Duncker, 1945; Katona, 1940; Luchins, 1942; Maier, 1930, 1970). These studies demonstrated that prior habits could interfere with the discovery of problem solutions and raised the issue of discovery versus expository learning.

The stages of problem solving

Several authors have analysed problem solving into a series of stages. Wallas (1926) described the stages of (1) preparation, (2) incubation, (3) inspiration, and (4) verification. In the *preparation stage*, the problem solver analyses the problem, tries to define it clearly, and gathers relevant facts and information. In the *incubation* stage, the problem is considered subconsciously while the problem solver is relaxing or considering something else. During the *inspiration* stage, the solution to get the problem comes to the learner unexpectedly in the sort of 'light bulb lights' experience illustrated in cartoons. The inspiration stage corresponds to the insight experience of the Gestalt psychologists. The *verification* stage involves checking the solution and working out the details. [. . .]

Not all stage descriptions place a strong emphasis on the subconscious processes of incubation and inspiration. Many describe a rational series of steps that the problem solver presumably goes through in solving a problem (Adams, 1974; Hayes, 1981; Kingsley and Garry, 1957; Osborn, 1963). An intuitive average of these stages is shown in Table 2. Descriptions such as shown in Table 2 are

Table 2   *Analytic stages of problem solving*

1 *Problem noticing*: Some discrepancy between what you have and want is noted.
2 *Problem specification*: A more precise description of the problem is worked out.
3 *Problem analysis*: The parts of the problem are figured out, and relevant information is gathered.
4 *Solution generation*: Possible solutions are considered.
5 *Testing of solutions*: The various possible solutions are considered and evaluated for likelihood of success.
6 *Solution selection and implementation*: The most likely solution is implemented in detail and evaluated for success.
7 *Solution revision* as necessary.

both very rational and gross. They are *rational* in the sense that they emphasise conscious thought and a logical analytic approach to problem solving. They are *gross* in the sense that they provide a molar and imprecise description of the mental activities in problem solving. They do not say what the mind or brain does when problems are noticed or solutions are generated. An adequate theory of problem solving will have to explain how problems are noticed or solutions generated, etc. However, these stage descriptions may be a useful starting place for an adequate theory.

Stage descriptions may also have a heuristic value in teaching learners to be more effective problem solvers. The steps can be considered as directions to learners to engage in activities that might facilitate problem solving. When considered as directions, such steps form a basis for most problem-solving training courses. Training with such directives has also been used to help individuals to solve interpersonal and emotional problems in counselling (Craighead, Kazdin, and Mahoney, 1981; Goldfried and Goldfried, 1980).

The Piagetian approach to problem solving
Piaget and his followers have developed an approach to problem solving that focuses on the mental logic that supports problem solving and how that logic develops (see Chapter 1.2 by Lunzer). [. . .]

A cognitive information-processing model of problem solving

Since the early 1960s, the dominant position in American psychology has moved from a behavioural position to a cognitive information-processing position. This position is based on a metaphor that the brain is like a programmed computer. From this position, problem solving is viewed as the processing of information by an information-processing system (brain, computer), such that the information in an initial state is transformed into the information of a desired end state. An adequate theory of problem solving would consist of (1) a complete description of the architecture and capabilities of the information-processing system and (2) a description of the step-by-step processes by which a problem-solving activity is carried out. The level of description in such a theory would be sufficiently precise to simulate the entity being described in an actual or conceptual computer. Often information-processing descriptions are actually programmed into a computer (e.g. Newell and Simon, 1972), and the adequacy of the description is tested by comparing the computer simulation to the behaviour of humans. Unlike the behavioural position, the cognitive focus has mostly been on the description of how problem solving occurs rather than how individuals learn to become problem solvers. Only recently has learning received attention within the information-processing tradition.

A general problem-solving model

Most cognitive psychologists would agree to a description of prob-

Table 3 *An information-processing description of problem solving*

1 A problem consists of a situation where you want something and do not know the precise steps to get it.
2 The problem solver analyses the problem into goals and givens as defined in Table 2 and forms an initial representation of the goals and givens in memory.
3 The problem solver operates on the representations of the givens and the goals in order to reduce the discrepancy between the givens and the goals. A solution to the problem consists of the path of operations that can transform the givens into the goals.
4 In operating on the givens and goals, the problem solver may use the following, not necessarily exclusive, approaches:
   (a) Information or schemata (productions) in long-term memory
   (b) Heuristic approaches to solving problems
   (c) Algorithms for problem solution if they are available
   (d) Metaphorical relationships with other representations.
5 The process of operating on an initial representation to find a problem solution is called *search*. As part of the solution-search process, the representation may be transformed into other representations.
6 Search continues until either a solution is found or the problem solver gives up.

lem solving that is similar to that described in Table 3 (Anderson, 1980; Hayes, 1981; Mayer, 1983; Newell and Simon, 1972). The description in Table 3 is similar in some ways to the steps of problem-solving notions described above, but has the advantage of telling us issues that need to be investigated in order to understand problem solving. If this description of problem solving is accurate, then areas to be researched include:

1 The processes by which a problem description is converted to an internal representation.
2 The role of representation in problem solving.
3 The role of prior knowledge in problem solving – this issue subsumes questions about:
   (a) the nature of knowledge in our memory
   (b) factors that cause stored knowledge to be activated
   (c) differences between verbal knowledge and skill knowledge
   (d) the arrangement of knowledge in memory.

Specific heuristics and domain-specific knowledge

While early studies of problem solving emphasised general heuristics, more recent work has recognised that expert problem solvers amass a large amount of domain-specific knowledge. Such knowledge can include larger structures for recognising problems, more complicated algorithms, and a large number of specific heuristics. Lenat (1983) developed a computer simulation that was able to learn and discover fundamental laws of basic arithmetic from an initial base of fundamental mathematical facts. The programme consisted of only a few basic facts but a large number of quite specific heuristics that controlled the exploration process. In addition, the programme had to develop new specific heuristics as it learned about the subject matter. Champagne, Klopfer, and Chaiklin (1984) studied what physics students needed to know to solve transfer problems. They found that the learners needed much more domain-specific knowledge than is commonly given in physics instruction. Without such knowledge, students were not able to do much more than rotely memorise solutions to problems and were unable to transfer what they had been taught to new situations. For example, Simon (1980) estimates that a chess master has approximately 50,000 general patterns of chess pieces stored in memory. Each pattern includes a pattern of pieces and a procedure to follow when that pattern is encountered. Simon estimates a minimum of eight seconds of learning are required to master each chunk. More complicated chunks would take longer; Simon believes that expertise in a subject matter area probably requires 10 years of study of that area. Other authors (Goldstein and Papert, 1977; Norman,

1980) also support the notion that efficient problem solving requires considerable domain-specific knowledge.

To illustrate the kinds of knowledge necessary for a particular domain, consider the kinds of knowledge Mayer (1983) identifies as necessary knowledge for solving mathematical story problems. Mayer's list includes

1 Linguistic knowledge – recognising words, parsing sentences, etc.
2 Semantic knowledge – knowledge of the world relevant to the problem.
3 Schematic knowledge – knowledge of problem types.
4 Procedural knowledge – knowledge of the algorithms necessary for problem solution.
5 Strategic knowledge – techniques for using types of knowledge and heuristics.

[. . .] Superficial analyses of problem solving have often given the impression that much creativity and problem solving depends on the unlocking of hidden potential and general tricks of thinking (André, 1979). Rather effective problem solving in a domain relies both on considerable domain-specific knowledge and on general heuristics. This fact emphasises the importance of the preparation stage of problem solving discussed by Wallas (1926). It also argues that education must provide learners with an extensive knowledge base if they are to develop problem-solving skills.

The nature of domain-specific knowledge – intellectual skills

If domain-specific knowledge is critical to understanding problem solving, an important question is how knowledge is stored and organised in memory to facilitate problem solving. The basic approach that cognitive psychologists and artificial intelligence researchers have adopted is the production system. A production system consists of a network of condition–action sequences. The *condition* refers to the set of circumstances that will activate the production; the *action* refers to the set of activities that will occur if the production is activated. Both the conditional and the action part of a production can vary from simple to complex. [. . .]

Productions, schemata, and intellectual skills

I believe that the idea of a production system provides a unifying theme for representing *what* one knows when one knows concepts, principles, mental skills, and problem-solving abilities. Gagne (1977) has called knowledge of such entities *intellectual skills*. The word *schemata* is also commonly used. The formalism of a production can be used to represent each of these notions. This section describes what individuals know when they know concepts, principles, and mental and problem-solving skills, and it shows how the general idea of a production can be used to represent that information in memory.

Concepts

In the traditional psychological view, concepts are generally viewed as rules for classifying (Anderson and Faust, 1973; Gagne, 1977). In knowing a concept, a person is assumed to have knowledge of the rule that defines the critical features of the concept and to be able to use these critical features to recognise unfamiliar instances of the concept. Both philosophical analysis (Wittgenstein, 1953) and recent research in cognitive psychology suggests that this traditional view is insufficient. One prediction of a strict critical-feature model would be that all instances of the category should be recognised equally quickly because each instance should be tested against the same critical features.

However, this is not the case. For example, Rosch (1973) demonstrated that individuals' knowledge of the concept *bird* seemed to be dependent on a having a prototype of the concept *bird*. A *prototype* is a sort of generalised image, not necessarily visual, of the concept. Birds closer to the prototype (e.g. robins, sparrows) were recognised more quickly, while non-typical birds (e.g. owl, ostrich) took a longer time to identify. Clear non-bird silhouettes were quickly dismissed as noninstances. [. . .]

In cognitive psychology, prototypes/concepts are often called *schemata* (frames, scripts, patterns, gestalts). A *schema* is an organisational form for the knowledge we have about a particular concept. A schema usually has default values for the parts of the concept. The totality of the default values would represent the prototype for the schema.

One metaphor that may help to conceptualise what a schema/prototype might be like is to imagine making black-and-white silhouette slides of a variety of birds so that the birds are about the same height. Then imagine projecting a very bright light through the entire set of slides. What would emerge would be a centralised dark image (the prototype) that would be the most typical bird. Non-typical birds would be represented by lighter grey fuzzy boundaries around the central prototype.

I am generally comfortable with the idea of a schema/prototype for most naturally acquired concepts. However, I think that many school-learned concepts may be acquired both as a set of learned critical features and as a prototype. The prototype is used to identify instances that are fairly typical, as well as clear non-instances.

Typical instances possess many commonalities with the prototype, while noninstances possess few commonalities. However, for examples that are ambiguous, learned critical features are used to determine if the example is valid. [. . .]

The idea that conceptual knowledge may include both prototypical information and critical-feature information is consistent with the research on conceptual development carried out by Klausmeier and his associates (Klausmeier and Allen, 1978; Klausmeier, Ghatala, and Frayer, 1974; Tennyson and Park, 1980). Klausmeier and his co-workers see conceptual development occurring in four stages, running from discrimination of individual instances, through classifying instances as category members, to being able to verbally and formally describe the concept and relate it to other concepts. In a longitudinal study of conceptual development in children, they show that this is how children acquire concepts (Klausmeier and Allen, 1978).

Concepts also relate to other concepts by means of superordinate, coordinate, and subordinate relationships (Klausmeier and Allen, 1978; Klausmeier, Ghatala and Frayer, 1974; Tennyson and Park, 1980). Acquiring a knowledge of such relationships is necessary to gaining an understanding of the concept (Tennyson and Park, 1980). In addition, concepts may be related metaphorically to other concepts. The implications and importance of such metaphorical relationships are beginning to be understood. Such metaphorical relationships may represent a fundamental process in understanding new situations and acquiring new concepts (Ortony, 1980).

Rules, principles, and skills

Rules or principles are statements that relate concepts and tell how changes or alterations in one concept influence other concepts. A person who knows a rule has an 'inferred capability that enables the individual to respond to a class of stimulus situations with a class of performances' (Gagne, 1977). Just as do concepts, principles and skills have a set of critical features that give rise to their operation or identify situations to which they apply. [. . .]

The nature of rules can be illustrated by work on story schemata (Bower, Black and Turner, 1979; Schank and Abelson, 1977). Schemata have been used to explain how we understand language and events in the world. [. . .]

Schemata are also used to tell us what to do in particular situations. Schank and Abelson (1977) discussed the role of schemata in determining appropriate behaviour in a restaurant. When we enter a restaurant, we have certain expectations: a waiter will come with a menu, we will order food, etc. These schema-based expectations determine our behaviour. It may make this more clear to note that we have schemata for different classes of restaurants. You probably have no trouble identifying schemata for plastic fast food place, fine restaurant, greasy spoon, bar and grill. We have a different schema for each of these different categories of restaurants which allows us to recognise the type and tells us how to behave in that type of restaurant. We would not expect to order wine at McDonald's and we would not expect to stand at a counter for food at the Ritz. [. . .]

Productions and education

As noted, I believe that it is valuable to think about the learning of concepts, principles/rules, skills, and problem-solving abilities as the development of production systems. Each of these intellectual skills is activated by some set of conditions (the *conditional* part of a production), carries out some task (the *action* part of a production), and is associated in particular ways to other productions in memory. By thinking about knowledge as a production system, we have a unified means of describing what students must acquire to learn intellectual skills and what teachers and instruction should do to help the acquisition of intellectual skills. The conception of concepts, rules, and problem-solving skills as elements in a production system is consistent with Gagne's (1977) common description of these as intellectual skills and with current cognitive models of learning (Anderson, 1980; Anderson, Kline and Beasley, 1979; Goldstein, 1980, Lenat, 1983; Simon, 1980).

Declarative and procedural knowledge

Production-system learning models make a distinction between declarative versus procedural knowledge. The distinction is usually described as the distinction between *knowing that* and *knowing how. Knowing that* refers to being able to talk about something; *knowing how* refers to being able to do that something (e.g., being able to describe a tennis service versus being able to hit one). The importance of this distinction is not that declarative and procedural knowledge are fundamentally different in the way that they are stored in memory, but rather that they involve two different aspects of teaching intellectual skills or productions. Teaching someone to hit a serve is different from teaching them to describe a tennis serve. For most school-learned intellectual skills, the objectives of instruction involve both declarative and procedural knowledge about a skill. [. . .]

Acquiring procedural knowledge does *not* ensure that declarative knowledge will be acquired and vice versa. Keeping the distinction in mind helps teachers and instructional designers to focus on the need to develop instruction that leads to *both* procedural *and*

Table 4 *Model for developing instruction for training in intellectual skills*

Step 1 Analyse the subject-matter domain for intellectual skills required in that domain, and develop a map of skills and their relationship. Develop a behavioural–cognitive task analysis for each skill.

Step 2 Provide for an appropriate emotional–motivation setting.

Step 3 Acquire the conditional component of the production.
  (a) Identify the subcomponents of the conditional (identify the critical features of exemplar situations that will activate the concept insofar as possible. Collect exemplar situations that represent the range of situations that will activate the conditional).
  (b) Test students to determine if they have the subcomponents available to them. Provide training as necessary.
  (c) Activate relevant prior learning by
    (i) Subsumatory or comparative advanced organisers
    (ii) Meaningful metaphors that provide a model for understanding.
  (d) Provide a range of examples that illustrate the discriminative features of exemplar situations that activate the conditional to allow development of a prototype.
  (e) Lead the student to attend to discriminative features of examples by appropriate adjunct aids, such as
    (i) inserted questions that ask why examples are examples
    (ii) text cues
    (iii) diagrams/illustrations.
  (f) Lead the student to attend to discriminative features by activating relevant learning strategies or tactics.

Step 4 Acquire the network relationships of a production by
  (a) Presenting an organiser that demonstrates relationships between superordinate, coordinate, and subordinate concepts
  (b) Leading the student to analyse relationships between productions by requiring him/her to respond to compare–contrast type questions
  (c) Providing metaphors that illustrate relationships among concepts
  (d) Teaching related productions simultaneously to illustrate relationships
  (e) Using pictorial–graphic material that illustrates relationships.

Step 5 Acquire the action part of a production
  (a) Identify the steps in the action, and communicate the steps to the learner – this may involve both behavioural and cognitive task analysis.
  (b) Provide the learner with sufficient opportunity to practice the skills so that its use becomes relatively automatic.
  (c) Provide feedback to the learner about the quality of his/her action.

---

declarative knowledge and not to the slighting of one for the other. I might raise the point that subject matter fields tend to differ in their emphasis on one or the other. [. . .] Perhaps instructional designers need a more careful analysis of their subject matter in terms of its declarative and procedural knowledge and to consider these more carefully in the design of instruction.

Facilitating the learning of intellectual skills

[. . .] *Can we use this information to teach intellectual skills better?* André (1984) suggested that such a review would be useful by leading to a set of general guidelines developing instruction on intellectual skills. In André's view, every time a production (concept, rule, skill, or problem-solving ability) is to be taught, the production needs to be analysed into its components and the instruction should ensure that the learner acquires each of the components. In André's model, once the components are identified, then instructional moves can be planned. The model is presented in Table 4.

The recommendations in Table 4 are still very general. To be used, they have to be operationalised in a particular educational situation. The list in Table 4 should be considered a checklist of possible activities in which a learner may engage in order to promote the development of productions that represent intellectual skills. Instructional developers should use this list to consider possible instructional moves. In addition, the model provides a programme for future investigation on instructional processes.

References

Adams, J. L. (1974) *Conceptual Blockbusting*. New York: Norton.
Anderson, J. R. (1980) *Cognitive Psychology and its Implications*. San Francisco: Freeman.
Anderson, J. R., Kline, P. J. and Beasley, C. M. (1979) 'A General Learning Theory and its Application to Schema Abstraction', in G. H. Bower (ed.), *The Psychology of Learning and Motivation*, Vol. 13. New York: Academic Press, pp. 249–96.
Anderson, R. C. and Faust, G. W. (1973) *Educational Psychology*. New York: Dodd, Mead.
André, T. (1979) 'On Productive Knowledge and Levels of Questions', *Review of Educational Research*, 49, pp. 280–318.
Bower, G. H., Black, J. B. and Turner, T. J. (1979) 'Scripts in Memory for Text', *Cognitive Psychology*, 11, pp. 177–220.
Campbell, D. T. (1960) 'Blind Variation and Selective Retention in Creative Thought as in Other Knowledge Processes', *Psychological Review*, 67, pp. 380–400.
Champagne, A. B., Klopfer, L. E. and Chaiklin, S. (1984) *The Ubiquitous

Quantities. Paper presented at the annual meeting of the American Educational Research Association, New Orleans.

Craighead, W. E., Kazdin, A. E. and Mahoney, M. J. (1981) *Behavior Modification*. Boston: Houghton Mifflin.

Davis, G. A. (1973) *Psychology of Problem Solving*. New York: Basic.

Duncker, K. (1945) 'On problem solving', *Psychological Monographs*, 58, 5, whole no. 270.

Gagne, R. M. (1977) *The Conditions of Learning*. New York: Holt.

Goldfried, M. R. and Goldfried, A. P. (1980) 'Cognitive change methods', in F. H. Kanfer and A. P. Goldstein (eds), *Helping People Change*. New York: Pergamon, pp. 97–130.

Goldstein, I. (1980) Developing a Computational Representation for Problem-Solving Skills, in D. T. Tuma and F. Reif (eds), *Problem Solving and Education*. Hillsdale, NJ: Erlbaum, pp. 53–80.

Goldstein, I. and Papert, S. (1977) 'Artificial Intelligence, Language, and the Study of Knowledge', *Cognitive Science*, 1, pp. 84–124.

Hayes, J. R. (1981) *The Compleat Problem Solver*. Philadelphia: Franklin Institute Press.

Katona, G. (1940) *Organizing and Memorizing*. New York: Columbia University Press.

Kingsley, H. L. and Garry, R. (1957) *The Nature and Conditions of Learning* (2nd edn). Englewood Cliffs, NJ: Prentice-Hall.

Klausmeier, H. J. and Allen, P. S. (1978) *Cognitive development of children and youth: A longitudinal study*. New York: Academic Press.

Klausmeier, H. J., Ghatala, E. S. and Frayer, D. A. (1974) *Conceptual Learning and Development: A Cognitive View*. New York: Academic Press.

Kohler, W. (1925) *The Mentality of Apes*. New York: Harcourt Brace Jovanovich.

Lenat, D. B. (1983) 'Toward a Theory of Heuristics', in R. Groner, M. Groner and W. F. Bischof (eds), *Methods of Linguistics*. Hillsdale, NJ: Erlbaum, pp. 351–404.

Luchins, A. S. (1942) 'Mechanization in Problem Solving', *Psychological Monographs*, 54, 6, whole no. 248.

Maier, N. R. F. (1930) 'Reasoning in Humans, I: on direction', *Journal of Comparative Psychology*, 10, pp. 115–43.

Maier, N. (1970) *Problem Solving and Creativity: In Individuals and Groups*. Belmont, CA: Brooks/Cole.

Mayer, R. E. (1983) *Thinking, Problem Solving, Cognition*. New York: Freeman.

Newell, A. and Simon, H. (1972) *Human Problem Solving*. Englewood Cliffs, NJ: Prentice-Hall.

Norman, D. A. (1980) 'Cognitive Engineering and Education', in D. T. Tuma and F. Reif (eds), *Problem Solving and Education*. Hillsdale, NJ: Erlbaum, pp. 97–140.

Ortony, A. (1980) 'Metaphor', in Spiro, R. J., Bruce, B. B. and Brewer, W. F. (eds). *Theoretical Issues in Reading Comprehension*. Hillsdale, NJ: Erlbaum, pp. 349–61.

Osborn, A. F. (1963) *Applied Imagination*. New York: Scribner's.

Rosch, E. (1973) 'On the Internal Structure and Perceptual and Semantic Categories', in T. E. Mooze (ed.), *Cognitive Development and the Acquisition of Language*. New York: Academic Press, pp. 213–53.

Schank, R. C. and Abelson, R. P. (1977) *Scripts, Plans, Goals, and Understanding*. Hillsdale, NJ: Erlbaum.

Simon, H. A. (1980) 'Problem Solving in Education', in D. T. Tuma and F. Reif (eds), *Problem Solving and Education: Issues in Teaching and Research*. Hillsdale, NJ: Erlbaum, pp. 81–96.

Skinner, B. F. (1966) 'An Operant Analysis of Problem Solving', in B. Kleinmuntz (ed.), *Problem Solving: Research, Method and Theory*. New York: Wiley, pp. 127–59.

Staats, A. W. (1966) 'An Integrated-Functional Learning Approach to Complex Human Behaviour', in B. Kleinmuntz (ed.), *Problem Solving: Research, Method and Theory*. New York: Wiley, pp. 261–98.

Tennyson, R. D. and Park, O. (1980) 'The Teaching of Concepts: A Review of Instructional Design Literature', *Review of Educational Research*, 50, pp. 55–70.

Thorndike, E. L. (1898) 'Animal Intelligence: An Experimental Study of the Associative Processes in Animals', *Psychological Monographs*, 2, 8.

Wallas, G. (1926) *The Art of Thought*. New York: Harcourt Brace Jovanovich.

Wittgenstein, I. (1953) *Philosophical Investigations*. New York: Macmillan.

1.7

Knowledge as Action*

Douglas Barnes

[. . .]

Educational knowledge and knowledge for action

It is a commonplace of writing about school knowledge that it is radically different from the knowledge used and valued outside education systems. School knowledge is typically described as generalised, theoretical and explicit rather than particular, applied and implicit; as descriptive, analytical and passive rather than engaged or oriented towards action (Young, 1971; Saunders, 1982); expressed in writing rather than orally (Young, 1971); and distant from children's everyday cultural realities. School work requires the young to grapple with tasks which they themselves have not formulated and which may have little relevance to what they believed to be their concerns (Neisser, 1976; Wagner and Sternberg, 1986; Young, 1971). Demands for academic intelligence begin early: talk in the nursery school deals with a narrower range of topics than talk at home and is so dominated by adults that children are unable to play an active part. It fails to engage with the real world because teachers pursue their educational aims without regard to children's perspectives and priorities (Tizard and Hughes, 1984). Classroom discourse is believed to be different from much of the discourse young people take part in during their lives: children must learn to 'answer the question', that is, to look for an answer that conforms to the teacher's unstated expectations (Edwards and Mercer, 1986). School tasks are well defined – there are unambiguous criteria for successful conclusion – all the necessary information is provided and there is a single right answer (Wagner and Sternberg, 1986). Children learn that in school they must not use their existing knowledge of the world but pretend that only the

---

* Barnes' original chapter presents his detailed case for a 'practical' curriculum, 'which would arise from closer involvement in the world of action, and which would also include access to more decontextual ways of thinking, approaching these in a critical manner'. This chapter discusses the nature of educational knowledge.

information 'given' by the teacher is valid, so that they have to ignore many of the considerations that influence us in our everyday lives in favour of solving idealised logical problems posed by the teacher. (In the familiar question about men digging holes, did we ever ask ourselves whether they all worked equally hard?) This faces them with the task of internalising sets of unfamiliar social norms; success in doing so is a crucial part of academic 'intelligence' and school success (Edwards and Mercer, 1987; Hammersley, 1974).

Many commentators refer to the wide gulf between decontextualised school knowledge and the knowledge that the children bring to school with them (Olson, 1977, quoted by Edwards and Maybin, 1987). Schutz and Luckmann (1973), (quoted by Soloman, 1983) distinguished 'life-world structures' from 'symbolic universes'. 'Life-world structures are those pictures of the world that we live by; according to Schutz and Luckmann, they are based on loose typifications yet are strong because they are shared with other people. 'Symbolic universes' refers to school subjects which are kept separate from everyday life. It is important to realise that the life-world structures are upheld because they have a function: the school pupils who refused to accept their biology teacher's assertion that human beings are animals were influenced by the fact that for most of our everyday purposes it is more useful to emphasise the difference than the similarity (Hills, 1983). Moreover there seems to be a value judgement implicit in the shift from 'structures' to 'universes' which deserves to be unpacked. 'Children come to school with a practical conception of reality only to encounter a theoretical conception of reality' (Edwards and Maybin, 1987). Schooling substitutes decontextualised logic for the purpose-driven thinking which binds our normal behaviour to the here and now. Their home lives offer children from different families very different levels of assistance in the task of bridging this cultural gulf, which may be one of the most difficult demands that school lays upon the young.

It is important to understand what constitutes this task. Meaning does not lie in words but in the cultural competences which we bring to the words. Joining in the cultural life of a group (such as that of a classroom) is not merely a matter of being able to manage the expected patterns of interaction; we need appropriate knowledge. 'Children who fail in school are those who operate with ways of meaning different from those of schooling, (Christie, 1985). What is meant is not inherent in the words spoken; the words have to be reconstituted as meaning by the hearers on the basis of whatever cultural competences they can bring to the task. Behind every utterance lies 'the unspoken backcloth of meaning' (Edwards and Furlong, 1978). When education is seen as 'the induction of learners into "preferred discourses" or "genres" (Whitty, 1985; Christie, 1985), what is being referred to is not just linguistic forms or even patterns of social exchange. To take part in lessons requires 'sharing general epistemological frameworks, pragmatic and communicative assumptions and purposes, particular knowledge and experience' (Edwards and Mercer, 1986, 1987). Those students who in a public examination in English language wrote about a pop music idol in the language of a favourite magazine had seriously misread the tacit meaning of the task.

There are other ways in which school curricula differ radically from the competences required in everyday living. It is a normal part of teachers' work to give exercises to their students; typically they prescribe a rule and then set tasks which are intended to exemplify that rule. Very often what is demanded of the pupil is that he or she should operate a routine procedure, in some subjects even an algorithm, which does not always necessitate the student having much grasp of when this procedure is appropriate or how it is related to the principle that the teacher has enunciated. Traditional 'academic' pedagogy rests upon the hope that through rehearsing the procedures the pupil will eventually gain access to the principle, but since a procedure does not necessarily imply its own justification, this often happens very slowly and only for a minority of students.

It is in response to this that it is now commonly recommended that students be given 'problems' to solve, but even the word 'problem' is ambiguous. A good problem would require more than the application of a routine procedure and would be different enough from any example already discussed in class to require choice and reinterpretation by the student. Perhaps some transformation would be required; perhaps it would be necessary for the pupil to construe the terms of the problem and then decide what model or procedure was most appropriate as a basis for solving it. Some cases would need one treatment and some another, thus requiring the learner to have enough understanding of underlying principles to choose from a repertoire of models and methods. This would already have been built up by experience with other similar and dissimilar problems. These steps would perhaps lead to better textbook problems but would not make them like problem solving in everyday life. In pursuing everyday goals, such as organising a family trip, we are at the very same time deciding what we want, gathering information, considering possibilities for action and trying things out: there is no clear logical sequence. In real-life problems the choice of method is often far from clear. This is true even of technical problems: can I fasten this spring under tension using a hammer and a staple or should I use a screw hook? If the spring is too taut for either, I must look still further for a method. How much more true this is of interpersonal projects. I wish to influence a colleague and so embark on persuasion or bargaining, yet I modify and redirect these according to the response I receive. Of course, sometimes we know exactly what to do, but we usually call these 'tasks' rather than 'problems'. In real life we struggle at one and the same time to determine what should count as success and what methods are worth trying. The goal itself is often open to redefinition: one is often 'responding appropriately in terms of one's long-range and short-range goals, given the actual facts of the situation as one discovers them' (Neisser, 1976). Constructing the problem and the criteria that shall determine what constitutes success are as much part of the problem solving as working through to a solution.

There is no qualitative difference between thinking in an academic and an everyday context; the characteristics of everyday reasoning arise from the interaction of the actor's goals and the perceived possibilities and constraints of the situation (Lave, Murtaugh and de la Roche, 1984). What may differ is the value loading of problems met in and out of the classroom; understanding the diets of animals in a biology textbook is a different matter from understanding the needs of a pet, not because the principles involved are different but because the new ideas are brought into a different relationship with what the learner already knows. Feeling and values play an essential role in action-oriented uses of intelligence, since in the real world intellectual performance involves satisfying one's own motives (Neisser, 1976). It is true that there are occasions outside school when we find ourselves constrained to follow purposes not our own, as, for example, at work, which offers us money or other extrinsic inducements to accept others' goals. Do these occasions justify an education which requires young people to demonstrate their willingness to pursue goals whose value they are not in a position to appreciate? It is not an easy question to answer. Central to critiques of schooling, whatever political perspectives they come from, is its frequent failure to coopt the learners' purposes.

We must ask ourselves whether we are using an accurate account of academic schooling. If we compare it with the work of outstanding teachers, or perhaps of most teachers in their more inventive moments, the picture of abstract theorising seems something of a caricature. Teaching large groups of youthful conscripts under pressure of time and for tests designed by others often does push teachers in that direction, however, even against their will. Moreover, there is a considerable divergency in the traditional curriculum, which has never been simply a matter of transmitting 'objective knowledge'. Much of the curriculum has always been heavily value-laden, as witness the kinds of history or literature commonly

taught or the older emphasis upon 'character building' and the more recent one of 'personal and social education'. Nor has traditional education been concerned only with cognition: skills and motor activities have always played a part, not only in physical education and in craft but also, for example, in the academic subjects in the form of the teaching of handwriting or laboratory skills. Some teachers of geography, English, history, religious education, social studies and even science have made it their business to deal overtly with moral and social issues. However carefully teachers avoid overt indoctrination, it is impossible to teach any of these subjects without implying some perspective and making some choices which will be implicitly value-laden. The British Government's attempt to banish values from the curriculum is in danger of becoming an attempt to banish all values except their own.
[. . .]

References

Christie, F. (1985) 'Language and Schooling', in S. N. Tchudi (ed.), *Language, Schooling and Society*. Upper Montclair, NJ: Boynton/Cook.

Edwards, A. D. and Furlong, V. J. (1978) *The Language of Teaching*. London: Heinemann.

Edwards, D. and Maybin, J. (1987) *The Development of Understanding in the Classroom*. Milton Keynes: Open University Press. (EH207, Communication and Education.)

Edwards, D. and Mercer, N. (1986) 'Context and Continuity: Classroom Discourse and the Development of Shared Knowledge', in K. Durkin (ed.), *Language Development in the School Years*. London: Croom Helm.

Edwards, D. and Mercer, N. (1987) *Common Knowledge: The Development of Understanding in the Classroom*. London: Methuen.

Hammersley, M. (1974) 'The Organisation of Pupil Participation', in A. Hargreaves and P. Woods (eds), *Classrooms and Staffrooms*. Milton Keynes: Open University Press.

Hills, G. (1983) 'Misconceptions Misconceived: Using Conceptual Change to Understand Some of the Problems Pupils Have in Learning Science', in H. Helm and J. D. Novak (eds), *Misconceptions in Science and Mathematics*. Proceedings of the International Seminar.

Lave, J., Murtaugh, M. and de la Roche, O. (1984) 'The Dialectic of Arithmetic in Grocery Shopping', in B. Rogoff and J. Lave (eds), *Everyday Cognition: Its Development in Social Context*. Cambridge, Mass.: Harvard University Press.

Neisser, U. (1976) 'General, Academic and Artificial Intelligence', in L. B. Resnick (ed.), *The Nature of Intelligence*. Hillsdale, NJ: Erlbaum.

Olson, D. R. (1977) 'Oral and Written Language and the Cognitive Processes of Children', *Journal of Communication*, 27, 3, pp. 10–26.

Saunders, M. (1982) 'Productive Activity in the Curriculum: Changing the Literate Bias of Secondary Schools in Tanzania', *British Journal of the Sociology of Education*, 3, 1.

Schutz, A., and Luckmann, T. (1973) *The Structures of the Life World*. London: Heinemann.

Soloman, J. (1983) 'Learning About Energy: How Pupils Think in Two Domains', *European Journal of Science Education*, 5, 1, pp. 49–59.

Tizard, B. and Hughes, M. (1984) *Young Children Learning*. London: Fontana.

Tough, J. (1979) *Talk for Teaching and Learning*. London: Ward Lock.

Wagner, R. K. and Sternberg, R. J. (1986) 'Tacit Knowledge and Intelligence in the Everyday World', in R. K. Wagner and R. J. Sternberg (eds), *Practical Intelligence*. Cambridge: Cambridge University Press.

Whitty, G. (1985) *Sociology and School Knowledge*. London: Methuen.

Williams, J. T. (1977) *Learning to Write or Writing to Learn*. Slough: National Foundation for Educational Research.

Young, M. F. D. (1971) 'An Approach to the Study of Curricula as Socially Organised Knowledge', in M. F. D. Young (ed.), *Knowledge and Control*. London: Collier Macmillan.

SECTION 2

Learning in Domains

Introduction

In planning a curriculum decisions are made about how knowledge is organised. This can be the total responsibility of the teacher and pupil or choices may be circumscribed by local or national regulation. The definition of a domain is based on views of how subject knowledge is constructed, represented, acquired and used. As such it is a critical feature of the learning process and its assessment.

The readings in this section explore learning from different domain perspectives and represent challenges to traditional domain definitions. Research and development indicates both domain specific and common features in the learning process.

The traditional view of the mathematical domain as culture and value free is explored by Alan Bishop who promotes the view that mathematics must be understood as a kind of cultural knowledge, which all cultures create but not in the same way. He outlines the implications of enculturation and acculturation in the mathematics curriculum focusing on the 'intentionally accultural' nature of traditional Western mathematics. By proposing 'universal' mathematical activities, Bishop aims for a culturally-fair curriculum which incorporates the ideas of other cultures whilst retaining a general overarching mathematical structure. He further challenges the values of the traditional mathematics curriculum and argues for children being taught *about* values rather than inducted into them, a curriculum for training rather than education.

The introduction of other culturally construed worlds into subject teaching is raised again in Claire Woods' extract. She outlines the contradiction between a view of language which sees children as evolving world representations and the restrictive nature of the texts constructed in English lessons. She recommends a widening of the English curriculum to include the discourse of other domains of inquiry to allow children to see how other world views are constructed. Medway is quoted to show how the treatment of children's pre-disciplinary knowledge varies between domains allowing teaching and learning to be compartmentalised and the knowledge acquired limited in its application. To alter this Woods details the need for changes in the view of subject knowledge.

The failure of the science curriculum to enable pupils to develop scientific understanding is the central issue in Susan Carey's article. She focuses on the paradox that to understand science lessons pupils' existing conceptual schemata must allow them to construct meaning in presented information yet the goal of science teaching is to impart new schemata for establishing new understanding. Carey questions how pupils are to make sense of new information given this goal. The alternative frameworks position in science is explored and the nature of the change from novice schemata to expert schemata considered in the light of alternative views of knowledge restructuring. The need for collaboration between cognitive scientists and science educationists is seen to arise from their converging aims, to represent pupils' knowledge and to understand the mechanisms for conceptual change.

The role of discussion in mathematics learning and the implications for the definition of the domain is explored in the chapter by Celia Hoyles. She sees the focus on discussion in the mathematics curriculum as reflecting a move away from the transmission model of learning and a view of the domain located within the framework of Piagetian developmental psychology. She typifies the domain innovations as: a collaborative model of learning; an increased emphasis on the socio-cultural setting of mathematical development; a reorientation away from the teacher to the pupil; and a recognition of maths learning occurring outside the discipline. That discussion in only one aspect of the learning process is recognised and Hoyles highlights the significance of the social atmosphere in which discussion takes place, the nature of the learning activity (here she discusses computer work) and the role of the teacher in encouraging reflection. Finally she describes a view of mathematical development and what mathematical understanding from a social interaction perspective might look like.

The consequences of a shift in the view of learning within a domain is considered again by Marion Whitehead who looks at approaches to the teaching of reading. She details the transformation of reading from a decoding task to a 'meaning-making' enterprise. The implications of this transformation are explored with particular reference to the social and cultural features of learning and the teacher's role as the mediator between the reader and the text. In her final comments she raises the important point that the developments within the reading domain highlight increasingly 'complex, variable and sophisticated processes' yet the present curriculum trends are towards simplistic and inappropriate interventions.

In a quite different vein, Madeleine Atkins analyses the pre-vocational curriculum from alternative sociological perspectives. She juxtaposes views of the curriculum's aims, forms, structure, assessment and content as positive or negative depending on the perspective adopted. In so doing she raises the potential for a range of fundamental paradoxes within the aims and assessment of various pre-vocational curricula. The serious consequences for initiatives such as Records of Achievement are self-evident. Her final concern is the relationship of the curriculum to the employment market which she sees as challenging the aims and content of the pre-vocational curriculum.

The section finishes with a description of a piece of curriculum development – the National Writing Project. The problems of implementation of curriculum change highlight the mismatch between teachers' implicit models of practice and their intentions. This mismatch is evidenced in children's perceptions of the learning process. During the process of curriculum development the implicit views of the teachers emerged and were the subject of reflection and action. At the end of the project views of writing as an activity and the role of the learner were made explicit which allowed a clearer identification of learner needs and teacher needs.

2.1

Mathematics Education in its Cultural Context

Alan J. Bishop

[...]
In this chapter I shall summarise the results of the analyses and investigations which have engaged me over the past fifteen years [...]. There have been two major and related areas of concern in that time, and both seem to have important implications for research, for theory development and for classroom practice.

Cultural interfaces in mathematics education

The first concern is with what I think of as 'cultural interfaces'. In some countries like the UK pressure has mounted to reflect in the school curriculum the multicultural nature of their societies, and there has been widespread recognition of the need to re-evaluate the total school experience in the face of the education failure of many children from ethnic minority communities. In other countries, like Papua New Guinea, Mozambique and Iran, there is criticism of the 'colonial' or 'Western' educational experience, and a desire to create instead an education which is in tune with the 'home' culture of the society. The same concern emerges in other debates about the formal education of Aborigines, of Amerindians, of the Lapps and of Eskimos. In all of these cases, a culture-conflict situation is recognised and curricula are being re-examined.

One particular version of this problem relates to the mathematics curriculum and its relationship with the home culture of the child. Mathematics curricula though, have been slow to change, due primarily to a popular and widespread misconception. Up to five or so years ago, the conventional wisdom was that mathematics was 'culture-free' knowledge. After all, the argument went, 'a negative times a negative gives a positive' wherever you are, and triangles the world over have angles which add up to 180 degrees. This view though, confuses the 'universality of truth' of mathematical ideas with the cultural basis of that knowledge. The ideas are decontextualised and abstracted in such a way that 'obviously' they can apply everywhere. In that sense they are clearly universal.

But as soon as one begins to focus on the particulars of these statements, one's belief in that universality tends to feel challenged. Why is it 180 degrees and not, say, 100 or 150? Where does the idea of negative number come from? Authoritative writers on mathematical history have given answers to these kinds of questions, of course, and they demonstrate quite clearly that mathematics has a cultural history.

But whose cultural history are we referring to? Recently, research evidence from anthropological and cross-cultural studies has emerged which not only supports the idea that mathematics has a cultural history, but also that from different cultural histories have come what can only be described as different mathematics. One can cite the work of Zaslavsky (1973), who has shown in her book *Africa Counts*, the range of mathematical ideas existing in indigenous African cultures. Van Sertima's *Blacks in Science* (1986), is another African source as is Gerdes (1985). On other continents, the research of Lancy (1983), Lean (1986) and Bishop (1979) in Papua New Guinea, Harris (1980) and Lewis (1976) in Aboriginal Australia, and Pinxten (1983) and Closs (1986) with the Amerindians, has also added fuel to this debate. The term 'ethnomathematics' has been revived (d'Ambrosio, 1985) to describe some of these ideas, and even if the term itself is still not yet well defined, there is no doubting the sentiment that the ideas are indeed *mathematical* ideas.

The thesis is therefore developing that mathematics must now be understood as a kind of cultural knowledge, which all cultures generate but which need not necessarily 'look' the same from one cultural group to another. Just as all human cultures generate language, religious beliefs, rituals, food-producing techniques, etc., so it seems that all human cultures generate mathematics. Mathematics is a pan-human phenomenon. Moreover, just as *each* cultural group generates its own language, religious belief, etc., so it seems that each cultural group is capable of generating its own mathematics.

Clearly this kind of thinking will necessitate some fundamental re-examinations of many of our traditional beliefs about the theory and practice of mathematics education, and I will outline some of these issues below.

Values in mathematics education

The second area of concern has been our ignorance about 'values' in mathematics education. In the same way that mathematics has been considered for many years to be culture-free, so it has also been considered to be value-free. How could it be concerned with values, the argument goes, when it is about indisputable facts concerning triangles, fractions or multiplication? Once again anthropologically-oriented researchers like Pinxten (1983), Horton (1971), Lewis (1976) and Leach (1973) have presented us with plenty of evidence with which to challenge that traditional view. Moreover any mathematics educator who works in cultural-interface situations [. . .] soon becomes acutely aware of the influence of value-conflicts on the mathematical learning experience of the children they are responsible for.[1]

Moreover one can argue that a mathematical education is no education at all if it does not have anything to contribute to values development. Perhaps that is a crucial difference between a mathematical training and a mathematical education?

Indeed it would seem to me to be thoroughly appropriate to conceptualise much current mathematics teaching as merely mathematical training, in that generally there is no *explicit* attention paid to values. I am not saying that values are not learnt – clearly they are – but implicitly, covertly and without much awareness or conscious choice. Surely a mathematical *education*, on the other hand, should make the values explicit and overt, in order to develop the learner's awareness and capacity for choosing?

There is even more of a pressing need today to consider values because of the increasing presence of the computer and the calculator in our societies. These devices can perform many mathematical techniques for us, even now, and the arguments in favour of a purely mathematical *training* for our future citizens are surely weakened. Society will only be able to harness the mathematical power of these devices for appropriate use if its citizens have been made to consider values as part of their education. For some pessimists however, like Ellul (1980) the situation is far too out of control in any case for education to be able to do anything constructive at this stage. Nevertheless the ideas of other analysts such as Skovsmose (1985) do offer, in my view, the potential for developing strategies for change.

My own perspective on this area of values has been stimulated by the culture-conflict research mentioned earlier and it is this perspective which I propose to enlarge on here. The fundamental task for my work was to find a rich way to conceptualise mathematics as a cultural phenomenon.

Mathematics as a cultural phenomenon

The most productive starting point was provided by White (1959) in his book *The Evolution of Culture* in which he argues, as others have done, that 'the functions of culture are to relate man to his environment on the one hand, and to relate man to man, on the other' (p. 8). White, though, went further, and divided the components of culture into four categories:

1 ideological: composed of beliefs, dependent on symbols, philosophies;
2 sociological: the customs, institutions, rules and patterns of interpersonal behaviour;
3 sentimental: attitudes, feelings concerning people, behaviour;
4 technological: manufacture and use of tools and implements.

Moreover while showing that these four components are interrelated White argues strongly that 'the technological factor is the basic one; all others are dependent upon it. Furthermore, the technological factor determines, in a general way at least, the form and content of the social, philosophic and sentimental factors' (p. 19).

Writers such as Bruner (1964) and Vygotsky (1978) have also shown us the significance of written language, and one of its particular conceptual 'tools', mathematical symbolism. Mathematics, as an example of a cultural phenomenon, has an important 'technological' component, to use White's terminology. But White's schema also offered an opportunity to explore the ideology, sentiment and sociology driven by this symbolic technology, and therefore to attend to values as well.

Mathematics in this context is therefore conceived of as a cultural *product*, which has developed as a result of various activities. These I have described in other writings (Bishop, 1986; Bishop, 1988) so I will just briefly summarise them here. There are, from my analyses, six fundamental activities which I argue are both universal, in that they appear to be carried out by every cultural group ever studied, and also necessary and sufficient for the development of mathematical knowledge.

They are as follows:

1 *Counting.* The use of a systematic way to compare and order discrete phenomena. It may involve tallying, or using objects or string to record, or special number words or names. (See for example, Lean, 1986; Menninger, 1969; Ascher and Ascher, 1981; Closs, 1986; Ronan, 1981; Zaslavsky, 1973.)
2 *Locating.* Exploring one's spatial environment and conceptualising and symbolising that environment, with models, diagrams, drawings, words or other means. (See for example, Pinxten, 1983; Lewis, 1976; Harris, 1980; Ronan, 1983.)
3 *Measuring.* Quantifying qualities for the purposes of comparison and ordering, using objects or tokens as measuring devices

with associated units or 'measure-words'. (See for example, Menninger, 1969; Gay and Cole, 1967; Jones, 1974; Harris, 1980; Zaslavsky, 1973.)

4 *Designing.*   Creating a shape or design for an object or for any part of one's spatial environment. It may involve making the object, as a 'mental template', or symbolising it in some conventionalised way. (See for example, Gerdes, 1986; Temple, 1986; Ronan, 1981; Bourgoin, 1973; Faegre, 1979; Oswalt, 1976.)

5 *Playing.*   Devising, and engaging in, games and pastimes, with more or less formalised rules that all players must abide by. (See for example, Huizinga, 1949; Lancy, 1983; Jayne, 1974; Roth, 1902; Falkener, 1961; Zaslavsky, 1973.)

6 *Explaining.*   Finding ways to account for the existence of phenomena, be they religious, animistic or scientific. (See for example, Lancy, 1983; Horton, 1971; Pinxten, 1983; Ronan, 1981; Gay and Cole, 1967.)

Mathematics, as cultural knowledge, derives from humans engaging in these six universal activities in a sustained, and conscious manner. The activities can either be performed in a mutually exclusive way or, perhaps more significantly, by interacting together, as in 'playing with numbers' which is likely to have developed number patterns and magic squares, and which arguably contributed to the development of algebra.

I would argue that, in the mathematics which *I* and many others have learnt, these activities have contributed at least the following highly significant ideas:

1 *Counting.*   Numbers. Number patterns. Number relationships. Developments of number systems. Algebraic representation. Infinitely large and small. Events, probabilities, frequencies. Numerical methods. Iteration. Combinatorics. Limits.

2 *Locating.*   Position. Orientation. Development of coordinates – rectangular, polar, spherical. Latitude/longitude. Bearings. Angles. Lines. Networks. Journey. Change of position. Loci (circle, ellipse, polygon . . .). Change of orientation. Rotation. Reflection.

3 *Measuring.*   Comparing. Ordering. Length. Area. Volume. Time. Temperature. Weight. Development of units – conventional, standard, metric system. Measuring instruments. Estimation. Approximation. Error.

4 *Designing.*   Properties of objects. Shape. Pattern. Design. Geometric shapes (figures and solids). Properties of shapes. Similarity. Congruence. Ratios (internal and external).

5 *Playing.*   Puzzles. Paradoxes. Models. Games. Rules. Procedures. Strategies. Prediction. Guessing. Chance. Hypothetical reasoning. Games analysis.

6 *Explaining*.   Classifications. Conventions. Generalisations. Linguistic explanations – arguments, logical connections, proof.
Symbolic explanations – equations, formulae, algorithms, functions. Figural explanations – diagrams, graphs, charts, matrices.
(Mathematical structure – axioms, theorems, analysis, consistency.) (Mathematical model – assumptions, analogies, generalisability, prediction.)

From these basic notions, the rest of 'Western' mathematical
knowledge can be derived,[2] while in this structure can also be
located the evidence of the 'other mathematics' developed by other
cultures. Indeed we ought to re-examine labels such as 'Western
Mathematics' since we know that many different cultures contributed to the knowledge encapsulated by that particular label.[3]

However, I must now admit to what might be seen as a conceptual
weakness. There is no real prospect of *my* being able to test whether
or not this 'universal' structure will be adequate for describing the
mathematical ideas of other cultural groups. On the contrary, I
would maintain that it must be for others from those cultural groups
to determine this. Far from my inability being interpreted as a
weakness, I believe it is important to recognise that in this kind of
analysis one must be constantly aware of the dangers of culturo-
centrism. It may well be the case that my analysis will not hold up
under cross-cultural scrutiny – it is my hope that it may in fact
stimulate some other analytic developments, which again could be
tested cross-culturally.

This kind of culturo-centrism is well explained by Lancy (1983)
who has proposed a 'universal' stage theory of cognitive development. Lancy shows that his *Stage 1* corresponds to Piaget's sensory-
motor and pre-operational stages 'the accomplishments of this stage
are shared by all human beings' (p. 203). Stage 2 is where
enculturation begins: 'What happens to cognition during Stage 2,
then, has much to do with culture and environment and less to do
with genetics' (p. 205). This, for me, is the stage where different
cultures develop different mathematics.

However Lancy also has a Stage 3 in his theory, which concerns
the metacognitive level: 'In addition to developing cognitive and
linguistic strategies, individuals acquire "theories" of language and
cognition' (p. 208). For Lancy, therefore, the 'formal operation'
stage of Piaget's theory represents the particular theory of knowledge which the 'Western' cultural group emphasises. Other cultural
groups can, and do, emphasise other theories of knowledge.

This idea gives a useful cultural entrée into the area of values,
linking as it does with White's idea that the technology of a culture
(in our case the symbolic technology of mathematics) not only
relates humans to their environment in a particular way, but also

'drives' the other cultural components – the sentimental, the ideological and the sociological. It is these that are the heart of the values associated with mathematics as a cultural phenomenon.

Before turning to examine these in more detail it is necessary to point out that my own cultural predisposition makes it very difficult to attempt any more at this stage than merely outlining the values which I feel are associated with the 'Western Mathematics' with which I am familiar. I do know that enough evidence exists to suggest that White's schema does have some credibility in 'Western' culture. I am in no position however to argue that for any other culture. Once again that verification must be left to those in the other cultural groups.

The three value components of culture – White's sentimental, ideological and sociological components – appear to me to have pairs of complementary values associated with mathematics, which give rise to certain balances and tensions. If we consider first the 'sentimental' component we can see that so much of the power of mathematics in our society comes from the feelings of security and *control* that it offers. Mathematics, through science and technology has given Western culture the sense of security in knowledge – so much so that people can become very frustrated at natural or man-made disasters which they feel shouldn't have happened! The inconsistency of a Mathematical argument is a strong motive for uncovering the error and getting the answer 'right'. The mathematical valuing of 'right' answers informs society which also looks (in vain of course) for right answers to its societal problems. Western culture is fast becoming a Mathematico-Technological culture.

Where control and security are sentiments about things remaining predictable, the complementary value relates to *progress*. A method of solution for one mathematical problem is able, by the abstract nature of mathematics, to be generalised to other problems. The unknown can become known. Knowledge can develop. Progress, though, can become its own reward and change becomes inevitable. Alternativism is strongly upheld in Western culture and as with all the values described here, contains within itself the seeds of destruction. It is therefore important to recognise that it is the interactions and tensions between those values of control and progress which allow cultures to survive and to grow.

If those are the twin sentiments driven by the mathematical symbolic technology then the principle *ideology* associated with Western Mathematics must be *rationalism*. If one were searching for only one identifiable value, it would be this one. It is logic, rationalism and reason which has guaranteed the pre-eminence of mathematics within Western culture. It is not tradition, not status, not experience, not seniority, but logic which offers the major criterion of mathematical knowledge. With the advent of computers the ideology is extending even further, if that is possible.

The Indo-European languages appear to have rich vocabularies for logic – Gardner (1977) in his (English) tests used over 800 different logical connectives. The rise of physical technology has also helped this development, in that 'causation', one of the roots of rational argument, seems to be developed much easier through physical technology than through nature – the time-scales of natural processes are often too fast or too slow. It was simple physical technological devices which enabled humans to experiment with process, and to develop the formidable concept of 'direct causation'.

However there is also a complementary ideology which is clearly identifiable in Western culture, and that is *objectism*. Western culture's worldview appears to be dominated by material objects and physical technology. Where rationalism is concerned with the relationship between ideas, objectism is about the genesis of those ideas. One of the ways mathematics has gained its power is through the activity of objectivising the abstractions from reality. Through its symbols (letters, numerals, figures) mathematics has taught people how to deal with abstract entities, *as if they were* objects.

The final two complementary values concern White's *sociological* component, the relationships between people and mathematical knowledge. The first I call *openness* and concerns the fact that mathematical truths are open to examination by all, provided of course that one has the necessary knowledge to do the examining. Proof grew from the desire for articulation and demonstration, so well practised by the early Greeks, and although the criteria for the acceptibility of proof have changed, the value of 'opening' the knowledge has remained as strong as ever.

However there is a complementary sociological value which I call *mystery*. Despite that openness, there is a mysterious quality about mathematical ideas. Certainly everyone who has learnt mathematics knows this intuitively, whether it is through the meaningless symbol-pushing which many children still unfortunately experience, or whether it is in the surprising discovery of an unexpected connection. The basis of the mystery again lies in the abstract nature of mathematics – abstractions take one away from a context, and decontextualised knowledge is literally meaningless. Of course mathematical ideas offer their own kind of context so it is very possible to develop meanings within mathematics.

These then are the three pairs of values relating to Western mathematics which are shaped by, and also have helped to shape, a particular set of symbolic conceptual structures. Together with those structures they constitute the cultural phenomenon which is often labelled as 'Western Mathematics'. We certainly know that different symbolisations have been developed in different cultures and it is very likely that there are differences in values also, although detailed evidence on this is not readily available at the present time. How unique these values are, or how separable a technology is from its values must also remain open questions.

Some issues arising from this analysis

White's (1959) view of culture has enabled us to create a conception of mathematics different from that normally drawn. It is a comparison which enables mathematics to be understood as a pan-cultural phenomenon. It seems that what I have been referring to as 'Western' mathematics must be recognised as being similar to, yet different from, the mathematics developed by other cultural groups. There appear to be differences in symbolisation and also differences in values. Just how great those differences are will have to be revealed by further analysis of the available anthropological and cross-cultural evidence. Hopefully the analysis here will help to structure the search for that evidence.

But what educational issues has this analysis revealed to us? From an anthropological perspective mathematical education is a process of inducting the young into part of their culture, and there appear initially to be two distinct kinds of process. On the one hand there is *enculturation*, which concerns the induction of the young child into the home or local culture, while on the other there is *acculturation*, which is to do with the induction of the person into a culture which is in some sense alien, and different from that of their home background.

Appealing as this simple dichotomy is, the real educational situation is rather more complex. Consider inducting a child into 'Western' mathematics – for which children is enculturation the appropriate model? Is it really part of anyone's *home* and *local* culture? It is certainly not the product of any *one* culture and therefore no-one could claim it as theirs exclusively. Moreover there are plenty of practising mathematicians in Universities all over the world who would object fundamentally (and rightly so in my opinion) to the suggestion that they were engaged in developing *Western* cultural knowledge.

So what, *culturally*, is the mathematics which until a few years ago was generally thought to represent the only mathematics? Is it better to think of it as a kind of internationalised mathematics which all can learn to speak and understand? Or is it more a sort of Esperanto of the mathematical world, an artificial, pragmatic solution to a multicultural situation? That does not seem to be a good analogy because of the strong cultural values associated with it, and the fact that it was not deliberately created in the way Esperanto was.

Perhaps it is more appropriate educationally to recognise that different societies are influenced to different degrees by this international mathematico-technological culture and that the greater the degree of influence the more appropriate would be the idea of enculturation?

What of acculturation? That clearly does raise other educational issues. Whilst acculturation is a natural kind of cultural development when cultures meet, there is something very contentious to me about an education which is *intentionally* acculturative. There is a clear intention implied in that notion to induct the child into an alien culture without any concern for the ultimate preservation of that child's home culture.[4] Those whose children are being so acculturated have a perfectly understandable right to be concerned.

Moreover I would stress that only those people for whom Western mathematics *is* an alien cultural product should decide what to do in the culture-conflict situation so created. It might be possible to develop a bi-cultural strategy, but that should not be for 'aliens' like me to decide. In my view the same questions arise over choice of teacher, and choice of educational environment. I would argue that in general in a culture-conflict situation it is better in the long run for the teacher to be from the 'home' culture, and for that teacher to be closely linked with the local community. If culture-conflict is to be handled sensitively, then schooling, and the teacher, should stay close to the people affected, in my view.[5]

Another set of issues relate to the mathematics curriculum in schools, particularly in those societies where there are several ethnic minority groups. What ideas should we be introducing the children to? To what extent should any of the mathematical ideas from other cultures be used? And how is it possible to structure the mathematics curriculum to allow this to happen?

It certainly would seem valuable to use mathematical ideas from the child's home culture within the overall mathematical experience, if only to enable the child to make good contact with the construct of *mathematics* per se. We know only too well some of the negative effects of insisting on children only experiencing alien cultural products – the meaninglessness, the rote-learning syndrome, the general attitude of irrelevance and purposelessness. So how can we overcome this?

One possible way is to use as a structural framework the six *activities* which I described earlier. If those activities are universal, and if they are both necessary and sufficient for mathematical development, then a curriculum which is structured around those activities *would* allow the mathematical ideas from different cultural groups to be introduced sensibly. Is it indeed possible by this means to create a culturally fair mathematics curriculum – a curriculum which would allow all cultural groups to involve their own mathematical ideas while also permitting the 'international' mathematical ideas to be developed?

Finally, what about the education of values? One implication of the values analysis earlier could be a consideration of the emphasis given in present mathematics education to certain values. I do not think it would be too cynical to suggest that a great deal of current mathematics teaching leans more towards control than to progress, to objectism rather than to rationalism, and to mystery rather than to openness. Perhaps a greater use of such teaching activities as group work, discussion, project work and investigations could help to redress the balances in each of the complementary pairs. We may then move our mathematical education more towards 'progress', 'rationalism' and 'openness', a goal with which several recent writers appear to agree.

Certainly I believe that we should educate our children *about* values and not just train them into adopting certain values, although I realise that different societies may desire different approaches. (Nevertheless I can't imagine how, or why, one would *train* a child to adopt a value like openness!) Again it seems to me to depend on the extent to which the particular society is influenced by these mathematico-technological cultural values, and relates once again to the enculturation/acculturation issue I described earlier.

In conclusion

Perhaps the most significant implication for mathematics education of this whole area lies in teacher education. It is clear that teacher educators can no longer ignore these kinds of issues. Mathematics education in practice is, and always should be, mediated by human teachers. Inducting a young child into part of its culture is *necessarily* an interpersonal affair, and therefore teachers must be made fully aware of this aspect of their role. More than that, they need to know about the values inherent in the subject they are responsible for, they need to know about the cultural history of their subject, they need to reflect on *their* relationship with those values, and they need to be aware of how their teaching contributes not just to the mathematical development of their pupils, but also to the development of mathematics in their culture. Teacher education is the key to cultural preservation and development.

Notes

1 Fasheh (1982) and Kothari (1978) are educators who also express the values-conflict clearly.
2 As mathematical ideas develop, of course, they become part of the environment

also, ready to be acted on as with any other part of the environment.

3 Kline (1962) and Wilder (1981) are two authors who have explored the cultural history of 'Western' mathematics.

4 The papers by Graham, Gerdes and Presmeg in this issue are concerned with this area.

5 Taft (1977) in a wide-ranging article describes many of the complex issues surrounding people in culture-conflict situations, and also indicates just how widespread a phenomenon it is.

References

d'Ambrosio, U. (1985) 'Ethnomathematics and its place in the history and pedagogy of mathematics', *For the Learning of Mathematics*, 5, 1, pp. 44–8.

Ascher, M. and Ascher, R. (1981) *Code of the Quipu*. Chicago: University of Michigan Press.

Bishop, A. J. (1979) 'Visualising and Mathematics in a Pre-technological Culture', *Educational Studies in Mathematics*, 10, 2, pp. 135–46.

Bishop, A. J. (1986) 'Mathematics Education as Cultural Induction', *Nieuwe Wiskrant*, October, pp. 27–32.

Bishop, A. J. (1988) *Mathematical Enculturation: A Cultural Perspective on Mathematics Education*. Dordrecht, Reidel.

Bourgoin, J. (1973) *Arabic Geometrical Pattern and Design*. New York: Dover.

Bruner, J. S. (1964) 'The course of cognitive growth', *American Psychologist*, 19, pp. 1–15.

Closs, M. P. (ed.) (1986) *Native American Mathematics*. Austin: University of Texas Press, Texas.

Ellul, J. (1980) *The Technological System*. New York: Continuum Publishing.

Faegre, T. (1979) *Tents: Architecture of the Nomads*. London: John Murray.

Falkener, E. (1961) *Games Ancient and Oriental – How to Play Them*. New York: Dover.

Fasheh, M. (1982) 'Mathematics, Culture and Authority', *For the Learning of Mathematics*, 3, 2, pp. 2–8.

Gardner, P. L. (1977) *Logical Connectives in Science*. Melbourne: Monash University, Faculty of Education.

Gay, J. and Cole, M. (1967) *The New Mathematics in an Old Culture*. New York: Holt, Rinehart and Winston.

Gerdes, P. (1985) 'Conditions and Strategies for Emancipatory Mathematics Education in Under-developed Countries', *For the Learning of Mathematics*, 5, 1, pp. 15–20.

Gerdes, P. (1986) 'How to Recognise Hidden Geometrical Thinking: A Contribution to the Development of Anthropological Mathematics', *For the Learning of Mathematics*, 6, 2, pp. 10–17.

Harris, P. (1980) *Measurements in Tribal Aboriginal Communities*. Northern Territory Department of Education, Australia.

Horton, R. (1971) 'African traditional thought and Western Science', *Africa*, Vol. XXXVII, also in M. F. D. Young (ed.), *Knowledge and Control*, pp. 208–66. London: Collier-MacMillan.

Huizinga, J. (1949) *Homo Luden*. London: Routledge and Kegan Paul.

Jayne, C. F. (1974) *String Figures and How to Make Them*. New York: Dover (first published as 'String Figures' by Scribner in 1906).

Jones, J. (1974) *Cognitive Studies with Students in Papua New Guinea* (Working Paper, No. 10), University of Papua New Guinea, Education Research Unit.

Kline, M. (1962) *Mathematics: A Cultural Approach*. Mass.: Addison Wesley.

Kothari, D. S. (1978) Keynote address in *Proceedings of Asian Regional Seminar of the Commonwealth Association of Science and Mathematics Educators* (New Delhi). London: British Council.

Lancy, D. F. (1983) *Cross-cultural Studies in Cognition and Mathematics*. New York: Academic Press.

Leach, E. (1973) 'Some anthropological observations on number, time and common-sense', in A. G. Howson (ed.), *Developments in Mathematical Education*, Cambridge: Cambridge University Press.

Lean, G. A. (1986) *Counting Systems of Papua New Guinea*, Research Bibliography, 3rd edn, Lae, Papua New Guinea. Department of Mathematics, Papua New Guinea University of Technology.

Lewis, D. (1972) *We the Navigators*. Hawaii: University Press of Hawaii.

Lewis, D. (1976) 'Observations on Route-Finding and Spatial Orientation Among the Aboriginal Peoples of the Western Desert Region of Central Australia', *Oceania*, XLVI, 4, pp. 249–82.

Menninger, K. (1969) *Number Words and Number Symbols – A Cultural History of Numbers*. Cambridge, Mass.: MIT Press.

Oswalt, W. H. (1976) *An Anthropological Analysis of Food-getting Technology*. New York: Wiley.

Pinxten, R., van Dooren, I. and Harvey, F. (1983) *The Anthropology of Space*. Philadelphia: University of Pennsylvania Press.

Ronan, C. A. (1981) *The Shorter Science and Civilisation in China: Vol. 2*. Cambridge: Cambridge University Press.

Ronan, C. A. (1983) *The Cambridge Illustrated History of the World's Science*. Cambridge: Cambridge University Press.

Roth, W. E. (1902) 'Games, Sports and Amusements', *North Queensland Ethnographic Bulletin*, 4, pp. 7–24.

van Sertima, I. (1986) *Black in Science*. New Brunswick: Transaction Books.

Skovsmose, O. (1985) 'Mathematical education versus critical education', *Educational Studies in Mathematics*, 16, 4, pp. 337–54.

Taft, R. (1977) 'Coping with Unfamiliar Cultures', in N. Warren (ed.), *Studies in Cross-Cultural Psychology*, Vol. 1. London: Academic Press.

Temple, R. K. G. (1986) *China, Land of Discovery and Invention*. Wellingborough: Stephens.

Vygotsky, L. S. (1978) *Mind in Society*. Cambridge, Mass.: MIT Press.

White, L. A. (1959) *The Evolution of Culture*. New York: McGraw-Hill.

Wilder, R. L. (1981) *Mathematics as a Cultural System*. Oxford: Permagon Press.

Zaslavsky, C. (1973) *Africa Counts*. Boston, Mass.: Prindle, Weber and Schmidt.

2.2

Places for Evolving Autobiography: English Classes at Work in the Curriculum*

Claire Woods

[. . .]

Our lives and those of our students are spun in words. There is no tie on time or place for such spinning. Professional writers and raconteurs know this only too well. Their chosen craft is word spinning, snatching the main threads and offcuts of their own and others' lives and shaping them for us to read or hear. The rest of us do not choose to craft as formally perhaps, but we do construct our lives with narratives. The child racing home to tell someone the dramatic moment of the school day; each of us turning to a friend to recount *our* version of an event; individuals offering their individual interpretations of and feelings about the headline news – 'I feel so sad for . . .', 'it reminds me of . . .', 'you can't believe it, can you?', 'remember when . . .', the cues to narratives and anecdotes of personal lives. They are also the narratives of lives shared in time and place. In these narratives is a meeting ground of the personal and the social, the individual and the shared, the private and the public.

They are narratives from individuals in their worlds and their cultures. A personal narrative is a cultural narrative, spun as it is within the understandings, traditions, ways of knowing, ways of speaking into which each of us is born and in which we each live and grow. We are constantly evolving our own autobiographies and thus constructing consciously and unconsciously our individual versions

---

* Claire Woods' original chapter explores the English curriculum from the perspective that 'it must ensure that students hear and discover the voices and texts of others'. She considers the teacher's role as a constructor and interpreter of 'a full range of texts where these reflect the world representations of different cultures and of different domains of knowing or knowledge'. The chapter presented here focuses on her discussion of how the English curriculum should be widened to include the texts and narratives of other domains of inquiry.

of ourselves and the pathways we tread through the worlds, spiritual and temporal, public and private, real and fantastical, we inhabit.

Thus evolving autobiographies are both about one's self alone and about one's self in community. Into each evolving autobiography are threaded the events of daily lives and of school days, snatches of other people's conversations, teachers' ideas and prejudices, the books read, the films seen and the ideas and experiences of countless others. These jostle for a place in the patterns we seek to create for ourselves of our own way of being or our own 'world representation'. [. . .] 'Our world representation is a storehouse of the data of our experience . . .' Britton (1970) continues:

What I have loosely referred to as 'world representation' has been more elaborately christened 'a verbally organised world schema'. *Verbally organised*: what is organised is far more than words. Woven into its fabric are representations of many kinds: images directly presented by the senses, images that are interiorised experiences of sight, sound, movement, touch, smell and taste: pre-verbal patterns reflecting feeling responses and elementary value judgements: post-verbal patterns, our ideas and reasoned beliefs about the world: images derived from myth, religion and the arts [. . .]. We build in large measure a common world, a world in which we live together: yet each of us builds in his own way. My representation differs from yours not only because the world has treated us differently but also because my way of representing what happens to both of us will differ from yours. We are neither of us cameras. Admittedly, we construct a representation of the world we both inhabit: on your screen and mine, as on the sensitive plate in the camera, is reflected that world. But we are at the same time projecting on to the screen our own needs and desires. In this sense then, we build what is for each of us a representation of the world and at the same time is to each other a representation of a different individuality, another self (Britton, 1982, first published in Jones and Mulford, 1971).

As we evolve our world representations we each construct a text for ourselves in which we are the main character. Each text is thus an evolving autobiography, filled with different versions of times, places, people and events. Each text evolves across the different spaces we occupy – school, home, work; across, therefore, the public and the private, the social and the personal. Each text evolves as an attempt to make sense of the discontinuities, the similarities, the certainties and the ambiguities. We construct our texts; we evolve our autobiographies; we learn. Schooling experienced is a sub-text within the text. Each child therefore is engaged in constructing many texts. This is a significant part of an evolving autobiography built upon the different contexts for learning in which each participates. The worlds of science, history, technical studies or geography are ripe for appropriation to each individual's story of learning.

What then of the role of English in the curriculum, in the experience of schooling? English, the subject, is predicted upon ways of representing the world and of acting upon the world with words. [. . .]

In the past twenty years English teachers have allowed the experiences of their students to take centre stage in their classroom. They have also begun to extend the range of texts they make available to students so that the writings of the cultures of all our students are seen as more acceptable within English. There is a long way to go in this regard. The worlds of immigrant or ethnic minority writers are not yet widely introduced in English classes. One day the wealth of literature – the heritage of the diverse cultures represented by the children (of whatever race or gender) in our classes – will truly be shared within the context of English.

What of the other connections to be made within the subject English in practice? What is the evolving autobiography of the student in the rest of the school? What role is there for English and the English teacher in relation to the rest of the curriculum? All classes, all subjects should be an obvious link in the continuum of learning. We know they are not. Schooling is not. In English, however, the continuity should be made most obvious. It is in this focused time in the school day that children, students and teachers by the very nature of language at work are engaged in consciously constructing their own texts both literally and metaphorically. When you put your language out in front of you and when you announce 'I am a writer, reader, speaker and so on', you deliberately grasp your own text. Then it can be shaken, turned upside down for a time or refashioned. You also offer your narrative and its cultural contexts and meanings to others. The texts of others and thus of other ways of perceiving the world, can be shaken, questioned and interpreted too.

This is not easy. The English curriculum at work must recognise the realities of the world and at the same time the vulnerabilities of each individual. In the toughest and most sensitive way it must add to each child's repertoire of ways of acting in and upon the world. Its foci are the language and texts of spectators and participants. It must ensure that each child's voice has its own strength. It must ensure that children hear and discover the voices and texts of others.

Since English teachers have not yet ventured into the texts or the stories of the scientist or biologist or the historian or the geographer, we have not been able to help children evolve their autobiographies of their schooling in anything other than a limited way. Similarly we have been loath to tread into the discourse and texts of the action of the world beyond school in any substantial way. And our forays into a diversity of cultural experiences through non-Anglo-Celtic literary resources have been but tentative. [. . .] Making the shift to seeing the texts of the world of action outside and those of the other domains of knowing, of other subjects, as part of the work of English is for most of us difficult to accept. [. . .] The time has come when the English teacher (who draws children into particular relationships with texts, inviting them to read, respond to, generate and act through texts) should widen the range of discourse to include the texts, indeed the narratives, of other domains of inquiry and knowing. I choose my words carefully because I do not mean that the standard school textbooks of other subject areas should be included in English (although there may be a place for deconstructing them with vigour). Rather, if we accept that there are different ways of construing the world, then we should be showing children how the lens of the scientist or of the historian or the anthropologist allows for particular world representations. We should be helping children discover how, in their writings, scientists or anthropologists, for example, construct their worlds.

The English classroom focuses on texts, written, spoken, and visual. It invites students into the 'spectator' mode, just as it invites them to be 'participants' in using language. If the texts and narratives of historians or natural scientists are drawn into English, then the English teacher and her students as spectators can share something of the former's perspectives on the world. Students as critical and reflective readers can explore how these different texts work and, in trying to create similar texts for themselves, move from reflection to action with their language. What reading might we lure into English – popular writings about biology, economics, archaeology, anthropology, political essays, social commentaries, the biographies of scientists and mathematicians, the autobiographical essays of Primo Levi or E. B. White, articles from *National Geographic* or *Scientific American*, journal observations of field naturalists or what? Can we invite other colleagues, teachers of science or geography for example, into the English class to help us and our students read these texts?

There is room in English for the reading of expository writing; writing that argues a case, describes, explains, defines, persuades, classifies and reports, that covers a breadth of contexts, situations and topics. Some of this writing might have an expressive function and some clearly serves the poetic. Other examples of such writing will fall into the kinds of informative and conative categories of the transactional. The consciously crafted essay, the specialist report in a journal, the diary observations of a scientist or explorer or a first-person account with technical detail of a motorcycle race invites particular engagement from students as readers and thence as writers. Such writing would be the models for many of the texts students encounter in their other subjects.

What writing might we find in English if we adopt a notion of the English teacher and students as discoverers and makers of texts? Obviously we would find writing of the kind just mentioned. We might also make the opportunity to work closely with other teachers; not to focus on a topic or theme in ways advocated by integrated studies or humanities courses but to help students to use their writing to learn.

Can the English class be a place for making texts of all kinds? A geography essay, a science report, a project diary in technical studies, a technical description of a geology excursion? English is concerned with students as writers and readers and with their being readers and writers for many purposes. We seek our different audiences for student writing. We talk of seeking the real purposes of writing and reading. Yet we have tended to ignore the real purposes and situations close at hand in the school, those in which students are engaged as writers and readers. Can the English class be a workshop where they read and reflect as scientists or geologists? Can they begin to see themselves as writers of science and of history in an English class where they are helped to make the connections between the texts of different subjects? What kind of reading or writing of texts do we encourage in English? We encourage our students to predict, to speculate, to reflect, to share through talking their current understandings. We encourage them to approach new material through personal and expressive language. We encourage them 'to shape at the point of utterance' as writers and as readers.[1]

Peter Medway (1980) sums up the distinction and yet underlying similarity between learning in other subjects and learning in English when he writes:

> English at its best recognises the validity of the knowledge that students bring to school with them, and provides means of expression – from informal conversation to consciously structured poetic writings – which allow it to be considered and made more of. Much of this knowledge falls within the fields of other school subjects – for instance children's knowledge of nature. Yet the other subjects tend to ignore this 'pre-disciplinary knowledge' and start from the assumption that students know nothing, or nothing that is 'real knowledge' – even though adult practitioners could not practise their disciplines without these unspecifiable awarenesses and sensitivities.

Medway comments that these 'awarenesses and sensitivities' or 'the personal and unstateable knowledge' of the different disciplines are similar to the kind of knowledge encouraged in English.

Yet these ways of learning with language which support such knowing have been difficult for most other subject teachers to recognise as valid and to adopt in their contexts. Language across the curriculum has foundered on this because what is demanded of teachers is a new conceptualisation of who owns subject 'knowledge', of ways of knowing and thus of learning and of teaching. English teachers too have been unable generally to build the bridges between the processes of language and learning in English and other subjects. Often the differences between the intentions of the English teacher and those of other teachers have been insurmountable barriers in schools. [. . .] The barriers to the exchange of texts and processes across subject areas lie, however, not only with teachers but with children whose experience of education has led them to compartmentalise their learning. Medway notes:

> The separation in the secondary curriculum of the scientific (in the broad sense) from the personal and intuitive ways of knowing fails to reflect the psychological realities of most of (the) students under 16 that I have known.
>
> It does not correspond to any achieved differentiation in their thinking; few of them have come to regard objectivity and the establishment of impersonal truth as values in themselves. Arrival at that stage appears indeed to be hindered by teaching approaches which insist on the outward forms of objectivity and which exclude the larger part of the child's response (1980, p. 10).

Perhaps, as we include alternative texts, the writing of other domains of knowing the world, and help children into the language of action in the world and community, we will be forced to be learners again ourselves. For we will have to uncover the structures and insights of quite different texts and topics. We will see the world through new lenses. We might begin to wonder again, to be delighted by new reflections on the world. Why should we be trapped in a genre of English teaching because of the texts we have traditionally chosen? And in the ways we have traditionally *taught* them?

Making connections across the curriculum with texts, reflects a view of our children as active and not passive text discoverers and makers. [. . .] We can offer our children the chance to develop power over and through texts and discourse. We can do this by enabling them to examine the metaphors, tropes, images and structures of the scientist's or anthropologist's writing or the television documentary or the picture book or the politician's speech. To do this is to offer children a way of reading, interpreting and thus commanding the world. English ought therefore be the place for 'authentic engagements' of the kind encouraged by a different set of activities relating to the world and its discourse and permitted by an altered range of texts. Thus children should be involved in reflection and action with their language.

Note

1 For a discussion of reading for meaning as 'shaping at the point of utterance', see Pradl (1987), pp. 66–9.

References

Britton, J. (1970) *Language and Learning*. London: Allen Lane.

Britton, J. (1982) *Prospect and Retrospect: Selected Essays of James Britton* (ed. G. Pradl). London: Heinemann.

Medway, P. (1980) *Finding a Language*. London: Chameleon.

Pradl, G. (1987) 'Close encounters of the first kind: teaching the poem at the point of utterance', *English Journal*, 76, 2, pp. 66–9.

2.3

Cognitive Science and Science Education

Susan Carey

[. . .]

To understand some new piece of information is to relate it to a mentally represented schema, to integrate it with already existing knowledge. This may also seem self-evident, but a simple demonstration from over a decade ago might show the force of this idea. Try to make sense of the following text (from Bransford and Johnson, 1973):

> If the balloons popped the sound wouldn't be able to carry since everything would be too far away from the correct floor. A closed window would also prevent the sound from carrying, since most buildings tend to be well insulated. Since the whole operation depends on a steady flow of electricity, a break in the middle of the wire would also cause problems. Of course, the fellow could shout, but the human voice is not loud enough to carry that far. An additional problem is that a string could break on the instrument. Then there could be no accompaniment to the message. It is clear that the best situation would involve less distance. Then there would be fewer potential problems. With face to face contact, the least number of things could go wrong (pp. 392–3).

If understanding of this passage eludes you, turn the page and look at Figure 1, a context that provides a key. Bransford and Johnson (1973) showed that subjects who were denied access to the context rated the text as fairly incomprehensible and, when asked to recall the text, remembered very little of it. Apparently, the figure allows access to a known schema (the serenade), which, in turn, provides a framework for comprehension. Simple demonstrations such as these set the stage for analyses of the schemata people have for understanding the world and for techniques that ensure that many different types of connections are made between what is being read and what is already known.

What does all this have to do with science education? Surely, understanding should also be at the core of the science curriculum. Our scientific heritage has provided us with deep and counter-intuitive understanding of the physical, biological, and social worlds, and we want to teach at least some aspects of that understanding to

Figure 1   Context sufficient to make sense of balloons passage

Note. Reprinted from 'Consideration of Some Problems in Comprehension' (p. 394) by J. D. Bransford and M. K. Johnson. In *Visual Information Processing* by W. G. Chase (ed.) (1973) New York: Academic Press. Copyright 1973 by Academic Press. Reprinted by permission.

youngsters. We also want them to grasp the nature of the scientific process, especially how it yields scientific understanding of the natural world.

The immediate lessons of the research on reading are clear. Students reading a science text or listening to a science teacher must gain understanding by relating what they are reading (hearing) to what they know, and this requires active, constructive work. This is the cognitive rationale (as opposed to the motivational rationale) for making science lessons relevant to students' concerns. But the serenade example is fundamentally misleading as applied to the problem of gaining understanding of a science text. In the case of science learning, students do not already have the schemata, such as the schema of the serenade, available to form the basis of their understanding.

We have arrived at a paradox: to understand text or spoken language, one must relate it to schemata for understanding the world. But the goal of science teaching is imparting new schemata for understanding, schemata not yet in the student's repertoire. So how is the student to understand the texts and lessons that impart the new information? This paradox is real, and failure to grasp its full import is the source of many of the current problems in our science curriculum. It has been noted that junior and senior high school texts often introduce more new vocabulary per page than foreign language texts. But in foreign language texts the concepts denoted by the new words are already known to the student; that is, they already function in mentally represented schemata. But this is not so for new scientific vocabulary. Science as vocabulary lesson is a recipe for disaster, especially if understanding is the goal.

Indeed, the full force of students' *lack* of understanding of what they have been taught in science has begun to be grasped. Phenomena independently discovered by cognitive scientists and by educational researchers dramatically demonstrate this lack.

The phenomena of misconceptions

The phenomena I refer to are the misconceptions that prove so resistant to teaching. The diagnosis of misconceptions has become a highly productive cottage industry (see, e.g. the proceedings of the International Seminar on Misconceptions in Science and Mathematics, Helm and Novak, 1983). To illustrate the independent discovery of this phenomenon by educators and cognitive scientists, let me give two examples from mechanics. Remember your mechanics from high school or college physics? If you had no high school or college physics, see how you would answer the questions anyway, for your intuitions should be the same as those of the novices. If you had some physics but still have the novice intuitions, don't worry, that's part of the phenomenon of interest here.

Consider the problem in Figure 2, panel A. A coin is tossed; in position (a) it is on the upward part of its trajectory and in position (b) it is on the downward part of its trajectory. Your task is to indicate, with little arrows, the forces that are acting on the coin at position (a) and at position (b). Novice physicists (even those who have had a year of college physics in which they have been taught the relevant part of Newtonian mechanics) draw the arrows as in panel B; experts draw the arrows as in panel C (Clement, 1982). The novices explain their two arrows at position (a) as follows:

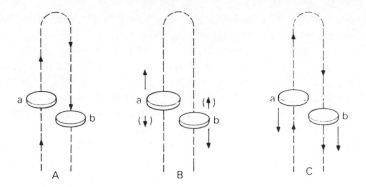

Figure 2   Problem (A), novice solution (B), and expert solution (C)

Note.   Adapted from 'Students' Preconceptions in Introductory Mechanics' by J. Clement (1982) *American Journal of Physics*, 50, 1, p. 68. Copyright 1982 by the American Association of Physics Teachers. Adapted by permission.

There are two forces acting on the coin in its upward trajectory – the force imparted when it was thrown up and the force of gravity. The former force is greater in the upward trajectory; that's why the coin is going up. In the downward trajectory the force of gravity is the only force, or else it is the greater of the two, which is why the coin is descending.

Newtonians, in contrast, recognise only the force of gravity once the coin has been set in motion. Apparently, novices have a misconception about motion, one highly resistant to tuition, something like 'no motion without a force causing it'. This violates Newton's laws, which recognise a related conception: 'no acceleration without a force causing it'.

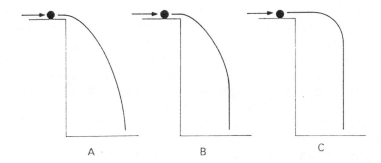

Figure 3   Expert solution (A) and two novice solutions (B and C)

Note.   Adapted from 'Naive Theories of Motion' by M. McCloskey. In *Mental Models* by D. Gentner and A. Stevens (eds) (1983) Hillsdale, NJ: Lawrence Erlbaum. Copyright 1983 by Lawrence Erlbaum Associates, Inc. Adapted by permission.

Closely analogous misconceptions have been documented by other science educators, such as Viennot (1979), McDermott (1984), and Champagne and Klopfer (1984). Cognitive psychologists have also contributed to this documentation. For example, McCloskey (1983) described a slight variant of Clement's problem, with identical results. McCloskey also contributed several new cases of mechanics misconceptions. Consider the following problem. The subject is to imagine a ball going off a frictionless cliff at 50 mph and is to draw its trajectory as it falls to the ground. The correct answer is a parabolic trajectory (Figure 3, panel A), because the ball continues to travel horizontally at 50 mph but accelerates in its downward motion due to gravity (the only force acting on the ball). Most subjects draw a roughly parabolic curve, but some (about one fourth) draw curves such as those in panels B and C, in which there is a period of pure downward motion, sometimes following a period of pure horizontal motion (panel C). Subjects explain these trajectories by saying that the force causing the horizontal motion is dissipating and that gravity then takes over.

Analogous misconceptions are observed at other levels of the science curriculum. Johnson and Wellman (1982) documented that young children misconceive what the brain is for; they consider it the organ of mental life and thus deem it necessary for thinking, dreaming, remembering, solving problems, and so on, but deem it irrelevant to walking, breathing, sneezing, or even talking. One of the fifth grades in which Johnson and Wellman did their research had a two-week curricular unit on the brain, complete with a discussion of the autonomic as well as the central nervous system. Children who had completed this unit were just as likely to see the brain as irrelevant to breathing and sneezing as were those who had not yet had the unit.

Let me re-emphasise that the mechanics misconceptions are also common *after* students have had relevant instruction (*two years* of physics – high school and college). The teachers in the courses whose students make these responses are surprised, even incredulous. The point here is that these misconceptions document failure of the curriculum to impart the hoped-for understanding. But much deeper points can be made about the same phenomena.

Remember the paradox with which I began. Students, like anybody else, understand by relating incoming information to currently held knowledge schemata. Information presented in science lessons, even whole courses, is assimilated to existing knowledge structures, which differ in systematic ways from the knowledge structures the curriculum is intended to impart. Part of the paradox is resolved. Although students do not yet have the experts' mental schemata, they bring *some* schemata for understanding the physical, biological, and social worlds. This ensures *some* understanding of curricular materials. They are not in the position of readers of the serenade text, with no clues to any relevant schema for understanding the text or, worse, with no relevant schemata at all. But now we have another, much more difficult problem. *How* do the students' schemata differ from those of the experts? In the rest of this brief essay, I will discuss several proposals for how scientific schemata change in the course of acquiring more scientific knowledge. I hope to provide a feel for the complexity of the issues, to show that progress is being made, and to suggest that success will require the collaboration of cognitive scientists and science educators, who together must be aware of the understanding of science provided by both historians and philosophers of science. In my view, answering this question should be our top priority. The answer provides the instructional challenge – it tells us what changes our science curriculum must effect.

Knowledge restructuring – the view from cognitive science

Cognitive scientists place the work on misconceptions in the context of other research on the so-called novice–expert shift. As the name implies, the novice–expert shift is the change that occurs as a beginner in some domain gains expertise. Many domains have been studied – most extensively, expertise at the game of chess and expertise in the physical sciences, particularly mechanics. Chi, Glaser, and Rees (1982) provided an excellent review of the cognitive science research on the novice–expert shift. As they pointed out, three methods have been brought to bear on the description of how novices differ from experts. The first (and most important) is the documentation of misconceptions, such as those sketched above. Other methods include analyses of perceived similarities among elements in the domain and information-processing analysis of how problems are solved.

Research by Chi and her colleagues illustrates the use of the second method. Novices and experts were asked to group physics problems according to similarity. Novices put together those problems that mentioned the same kinds of objects – problems about pulleys were grouped together, problems about inclined planes were grouped together, and so on. Experts, in contrast, placed together those problems solvable with Newton's laws of motion, on the one hand, and those solvable using energy equations, on the other (Chi *et al.*, 1982). These two ways of classifying the problems were orthogonal; inclined plane problems, for example, can be of both types. The expert apparently organises his or her knowledge of physics in terms of abstract schemata not salient to the novice.

The force of this difference is brought home by studies using the third method: information-processing analyses of how problems are solved. Larkin and her co-workers (Larkin, McDermott, Simon, and Simon, 1980) showed that when solving mechanics problems, novices use painful means–end analyses, working with equations that they hope are relevant to the problem. Experts, in contrast, apply correct equations in a forward direction, indicating that they have a whole solution plan in place before they begin. The schemata in terms of which experts organise their knowledge of physics enable them to grasp the structure of problems in a way that novices cannot.

These first two methods discussed by Chi *et al.* (1982) – analyses of misconceptions, analyses of similarity judgements – have been used by science educators as well. Science educators have also developed the technique of 'concept mapping', in which the student and teacher, or the student and researcher, together produce a representation of the student's concepts in the domain. This process serves both research and pedagogical goals. By comparing successive concept maps, produced as the student gains mastery of the domain, the researcher can see how knowledge is restructured in the course of acquisition. By participating in the production of maps for his or her own concepts, and monitoring how they change, the student sees what it is to gain understanding of a new domain.

All these techniques have as their goal the description of the novice's (and expert's) structuring of the domain, so that the two structures may be compared and the question of 'restructuring' addressed. Chi *et al.* (1982) provided a precise statement of what might be meant by 'restructuring'. First, experts represent relations among concepts different from the relations novices represent among them (as in the change from 'no motion without a force' to 'no acceleration without a force'). Secondly, patterns among these new relations motivate the creation of new, abstract concepts and schemata that are either not represented by novices at all or are not very accessible to them (as reflected in the changes in perceived similarity among physics problems and in the changes in the ways in which problems are attacked when solved). As Chi *et al.* (1982) put it, what is basic level for the novice is subordinate level for the expert.

So far, what I have said about the novice–expert shift suggests that the two systems share many concepts. Nodes corresponding to concepts such as *force*, *energy*, and so on, can be identified in both systems, and the terms for these concepts are identical or can easily be translated from one system to the other. Only if this is so may we conceive of the novice's misconceptions as beliefs different from the expert's about the same physical magnitudes or as the novice's representing relations among the same concepts different from those of the expert. Only if this is so may we credit novices with understanding when they manage to choose the correct equations, even in their bumbling way, to apply to a given problem. And only if this is so may we think of restructuring primarily as the building of more abstract schemata to incorporate the same subordinate schemata.

Knowledge restructuring – the view from the history of science

The study of conceptual change in the history of science has led to a much more radical view of restructuring of knowledge (Feyerabend, 1962; Kuhn, 1962; Toulmin, 1953). The original formulations of this radical view embraced a kind of meaning holism in which the meaning of each concept in a theory is determined by its relations with all other concepts in the theory. In this view, any theory change necessarily involves conceptual change. This view has other consequences: that successive theories are incommensurate and that each theory is unfalsifiable. These extreme formulations have been rejected by most philosophers of science (see Suppe, 1974, for extensive discussion), but a strong view of restructuring has survived, one that allows for true conceptual change among core concepts of successive theories (see Kuhn, 1982). In the strong view, successive conceptual systems differ in three related ways – in the domain of phenomena accounted for, in the nature of explanations deemed acceptable, and even in the individual concepts in the centre of each system. These three types of differences sometimes result in one theory's terms not even being translatable into the terms of the other (Kuhn, 1982). For example, in successive theories of mechanics each of the core terms, such as *force*, *velocity*, *time*, and *mass*, has fundamentally different meanings in the earlier as compared to the later theory.

As an example, consider the concepts *motion* and *velocity* in Aristotelian and Galilean mechanics. For Aristotle, motion included all change over time – movement, growth, decay, and so on. He distinguished two fundamentally different types of motion – natural and violent. His physics accounted for the two in quite different ways. Natural motions included objects falling to the earth, smoke rising, plants growing, and so on and were explained in terms of each kind's natural place or state. Violent, or artificial, motions were those caused by an active agent, such as the movement of a person or the heat of a fire, and were explained in terms of entirely different mechanisms. Galileo, in contrast, restricted his study to movement through space, saw that the distinction between natural and violent motion was a distinction without a difference, and collapsed the two kinds of motion, bringing both into the domain of a single mechanical theory. Galileo's system had no concept of natural place or natural state. Moreover, Aristotle did not distinguish between average velocity and instantaneous velocity – the key distinction that got Galileo's kinematics off the ground (Kuhn, 1977). These changes at the level of individual concepts are the reason that the core terms of Aristotelian mechanics and Galilean mechanics are not intertranslatable (Kuhn, 1982). The changes from Aristotelian to Galilean mechanics did not come easily. One cannot understand the process by which they occurred without considering the changes in the whole theory – in the domain of phenomena to be explained and in the kinds of explanations considered acceptable. All three kinds of change – in domain, concepts, and explanatory structure – come together. Change of one kind cannot be understood without reference to the changes of the other kinds.

I have contrasted two different senses of 'restructuring'. The first, weaker sense is the one spelled out in Chi *et al.* (1982). With expertise, new relations among concepts are represented, and new schemata come into being that allow the solution of new problems and change the solutions to old problems. The second, stronger sense includes not only these kinds of change but also changes in the individual core concepts of the successive systems. The analysis of conceptual change is extremely difficult. I will not attempt to provide criteria for telling whether a particular case of restructuring involves this type of change. None the less, consideration of clear examples such as the transition from Aristotelian to Galilean mechanics can help us decide other cases. In this transition several differentiations and coalescences occurred, which are both paradigm cases of conceptual change. Furthermore, the ontological commitments of the theories differ. Aristotle was committed to the existence of natural places and natural states, for these played a central explanatory role in his theory. According to Galileo's theory, however, such things did not exist. These changes – differentiations, coalescences, changes in ontological commitments – are understandable only in terms of the changes in domains and causal notions between the successive theories. When all these changes are found, we should be confident that the knowledge reorganisation in question is of the stronger kind, involving conceptual change.

The discussion of theory change by historians and philosophers of science poses a question for cognitive scientists. Does the novice–expert shift among adults involve conceptual change? There are certainly reasons to doubt it. Convincing examples in the history of science occur over years, even centuries, of conscious theory building by mature scientists. Nevertheless, recent work by students of the novice–expert shift begins to suggest that such restructuring does occur as individuals learn a new domain of science. Larkin (1983) proposed that novices think of physical causality in terms of time based propagation of physical effects. In similar contexts experts explain phenomena in terms of state equations. Wiser and Carey (1983) documented a similar change in the historical development of thermal theories in the century between Galileo and Black. McCloskey and his colleagues (e.g. McCloskey, 1983) claimed that the beginner at mechanics brings a theory of mechanical phenomena to his or her study of mechanics in school and that this theory is identical to the pre-Galilean impetus theory of the Middle Ages. The misconceptions in Figures 2 and 3 are one source of evidence for this claim; the novice's upward force is the impetus imparted to the coin when it is tossed; it is horizontal impetus that maintains the horizontal trajectory after the ball has left the cliff. The reason that students' misconceptions are so resistant to tuition is that learning mechanics requires a theory change of the sort achieved by Galileo – indeed, even more than that achieved by Galileo, all the way from impetus theory to Newton. If McCloskey is correct, strong restructuring involving conceptual change occurs, because many simultaneous adjustments at the level of individual concepts make the core notions of Newtonian mechanics unstatable in terms of the concepts of pre-Galilean impetus theory.

We are now in a position to understand the true importance of the study of student misconceptions. True, they show us the failure of our curricula. More important, they provide one clue as to the content of the student's schemata for understanding nature and as to how those schemata differ from the expert's. We cannot effect scientific understanding without grasping the depth and tenacity of the student's preexisting knowledge.

The above examples of conceptual change in the course of learning scientific knowledge come from the high school and college curricula. In two recently published case studies of knowledge restructuring in childhood, my colleagues and I argued that cognitive development also involves conceptual change. Carey (1985b) analysed the interrelated changes in the concepts of animal, person, plant, living thing, death, reproduction, gender, and so forth, in the years from age 4 to 10 and argued that these years witness the emergence of an intuitive biology as an independent domain of theorising. The young child has not differentiated two senses of *not alive* – namely, *dead* and *inanimate*. At age 4, these concepts are embedded only in an intuitive psychology. Neither dead things nor inanimate things are capable of behaviour, and biological relations such as parentage are seen as social relations. The misconceptions about the brain described by Johnson and Wellman (1982) should be seen in this context. Analogously, Smith, Carey, and Wiser (1986) documented the differentiation of *weight* and *density* over

these same years and argued that the same analysis of differentiation that applies in historical cases (such as Black's differentiation of
heat and *temperature*, see Wiser and Carey, 1983) is required to
describe this childhood case. The differentiation occurs in the
context of developing an intuitive theory of matter. Piaget and
Inhelder (1941) and Smith *et al.* (1986) documented many misconceptions in support of this claim. Young children think that sugar
ceases to exist when it is dissolved in water; young children maintain
that a small piece of styrofoam weighs nothing at all; young children
think shadows are made out of some kind of stuff in the same sense
that tables are, and so forth.

Knowledge restructuring – the view from science education

Like cognitive scientists concerned with the novice–expert shift,
most science educators have underestimated the degree to which
students' alternative conceptual frameworks differ from the science
being taught. When misconceptions are cited, they are often given
one-sentence characterisations, as in the following list taken from a
recent review in *The Research Digest* (Capper, 1984, p. 4):

> Examples of misconceptions include the following:
> 'Light from a candle goes further at night' (Stead and Osborne, 1980)
>
> 'Friction only occurs between moving surfaces' (Stead and Osborne, 1981)
>
> 'Electric current is used up in a light bulb' (Osborne, 1981)
>
> 'A worm is not an animal' (Bell, 1981)
>
> 'Force is a quantity in a moving object in the direction of motion' (Osborne and
> Gilbert, 1980)
>
> 'Gravity requires the presence of air' (Stead and Osborne, 1981; Minstrell, 1982)

Such a list seems to presuppose the weaker sense of restructuring
(different relations among core concepts) because the misconceptions are characterised simply as false beliefs that are highly
resistant to tuition. It is perfectly possible, of course, that the
weaker sense of restructuring properly captures some of the above-
cited mismatches between novice and expert conceptual systems. In
another example, Champagne and Klopfer (1984) described studies
showing that novices believe that heavier objects fall faster than
lighter objects. This misconception truly may be a proposition stated
over the same concepts as the expert's *faster* and *heavier*, such that
the restructuring involved in attaining the expert conceptual
framework does not require conceptual change.

In spite of this very real possibility, I doubt that weak restructuring characterises most changes in conceptual frameworks achieved

by successful science education. The source of my suspicion is the fifth misconception on the above list, 'Force is a quantity in a moving object in the direction of motion'. This is the 'no motion without a force' misconception supported by demonstrations such as those depicted in Figures 2 and 3. But these are the very demonstrations that have been analysed by McCloskey (1983) as part of an extensive alternative theory articulated in terms of concepts different from those of Newtonian physics. Science educators, as well, have challenged the simple false-belief characterisation of the source of subjects' errors (e.g. McDermott, 1984):

> The students' responses, both in word and action, indicated that they lacked a consistent conceptual system. Their use of the word 'force' and other technical terms was ambiguous and unstable. . . . (It) could not be adequately summarised as a simple belief in the necessity of a force in the direction of motion. (p. 8)

Indeed, Vienott (1979) anticipated McCloskey's (1983) claims that the students' conceptual system resembles an evolved scheme of historical thought, 'closer to the Impetus theory than to Aristotle' (Viennot, 1979, p. 213), and provided an elegant analysis of how some of the core concepts of the student differ from the core concepts of Newtonian mechanics. Her central claim was that the student's concept of force conflates two distinct components, each called upon in different contexts. She dubbed the two components of the students' undifferentiated concept 'force of interaction' and 'supply of force', respectively. The former, force of interaction, is a function of the position of a moving body, and it determines the rate of change in velocity. Force of interaction satisfies the equation $F = ma$. It is appealed to whenever the problem calls forth a local analysis of the situation or when the force acts in the same direction as the motion. Thus students speak of 'the force acting on the mass'. Students speak of the latter, supply of force, as 'the force *of* the mass' and think of it as the force in a body that keeps it moving. This is the notion appealed to when motion is made obvious in the statement of the problem and especially when the motion is in the opposite direction to the (true) resultant forces.

Viennot (1979) analysed the relation of this undifferentiated concept of force to the concept of energy, noting that 'energy' is sometimes used correctly and sometimes inextricably linked with the concept of force in a single undifferentiated explanatory concept. Besides being undifferentiated relative to the Newtonian concepts, the student's concepts differ from those of Newtonian concepts in other ways as well. Another key difference (also noted by Larkin, 1983) is that the students attribute physical quantities such as force and energy to the objects themselves, whereas the Newtonian system does not.

Viennot's analysis, then, complemented and extended that of the cognitive scientists who worked on the same misconceptions and provided a convincing example of conceptual change. It is very likely that other misconceptions also require conceptual change before being abandoned.

A different challenge to weak restructuring

McDermott (1984), quoted earlier, expressed dissatisfaction with the summary of the student's misconception as a simple belief in the necessity of a force in the direction of motion. I chose to explicate her dissatisfaction by presenting Viennot's (1979) analaysis of the conceptual change involved, of the strong restructuring required to bring the novice and the expert into alignment. However, there is another thread of McDermott's dissatisfaction, one that denies the 'alternative conceptual framework' approach altogether; in this interpretation, both weak and strong restructuring are denied. McDermott suggested that students lack a consistent conceptual system at all. Others have noted the inconsistencies in students' solutions to problems (e.g. White, 1981) and have wondered whether it is justifiable to credit students with 'alternative conceptual frameworks' or 'intuitive theories', rather than with bags of tricks that they call upon haphazardly.

One cannot deny the inconsistencies noted by the doubters. But inconsistency and apparent confusion are not sufficient to disprove the 'alternative conceptual framework' picture of the learner. An intuitive theory is characterised by its core concepts, the phenomena in its domain, and its explanatory notions. It is only with respect to its explanations of the phenomena in its domain that consistency is expected. It is easy to push any historical theory into inconsistency and its adherents into apparent confusion by probing at its periphery, rather than examining it at its core.

Whether the 'alternative conceptual framework' position is correct is an empirical question. Its answer depends on finding a domain of phenomena consistently handled by the candidate intuitive theory. Carey (1985b) provided an analysis of at least one intuitive theory, the intuitive biological theory achieved by age 10. Carey also discussed the need for appeals to intuitive theories in cognitive science. We must appeal to intuitive theories to state constraints on induction, to explicate ontological commitments and causal notions, to analyse conceptual change, and so on. For these reasons, I cannot take seriously the denial of the 'alternative conceptual framework' position.

A different view of restructuring – Piaget's

Thus far, we have been discussing how the student's conceptual frameworks for explaining natural phenomena differ from the experts. Through this analysis we gain insight into the barriers students face to the understanding of newly presented scientific knowledge. Piaget gave us a quite different picture of the barriers to learning in young children. Piaget taught us that young children are fundamently different kinds of thinkers and learners from adults – that they think in concrete terms, cannot represent concepts with the structure of scientific concepts, are limited in their inferential apparatus, and so forth. His stage theory described several general reorganisations of the child's conceptual machinery – the shift from sensorimotor to representational thought, from pre-logical to early concrete logical thought, and finally to the formal thinking of adults. In Piaget's system, these shifts are domain independent. That is, they were meant to explain the child's limitations in learning new information with certain formal properties, no matter what domain of knowledge that information pertained to. Piaget's stage theory has come under fire and has been abandoned by many developmental psychologists. It is probably fundamentally misleading (see Carey, 1985a; Gelman and Baillargeon, 1983, for reviews). That is, many developmental psychologists now believe that the young child does *not* think differently from the adult, is *not* concrete, illogical, and so forth. Phenomena that were interpreted in terms of Piaget's stage theory are better interpreted in terms of specific alternative conceptual frameworks – novice-expert shifts and theory changes in particular domains.

The Piagetian work is closely related to that reviewed in this essay. Piaget and his colleagues have given us a rich stock of the misconceptions of young children. The non-conservations can be seen in this light, as can childhood animism, the child's beliefs about phase change and dissolving sugar, and so forth. Insofar as Piaget interpreted these misconceptions in terms of the child's changing theories (as when conservation of weight, mass, and volume, the dissolving of sugar, the differentiation of weight and density, etc., were all interpreted in terms of the child's inventing a naive particulate theory of matter; see Piaget and Inhelder, 1941; Smith, Carey and Wiser, 1986), his work was the direct forerunner to the research under discussion here. It is only when Piaget sought to further explain the differences between young children and adults in terms of domain-general limitations on the child's representational or computational abilities that his interpretations have come under fire. However, the question is still very much open. One goal of further research is to discover the relative roles of domain-specific and domain-general developmental changes in the description of cognitive development.

The challenges

Some version of the 'alternative conceptual framework' view is undoubtedly correct. I have argued that it is important to state the alternative versions clearly and to discover which are correct for which cases. I see two further challenges: the representational problem and the mechanism-of-change problem. First, we must find much better ways of *representing* conceptual structures so as to be able to analyse conceptual reorganisation. Secondly, we must develop theories of what causes change.

Why cognitive scientists and science educators need each other

The independent convergence on the same phenomena as central to the concerns of both groups sets the stage for successful collaboration between cognitive scientists and science educators. A second requirement for successful collaboration is complementary strengths – each group should bring something different to the collaboration. I believe this condition is met as well.

The representational problem will be solved, if at all, by cognitive scientists. Many are dissatisfied with current network representations of conceptual structures and are working on new formalisms for the representation of scientific knowledge. For example, Forbus and Gentner (1984) described a formalism for representing knowledge that models qualitative reasoning; most intuitive theories provide qualitative rather than quantitative explanations of natural phenomena. Cognitive scientists are also working on the relation of causal notions to the nature of human concepts (e.g., Murphy and Medin, 1985) and on the analysis of ontological notions (e.g. Keil, 1979; Macnamara, 1982; Carey, 1985b). Such work will undoubtedly aid the joint enterprise of stating more precisely how knowledge is restructured in the course of acquisition.

The mechanism-of-change problem will be solved, if at all, by collaboration of the two groups. It is science educators who must test any ideas about how to effect knowledge restructuring in the classroom. In a recent article, Posner, Strike, Hewson, and Gertzog (1982) accepted the challenge of the 'alternative conceptual framework' point of view and proposed instructional strategies that will effect knowledge reorganisation. Much more work along these lines is called for. Never again must ideas about knowledge acquisition be tested against cases that do not pose the difficult issue of its restructuring.

References

Bell, B. F. (1981) 'When is an Animal not an Animal?' *Journal of Biology Education*, 15, 3, pp. 213–18.

Bransford, J. D. and Johnson, M. K. (1973) 'Consideration of Some Problems in Comprehension', in W. G. Chase (ed.), *Visual Information Processing*. New York: Academic Press, pp. 383–438.

Capper, J. (1984) 'Research in Science Education: A Cognitive Science Perspective', in *The Research Digest*. Washington, DC: Available from Center for Research Into Practice.

Carey, S. (1985a) 'Are Children Fundamentally Different Thinkers than Adults?' in S. Chipman, J. Segal and R. Glaser (eds), *Thinking and Learning Skills*, Vol. 2, pp. 485–518. Hillsdale, NJ: Erlbaum.

Carey, S. (1985b). *Conceptual Change in Childhood*. Cambridge, MA: MIT Press.

Champagne, A. B. and Klopfer, L. E. (1984) 'Research in Science Education: the Cognitive Psychology Perspective', in D. Holdzkom and P. B. Ludz (eds), *Research within Reach: Science Education*. Washington, DC: National Science Teachers Association.

Chi, M., Glaser, R. and Rees, E. (1982) 'Expertise in Problem Solving', in R. Sternberg (ed.), *Advances in the Psychology of Human Intelligence*, Vol. 1. Hillsdale, NJ: Erlbaum.

Clement, J. (1982) 'Students' Preconceptions in Introductory Mechanics', *American Journal of Physics*, 50, 1, pp. 66–71.

Feyerabend, P. (1962) 'Explanation, Reduction and Empiricism', in H. Feigl and G. Maxwell (eds), *Minnesota Studies in Philosophy of Science*, Vol. 3. Minneapolis: University of Minnesota Press.

Forbus, K. D. and Gentner, D. (1984) *Learning Physical Domains: Towards a Theoretical Framework* (Report No. 5699). Cambridge, MA: Bolt, Beranek and Newman.

Gelman, R. and Baillargeon, R. (1983) 'A Review of Some Piagetian Concepts', in J. H. Flavell and E. M. Markman (eds), *Carmichael's Manual of Child Psychology*, Vol. 3. New York: Wiley.

Helm, H. and Novak, J. D. (1983) *Proceedings of the International Seminar on Misconceptions in Science & Mathematics*. Unpublished manuscript, Ithaca, NY.

Johnson, C. N. and Wellman, H. M. (1982) 'Children's Developing Conceptions of the Mind and the Brain', *Child Development*, 53, pp. 222–34.

Keil, F. (1979) *Semantic and Conceptual Development: An Ontological Perspective*. Cambridge, MA: Harvard University Press.

Kuhn, T. S. (1962). *The Structure of Scientific Revolutions*. Chicago: University of Chicago Press.

Kuhn, T. S. (1977) 'A Function for Thought Experiments', in T. S. Kuhn (ed.), *The Essential Tension*. Chicago: University of Chicago Press.

Kuhn, T. S. (1982) 'Commensurability, Comparability, Communicability', in *Philosophy of Science Association*, Vol. 2. East Lansing, MI: Philosophy of Science Association.

Larkin, J. H. (1983) 'The Role of Problem Representations in Physics', in D. Gentner and A. Stevens (eds), *Mental Models*. Hillsdale, NJ: Erlbaum.

Larkin, J. H., McDermott, J., Simon, D. P. and Simon, H. A. (1980) 'Models of Competence in Solving Physics Problems', *Cognitive Science*, 4, pp. 317–45.

Macnamara, J. (1982) *Names for Things*. Cambridge, MA: MIT Press.

McCloskey, M. (1983) 'Naive Theories of Motion', in D. Genter and A. Stevens (eds), *Mental Models*. Hillsdale, NJ: Erlbaum.

McDermott, L. C. (1984, July) 'Research on Conceptual Understanding in Mechanics', *Physics Today*, pp. 1–10.

Minstrell, J. (1982) 'Conceptual Development Research in the Natural Setting of a

Secondary School Classroom', in H. B. Rowe (ed.), *Science for the 80s*. Washington, DC: National Education Association.

Murphy, G. L. and Medin, D. L. (1985) 'The Role of Theories in Conceptual Coherence', *Psychological Review*, 92, 3, pp. 289–316.

Osborne, R. J. (1981) 'Children's Ideas about Electric Current', *New Zealand Science Teachers*, 29, pp. 12–19.

Osborne, R. J. and Gilbert, J. K. (1980) 'A Technique for Exploring Students' View of the World', *Physics Education*, 15, 6, pp. 376–9.

Piaget, J. and Inhelder, B. (1941) *Le Developpement des Quantities Chez l'Enfant* [*The development of quantity in the child*]. Neuchatel, France: Delachaux et Niestle.

Posner, G. J., Strike, K. A., Hewson, P. W. and Gertzog, W. A. (1982) 'Accommodation of a Scientific Conception: Toward a Theory of Conceptual Change', *Science Education*, 66, pp. 211–27.

Smith, C., Carey, S. and Wiser, M. (1986) 'On Differentiation: A Case Study of the Development of the Concepts of Size, Weight, and Density', *Cognition*, 21, pp. 177–237.

Stead, B. F. and Osborne, R. J. (1980). 'Exploring Science Students' Concepts of Light', *Australian Science Teachers Journal*, 26, 3, pp. 84–90.

Stead, B. F. and Osborne, R. J. (1981) 'What is Friction: Some Children's Ideas', *Australian Science Teachers Journal*, 27, 3, pp. 51–7.

Suppe, F. (1974) *The Structure of Scientific Theories*. Urbana: University of Illinois Press.

Toulmin, S. (1953) *The Philosophy of Science: An Introduction*. London: Hutchinson.

Viennot, L. (1979) 'Spontaneous Reasoning in Elementary Dynamics', *European Journal of Science Education*, 1, pp. 205–21.

White, B. (1981) *Designing Computer Games to Facilitate Learning*. Unpublished doctoral dissertation, Massachusetts Institute of Technology.

Wiser, M. and Carey, S. (1983) 'When Heat and Temperature Were One', in D. Gentner and A. Stevens (eds), *Mental Models*. Hillsdale, NJ: Erlbaum.

2.4

What is the Point of Group Discussion in Mathematics?

Celia Hoyles

[...]
Traditionally school mathematics, particularly at secondary level, has tended to be concerned with the transmission of a body of knowledge from teacher to pupil. Implicit in this model of education is the idea that what is learned exists in some way independently of the participants in the learning process. Mounting evidence of the inadequacies of this mode of teaching and learning has led to a search for more effective teaching methods and ways of organising the mathematics classroom. Within this context mathematics educators have turned their attention to collaborative modes of learning and to the potential role of discussion in mathematics classrooms. For example, in the recent influential report of the Cockcroft Committee in the United Kingdom (Cockcroft, 1982) it was stated that: 'Language plays an essential part in the formation and expression of mathematical ideas. School children should be encouraged to discuss and explain the mathematics which they are doing' (Cockcroft 1982, para. 306).

In a too ready acceptance of this statement it might be easy to fail both to recognise some of its fundamental implications for mathematics education and to face up to some of the many questions it raises. Using discussion in the mathematics classroom suggests a recognition of the significance of the sociocultural setting in the development of a child's mathematical knowledge. Despite research within psychology which has uncovered contextual determinants of task performance and deployment of previously learned skills (Donaldson, 1978; Light and Gilmour, 1983), investigations within mathematics education have tended to remain within a traditional framework of Piagetian developmental psychology, with development seen as a process of the construction of ever more powerful forms of logical inference. Encouraging pupils to talk about their conceptions and to justify their own strategies of exploration or proof represents a shift in the social relations in the classroom from a 'teacher-centred' to more 'pupil-centred' approach.

It also implies a recognition that a pupil develops mathematical concepts from sources outside school as well as from experiences within school, and part of the teacher's role is to facilitate the integration of possibly contradictory perceptions within a pupil's mind. A characteristic of development in mathematical understanding could be seen therefore as an increasing ability to move from the performance of operations in context specific 'special cases' towards generalisation and abstraction.

The main focus of this paper is with pupil–pupil rather than pupil–teacher discussion. There are different aspects of such a discussion which could facilitate a pupil's integration of her 'fragmented knowledge'. First, an active participant in a discussion will be either talking or listening, but this 'talk' has two qualitatively different functions, namely the cognitive function for the articulation of one's own thought processes, and the communicative function for making one's ideas available to another. The cognitive function of language has been extensively researched and debated (Piaget, 1926; Bruner, 1964; Vygotsky, 1962) and despite arguments about the relationship between language structures, concept formation, and action, there appears to be some agreement that, at least at post-primary level, when structures of thought are more defined, language facilitates reflection and internal regulation since difficulties in formulating the language to describe a situation may lead the speaker to modify her analysis of that situation. Language also provides the potential for hypothetical and abstract argument. However, the following questions remain for mathematics educators: does talk necessarily improve one's awareness of one's own thinking processes in mathematics and does any improved awareness facilitate the employment of the strategies used in this situation to other problem solving contexts? Or put another way, is the potential for mathematical abstraction enhanced by the linguistic variability provided by talk?

A second aspect in any discussion is that the demand for verbalisation arises from the social situation itself and from the need to communicate. When the aim of the language is the communication of a mathematical idea or process, the communicator is forced to frame thoughts in language which has to be recognised and accepted by others as a conveyor of meanings. This compels the communicator therefore, to identify those parts of a mathematical situation seen as important for meaning and those that are not, and how the former relate to one another. Thus, in line with the arguments of Walkerdine and Sinha (1978), the language of the communicator will define a specific interpretation of the context (see also Walkerdine, 1982). Crucial to communication through discussion in mathematics classrooms is therefore an awareness that mathematical ideas are susceptible to a variety of interpretations and that meaning can only in reality be shared after careful elaboration of one's own interpretation of the given context.

A third aspect in discussion is that of listening and this also can be seen as having a positive role. It is perhaps in silences that real 'learning' can take place. The ideas of others can suggest modifications to one's own thoughts, clarify half-worked out predictions or explain half-understood processes. Listening for learning is not passive; it is an active attempt to incorporate another's scheme into one's own; it stimulates one to go outside oneself and look again at the arguments.

Although the component parts of a discussion have been described separately in order to clarify their different functions, it is important to recognise their creative interaction. We can all recall how a chance comment of another person can trigger off a whole new avenue for exploration. Bruner (1962) talks about this 'dynamic relationship' in his description of 'reciprocal learning'. He suggests that even while one participant is talking, she will be receiving information from her partner which leads her to reshape what she is saying *while* she is actually saying it. Additionally, the listening partner, while in the process of finding a verbal form for her thoughts will modify them as a result of signals from the 'talker'. Bruner argues that it is this *immediacy* of feedback, taking place at the moment of choice, which facilitates the internalisation of another's point of view. Or, as argued by Balacheff and Laborde (1985) it is the interactions between the construction of meanings by the speaker, their reconstructions by the listener, and the contradictions that can arise, which can generate increased understanding.

It can be argued therefore that conflict within a discussion can arise merely in the *process* of communication of an idea. Obviously, it can also arise when the participants in a discussion disagree as to their goals or strategies. One is then led to ask if conflict is important for learning. In early Piagetian work, social cooperation and conflict were cited as prime instigators of development, and cognitive psychologists such as Smedslund (1966) and Damon (1979) have urged that more attention should be given to this. It is suggested that confrontation with a different cognitive model offers 'some relevant dimensions for a progressive elaboration of a cognitive mechanism' (Mugny *et al.*, 1981 quoted in Light, 1983, p. 7) which is new to the participant. It is argued therefore that it does not matter 'if both partners are equally wrong, as long as they are wrong in different ways' (Light, 1983)! Decentration, that is, the ability to take one's own activity as an object of thinking, is facilitated by the differing points of view among participants in a discussion and this on its own may stimulate progression.

The role of conflict in discussion can therefore be seen as 'pushing' the participants towards an 'objective' as opposed to a 'subjective' approach to a problem. Bernstein's (1965) work on linguistic codes would support this view. He suggests that it is the conflict within social interaction which stimulates a child to move from context-specific arguments with undefined terms and built-in assumptions to 'unsupported' and explicit formulations (see also Bernstein, 1970, on the speech of 'position-oriented' and 'person-oriented' families). It is possible therefore that argument and discussion within a mathematics classroom could help initiate children into a 'disembedded' use of language, which is regarded as important for an appreciation of formal mathematics (see for example Booth, 1981).

The situation is however by no means straightforward. The effectiveness of any discussion necessarily depends on a number of conditions relating to the structure of the task, the age and motivation of the children and the social relations within the group. In addition, although the importance of verbal communication within problem situations has been shown by, for example, Doise (1978) there is also evidence of a need for opportunity for resolution of conflict by activity other than talk (Russell, 1978, quoted in Glachan and Light, 1982). Experimental work reported by Balacheff (1980), and Balacheff and Laborde (1985), admirably conveys the complexity of the situation and since this is concerned specifically with mathematics education it will be summarised briefly here.

Pupils in this study were required to elaborate an explanation of their solutions to a combinational problem. The context was designed in such a way that propositions would not be accepted or refused without discussion. The aim of the researchers was therefore to observe how pairs of school children go about producing a mathematical description of a given problem situation, establishing the proof of this description and communicating this proof to others. No clear-cut conclusions can be drawn from this experimental work, but Balacheff and Laborde make several observations. First, the 10–11 year old children recognised the need to explain their solutions in order that their partners could follow the arguments and participate in the 'game', but none the less had difficulty in articulating their thought processes. They often therefore tended to resort to simple enumeration and description of the given problem. Older children, however, by way of contrast, frequently lost sight of the given problem in their search for a mathematical explanation. In the first experiment (Balacheff, 1980) it was found that pupils tended to judge the clearness of their explanation on the basis of its clarity to themselves (rather than on its predicted clarity for others). However, in the second experiment Balacheff and Laborde (1985) reported that it was the very discussions about the ability of team mates to 'decode messages' which tended to 'push' the children into a suitable coding system. Conflict too was found to play an ambiguous role; sometimes conflict ended with a 'better' final solution, sometimes it was avoided by the production of a joint answer incorporating both suggestions side by side and sometimes it was 'resolved' by authority argument. It would be worth investigating which factors in the particular situations appeared to provoke these different outcomes. Despite all their reservations as to the positive effects of the discussion, Balacheff and Laborde (1985) do state: 'We have observed there is a close relationship between the evolution of the process of solution and the search for the means of explanation . . . if this is the case we must investigate further and consider the types of situations which most likely would produce positive outcomes.'

One obvious factor within a situation which would influence the value of any discussion is the social atmosphere in which it takes place. Balacheff and Laborde's results arose for example from an experimental situation in which goals and rules were given by the researchers and teams competed for the reward of 'winning'. It is possible that a working context in which a goal is jointly chosen by the participants and cooperatively worked upon might throw up rather different results (see for example Johnson and Johnson, 1980); De Vries and Slavin, 1978 and Yeomans, 1983 on the influences of cooperative goal structures on learning and on feelings of self-worth). The pattern of dominance in the group is also important. The question as to whether the presence of an 'expert' with exclusive access to knowledge and the 'right answer' inhibits discussion, as participants are afraid to take risks for fear of ridicule, or facilitates it, since 'disputes' can be managed more efficiently, must be faced. Children must be helped to work together, to tolerate disagreements, to challenge each other and to avoid premature closure of argument.

As well as these social aspects the nature of the activity undertaken and the way it is structured is bound to influence outcomes. There must be, for example, sufficient motivation for the task, and preferably for the task *itself* and not for any reward. Mathematics educators could easily generate a list of potential tasks, activities and investigations. One given as an example here concerns working with a computer. The interactive nature of the activity and the ease with which 'errors' can be corrected certainly captures pupils' attention. 'Pupils in large numbers are finding a joy and zest in some aspects of mathematics which they did not find before' (Fletcher, 1983). Computer work can quite naturally be individual. If however it is structured as *joint* activity, the public character of the screen and the speed of response to pupil inputs readily encourage the discussion of strategy and outcome, provided, of course, that these are in the control of the pupils rather than the machine or teacher!

Research is at present under way to try to discover how the cognitive and communicative functions of the social interactions between pairs of children learning the computer language Logo contribute both to the construction of their own learning goals, and also to development in mathematical processes and programming strategies (Hoyles and Sutherland, 1983). Evidence to date suggests that, provided choices and criteria for decision are left to the pupils with no hidden curriculum, genuine discussion is possible. Children have, however, needed time to develop ways of working together; but *if* this is available their collaborative activity has stimulated numerous insights and more reflective attitudes (Hoyles, Sutherland, Evans, 1984). It should be noted here that the dynamic interaction with the computer and the ease with which disputes can be resolved by action, factors which undoubtedly stimulate discussion, also tend to mitigate against the reflective elaboration of a pupil's arguments. The role of the teacher has therefore been found to be important in the learning process in order to encourage reflection on what has been done and on what further outcomes could arise.

The interpretation and analysis of transcripts is a difficult and laborious task. It is neither desirable nor possible to sort out what exactly provokes a new insight. It is often a combination of the talk between the pairs of participants and the feedback of the computer. The following serves as illustration of this point.

John and Jean, two adults, have been learning Logo for approximately three hours. They have already defined a circle (called a 'cobweb') and want to draw a big tent, consisting of a rectangle with a semi-circular roof. It is evident from the transcript that they start with a clear goal in mind but with little idea as to how to achieve this goal.

John	*Jean*
1 'We could get a nice cobweb, but how do we stop it going underneath?'	
	2 'We've got to redefine.'
3 'How can we define a half circle?'	
	4 'Lets put our circle formula in and then we shall say "half circle" and we shall type it in. Then at the end divide by 2 and that will be the programme half circle.'

5 'Define half circle and add a
   rectangle to it. To half circle
   and put the formula in and
   halve it?'

6 'We'll still have to type the
   whole thing it.'

7 'But we don't want to do
   that. We don't know which
   half it will take away, do
   we?'

8 'We can only try, can't we?'

9 'Would it be safer to specify
   which half we want.'

10 'Well what do we call it?'

11 'Say, 'To half circle' start
    here, turn right and take
    away the bit we don't want.'

They then position the turtle at A (see Figure 4) that is at the end of
the diameter upon which the semicircle is to be drawn.

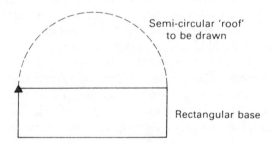

Semi-circular 'roof'
to be drawn

Rectangular base

Figure 4   Big top (tent)

12 'Now what do we do?'

This is the point at which 'the penny drops'.

13 'Oh, so we just want "Repeat
    180". All we want is half and
    we know which half we'll get
    don't we?'

The sequence above starts with a genuine question from John. He
knows how a complete circle can be drawn but does not see how this
can be adapted to make half a circle. His contributions (1), (3), (7),
(9) are all expressing these doubts, Jean answers his first question
directly by observing that a new procedure is required (2) and then
explains how this can be done (4 and 6) although she obviously has

not worked out how exactly 'half can be taken away'. Her communications are echoed by John (5 and 11), who then 'sees' the first steps he has to take. Jean encourages John to experiment (8) and they move the turtle to A, the point at which they would start drawing their semi-circle. They still have not worked out the critical step of halving their circle procedure (as John points out in (12)). It is at this point, after Jean has articulated a strategy, the incompleteness of which has been noticed by John but none the less they have started to act, that the 'solution' appears, i.e. that 180 repeats are needed as opposed to the 360 used for the complete circle.

Thus the solution emerged from a combination of trying to work out and communicate a way forward in a very mundane step-by-step manner; sensing 'gaps' in the strategy but nevertheless, through mutual encouragement, 'having a go' and finding the answer after the visual stimulation on the screen. It appears that the pressure of another encouraged both the elaboration of ideas and 'steps into unknown territory' as well as providing sensitising feedback as to where the problems might lie.

Group work and discussion in mathematics classes are not panaceas. Their effects may depend on so many elusive and subtle conditions.

However, against a background in which it has been shown over and over again that pupils feel either alienated and bored with their mathematics, or helpless and dependent on their teachers (Hoyles, 1982), it is important that mathematics educators both accept the notion of discussion *and* probe further. With this in mind, I would suggest that we might consider mathematical understanding from a social interaction perspective and perhaps define it as the ability to:

1 form a view of the mathematical idea
2 step back and reflect upon it
3 use it appropriately and flexibly
4 communicate it effectively to another
5 reflect on another's perspective of the idea
6 incorporate another's perspective into one's own framework or challenge and logically reject this alternative view.

The helpfulness of such a description will emerge if it is usable and useful. Having opened the discussion I look forward to criticism and comment!

References

Balacheff, N. (1980) 'The Sense of Mathematical Explanation', *Proceedings of IGPME*, Berkeley, California.
Balacheff, N. and Laborde, C. (1985) 'Language Symbolique et Preuves dans l'Enseignement Mathematique: Une Approache Socio-Cognitive', in Mugny, G. (ed.), *Psychologie Sociale du Dévelopement Cognitif*, P. Lang, Berne.
Bernstein, B. (1965) 'A Socio-linguistic Approach to Social Learning', in Gould, J.

(ed.), *Social Science Survey*. London: Penguin.

Bernstein, B. (1970) 'A Socio-linguistic Approach to Socialisation with Reference to Educability', in Gumper, J. and Hynes, D. (eds), *Directions in Socio-linguistics*. Eastbourne: Holt, Rinehart and Wilson.

Booth, L. R. (1981) 'Child Methods in Secondary Mathematics', *Educational Studies in Mathematics*, 12, pp. 29–41.

Bruner, J. (1962) *On Knowing*. Cambridge, Mass.: Harvard University Press.

Bruner, J. S. (1964) 'The Course of Cognitive Growth', *Am. Psych.*, 19, pp. 1–15.

Bruner, J. S. (1975) 'Language as an Instrument of Thought', in Davies, A. (ed.), *Problems of Language and Learning*. London: SSRC.

Cockcroft, W. *et al.* (1982) *Mathematics Counts*. London: HMSO.

Damon, W. (1979) 'Why Study Social-cognitive Development', *Human Development*, 22, pp. 206–11.

De Vries, D. and Slavin, R. (1978) 'Team Games – Tournaments: A Research Review', *J. Research Development in Education*, 12, pp. 28–38.

Doise, W. (1978) *Groups and Individuals*. Cambridge: CUP.

Donaldson, M. (1978) *Children's Minds*. London: Fontana/Collins.

Fletcher, T. J. (1983) *Microcomputers and Mathematics in Schools – a discussion paper*, DES, London.

Glachan, M. and Light, P. (1982) 'Peer Interactions and Learning: Can Two Wrongs Make a Right?' in Butterworth, G. (ed.) *Social Cognition in the Development of Understanding*. Brighton: Harvester.

Hoyles, C. (1982) 'The Pupil's View of Mathematics Learning', *Education Studies in Mathematics*, 13, pp. 349–72.

Hoyles, C. and Sutherland, R. (1983) 'An Investigation of the Pupil-centred Approach to the Learning of Logo in the Secondary School Mathematics Classroom', *Research Proposal Leverhulme Trust*.

Hoyles, C., Sutherland, R. and Evans, J. (1984) 'Pairs of Children Working with Logo in their Mathematics Classrooms', *Report to Leverhulme Trust*.

Johnson, D. and Johnson, R. (1980) 'The Instructional use of Co-operative Competitive and Individualistic Goal Structures', in Walbert, H. (ed.), *Educational Environments and Effects*. Berkeley, CA: McCuthchan.

Light, P. (1983). 'Social Interaction and Cognitive Development: a Review of Post-Piagetian Research', in Meadows, S. (ed.), *Developing Thinking*. London: Methuen.

Light, P. H. and Gilmour, A. (1983) 'Conservation or Conversation? Contextual Facilitation of Inappropriate Conservation Judgements', *Journal of Experimental Child Psychology*, 36, pp. 356–63.

Mugny, G. *et al.* (1981) 'Interpersonal Co-ordination and Sociological Differences in the Construction of the Intellect', in Stevenson, G. and Davis, G. B. (eds), *Applied Social Psychology*, Vol. 1, Chichester: Wiley.

Smedslund, J. (1966) 'Les Origenes Sociales de la Decentration', in Grize, J. and Inhelder, B. (eds), *Psychologie et Epistemiologie Genetique: Theories Piagetians*. Montrouge: Dunod.

Piaget, J. (1926) *The Language and Thought of the Child*. London: RKP. New York.

Vygotsky, L. S. (1962) *Thought and Language*. Cambridge, Mass.: MIT. J. Wiley. New York.

Walkerdine, V. (1982) 'From Context to Text: a Psychosemiotic Approach to Abstract Thought', in Beveridge, M. (ed.), *Children Thinking Through Language*. London: Edward Arnold.

Walkerdine, V. and Sinha, C. (1978) 'The Internal Triangle: Language, Reasoning and the Social Context', in Markova, A. (ed.), *The Social Context of Language*. Chichester: Wiley.

Yeomans, A. (1983) *Collaborative Group Work: A Research Review*, University of Leicester School of Education, Leicester.

2.5

Reading – Caught or Taught? Some Issues Involved in Changed Approaches to the Teaching of Reading

Marian Whitehead

Has there really been a revolution in the teaching of reading? Are the frequently encountered phrases such as 'hooked on books', 'read with me' and 'reading at home' no more than a seductive new jacket design hiding the same old grind of the graded reading book? The phrases suggest the enticement and pleasure of an informal, sociable and relaxed approach to the tasks of early literacy and are in marked contrast to the rigours of phonics, grapheme-phoneme correspondence and reading and comprehension tests. But these are caricatures and in order to move beyond the emotive vocabulary of this polarised presentation I shall discuss four issues which appear to me to be raised by the 'caught or taught' arguments about early reading. These issues are all aspects of change and concern changed views of reading, changed views of teaching and learning, changed views of 'caught' skills and attitudes and changing metaphors for education.

The issue of changed views of reading and learning to read is central to the claim that there has been a revolution in reading. As with all revolutions, one is able to identify an old order and the emergence of a new and radically different situation. But there the analogy ends for the processes of educational research and changing perceptions do not lend themselves to sudden 'coups' and 'revolts'. What is clear is that there has been a significant move from one dominant view of learning to read to a very different kind of approach. There is, however, one element which may be identified as the catalyst for this change. This is the study of linguistics which has brought new understanding of the processes of language and of language learning to bear on all aspects of spoken and written language forms. Before this particular linguistic revolution made any impact on education reading was thought of as a discrete and separate skill, or, perhaps, a bundle of special skills.

Learning to read was a decoding task which could be approached by learning rules formulated in a hierarchical order of difficulty and then applying the rules to limited and controlled samples of written language. These samples were controlled for numbers of new words, complexity of vocabulary – usually judged on word length or conceptual sophistication – and sentence length and complexity. Repetition was believed to be essential and words, phrases and sentences were repeated or 'drilled' to an extent which clearly reflected the influence of behaviourist psychology on the approach. This way of teaching reading is still with us and accounts for all the schemes and methods which stress phonics, words out of context, coding and grading, reading 'laboratories' and 'powerbuilders'. In essence it is a view of reading which isolates the business of learning to do it from the purposes and processes involved when people do it 'for real'.

The recent and more 'linguistic' approach focuses upon literacy, not just reading, as a development and extension of language learning and communication. The approach is often described as psycholinguistic because it highlights psychological and linguistic aspects of learning which are particularly significant for literacy, although not restricted to the learning of literacy. These aspects could be broadly described as knowledge about the nature of human learning, knowledge about the nature of language and knowledge of the world of persons and objects. It follows that the approach will place great emphasis on the social and cultural features of learning to read and write and on the role of literature in providing significant material to read and motivation for going on reading. Reading and writing are seen as complementary and mutually enriching and the dual role of literacy in a community and in the lives of individuals is underlined by the focus on reading and writing genuine messages and narratives.

The process of reading is seen to be like other forms of human learning, a meaning making enterprise. Readers are engaged upon questioning any text and reconstructing its meanings. The approach acknowledges the special nature of written language forms: print is a system of signs which is comparatively disembedded or 'decontextualised' and presents the learner with articular problems. Compared with spoken communications, the 'stream of ink' lacks much of the social and situational support of the 'stream of air' (Uldall, 1944). Beginning readers must work hard to fill in all the essential background to the text but many start at a surprisingly early age (Butler, 1979: Scollon and Scollon, 1981; Payton, 1984). Before noting the ways in which young learners go about making sense of print we need to be clear that the approach depends on the use of complex human texts as reading material. Complex human texts embody recognisable issues, motives and emotions in recognisable language. In other words, stories, anecdotes and real books are the ideal narrative texts for beginning readers. Initially the books are shared with a more experienced partner and the focus of attention is on re-creating meanings and exploring the ideas and experiences of the authors' possible worlds. Simultaneously the children will also be involved in creating messages and texts, practising becoming writers and authors.

These changes in approaches to reading and learning to read are inevitably paralleled by changing views of teaching and learning. It follows that teachers are no longer simply checking off children's progress through graded reading schemes and lists of isolated 'test' words. Pedagogy is more likely to involve sharing the burden of the new learning with children and judging the degree of support they need and the manner and timing for progressively lessening this support. The essential scaffolding provided by the reading teacher is a matter of helping children relate the new and unknown to the familiar and experienced. It is more complex than simply giving linguistic information about words and textual conventions and involves the teacher in understanding the children's world outside the school. It necessitates some degree of involvement with the children's communities and their particular ways with words, literacy and child rearing (Heath, 1983). The teacher as linguistic informant is required to operate above the level of 'giving words' and needs to know something of how language varies in particular contexts, how children learn their first languages and how all human languages and dialects are creative and rule-governed. Above all, the enabling reading teacher uses children's miscues in reading as valuable insights into the learning process.

Sharing real books with beginning readers is a great pleasure but it is no less intellectually demanding because it is enjoyable! When it occurs, teachers and children are involved in a complex interaction with text and a resulting re-ordering of their individual experiences and understandings. Detailed evidence of young children and adults engaged in this process can be found in Wells (1985), Clark (1985) and Bruner (1984). The model of an apprenticeship start to reading (Waterland, 1985) does highlight the essential feature of gradually handing over power and independence to the emergent reader. Perhaps the real revolution in reading is the acceptance in educational institutions that reading is something children have to do for themselves, not something that can be done to them or for them. Handing over control to child readers and listeners may be difficult for some teachers but it is the only way of ensuring that the reading goes on when the teaching stops. Bruner (1984) relates an incident in which a class of 4 year olds speak for themselves on this point:

I recall the account of a Head Start class whose teacher read them Little Red Riding Hood. When the story reached the climax at which the wolf, disguised as Grandmother, responds to Red Riding Hood's remark about her big teeth by proclaiming, 'All the better to eat you, hoho!' one of the children snarled, 'That mother-fucking son-of-a-bitch' ... the teacher was clever enough to ask the children how the story *should* have gone at that point, 'She shoulda killed the wolf!' was the response. (p. 197).

Early learning generally is now viewed as similar to a scientific process of exploration: young children are setting up hypotheses and monitoring feedback, 'She shoulda killed the wolf!' Early reading and early writing, like first language learning, are seen as processes of interaction and experimentation. Studies of young readers and writers teach us that they are actively generating theories, not just about writing but about symbols and a wide range of print. They are also evolving powerful communicative strategies (Clay, 1975; Bissex, 1980; Whitehead, 1985, 1986). Such evidence also suggests that we often underestimate the interests, abilities and self-motivation of very young children exploring the literate environment.

The success of all these endeavours depends on mutually satisfying relationships, on real needs and interests, and on access to real texts which embody interesting events and motives. The approach relies on sensible feedback to such questions as what's that say, or, how do you write? Time for mulling things over and a secure setting in which to make mistakes and hazard guesses are crucial to this approach to early literacy. These opportunities are more often found outside classrooms than in them and suggest reasons for the remarkable successes of 'reading at home' projects. The strengths of the home and the community in early literacy might be summarised as informality, sensible feedback, total adult commitment to the unique child and a shared past, present and future. The availability of a shared world to place alongside the worlds of stories, poems and books facilitates complex and powerful connections and meditation on the possibilities of life. This fascination with the rich variety and potential of human experience can create an irresistible invitation to become a reader.

Any attempt to dismiss recent changes in the teaching of reading as mere reliance on appropriate attitudes and skills being 'caught' raises some interesting questions. Is the 'caught' metaphor indicative of an invisible, silent and passive subjection to an infection like the common cold? Does this approach to reading relegate teachers and child-carers to waiting around, hoping literarcy will 'take a hold'. And how are attitudes 'caught' and why do they persist long after much of the factual information which we think we have 'taught' has been forgotten?

A growing body of research suggests that we may well underestimate the complex cognitive aspects of 'catching' literacy in a literate
community (Goelman, Oberg and Smith, 1984). Experiences with
print appear to be carefully structured and demonstrated for young
children by other people and then taken over and tried out and
modified by the young apprentice-learners. But these activities are
so much a taken for granted aspect of caring for young children in
particular communities that we do not always recognise them as
teaching. However, cross-cultural studies are able to foreground
this 'natural' teaching and indicate how thorough is the preparation
for becoming a reader and writer. Heath (1983) looked at language
and literacy in three adjacent but culturally very different American
communities and recorded the diverse attitudes and preparations
centred on 'literacy events' which surrounded infants from, and
even before, birth. In the more structured setting of a middle-class
American kindergarten, Cochran-Smith (1984) analysed the specific
preparations for becoming a reader which are built into story and
discussion sessions. These involved not only the technical matters of
handling books and relating text and pictures to a narrative but the
appropriate attitudes and behaviours for listeners and tellers. The
work of Tizard and Hughes (1984) indicates that in Great Britain
informal preparation for literacy is wide-ranging and pervasive in
working-class and middle-class homes. The 4-year-old girls in the
study were involved with their families as active participants in the
daily 'literacy events' of gossip, jokes, explanations, books, stories,
messages, shopping lists, labels and greetings cards. It would appear
that, to a surprising extent, children's developing awareness of print
is not left to chance. However, the 'what' and the 'how' of literacy
will vary across communities and the individual child will be unique
in his/her way of taking on the printed world, as 4-year-old Cecilia
Payton reminds us: 'Mum, you show me how to read the words and
then I read it' (Payton 1984, p. 94).

The words of Cecilia suggest that she has already learnt that with
some support and demonstration reading is something that you can
do for yourself. But the child's words can also remind us that new
approaches to reading, teaching and learning bring with them new
metaphors for talking about the processes. Metaphors permeate our
language and our lives and are powerful ways of talking about the
complex and the abstract. Used well, they enable us to approach the
new and the unknown in terms of the familiar and are 'bridges' or
even 'opening doors'. But metaphors can become 'traps' and this is
a particularly sensitive issue in education if our nineteenth century
inheritance of 'empty pitchers' and 'blank slates' still distorts our
thinking. Even in the age of new technology we have to be wary for,
as Frank Smith has indicated (1983), our metaphors for literacy
affect our teaching, our expectations and the learning outcomes. If

we go for 'shunting information' we are no more than a twentieth-century Gradgrind industry but if we are about 'creating new worlds' we are maximising human potential. The metaphors which are now associated with changed views of reading and learning to read encapsulate altered approaches to teachers, learners and literacy. The phrases are familiar but they are more than catch-phrases. Paired reading, shared reading, reading with parents, apprenticeship approaches, the making of readers, ways with words, are all significant descriptions. The new emphasis is on language, on the social world, on the communities outside schools, on shared tasks and on reading for real with real books and on writing real messages.

Conclusion

This brief overview of some aspects of what is often called a revolution in the teaching of reading leads me to two conclusions and a problem. My first conclusion is that reading is both caught and taught. Reading is caught in so far as children are born into literate communities and are drawn into the meaning-making literacy activities of these communities. Reading is taught by those more experienced individuals (not necessarily 'adult' or particularly 'bookish') who mediate helpfully between the beginning reader and the text. This teaching involves helping learners to develop, articulate and use their existing knowledge of the world, their knowledge of their language and their strategies and skills as story-makers. This conclusion is supported by long-established work in the fields of child development and language. Children develop through social interaction with other people. They learn how to achieve mastery of many skills by first performing those skills with the help of others. Shared reading and writing are instances of children working at the leading edge of their potential level of learning: 'What the child can do in cooperation today he can do alone tomorrow' (Vygotsky, 1962, p. 104).

My second conclusion is the straightforward one that all the changes I have referred to are examples of a move away from neat, stereotyped and simple explanations to the appreciation of complex, variable and sophisticated processes. It is this conclusion that raises the problem. Researchers, teachers and many parents are increasingly aware of the complexity involved in teaching and learning. They are also increasingly sensitive to the powerful, idiosyncratic strategies which young learners bring to bear on making sense of their worlds. However, the main thrust of government requirements and initiatives in the maintained sector is increasingly towards centralised, simplistic and inappropriate interventions in the curriculum. It is a sad fact that the most concerned and informed practitioners in education are now obstructed by ill-conceived and unhelpful directives.

Acknowledgements

My thanks to Cynthia James, Primary Adviser, and the primary teachers of Haringey who got me into this!

References

Bissex, G. L. (1980) *GNYS AT WRK, A Child learns to Write and Read*. Cambridge, Mass.: Harvard University Press.
Bruner, J. S. (1984) 'Language, Mind, and Reading', in Goelman, *et al.* (eds).
Butler, D. (1979) *Cushla and her Books*. Sevenoaks: Hodder and Stoughton.
Clark, M. M. (ed.) (1985) *New Directions in the Study of Reading*. Lewes: The Falmer Press.
Clay, M. M. (1975) *What Did I Write?* London: Heinemann.
Cochran-Smith, M. (1984) *The Making of a Reader*. Norwood, NJ: Ablex.
Goelman, H., Oberg, A., Smith, F. (eds) (1984) *Awakening to Literacy*. London: Heinemann.
Heath, S. B. (1983) *Ways with Words*. Cambridge: Cambridge University Press.
Payton, S. (1984) *Developing Awareness of Print*. A young child's first steps towards literacy. *Education Review*, University of Birmingham.
Scollon, R. and Scollon, S. B. K. (1981) *Narrative, Literacy and Face in Interethnic Communication*. Norwood, NJ: Ablex.
Smith, F. (1983) *Essays into Literacy*. London: Heinemann.
Tizard, B. and Hughes, M. (1984) *Young Children Learning*. London: Fontana.
Uldall, H. J. (1944) 'Speech and Writing', *Acta Linguistica*, IV, pp. 11–16.
Vygotsky, L. S. (1962) *Thought and Language*. Cambridge Mass.: MIT (orig. publ. Moscow 1934).
Waterland, L. (1985) *Read with Me*. Stroud: Thimble Press.
Wells, G. (1985) *Language, Learning and Education*, Windsor: NFER-Nelson.
Whitehead, M. R. (1985) 'On Learning to Write. Recent Research and Developmental Writing', *Curriculum*, 6, 2, Summer.
Whitehead, M. R. (1986) 'Breakthrough Re-visited. Some Thoughts on "Breakthrough to Literacy" and Developmental Writing', *Curriculum*, 7, 1, Spring.

2.6

The Pre-Vocational Curriculum: A Review of the Issues Involved

Madeleine J. Atkins

Introduction

The pre-vocational curriculum has grown with spectacular rapidity in the last decade. The introduction in 1985–86 of the Certificate of Pre-Vocational Education (CPVE), intended to rationalise provision at the post-compulsory stage, seems a good point at which to examine the alleged advantages and disadvantages of this emerging curriculum.

Pre-vocational courses and schemes have developed in response to various political and economic pressures. Their growth has also been fostered by educationists and practitioners who believed that the pre-existing, diluted, academic curriculum was inappropriate for many young people. With the emphasis on preparation for adult life including employment, the pre-vocational curriculum is claimed to be more relevant, motivating and useful for the young people concerned, while still ensuring that a good standard of general education has been achieved. It is also promoted on the grounds of its benefit to industry and society as a whole. Better training, extended to a larger proportion of each age group, will increase productivity and lead to more jobs.[1]

The pre-vocational curriculum is not, however, without its critics. At least two sources of criticism can be discerned. The first is that the pre-vocational curriculum is a second-class education and will function to the further disadvantage of those groups already failed by the formal education system. The second major criticism is that these courses and schemes are fundamentally misconceived for a society increasingly characterised by structural unemployment.

First-class or second-class education?

The arguments and counter-arguments about the worth of the pre-vocational curriculum can be examined in terms of its aims, structure and content. Although there are differences of emphasis between the various schemes and courses (for example, in the extent and nature of work experience provided), there is nevertheless an underlying unity of assumption and conception, both about the characteristics of the young people concerned and about the nature of the learning experiences they should receive.[2]

Aims and objectives

The general aim of the pre-vocational curriculum is the effective preparation of young people for adult life and particularly for waged employment. Permeating the thinking behind such courses are the concepts of transition and transfer. Such aims and objectives suggest that pre-vocational courses have a strong transmission function: young people are to be socialised into selected aspects of adulthood. It is anticipated that cultural norms and values will be internalised or reinforced in this process.

Functionalist theories of schooling, applied to this transmission aspect, lead either to approval or censure of the courses depending on the value position of the theorist. For those who perceive a corresponding relationship between the unequal treatment of pupils in school and the unequal treatment of different groups in society,[3] pre-vocational courses would be seen as instrumental in reproducing the economic and cultural dispossession of the already disadvantaged. In particular, the pre-vocational curriculum reinforces the class-based division of labour, and the separation of conception and execution characteristic of Western industrial society. It can be argued that these courses have been designed systematically to produce the hard-working and subservient employee, ready to accept uncritically the externally defined disciplines of the workplace. Young people will, therefore, emerge from the courses characterised by needs, aspirations and expectations which will ensure the perpetuation of their dominated status. More recently, such courses have also begun to transmit the knowledge, skills and values of the small-scale entrepreneur. This, it could be said, serves to strengthen the possessive individualism of the capitalist system and renders less likely any challenge to the powerful minority groups with vested interests in maintaining the current inequalities of advanced industrial capitalist societies.

Alternatively, more traditional structural – functionalist theories, when applied to the pre-vocational curriculum, yield a benevolent interpretation. Such courses, it can be said, enable society to pass on the generally held norms and values essential to its effective maintenance and development, encouraging the personal qualities which will enhance the life and work of the community. Among these can be identified the 'work ethic'; the desirability/normality of waged employment; individual ownership of skills and knowledge; technocratic efficiency; community participation; the fulfilment of the responsibilities of citizenship; and personal development, including the basis for continuing education and training.

Form and structure of the pre-vocational curriculum

Whereas the aims of the pre-vocational curriculum lend themselves to analysis through their transmission purposes, the form and structure of pre-vocational courses and schemes suggest an analysis of their allocation and selection functions. Pre-vocational courses tend to be integrated curricula rather than a collection of single subjects. They have a common core of general educational competencies compulsory for all students, complemented by a limited choice of more vocational modules, including some skills training and work experience. It is also possible in some schemes to take another qualification in the remaining discretionary time – students within the Technical and Vocational Education Initiative (TVEI) are expected to be entered for a range of nationally recognised qualifications: there is no 'TVEI Certificate' as such. Assessment is usually criterion- rather than norm-referenced. There is an emphasis on initial diagnosis of student strengths and weaknesses, especially in the basic educational competencies, and on student-centred formative assessment throughout the course or scheme. For these reasons, pre-vocational courses and schemes have tended to adopt profiles as the means of recording assessment. Once again, two conflicting interpretations of the form and structure of pre-vocational courses are possible.

Traditional functionalist analysis would see the emergence of such courses as a positive benefit. The existence of a pre-vocational curriculum, it could be argued, has extended the range of opportunities available to young people, has enabled a higher proportion of the age group to continue formal education, and has permitted for the first time a coherent scheme of skills-training to be offered to those best suited for it. In other words, the pre-vocational curriculum facilitates the appropriate, differentiated training of talent and skill in relation to various employment fields and occupational families. Students are progressively enabled to make a job choice which reflects their skills and interests and are not cut off from the benefits of education at the minimum school-leaving age.

Furthermore, it could be argued, the opportunity to study for extra qualifications provides a useful second chance for those who encountered artificial barriers to success in the earlier years of formal schooling. It reduces the wastage caused, historically, by the limited access to education for working-class pupils. Deficiencies in basic educational competencies can be diagnosed and remedied, while a common core ensures that a desirable balance is maintained between specific vocational training and broader general education. In this way, the old, unhelpful barrier between 'education' and 'training' can be broken down and a more enlightened, integrated policy introduced. Credit can be given for practical applied competencies as well as academic, theoretical understanding.

With such points in mind, the profile system can be seen as a way of recording success across a broader spectrum of skills and competencies than has been the case on traditional academic-style courses. It also facilitates the negotiation of learning goals between the young person and members of staff. Moreover, at the end of the course, potential employers and other 'end users' will have a clearer picture of the capabilities of the student or trainee. The job (or 'next-up') allocation function of schooling is thereby strengthened, the undesirable features of norm-referencing are avoided, and students will have become proficient in self-assessment – a valuable adult life asset.

Theorists influenced by neo-Marxist perspectives would place a different interpretation on the form and nature of the pre-vocational curriculum. At least six reasons would be advanced.

First, the existence of the pre-vocational curriculum alongside the 'academic' enables the education system to 'freeze out' certain students from the more prestigious of the two routes. It is no coincidence that research evidence reveals a tendency for working-class pupils to follow the pre-vocational courses, while children of professional groups tend to take the academic courses.[4] A similar differentiation may also exist in terms of racial grouping, with black 'West Indian' pupils overrepresented on pre-vocational courses and schemes compared [. . .] to 'A' level courses.[5]

Secondly, an integrated curriculum has traditionally had lower value in the education system than collection-type curricula.[6] [. . .] There is a less well defined ladder for pre-vocational courses, especially at 17+, while the economic benefit in terms of obtaining a job, or a job related to the content of the course, can be questioned.[7] Indeed, it can be argued that the very fact of being on a pre-vocational course indicates that the pupil, student or trainee is not considered a legitimate receiver of the cultural benefits of dominant elite groups in society.[8]

Third, since there is not an alternative to traditional academic study in the 16–19 age range, pressure to widen the clientele on the academic *cursus honorum* can be more easily resisted. The ideals behind comprehensive education which, for a while, seemed to threaten 'A' levels can be met through pre-vocational provision. 'A' levels, for example, have survived the restructuring proposals of N and F and Q and F.[9] [...] The fourth critique which might be offered by the 'new' school of sociology concerns the basis of selection for the different routes. It can be argued that the use of scholastic attainment as the criterion masks the true basis of selection behind a facade of apparent objectivity. Those students who are tracked into the pre-vocational curriculum are led to see this process as a reflection of their personal inadequacy for academic work, as 'proved' by their poor showing in school examinations and tests. The structural and class factors behind their low scores are ignored.[10] Thus, tertiary level institutions, while overtly adopting a policy of 'open access', in practice limit acceptance onto 'A' level courses to those who can already demonstrate that they have acquired the necessary middle-class linguistic and cultural capital to succeed. [...] Students who cannot meet these criteria take pre-vocational courses. There is no right to fail.

The fifth critique of the form of the pre-vocational curriculum is that, for all its apparent vocational emphasis, it effectively precludes students from entering jobs with real economic power. The deficiency model of education behind the diagnostic assessment and common core precludes students from specialising in any particular strength to a high level of marketable skill. [...] Finally, it can be argued that the profiling process also serves to increase the power of the staff at the expense of the student. Whereas on traditional academic courses assessment is limited to academic knowledge components, on the pre-vocational curriculum every attribute of the young person – cognitive, affective and psychomotor – is potentially open to scrutiny, comment and record. This is justified on the grounds that all these attributes are potential market commodities. However, the unequal power of distribution implicit in such an assessment scheme effectively corresponds to, and reproduces, the unequal relation of manufacturing production.[11] The correspondence can be taken further: just as on the pre-vocational course the student or trainee, once allocated, has a limited choice of what, how and when she/he will study, so as a waged employee, once a job is obtained, there will be little discretion in the nature, pacing and method of working allowed.

Subject content

The arguments and counter-arguments applied to the aims, form and structure of the pre-vocational curriculum can be extended in an analysis of its typical content matter. Although pre-vocational courses and schemes tend to allow schools and colleges to determine their own syllabus, characteristically a framework is provided. The framework usually consists of the following: a general education component including traditional and new 'basics', social education, vocational knowledge and skill, careers education and personal development, process skills, and recreation. The extent to which these elements are to be integrated may vary, CPVE, for example, aims at full integration of the general and vocational education components.

Traditional socialisation theories would suggest that such provision is in the dual interests of society and of the individual student. Relevance and practical application to work are the criteria for the inclusion of subject matter and the design of learning experience. For the young person this is motivating and rewarding. She/he is acquiring the knowledge, skill and understanding required to be successful in adult life. Careers guidance, the opportunity to 'taste' different jobs, real work experience and increased understanding of personal strengths, interests and capabilities ensure that an appropriate choice of job is made. For its part, society is acquiring a new member already partly trained and socialised into the performance of essential roles, less likely to change jobs in the early years, motivated, self-directing and socially mature.

The emphasis on information skills, computer literacy, microelectronics and technology – the so-called 'new' educational basics – can also be seen as beneficial. Students are more likely to find jobs in these new occupational fields than in traditional semi-skilled manufacturing concerns; there are skill shortages in these areas nationally. Similarly, vocational options in community care, the service sectors, in the media, in distribution, in catering, and in recreation and leisure industries, cover areas in which job opportunities need to be filled, or are likely to occur, or in which young people may have a reasonable chance of becoming self-employed and wealth-creating. Such areas represent a good investment, therefore, for society as a whole.

The components of such courses and schemes enable young people to become skill-owners and give them the techniques to appropriate knowledge for their own use. In this sense the courses serve the beneficent purposes of increasing individual autonomy and increasing the potential flexibility and adaptability of the nation's work-force. For not only are vocational skills learned, but essential process skills, such as hypothesis generation and testing, problem solving, learning to learn, transferring and applying knowledge to new situations, and self-assessment, are also acquired and practised. By equipping the majority of young people with appropriate vocational knowledge and with appropriate skills it should be possible to increase labour productivity and economic performance. Near universal training and education up to the age of 18 should also enable Britain to compete on more equal terms with countries such as West Germany, which have already developed coherent training systems.

What of the alternative perspective? Once again it is possible to analyse the pre-vocational curriculum and emerge with a negative judgement.

First, the emphasis on practical, applied knowledge and skills related to everyday life is an emphasis on the second-rate. The knowledge and skills which have traditionally been highly valued do not appear in the pre-vocational curriculum. For example, there is little theoretical knowledge, little emphasis on the mastery of abstract symbolic reasoning, and little attention paid to written argument, analysis and synthesis. The imaginative, creative aspects of language and literature are unlikely to feature prominently in 'communication studies', nor do foreign languages. In short, the pre-vocational curriculum can be seen as a 'new barbarism', denying access to the historically valued knowledge of the dominant groups. Moreover, training in specific computer related skills such as programming may be inappropriate in a rapidly developing field – it is not clear, for example, whether the fourth and fifth generation of computers will require programming skills or any technical knowledge of computers. An over-emphasis on technical computing skills may even stultify personal development.[12]

Secondly, the world of work, on which the pre-vocational courses are focused, is imposed on the students by the course and scheme designers. Even though it might have been expected that working-class students would have here, if anywhere, an opportunity to validate their own culture, contribute their own knowledge and create their own meanings about working life, in fact the view of waged employment, of social and life skills and of 'career' which has to be learned is that of the middle class. For example, 'transition to working life' is perceived in most course designs as a problematic process requiring facilitation, even though the research evidence indicates that transition to work as experienced by young people is *not* traumatic.[13] Similarly, exercises and activities in social- and life-skills sessions may grossly underestimate the coping abilities already developed by young people in their home life, or focus on aspects of adult life which have little actual, immediate relevance to the young person (for example, getting a mortgage or 'setting up on one's own').[14] Students are, accordingly, doubly disadvantaged. They are denied access to the forms of knowledge which count and they are expected to deny the validity of their own experience (including, at present, the reality of unemployment) for all its apparent relevance to the nature of the course. The extent of the freedom that they have to negotiate their own learning is thus severely limited.

The pre-vocational curriculum and unemployment

The second major area of debate concerns the relationship of pre-vocational courses and schemes to the employment market for young people. There is ample statistical evidence of an increase in registered unemployment for 16–18 year-olds. [. . .]

There is also clear evidence of growing participation in full-time education, so that, over the last decade, the proportion of 16–18 year-olds in employment has dropped from more than two-thirds to slightly over two-fifths.[15] Rather more doubt surrounds the figure of young people obtaining jobs at 17 or 18 who have completed a pre-vocational course or scheme.

[. . .] The national picture [. . .] presents a worrying paradox for teachers and others wishing to implement a pre-vocational curriculum. For, depending on whether the current level of youth (and adult) unemployment is temporary or permanent, so the pre-vocational curriculum can be commended or condemned.

Unemployment as a temporary phenomenon

It has been argued that the current high levels of unemployment are the result of the present recession rather than the product of deeper structural changes in the nature and distribution of paid jobs.[16] If this is the case, and if renewed economic growth does involve job creation, then one could expect the pre-vocational courses or schemes to act genuinely as a transition between formal schooling and full-time employment. The same situation might also arise if, for political reasons, permanent waged jobs were deliberately created through higher public-sector spending or in other ways. With either of these scenarios, the content and form of pre-vocational courses can be defined. Pending economic recovery, young people are acquiring skills, knowledge and practical competencies which will put them in a good position to obtain waged employment eventually. This is a constructive alternative to being 'on the dole', and a real alternative to continuing with inappropriate academic learning. It may also lay the foundation for a fully developed and coherent system of education and training constructively linked to the country's economic performance.

Unemployment as a permanent feature of society

Recent changes in the nature and amount of waged employment available both to young people and to adults can be interpreted as indicating that society has moved into a period of structural unemployment. Young people may, therefore, be facing a future of, at best, intermittent waged work.[17] If such arguments are accepted, then the current pre-vocational curriculum can be criticised both for its content and for the values implicit in it. By focusing so strongly on waged employment, the curriculum can be seen as irrelevant and potentially damaging to the self-concept of the young people concerned.

Three examples can be given. First, current pre-vocational courses tend to reinforce the link between identity and waged employment that has been a characteristic of Western industrial society. If, however, work for many young people will be non-waged, then transition courses should seek to establish alternative sources of status and identity.[18] Secondly, if young people are likely to experience long periods of 'leisure' time, then the curriculum, rather than externally structuring students' time, should enable students to acquire the skills of using free time in ways that seem valid to them.[19] Instead, therefore, of pre-determining and prescribing learning experiences, students should be given the opportunity genuinely to define and decide what they will learn to do. Various activities currently confined to the paracurriculum[20] might then be validated as part of the course or scheme. Thirdly, the current pre-vocational courses and schemes can be criticised for the absence of preparation for unemployment – the reality facing many young people on completion of their education and training. Survival skills and discussion of the socio-economic and political factors involved might, it is argued, assist young people to understand and cope better with the experience of being unemployed.[21]

Conclusion

The examination of the arguments in favour of pre-vocational courses, and against them, has revealed the extent of the dilemmas facing teachers and lecturers with responsibility for curriculum development, especially in the 16–19 age-range. Evaluation and interpretation of conflicting evidence is difficult and time-consuming, while on some key issues there is simply insufficient data to inform decision-making at local or regional levels. Yet the penalties for inappropriate choices are high. If the critics are correct, an irrelevant academic curriculum will simply be replaced by an equally limiting and damaging vocational curriculum. In such circumstances one can predict an accumulation of frustration both in the teachers and in the students or trainees, with the original pre-vocational aims and objectives eventually being subverted to other ends.[22]

CPVE can expect to be judged by the extent to which its status is comparable to the existing market benchmarks. It also needs to be assessed in terms of its relevance for those who may be unemployed at 18+ or who will undertake non-waged work in the home or community.

The situation is compounded by the apparent replication of pre-vocational courses on the market. In addition to the vexed questions of equivalence to [. . .] the General Certificate of Secondary Education (GCSE), there are also difficulties in gauging the comparative worth of pre-vocational courses for entry, say, to BTEC national diplomas or certificates. At present, [. . .] CPVE is in danger, through competing forces, of falling between the academic GCSE route and the vocational training route without achieving a marketable synthesis of them. In these circumstances, schools and colleges may consider developing the new course for a specific student target – e.g. those with special educational needs, or as an accompaniment for 'A' level TVEI students – rather than attempt to 'sell' it as a course that will enhance employability for a wide cross-section of young people at 16+.

Acknowledgements

The author is indebted to Dr G. D. Yeoman at the University of Nottingham for many discussions of the issues raised in this chapter, and to Professor A. D. Edwards at the University of Newcastle for access to his work while still in press.

References and Notes

1 For an analysis of these and related arguments, see Edwards, A. D. (1986) 'Education and Training 16–19: Rhetoric Policy and Practice', in Harnet, A. and Naish, M. (eds), *Education and Society Today*. Lewes: Falmer.
2 Brockington, D., White, R. and Pring, R. (1985) *The 14–18 Curriculum: Integrating CPVE, YTS, TVEI?* Bristol: Youth Education Service, p. 14.
3 For a summary and critique of such theories, see Giroux, H. A. (1981) *Ideology, Culture and the Process of Schooling*. London: Falmer, pp. 91–112.
4 Dean, J. and Steeds, A. (1981) *17 Plus: The New Sixth Form in Schools and FE*. Windsor: NFER-Nelson.
5 Atkins, M. J. (1982) 'Foundation Courses in a Sixth Form College: A Case Study'. Unpublished PhD thesis, University of Nottingham.
6 Bernstein, B. (1971) 'On the Classification and Framing of Educational Knowledge', in Young, M. F. D. (ed.) *Knowledge and Control*. London: Collier Macmillan, pp. 47–69.
7 Hurn, C. (1983) 'The Vocationalisation of American Education', *European Journal of Education*, 18, 1, pp. 45–64.
8 Bourdieu, P. and Passeron, J.-C. (1977) *Reproduction in Education, Society and Culture*. London: Sage. See also the arguments advanced by Young, M. F. D. (ed.) (1971) *Knowledge and Control: New Directions for the Sociology of Education*. London: Collier Macmillan, pp. 19–46.
9 Schools Council (1980) *Examinations at 18+: Report on the N and F Debate*. Schools Council Working Paper, No. 66. London: Methuen Educational.

10 Bourdieu and Passeron (1977) (see note 8).
11 Giroux, H. A. (1981) (see note 3).
12 See, for example, the arguments advanced by Cowie, A. (1985) 'Endangered Species', *Times Educational Supplement*, 26 April, p. 23.
13 Clarke, L. (1980) *The Transition from School to Work: A Critical Review of Research in the United Kingdom*. London: Department of Employment.
14 Atkins (1982) (see note 5).
15 *Ibid.*
16 Raffe, D. (1984) 'The Transition from School to Work and the Recession: Evidence from the Scottish School Leavers Surveys, 1977–1983', *British Journal of Sociology of Education*, 5, 3, pp. 247–65.
17 See, for example, Brockington, White and Pring (1985), p. 6 (see note 3); and Coffield, F. (1983) 'Learning to Live with Unemployment: What Future for Education in a World Without Jobs?' in Coffield, F. and Goodings, R. (eds) *Sacred Cows in Education* (Edinburgh University Press), pp. 191–207.
18 Of particular relevance to this point are the four alternative scenarios – unemployment, leisure, employment, work – advanced by Watts. See Watts, A. G. (1983) *Education, Unemployment and the Future of Work*. Milton Keynes: Open University Press.
19 Hendry, L. B., Raymond M. and Stewart, C. (1984) 'Unemployment, School and Leisure: An Adolescent Study', *Leisure Studies*, 3, pp. 175–87.
20 By 'paracurriculum' is meant those experiences such as leisure interests, hobbies or television viewing, outside formal schooling and training, through which young people acquire knowledge and skill.
21 There is conflicting evidence on the extent to which young people find difficulty in adapting to unemployment. See Coffield (1983) (see note 17) and Roberts, K., Noble, M. and Duggan, J. (1982) 'Youth unemployment: An old problem or a new life style?' *Leisure Studies*, 1, (1982), pp. 171–82.
22 Atkins, M. J. (1984) 'Pre-vocational Courses: Tensions and Strategies', *Journal of Curriculum Studies* 16, 4, pp. 403–15.

2.7

National Writing Project: A Story of Curriculum Change

Pam Czerniewska

The fact that those who advocate and develop change get more rewards than costs, and those who are expected to implement them experience many more costs than rewards, goes a long way in explaining why the more things change the more they remain the same. (Fullan, M. 1982, p. 113)

Background

In 1985 the School Curriculum Development Committee launched a major four-year project that aimed to change the writing curriculum: the National Writing Project. Of course, it was not put quite as baldly as that. In 1985, when many teachers were threatening to strike over pay and professional status and when the new GCSE examination was about to cause a most radical rethink of the secondary curriculum, nobody was going to say that here was a new project intent on changing the way writing was to be taught. Apart from the desire not to commit curriculum suicide, such an approach did not reflect the thinking of the small group of people given the task of implementing the Project.

In those early days, we did not articulate very clearly what our view of curriculum change was, and few of us had read much about curriculum models. Instead we had, as one coordinator later put it to me, a few stock phrases that abounded in our talk and publicity but whose meaning we only worked out as time went by; phrases like 'teacher-led', 'bottom-up', 'starting with practice', 'sharing ideas' and a 'network of teachers'.

Perhaps our model of curriculum change was best described for what it was not: it was not the introduction of new curriculum materials designed by a small group of researcher-practitioners, neither was it a select group of academics carrying out a systematic investigation of children's writing to test and refine a particular theory of development. Not being one of these approaches caused some consternation. Eve Bearne (1990), one of the Project Officers, writes that the two most common questions she met in her early days with the Project were 'What do you want me to do?' and 'What is the Project's theory of writing development?' The former came largely from teachers in the working groups, while the latter came mainly from academics and Inset providers. They reflected a familiar history of curriculum development in which usually very able and enlightened people have evolved models of development and learning which could dramatically affect the teacher's view of the child, or have designed programmes of work which would improve classroom practice. But too often such innovations were not accompanied by consideration of how they might be adopted and implemented. Many just stayed in textbooks; others fared poorly, perhaps because they failed to recognise the problem of 'brute sanity'.

> Brute sanity is the tendency to overlook the complexity and detailed processes and procedures required, in favour of more obvious matters of stressing goals, the importance of the problem and the grand plan. Brute sanity overpromises, overrationalises and consequently results in unfulfilled dreams and frustrations which discourage people from sustaining their efforts and from taking on future change projects (Fullan, M., 1988, p. 16).

Characteristics of the Project

To identify the distinctive characteristics of the Project it is important to allow for outside evaluation and possible replication. However, this is no easy task because of its inbuilt recognition of and accommodation to local variation.

The original proposal envisaged a small number of local education authorities forming the Project core: ten joining in the first year, and a further ten in the second year. (In the event, a total of twenty-four actually participated.) The LEAs were selected according to a variety of criteria. The Project wanted to have a number of writing issues covered – e.g. use of micros; bilingual writers; community involvement; writing and work – and to look at the whole age range 3–18. It aimed for geographical spread, a mix of shire and metropolitan authorities and a balance of authorities experienced and less-experienced in curriculum innovation. It did not aim to set up centres of excellence involving teachers of proven merit supported by maximum resources. Rather it wanted to represent the spread of experience among teachers and the diversity of local authority provision. In other words, it wanted to work within existing structures.

The personnel consisted of a small central team: a director, three Project Officers (two in the final implementation year) and an administrator. They were supported by a professional officer and a steering committee. At the local level, each authority was required, in order to participate, to support one full-time coordinator. They achieved this in various ways: most appointed one person for two or three years; one had four people on part-time release to equal one full-time equivalent; another seconded different people for each of the three years; the most fortunate had three full-time coordinators for three years. Most coordinators were seconded teachers or advisory teachers; some had been heads others had relatively little experience of group management or inservice provision. There were advantages and disadvantages to each arrangement: continuity was important and yet different people could bring new perspectives; status within the system helped to get things done, while acceptance as just an 'ordinary' teacher won credibility. The only characteristics which clearly correlated with local success were a commitment to improving children's writing and an understanding of the difficult process of change.

Each coordinator worked closely with their local adviser(s) and, in a few cases, HE lecturers, who had originally proposed the project theme. These partnerships were a crucial element in the effectiveness of the local activity.

The main element of the project structure was the teacher working groups set up within each authority. Again there was no fixed pattern. Most began with about twenty-five teachers from about twelve schools (though the range was from nine teachers from three schools to over a hundred teachers from sixty or so schools). Some teachers/schools were volunteers, others were nominated by their adviser either because they were known to have excellent ideas and practices or because 'it would do them good'. In most cases, supply cover was available for at least one meeting a term, very important to give the teachers a sense that they were being valued. In addition, there slowly grew an informal network of evening and weekend meetings in most authorities.

Starting points

It was not all smooth going. In fact, there were some rough beginnings. Excuses were available for these such as teacher action during the first term (September 1985), the delay in some appointments and so on. But these were not the main reasons for some tense meetings of teachers and many anxious discussions with coordinators. The initial difficulties came from the curriculum approach itself: no one said what the working groups were meant to do, beyond the initial very broad brief. There was an inevitable sense of unease as teachers faced basic questions like 'What do I think about the teaching of writing in my classroom?' 'What are the main issues to discuss with colleagues about school writing practices?' or even the more desperate 'Why involve me in this Project?' After her early meetings with teachers in the Project, one coordinator wrote in her diary 'I think one needs considerable nerve to keep fumbling on'. The different school positions that teachers held meant that there would be varied starting points within any one group. In the Project's national evaluation (White, J., 1988), four teachers interviewed in depth reflected this diversity. One was a primary teacher with no special responsibilities (apart from a class of thirty-eight juniors!), just a general concern with language development; another was a secondary head of English with a strong commitment to literature and a desire to implement change in her department; two others were middle school teachers constantly aware of the jostling demands of other school subjects. Such variety made the initial search for a coherent plan of action necessarily difficult.

But slowly, the groups began to respond to their role in the Project, to redefine what they were doing there and to review their writing practices. Some catalysts for this change have been identified. One coordinator tells of a group of different subject teachers within one school whose meetings were very hesitant until a geography teacher presented an account of his attempt to break away from his usual writing tasks by asking the children to take different points of view in a colliery closure plan. His initial scepticism that the syllabus would have to be abandoned if he spent time on children's writing was soon revised as the children demonstrated their sensitivity to the issues. His presentation of both what he did and his worries stimulated others in the group to discuss reservations and to explore new ideas. As Richard Landy, the local coordinator for the group put it, that first presentation of investigative work changed the group from just talking to *doing* and talking (Landy, R., 1990).

In other cases, a shared group task helped to orientate the group. For instance, a number of teachers began by looking at what they actually did in their classrooms. There were surveys of writing tasks carried out during a week or a term; interviews with children about what they thought about writing, who it was for and what made one piece of writing better than the next; there were observations made of the classroom itself: what writing was on the wall and who put it there. There were also explorations which involved teachers writing themselves and reflecting on the pain and pleasures experienced. Such blunt instruments, generally neither systematic nor scientific according to established canons helped teachers to set their agendas for action. The view that emerged from all these investigations was remarkably similar. Teachers from Reception classes to Sixth Forms found that children perceived writing as something they did for the teacher, to show that they knew and whose main purpose was to learn how to write. Far too rarely did pupils talk about writing as something that could achieve different purposes and that varied according to the reader; neither was writing as a tool for learning evident in children's responses. 'Good' writing was overwhelmingly judged by criteria of neatness, spelling and punctuation first, with content a poor second. When teachers reflected on their own writing behaviour, they realised how little they discussed with children about what it meant to be a writer – the processes of drafting; the choices to be made according to a text's function; the usefulness of discussions with others at all stages of a text's production. One coordinator wrote later 'enquiry, talk, collaboration, reflection and writing itself . . . altered teachers' perceptions' (Mawdsley, J., 1990).

Healthy tensions

The faltering beginnings reflected one of the 'healthy tensions' of our curriculum development approach. It resulted from an attempt to provide a supportive context for discussion and at the same time to create a momentum for change. Whereas there were working groups who were told that they were free to determine their own agendas for looking at the writing curriculum, there existed along-side a national brief, budget and timetable which had preempted who would be involved and what broad areas they would be concerned with.

This national versus local tension became more evident as time passed. For example, one national priority was for the Project to prepare documentary accounts of what was going on. With a three-year schedule (only extended to four at the last moment), this meant that publication plans had to be finalised when some of the groups were only beginning to think about where they were going. There was early resistance to preparing 'products' – after all, much of what we learned about writing development emphasised that learning was most effective when there was time to reflect on the process, not when end products were publicly displayed. A crisis point was almost reached at the end of the Project's second year (which for half the local projects was the end of their first year). The central team suggested and helped to stage a series of regionally based 'writing events' in which over two hundred teachers were to present their classroom investigations. Many felt they were not ready for such public exposure, that they wanted to go on discussing the issues within their groups before articulating them . . . meetings became tense. But with a lot of reassurance and practical support, the events happened and provided, in many cases, a major boost to the activities, giving teachers a large injection of self-confidence.

At each level these tensions emerged. Jay Mawdsley (1990), a local coordinator, for example, eloquently discusses her 'janus-like role of encouraging and supporting teachers whilst asking them at the same time to examine their own practice' concluding that 'it is in the nature of change to cause disequilibrium'.

Either because or despite of these conflicting pressures on the teacher groups, there emerged in practically every local authority, cohesive and self-supporting groups who were concentrating on particular aspects of the writing curriculum, exchanging ideas about practice and reflecting on how children learn to write and how teachers can best support that learning. They were developing what has been variously described by those involved as 'a common technical culture', 'a dialogic process' and 'a colloborative community for enduring change'. Although not articulated in this way at first, the model of learning that emerged owed much to the work of researchers such as Vygotsky (1978) and Bruner (1986). It is a model that recognises the social nature of learning and sees interaction as a vital way of 'scaffolding' cognitive processes such that the learner can achieve higher levels of abstraction.

A learning process

While this account is intended to focus more on the curriculum processes that developed than the model of writing, the two have much in common. A day spent with twenty-five HMIs and three coordinators from Dorset and Avon demonstrates this point. The HMIs were asked to think about some of the most successful examples of writing development work that they had observed in practice and to identify what such environments provided for learners. A ten-minute small group 'brainstorm' was followed by a pooling of ideas. Some quick and skilful writing on a flip chart produced the following list:

What do learners need to help them develop as writers?

1 the confidence and time to be tentative and to make mistakes
2 to see real purposes in the learning task and to have a stake in it
3 a sense of achievement
4 help in reshaping previous experience
5 control over the processes involved in writing (drafting, etc.)
6 opportunities for reflection
7 collaboration with others – teachers and pupils

Underlying all these statements, it was agreed, was a fundamental assumption about learning to write: that it was an active process, developed in interaction with others.

After some further discussion about the signs of an effective writing environment, the presenters asked the HMIs what parallels there were between what they identified as learners' needs in classrooms and what they thought teachers needed in curriculum development. The answer reached, not surprisingly, was that the learning needs were the same. The conclusions reached when thinking about children's writing that stressed the importance of experience, collaboration, control, and recursive development, were mirrored in their own feelings about teachers' learning. The fundamental assumption underlying learning that was being articulated is perhaps most elegantly put by Bruner when he writes:

> I have come increasingly to recognise that most learning in most settings is a communal activity, a sharing of the culture. It is not just that the child must make his knowledge his own, but that he must make it his own in a community of those who share his sense of belonging to a culture. It is this that leads me to emphasise not only discovery and invention but the importance of negotiating and sharing (Bruner, J., 1986, p. 127).

This example of people thinking about learning was repeated in many other groups: as teachers reflected on what they thought about children as learners, they recognised that they thought the same about themselves as agents of change.

Collaboration and consolidation

At first, for most, it was enough to be talking about what happened in classrooms, to experiment with new approaches and to discuss what the results meant. But, there grew a need – sometimes a demand – to confirm what they had discovered and shared, through reading and through more systematic research. As a result more formal links were made with HE institutions, some proposing certificated courses for teachers involved in the Project, and nationally, courses were offered during the Summer to write and to study writing in depth. These latter were organised jointly with the New York Writing Project.

Interesting parallels can be drawn with the US Writing Project which is based much more firmly in higher education structures. In their model, those colleges/universities wishing to participate begin by running Summer Institutes for chosen 'excellent' teachers. At these, teachers present examples of work, read, attend lectures and seminars and write. They then go back to their schools to form working groups, to act as teacher-consultants and so generate involvement of other teachers. (Of course, there is much variation in the ways of working between the different states involved but all share the initial 'Institute' and the teacher-as-consultant dissemination pattern.) While the British Writing Project began very differently, not excluding but certainly not based within higher education, after three years, many teachers felt the need to consolidate and find a framework for their thinking through colleges. Bridie Raban, a university based inservice provider who worked closely with one of the local groups, raises a question in her review of the project:

> How can we build and sustain bridges between the experiential craft knowledge and wisdom of teachers and the conceptual and theoretical base with which we wish to influence their work?

and concludes

> the chasm between classroom practice and belief systems is being bridged through supported reflection (Raban, 1988).

I understand her to mean that the model implicit in many curriculum projects of teachers who do things and academics who know things needs to be revised to show that teachers can only theorise on a base of experience. Through opportunities to revisit, review and reflect on that experience they can engage in new conceptual formulations. Where such reflection is supported by higher education, that thinking can shift in its level of abstraction. As one colleague put it, 'this moves collaboration up a notch'.

Towards a future

As this personal account of one project should have shown, curriculum development which starts from practice and tries to build itself within existing structures is a very messy process. You can never be quite sure where you have got to and can easily become complacent amid the testimonials from teachers delighted simply to have talked to each other. There is evidence of change happening in classrooms as a result of teachers' new approaches to writing and there is, within the new National Curriculum proposals, recognition of some of the teachers' conclusions about the writing curriculum. However, there are many aspects of writing where we have only begun to scratch the surface: issues of gender, bilingualism, writing in different subject areas are just a few examples where more work is urgently needed.

There are major reservations about the Project's future once national funding ends in 1989. More might have been done to help teachers institutionalise their practices within their own schools and authorities. Too often, the changes made were contained within individual classrooms and when a teacher left (and many were quite predictably promoted) so too did her/his experiences and ideas. But the most pressing concern that teachers have expressed is what happens when the support structures can no longer be maintained. What recognition is there likely to be in the future of teachers' need to come together in order to support and stimulate ideas. To rephrase a statement about evaluation written by Janet White:

> If we are to argue that curriculum development is best justified in terms of improvement in the quality of student learning, then we should also argue for improvement in the quality of teacher awareness of the kinds of processes by which this might be brought about (White, 1988).

Postscript

It was comforting when, towards the end of the Project's development phase, Michael Fullan gave a talk at the SCDC conference in which he offered eight basic guidelines or insights. I do not think we always managed to follow them but they did seem to reflect what we would also recommend in the light of our experience:

> – effective entrepreneurs exploit multiple innovations
> – overcome the 'if only . . .' problem, e.g. 'if only more heads were curriculum leaders . . .'; 'if only the government would stop introducing so many policies . . .'
> – manage multiple innovations. 'Do two well and the others as well as possible'
> – get better at implementation planning – more by doing than by planning, Start small but think big.
> – beware of implementation dip, i.e. the risk of temporary de-skilling as innovators learn new skills
> – remember that research shows that behaviour changes first and changes in belief follow
> – recognise that project leaders need to have a vision of content and process and the relationship between the two which will promote change. To have a vision of content of change without a vision of process of change is an example of 'brute sanity'
> – acknowledge the importance of ownership and commitment and that ownership is a process where commitment is increasingly acquired (Fullan, M., 1988, p. 18).

References

Bearne, E. (1990) 'Not Just in Theory', in *Ways of Looking*, 2. National Writing Project Reader. London: Thomas Nelson.

Bruner, J. (1986) *Actual Minds, Possible Worlds*. Cambridge, Mass.: Harvard University Press.

Fullan, M. (1982) *The Meaning of Educational Change*. Teacher's College Press/OISE.

Fullan, M. (1988) 'The Dynamics of Curriculum Change', in *Curriculum at the Crossroads*. SCDC.

Landy, R. (1990) 'Rewriting the Syllabus', in *Ways of Looking*, 2, National Writing Project Reader. London: Thomas Nelson.

Mawdsley, J. (1990) 'Instruments of Change', in *Ways of Looking*, 2, National Writing Project Reader. London: Thomas Nelson.

Raban, B. (1988) *Writing for Learning – a Curriculum Project*. Paper presented at IRA World Congress, Brisbane.

Vygotsky, L. S. (1978) *Mind in Society*. Cole, M. *et al.* (eds), Cambridge, Mass: Harvard Educational Press.

White, J. (1988) *Changing Practice: Part One*. Unpublished evaluation report.

SECTION 3
Changing Pedagogy

Introduction

It is an interesting paradox that in a period of major innovation in curriculum and assessment the role of the teacher in influencing development is diminishing. Increased central control of curricula has been accompanied by pressure for formal teacher appraisal and accountability, sometimes on the narrowest of criteria. New ambitions for curriculum and assessment systems are as yet unmatched by parallel capacities for a radical transformation of the content of in-service education. Within the implicit models of curricula developed by governments the teachers' pedagogical knowledge remains unproblematic, a perspective disputed by the readings in this section. Many contributors strongly indicate the need for a transformation of the teachers' role from a 'giver of knowledge' to an 'empowerer of learning'. What is entailed in such a transformation and the pedagogical implications of past and present educational positions provides the focus of this section. There is a particular emphasis on the pedagogical challenges implicit in a view of learning as a social and 'meaning making' enterprise.

Watts and Bentley consider the issue of conceptual change within a constructivist paradigm. They look critically at the cognitive conflict position advocated in view of the interdependence of the cognitive and affective domains in the process of learning. They highlight the subsequent need for teachers to create supportive learning atmospheres if a constructivist view of learning is to be achieved. They further suggest that teachers need to be aware of their actions and their purposes in this context.

Mason focuses more specifically on alternative approaches to teaching and identifies three prominent ones, behaviourism, Piagetian and information processing. He poses the problem of the relationship between learning theory and pedagogic practice. The contributors to this article look at the pedagogical implications of the alternative theoretical approaches by examining the teaching of a common problem and content. The discussion by Danner draws attention to the different foci of the three approaches and the quite distinct roles identified for teachers. The knowledge that teachers need of the learner, the process of learning and the learning activity are shown to be determined by the theoretical approach.

A more global perspective of pedagogy is presented by Walkerdine in her comprehensive chapter on developmental psychology and the child-centred pedagogy. Her starting point is the apparent failure of the liberating child-centred pedagogy. In the extract she argues cogently that the apparatuses of the child-centred pedagogy do not result from an *application* of the domain perspective, in this case, developmental psychology but are themselves 'a sight of production in their own right'. She describes how a pedagogy for the individual came to be associated with, and defined by, the notion of a normalised sequence of child development and presents the historical conditions for this occurrence. She locates Piaget's work within a particular body of scientific discourse and practices to explain how it was taken up in a particular way in early education. Finally she highlights the contradiction of a psychology and associated practices that are normalising providing the basis for a 'liberating' pedagogy and goes on to argue the need for a more effective psychology that 'tells us how children really learn'.

The learning of language is a central theme in Britton's article and in the extract from Applebee's chapter. Britton describes the contribution of Vygotsky and the challenge it presents to the traditional role of the teacher as the 'middle-man'. He argues from a Vygotskian position that education as 'an effect of community' means that teachers have to be aware of approaches to skilled behaviours and the obstacles to such behaviours and that this awareness should be made available to the learner. Hence the teacher is described as 'lending consciousness' to the learner.

Applebee, from a similar position, criticises the emphasis in teacher training on the teacher as a technocrat and a subject-knowledge specialist. Rather he suggests teachers need subject-specific knowledge of teaching which he defines as practical knowledge of the nature of a subject – the skills, procedures and concepts; how these develop and how such development is fostered. He challenges the training emphasis on expert practitioners which provides students with exemplar activities rather than the principles of good practice and argues that student teachers need to develop a repertoire of approaches to real problems.

Bennet provides a review of three research issues – teaching styles, opportunities for learning and classroom tasks to indicate changing perspectives on teaching and learning. He outlines the findings and the limitations of the research studies. He supports the constructivist perspective and argues the need for representations of teacher-knowledge systems which allow teachers to select tasks, diagnose pupils' understanding, teach cognitive processes and deal with the complexities of the learning environment. In this he appeals to the models developed by cognitive psychologists. He recognises that support for a constructivist view allows for the role of the pupil in mediating and structuring knowledge. This, however, places even greater emphasis on teacher competence in subject matter, pedagogical and curriculum knowledge.

3.1

Constructivism in the Classroom: Enabling Conceptual Change by Words and Deeds*

Mike Watts and Di Bentley

Introduction

This chapter follows a thread of argument that can be summarised as follows:

1 a major element of science education concerns enabling youngsters' conceptual change;
2 current theories of conceptual change require considerable self-exposure by youngsters of their existing ideas;
3 willingness to articulate and explore personal theories is dependent upon the learning environment that prevails in a classroom;
4 the learning environment is created both by what a teacher says and the way that he or she behaves;
5 youngsters are shrewd judges of behaviours which indicate trust, sympathy and empathy in teachers and prefer to work for and learn with teachers they trust;
6 effective conceptual change requires that teachers become skilled in both the verbal and the non-verbal cues they initiate.

The thread through the arguments is an attempt to bring together two distinctive and often separate research domains: cognitive development on the one hand, and non-verbal behaviour on the other. Within the paper we explore aspects of what we call a 'non-threatening learning environment' (NTLE).

At first glance it might seem a mildly eccentric inconsequence – rare are they who champion a *threatening* learning environment. It seems to us, however, a notion worth developing on two counts. The first relates to communicative acts within the psychological

---

* The extract presented below excludes the specific examples of evidence from pupil interviews cited in the article from the Bentley Study (1985).

atmospheres of school classrooms, while the second stems from recent research work and curriculum development in terms of cognitive structures and conceptual change. We develop our notional NTLE largely against a curriculum backdrop of school science education and from interview data as youngsters interpret teachers' postures and gestures.

Our experiences foster the conviction that, on the whole, life in school classrooms is conducted in a fairly robust atmosphere, redolent of the normal chiding, teasing and banter that occurs within pupil peer-group and teacher–pupil interactions. On the heavy-handed side, sarcasm, abrasive wit and verbal bullying are not uncommon tools in the armoury of the hard pressed teacher – or youngster. The model of the dour, humourless, disengaged authoritarian is sometimes offered as an appropriate role for initiate teachers at the outset of their careers – the old addage 'never smile before Easter' sometimes being proffered as having 'a germ of good psychological sense in it' (Marland, 1975). Needless to say, warmth, humour and sensitivity are also part of teachers' approach, though arguably perhaps not always with the same regularity and consistency as the caricature above.

Not all communicative acts, of course, are verbal: non-verbal actions, postures and expressions abound in the normal day-to-day discourse of school life. Clearly, the atmosphere of the classroom is of importance for learning and the teacher contributes to creating this by a variety of communicative means. Much of a teacher's communication within the classroom is geared to the pursuit of social control – communication which has to be encoded by the initiator and decoded by the recipient. Marland, for example, goes on to advise the beginning teacher to, whenever possible, influence the misbehaving pupil, or the pupil about to misbehave, silently and without the rest of the class knowing:

> Perhaps a small gesture will catch his eye and he will look up. Then a mere continuation of the stare may be sufficient, but it can be strengthened by a frown, or even a smile. This last may sound surprising, but a smile indicates you know the pupil is up to something he shouldn't have been, that you are not furious – yet, and that if he stops all will be well. A mouthed but soundless word or two can also be added occasionally. Such tactics avoid advertising the unsuitable behaviour to other pupils, and avoid the attendant risk of encouraging others to join in. This even creates a conspiratorial feeling between the teacher and the would-be wrong-doer that leaves a pleasurable rather than a thwarted feeling in the pupil.

Argyle (1969) has argued that as much as 60 per cent of the information gained in any communication between two individuals is gleaned from the non-verbal aspects of that communication. Feldman and Orchowsky (1982) report the use of non-verbal behaviours in teaching contexts. They add a further gloss to Argyle's figure:

That successful students received a more positive non-verbal behaviour than unsuccessful students seems quite reasonable ... the degree of *non-verbal* positiveness of the teacher could have potentially important effects, not only on student learning but upon their self-concept as well. (Our emphasis)

That is, differences in teachers' non-verbal behaviour might well facilitate learning because they enhance the clarity of the feedback given to youngsters. In our terms, actions which enable youngsters to feel positive about themselves aid the processes of cognitive change. But one might well ask, what are these 'positive non-verbal behaviours' that are so important? Richey and Richey (1982) and Bentley (1983), for example, have identified frequent eye contact, frequent hand gestures, open postures and physical closeness to be behaviours which indicate psychological acceptance.

The learning environment (non-threatening or otherwise), then, rests as much – if not more – on the way a teacher acts as it does upon what he or she might say. It also rests upon the ability of other participants in the room to decode the teacher's intended meanings.

Cognition and affect

In any environment the very act of learning is an emotional affair. The cognitive and the affective are not separate and distinct but are irrevocably intertwined. Learning brings with it a range of possible emotions from delight to fear, from satisfaction to frustration and despair. Our second strand of argument considers aspects of constructivist epistemology. As constructivist theories of learning have begun to be translated into classroom practice (see, for example, Horscroft and Pope, 1985; Driver and Oldham, 1985), the notion of a NTLE has grown in importance. In constructivist terms the classroom is often pictured as an arena in which youngsters are asked to consider the ideas and theories they hold for a particular topic, to explore these to some extent, to examine some of their consequences, to listen to and consider the ideas of others and to begin to re-shape their own ideas in order to take account of new factors. New additions or amendments to previous thinking might be brought about by either their teacher or peers.

When referring to conceptual change, some writers use the expressions 'cognitive *conflict*' and '*challenge*', and it is not difficult to see that the process of cognitive change, within the robust community of a school classroom, could be very intimidating. In fact, the act of self-exposure of well held, or even tentative, personally constructed ideas and beliefs can be a daunting task and – in certain inhospitable circumstances – quite counter productive. Minstrell (1982), for example, suggests that for conceptual development to take place within a school situation there needs to be an

> engaging, free thinking, free speaking social context . . . one in which students
> will put their thoughts up for consideration, free from fear of being chastised for
> being 'wrong'.

We would add that it might also need to be free of ridicule, supportive and empathetic of individuals needs and emotions. No one, at any stage in life, can consider their own beliefs and theories coldly and dispassionately – particularly at the point of change. They are inevitably invested with feelings, not least the feelings of personal ownership. We have recently (Watts and Bentley, 1984) attempted to draw out some implications for more 'personal' views of education (and in particular science education) and in doing so remarked that,

> A major implication of what has been said so far is for the 'atmosphere' of the
> classroom. It is an argument for a human climate that treats students as real
> persons, where attitudes and feelings can be expressed, where the student can
> choose from a range of feasible options, where the teacher serves as a facilitator
> of learning. The atmosphere in this sense is a supportive one where ridicule is
> avoided. Such a framework is likely to help students to feel sufficiently safe to
> help them interpret concepts in the light of their own experiences outside school
> and work in other parts of the school.

In the remainder of this paper we develop the notion of a NTLE in two main ways. We expand upon the two threads we have outlined above, of conceptual change and the atmosphere within which it is conducted. In particular we focus on students' views of teacher behaviour. We consider data derived from interviews with school children concerning their perceptions of the ways in which teachers act in generating part of that atmosphere. Finally, we summarise the arguments and speculate on some of the implications of what has been said.

Conceptual change

Much of the recent debate within science education circles has centred on theories of conceptual change. Books (for example West and Pines, 1985), conferences (Secondary Science Curriculum Review, 1983), complete editions of science education journals (*Physics Education*, 1985) review articles (Driver and Erickson, 1983; Gilbert and Watts, 1983) and research programmes (Children's Learning in Science Project, Bell and Driver, 1985) have all contributed to the field. The gradual and signally passive conceptual development of Piagetian persuasion (for example, Shayer and Adey, 1981) is giving way to more overtly interventionist approaches. Part of that intervention is to shape and manipulate the circumstances that will facilitate individuals in the process of conceptual change.

Policy and curriculum development, too, are shaping in similar directions. The Department of Education and Science (1985) say, as a matter of school science policy, that:

> In particular, opportunities for pupils to contribute their own ideas to discussion are important, with the object of establishing that in science recourse to experiment and experimental data is the principle means of testing whether a hypothesis is supported by evidence, and if so how far its implications extend. Pupils should be given the opportunity to test their own ideas.

As an organ of curriculum development, the Secondary Science Curriculum Review (1983) has included within its varied programme of work, such aims as the provision for all students of adequate opportunities to:

> study those aspects of science that are essential to an understanding of oneself and one's well being;
> discuss, reflect upon and evaluate their own personal understanding of key scientific concepts, theories and generalisations.

The bulk of the research informing the debate has focused upon the gulf between learners' own intuitive and personally constructed knowledge, and the formal, instructional, disciplined knowledge of schools. The former is individualised meaning-making and is characterised by being tentative, personal and part of the learner's belief system. The latter is well developed, highly structured, of high status and can be characterised in terms of authority. As West and Pines (1985) describe it:

> It is 'correct'; it is what the book says; what the teacher says. It is approved by a whole bunch of other people who are usually older and more highly regarded than the student.

Conceptual change is commonly portrayed as taking place from personal intuitive knowledge to correct (scientific) knowledge.

This sense of personally constructed meanings, varying between individuals and often at odds with the orthodoxy of school science, is a hall mark of the current constructivist approach. Driver (1984) draws out a series of features of such a view of learning and suggests it assumes:

> that learning outcomes depend not only on the learning environment but on the state of the learner, both on his or her conceptions and motivations. This implies that since learners may come to a learning task with different conceptions, they will learn different things from the same event.

She adds that constructivism also sees the learner as actively constructing his or her own meanings in any situation whether it is text, dialogue or physical experience, that construction of meaning is an active process of hypothesising and hypothesis testing, and has the consequence that the learner is seen as being ultimately responsible for their own learning. Clearly, two youngsters can carry away two distinctively different perceptions of a teacher's actions. A well articulated model for conceptual change is that developed by Strike and Posner (1985). They list four major conditions for a learner to undergo conceptual change:

1 there must be dissatisfaction with existing conceptions;
2 a new conception must be minimally understood, a person must be able to see how experience can be structured by a new conception;
3 a new conception must appear initially plausible, to have the capacity to solve problems that provoked dissatisfaction in the old one;
4 a new conception should suggest the possibility of being fruitful, of opening up new areas of thinking and explanation.

Swift (1984) has schematised this as shown in Figure 5.

The process of change is not seen necessarily as being either linear or abrupt but may, for some students, be a gradual and piecemeal affair.

Most classroom characterisations of this model of conceptual change envisage the teacher first assisting the learners to articulate and explore their own conceptions of some experience of phenomenon. The teacher then introduces anomalous features that are incapable of being easily interpreted by those conceptions and so induces dissatisfaction in the student. This kind of process is neatly summarised, for example, by Osborne and Freyberg (1985), and hinges upon the learner at some stage making explicit their own understandings either individually, in small groups or in a whole-class situation. They discuss four phases in the process: 'preliminary', 'focus', 'challenge' and 'application'. Focus, for the student, is the act of becoming familiar with classroom material concerning a particular concept: thinking and asking questions about the issue:

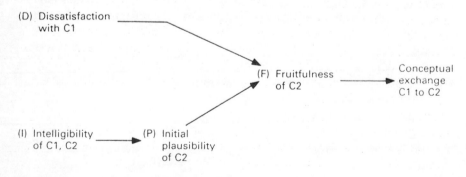

where C1, C2 = Concept 1, Concept 2

Figure 5   A model of conceptual change (Swift, 1984)

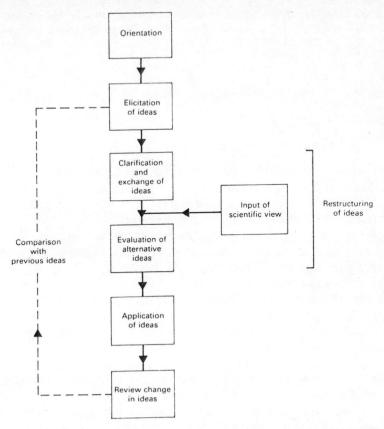

Figure 6 Constructivist teaching sequence (Driver and Oldham, 1985)

describing what he/she knows about it, and presenting own views to groups or discussion and display. Challenge is the consideration of individuals' views by other pupils in the class, seeking merits and defects; the testing of the validity of these views by seeking evidence, and the comparison of these views with the orthodox science view. An example of this in action is that described by Nussbaum and Novick (1981), where the issue is that of explaining the behaviour of a gas in terms of the particulate theory of matter. An example of a model for such a teaching scheme is that by Driver and Oldham (1985) (Figure 6).

As teachers we see ourselves in the business of encouraging conceptual change. Unfortunately the conceptual change model as outlined above could have some undesirable side affects (Watts and Pope, 1985). For instance, Clark (1985) notes that,

The theory of conceptual change (as articulated by Posner and Strike *et al.*, 1982) holds that the state of *readiness* for conceptual change ought best to arise from the learner's own attempts to make sense of experience . . . Yet a troublesome aspect of the way in which their work has been transformed into an instructional method is that the topics addressed arise from the wisdom of the curricularist, not the curiosity of the learner. The teacher is asked to *rush the students to readiness* by posing a question . . . that probably never occurred to the students, and then induce dissatisfaction with their own explanations by confrontation . . . The result is a kind of 'cognitive assault' in which students are *forced* to confront and abandon a part of self that has been, and is, serving them reasonably well.

Discussion

Let us take for granted, for a moment, that most teachers would want ideally to create a non-threatening learning environment if in the position to do so. Arguably most acts of social control are geared to generating an effective working (learning) environment, reaching apotheosis in a warm and trusting atmosphere. Recent science education policy and curriculum development is directed towards youngsters giving greater expression to their personally held ideas and conceptions of parts of science. Moreover, recently articulated constructivist theories of learning see processes of conceptual change in school science as being motivated by dissatisfaction with such existing ideas in the face of empirical evidence, images, analogies, or instruction. This motivation alone is insufficient for radical change in that the learner must also find any new ideas on offer to be plausible, intelligible and fruitful. The change being discussed is seen to take place in the context of a normal school setting and where students are encouraged (required) to make explicit their existing ideas in order that ensuing explorations will find them wanting. As Strike and Posner (1985) say:

> Dissatisfaction with the existing conception decreases its status, while exploring the fruitfulness of an alternative conception increases the alternatives's status . . . Therefore, competition between conceptions results in a process of accommodation characterised by temporary advances, frequent retreats and periods of indecision.

For us, this notion of cognitive change relies upon the development of a supportive classroom climate. The exposure of personally held ideas and beliefs, of personal 'retreats' and 'indecision' requires an atmosphere of warmth and trust. From our evidence (Bentley, 1985) it would seem that youngsters are highly attentive and sophisticated interpreters of teacher behaviour. Within a supportive atmosphere they are looking for high levels of trust, warmth and enthusiasm. They know they have found such attitudes when teachers engage in frequent eye contact, are alert, with quick body movements, listen carefully to youngsters' criticisms, and act on them. Such teachers laugh, with others and at themselves, stand close, touch from time to time, and use quick, bright voice tones that convey warmth and above all, respect for their co-learners. It is this interpretation of teachers as equals – in our terms as co-learners – that has some interesting implications for the way in which they manage classroom environments in terms of social control.

Our first implication concerns teacher awareness of their own actions. Youngsters seem to be asking for enthusiasm and, above all, teachers who make their lessons fun by being enthusiastic. This, it seems, encourages trust in learning. Moreover, these teachers show humility when things go wrong. All this implies that teachers need to consider the purposes of their actions. There would seem to be no immediate problem, [. . .] if teachers are disposed towards manifest social control. However, they must also develop the subtleties of being able to display a continuing respect that bridges difficult moments and situations. They must learn to make youngsters feel valued by warm, open friendliness. Many teachers are alive to [. . .] manipulative non-verbal behaviours – such as sarcastic tones, drawn brows to feign anger. In our view, they also display an amazing lack of sensitivity to the abilities of youngsters to read the other side of the cues they 'leak': the non-verbal actions that happen subconsciously as opposed to deliberately manipulated behaviour.

There is, however, a second major implication. The theoretical descriptions of constructivist conceptual change seem to require a non-threatening learning environment. There is a sense, though, that the kinds of actions and behaviours we are asking of teachers is more than can be expected of anyone in the essential hustle and bustle of everyday school life. That is, given that the less virtuous and normal human attributes of tension, tiredness, irritability, disapproval and altercation are ever present – then perhaps a non-threatening environment cannot be guaranteed for those prime moments of conceptual change. Which in turn must throw into question whether a theory that requires such a sensitive display of self-exposure can be viable in normal classroom situations. This leads us to three possibilities. First, as suggested earlier, teacher and student skills must be raised to the level where it is possible to fully engage youngsters in the processes involved. Secondly, theories of conceptual change need to be thoroughly re-considered in the light of inpracticability. Or, thirdly, some intermediate course is recognised. [. . .] Youngsters do not expect teachers to be paragons of virtue all of the time. They recognise the need for – and the associated behaviours to – teacher imposition of social control. They recognise the need for different behaviours in different circumstances. What youngsters want from a non-threatening learning environment is a sense of continuing trust consistently displayed. Further, exponents of theories of cognitive change must take into account the fact that neither they, nor the youngsters involved, will achieve the full explication of individual personal conceptions. In any class of more than two students, much of what eventuates from classroom interactions will be some admix of personal and group construction. It may well be that those youngsters most adept at social control, or at handling difficult classroom learning situations are the ones whose ideas will be heard. To gain some understanding of the conceptions of the less robust youngster might mean the direct teaching of personal skills in science as a precursor to classroom explication, that they might take a full part in the exercise. Whatever the case, it would seem to us that both theorists and the practitioners must reconsider and perhaps revisit the drawing board.

References

Argyle, M. (1969) *Social Interaction*. New York: Atherton Press.
Bell, B. and Driver, R. (1985) 'Childrens Learning in Science Project', *Education In Science*, 108, pp. 19–20.
Bell, B., Watts, D. M. and Ellington, K. (eds) (1984) 'Learning Doing and Understanding in Science'. The proceedings of a conference. London: SSCR.
Bentley, D. (1983) 'Teachers' Hidden Messages', *British Journal of Educational Psychology*, 53, pp. 121–7.
Bentley, D. (1985) 'It's not what you say . . .: youngsters' constructions of the meanings of teachers' non-verbal behaviour'. Paper presented to the 6th International Congress on Personal Construct Psychology, Cambridge, August.
Clark, H. (1985) Thoughts on the epistemological – effects of conceptual change teaching. Comments developed for the 1985 meeting of the Invisible College of Researchers on Teaching. Chicago, 20 March, personal communication.
Department of Education and Science (1985) *Science Education 5–16: a statement of policy*. London: HMSO.
Driver, R. (1984) 'A Review of Research into Children's Thinking and Learning in Science', in B. Bell, D. M. Watts and K. Ellington (eds), *Learning Doing and Understanding in Science*. The proceedings of a conference. London: SSCR.
Driver, R. and Erickson, G. (1983) 'Theories-in-action: Some Theoretical and Empirical Issues in the Study of Students' Conceptual Frameworks in Science', *Studies in Science Education*, 10, pp. 37–60.
Driver, R. and Oldham, V. (1985) 'A Constructivist Approach to Curriculum in Science'. Paper prepared for the Symposium 'Personal Construction of Meaning in Educational Settings', British Educational Research Association, Sheffield, August.
Feldman, R. S. and Orchowsky, S. (1982) 'Race and Performance of Students as Determinants of Teacher Non-verbal Behaviour', *Contemporary Education Psychology*, 4, pp. 324–33.
Gilbert, J. K. and Watts, D. M. (1983) 'Concepts, Misconcepts and Alternative Conceptions: Changing Perspectives in Science Education', *Studies in Science Education*, 10, pp. 61–98.
Horscroft, D. and Pope, M. L. (1985) 'Students and Teachers', Module A2 Study Guide, Diploma in the Practice of Science Education, University of Surrey/ Roehampton Institute.
Marland, M. (1975) *The Craft of the Classroom: a guide to survival*. London: Heinemann.
Minstrell, J. (1982) 'Explaining the 'at Rest' condition of an Object', *Physics Teacher*, 20 January, pp. 10–14.
Nussbaum, J. and Novick, S. (1981) 'Brainstorming in the Classroom to Invent a

Model: a Case Study', *School Science Review*, 62, pp. 771–8.

Osborne, R. and Freyberg, P. (1985) *Learning in Science*. London: Heinemann.

Physics Education (1985) Volume 20.

Posner, G. J., Strike, K. A., Hewson, P. W. and Gertzog, W. A. (1982) 'Accommodation of a Scientific Conception: Toward a Theory of Conceptual Change', *Science Education*, 66, 2, pp. 211–27.

Richey, A. and Richey, B. (1982) 'Nonverbal Behaviour in the Classroom', *Psychology in the Schools*, 19, pp. 224–31.

Secondary Science Curriculum Review (1983) *Science Education 11–16: proposals for action and consultation*. London: SSCR.

Shayer, M. and Adey, P. (1981) *Towards a Science of Science Teaching*. London: Heinemann.

Strike, K. A. and Posner, G. J. (1985) 'A Conceptual Change View of Learning and Understanding', in L. H. T. West and A. L. Pines (eds) *Cognitive Structure and Conceptual Change*. London: Academic Press.

Swift, D. J. (1984) 'Against Structuralism: is Genetic Epistemology a "Conservative-Activist" Theory of Knowledge?' Paper presented to the 10th Annual Conference of British Educational Research Association, University of Lancaster, August. Mimeograph, University of Surrey.

Watts, D. M. and Bentley, D. (1984) 'The Personal Parameters of Cognition: Two Aims in Science Education', *Oxford Review of Education*, 10, pp. 309–17.

Watts, D. M. and Pope, M. L. (1985) Modulation and fragmentation: some cases from science education. Paper presented to the 6th International Congress on Personal Construct Psychology, Cambridge, August.

West, L. H. T. and Pines, A. L. (1985) *Cognitive Structure and Conceptual Change*. London: Academic Press.

3.2

Three Approaches to Teaching and Learning in Education: Behavioural, Piagetian, and Information-Processing

Emanuel J. Mason
Patricia Cegelka, Rena Lewis, Suzanne Henry, Jill Larkin and Fred Danner

The problem: The relationship between theory and practice in teaching: *Emmanuel J. Mason*

In the education literature, three approaches to teaching seem prominent. The first, and perhaps the most well-known in education is behaviourism, both instrumental and classical. In this approach, focus is on behaviour external to the organism that can be observed. The behaviourist approach has produced a fairly consistent formula for instruction which involves reinforcement of correct responses, scheduling of reinforcement, and building complex behaviour by chaining simple behaviours, or shaping simple into complex behaviours (Snelbecker, 1974).

Another approach to how the child matures psychologically can be traced to the 'organismic' cognitive development model of Piaget (Inhelder and Piaget, 1958). According to this view, the child develops through a series of stages towards mature thinking. Educational programmes designed with this point of view would emphasise such Piagetian concepts as logic, classification, transitive ordering, and reversibility. For example, Kamii and De Vries (1976), and Copeland (1979) have discussed the teaching of number concepts to children using a Piagetian paradigm in which the child's ability to understand class and transitive ordering is emphasised.

The third approach to children's thinking is based on computer-like theoretical models of thinking. Among these approaches one might recognise information processing (e.g., Newell and Simon, 1972; Trabasso *et al.*, 1978), or memory (e.g. Loftus and Loftus, 1976; Kail, 1979). Such models of thinking tend to lead to algorithimic approaches to curriculum design (Brown, 1979; Shavelson, 1981).

There have been writers (e.g. Murray, 1980) who have argued convincingly that while theory may provide useful concepts for understanding the practice of teaching and learning, the translation of theory directly into techniques is not a simple matter. This is not a new position among behavioural scientists. For example, Murray cites William James' 1892 series of talks to teachers that 'Psychology is a science; and teaching is an art . . .', and that while psychology cannot contribute directly to teaching practice, it can help one to explain and understand the phenomenon of teaching.

In the following sections, each author was asked to explain how they would use their own theoretical orientation to teach secondary school students in a geometry class about the slope of a line. Commonalities and differences are explored in the final section by Fred Danner, a developmental and educational psychologist.

Teaching about slopes: A behavioural view: *Patricia Cegelka and Rena Lewis*

As behaviourists of long-standing we were instructed to analyse the problems of teaching slope from an 'operant conditioning point of view'. We feared that the term 'operant conditioning' might be construed too narrowly as involving only reinforcement of appropriate or target behaviours as they occur in the environment. As Skinner pointed out in *Technology of Teaching* (1968), simply waiting for behaviour to occur so that it may be reinforced is insufficient. '. . . Shaping behaviour by progressive approximation can be tedious [and] there are better ways' (p. 206).

This implies a broader approach to instruction than only contingent reinforcement. This broader approach is subsumed under the heading of Applied Behavioural Analysis, the primary features of which are:

1 statement of the desired behaviour in clearly observable terms,
2 identification of available reinforcers for shaping the behaviour,
3 specifying the contingent relationship between the target behaviours and the reinforcers,
4 developing the instructional programme.

Each of these considerations will be explored as a preface to presenting the instructional sequence we developed from the applied behavioural analysis perspective.

Statement of the desired behaviour in clear, observable terms

An applied behavioural analysis approach requires that the desired behaviour be stated in terms of instructional objectives that involve clearly observable behaviours. [. . .] The problem statement that we were given stated that 'at the end of instruction and as a result of it, the student will be expected to understand. . . .' As 'understanding' is itself a hypothetical condition observable only by learners themselves and not directly observable by others, it was necessary for us to further delineate the behaviours expected of the learners. This delineation in the form of behavioural objectives constitutes an important feature of the instructional programme we developed.

Specification of available reinforcers

The basic premise of applied behavioural analysis is that behaviour is a function of its consequences. Hence, the selection of consequences that act as reinforcers is of great importance. In approaching this task, one must be cognizant of the fact that not all consequences affect all learners in the same way. Some students may require arbitrary reinforcers – such as money, points, candy or any of a thousand others – while others will work for more 'natural' reinforcers, e.g., praise, knowledge of the results, grades. Generally the teacher will want to develop reinforcement hierarchies for each student. However, [. . .] we have assumed that knowledge of results, perhaps coupled with standard grading consequences, is sufficiently reinforcing for the desired problem-solving behaviours to occur.

Specifying the contingent relationship between the occurrences of the target behaviours and reinforcers

We have stated that we are approaching this task on the assumption that so-called natural reinforcers will maintain the specific behaviours. The contingent relationship of the standard grading procedures is generally of a delayed nature – delayed either by several hours, days or even weeks. The other assumed 'natural reinforcer', knowledge of accuracy of responses, implies a continuous schedule of reinforcement, such as that provided by programmed instruction. Here, for each problem-solving behaviour emitted, the student is provided with feedback as to the accuracy of his or her response. This type of reinforcement schedule is recognised as being particularly effective in building or developing a response. It is dependent on a carefully developed sequence of task components. The employment of task analysis is integral to a programmed approach to learning.

[. . .] It is through the careful sequencing of the task steps that the instructional programme is developed; it is through appropriate reinforcing of progress through these steps that effective learning is possible.

Development of the instructional programme

[. . .] A key element in an applied behavioural analysis approach is the skilfully developed instructional programme that moves the students through a series of progressive approximations to the target behaviour (Skinner, 1968). The physical structure of a programme usually makes the student's progress conspicuous, both to himself and to others (Skinner, 1968).

One of the really tragic misuses of so-called behaviour modification has been the attempt by teachers to maintain some level of classroom control through contingent reinforcement when the instructional programmes have been inappropriately and/or randomly presented. These attempts are based on a failure to grasp the importance of a sound instructional programme designed to move the learner through increasingly complex steps to the target behaviour.

The instructional programme developed by us for teaching the slope of the line is based on a task analysis of the target behaviours into discrete components that shape the correct behavioural responses and provide immediate feedback (reinforcement) to the student. An important component of the instructional programme is the specification of the prerequisite skills and an important step in implementing the programme is the assessment of students to determine the presence of the prerequisite skills. Further, it is also important to assess students to determine reinforcement hierarchies; in other words, the teacher must know for each student which consequences will serve to reinforce the desired behaviours.

An example of behavioural instruction: Programmed learning

An instructional programme may be delivered to students in a variety of ways. The teacher may structure the antecedent conditions through verbal presentations (with or without print and media aids), or an autoinstructional learning situation may be designed. For purposes of this discussion, we have selected the auto-instructional approach in which students are presented with a print programme which elicits written responses. Each student proceeds through the programme at his or her own pace; correct responses are provided to allow immediate confirmation or correction. More elaborate programmes include subroutines to which students may branch if responses are incorrect.

In order to design a programme for the teaching of slope, it is necessary to specify two major types of behaviours, the entry level skills of the students and the desired terminal behaviours. It is assumed that the [. . .] students in this situation are able to (1) perform simple arithmetic calculations with whole numbers, fractions, and negative numbers; (2) define trigonometric terms such as tangent and angle of inclination; and (3) plot points on a grid and, given a point, identify its coordinates. The target behaviours then become:

1 Given the coordinates of any two points of a straight line, the student will calculate slope,
2 Given grids with units of varying sizes, the student will identify lines of the same slope,
3 The student will demonstrate whether the slope of z with respect to y is equal to the slope of y with respect to x.

These three target behaviours represent a type of task analysis of the goal behaviour, the 'understanding' of the concept of slope. Since these are behavioural re-statements of the original three problem conditions, we shall retain them for purposes of discussion. However, it is likely that a behavioural task analysis of the goal behaviour would produce a different sequence of skills or even different target behaviours.

Let us consider the programme sequence for the first objective, the calculation of slope. One possible learning sequence is:

1 given coordinates of 2 points, plot line
2 given a line and 2 points, identify coordinates of the points
3 demonstrate that slope of a line is equal to the tangent of the angle of inclination
4 given a line and 2 points, describe procedure for calculation of tangent of the angle of inclination
5 given a line and 2 points, calculate slope using the formula

$$\text{slope} = \frac{Y_1 - Y_2}{X_1 - X_2}$$

6 given a line and 2 points, calculate slope.

Each of these subskills would require a sub-programme that would include (1) presentation of the task, (2) opportunity for practice and immediate feedback, and (3) assessment of mastery.

It is necessary to allow sufficient response opportunities within the programme. For example, in the fifth skill which deals with the calculation of slope given the formula, several practice problems would be provided.

Once the original programme is developed, individualisation may be incorporated into the system. The amount of practice may be varied according to the student's rate of correct responses. Or, students may branch to sub-programmes if they are deficient in prerequisite skills and/or if their incorrect responses typify certain types of errors. If such programme modifications do not reduce error rate to an acceptable level, the schedule of reinforcement and the reinforcement menu may be examined.

Throughout the programme, the student's mastery of skills is assessed. Mastery level may be set in various ways such as number of consecutive correct responses, or percentage of correct responses. Maintenance of acquired skills is monitored in later programme steps. Future response opportunities for target behaviours are assumed; if such opportunities did not exist, it is assumed that the skill would not be taught. Generalisation of skills to similar situations is also assessed as response opportunities occur.

In conclusion, the applied behavioural analysis approach to instruction is one that considers those variables in the environment that may be manipulated by the teacher – antecedent learning conditions, response opportunities, and contingent reinforcement of responses. The desired target behaviour is analysed and divided into subcomponents which are then arranged in an instructional sequence. This sequence is then presented to the learner by some means and appropriate responses are reinforced. In this way, the teacher can effectively control the conditions necessary for learning.

Development of knowledge of the slope of a line: A Piagetian approach: *Suzanne Henry*

In order to develop a Piagetian approach to the problem of teaching the slope of a line, some theoretical contexts must be set. Many highly qualified educators have written on the relationship between teaching and Piaget's theories, yet the relationship remains difficult to decipher. [. . .]

Two theoretical contexts are necessary for a Piagetian approach. One concerns world hypotheses, and the other, competence-performance models. A world hypothesis, as defined by Reese and Overton (1970) is an implicit metaphysical system which embodies a set of beliefs about the essential characteristics of man and the nature of reality. Piagetian theory is firmly rooted in the organismic world hypothesis and an understanding of the organismic hypothesis is important for a clear understanding of why Piagetian theory is what it is. The basic metaphor of the organismic view is a living organised system whose parts gain their meaning from their inter-relationship in a structured whole. The task of any organismic theory thus becomes the description of the organisation of these structures, and if it is a developmental theory, specification of the sequence of emergence of these structures. Ideally, the theory will also indicate how transition from one period of structural organisation to another occurs.

The organismic world hypothesis also views the individual as inherently and spontaneously active. As a result, change and developmental are given, and the individual is the source of action and knowledge. The epistemological position is that of constructivism and this implies that the individual actively participates in knowing the world. Thus knowledge about the world is organised as structures which have been constructed through the activity of the individual, and which mediate the individual's behaviour. Furthermore, as structures change developmentally, there is a qualitative change in how the individual knows the world because each structure has different organisational properties.

The second theoretical context within which I would like to place Piagetian theory is that of a competence model. Flavell and Wohlwill (1969) were among the first to relate the competence/performance distinction to cognitive development, and Overton and Newman (1981) have [. . .] provided a further elaboration of the distinction. As defined by these authors, a competence model is an idealised description of how the structures of knowledge within a given domain are organised. The description includes those general features which are necessary to account for the consistency of behaviour across individuals. However, competence models are not concerned with how knowledge is expressed as behaviour, specification of the efficient causal determinants of behaviour, and the role of individual differences in behaviour. These questions are left to performance or activation/utilisation models.

Piagetian theory reflects these two theoretical contexts in several ways. First, Piaget's description of how knowledge is acquired and changes developmentally is explicitly placed within the individual through the complementary processes of assimilation and accommodation, and the general developmental process of equilibration. Second, the emphasis placed on stages of development that are characterised by different organisational structures also emphasises the qualitative differences in the child's knowledge during the course of development. Finally, the structures which characterise each stage reflect different levels of cognitive organisation that differ in their formal descriptions. Thus Piagetian theory embodies the assumptions of the organismic world hypothesis in its description of stages of development with differing forms of structural organisation, and in its emphasis on the individual's accommodation and assimilation activities and the general process of equilibration. Furthermore, the formal, abstract description of each stage's structural organisation serves to define Piagetian theory as a competence model.

If Piagetian theory is based on an organismic world view and represents a competence model of cognitive development, what then are its implications for education? I think Piagetian theory has implications for two aspects of teaching – teacher training and student assessment. During the course of training the teacher needs to acquire two types of knowledge about the student: (1) What characteristics does that student share with his or her peers? (2) What is unique about a particular student? Piagetian theory provides a rich description of the consistencies across individuals within a given stage of cognitive development. It is critical, I believe, for teachers to have a clear understanding of the stage-related characteristics of the students' knowledge and thought. In addition, Piagetian theory provides a clear outline of the dimensions along which cognition changes during the course of development from one stage to another. Thus, I would argue that without a firm grounding in Piagetian theory, teachers cannot accurately understand their students. In order to know what is unique about a student's thought, one must first know the general features of thought that the student and his or her peers bring to the classroom. It is the cognitive consistencies within each stage and developmentally between stages that Piagetian theory has magnificently described, and teacher training curricula need to be firmly grounded in this theory.

The second area of education for which Piagetian theory has implications is student assessment. Here, I am not referring to assessment of normative achievement. I am defining assessment as a two stage procedure: first, development of research designed to describe the different levels in the student's changing knowledge about curriculum concepts and skills, and second, diagnosis of a particular student's level of knowledge with respect to this description. [. . .] Assessment of the interrelationships between structural knowledge, curriculum content, and some description of the student's changing knowledge is critical to the formulation of effective teaching techniques.

Teaching about slope

What then would be a Piagetian approach to the instructional problem of teaching the slope of a line [. . .]? An educator would begin by analysing how the concept of slope is related to the structural properties of the Piagetian stages. Thus, different definitions of the slope concept would be formulated and these definitions would be organised as a sequence that parallelled the structural differences associated with different levels of cognitive development.

Concrete operational thought is defined in terms of the logic of classes and the logic of relations and is directed to the organisation of objects in immediately given reality. The operations of class intersection and serial ordering would be reflected in a definition of the slope concept that included the ability to place a series of points at their intersect on the X and Y axes and organisation of points along either a vertical or horizontal line.

A second level of concrete operational knowledge of the slope concept relates to the correspondence operation and would be reflected in the child's discovery that there is a relationship between the horizontal and vertical dimensions as a result of observing concurrent changes of a series of points along the X and Y axes.

Formal operational thought is applied to propositions rather than discrete objects. As a result, the slope concept would be defined in terms of the horizontal and vertical dimensions of space. The [. . .] formal operations structure would be reflected in the slope concept as knowledge about how relative changes in distance on the horizontal and vertical dimensions interact to produce differences in the slope of a line. Thus, slope is now defined as a ratio between change in distance on the vertical axis and change in distance on the horizontal axis.

In summary, I have briefly outlined a sequence of levels of knowledge that define the concept of the slope of a line. Each level reflects the structural properties of a particular stage or substage within Piagetian theory. The sequence proceeds from (1) placement of actual points in space at their intersect on the X and Y axes and the ordering of points along a vertical or horizontal line, to (2) discovery of the qualitative relationship between the vertical and horizontal dimensions, to (3) discovery that the slope is determined by the ratio between a change in distance on the vertical axis and a change in distance on the horizontal axis.

Once a sequence such as I have outlined is formulated, the Piagetian educator would empirically determine its validity for teaching through a programme of research designed to assess students' knowledge of the slope concept. Further differentiation of the sequence of the slope concept might be made as a result of insights gained from these data. The final sequence of concept development could then be used for two purposes: (1) as a method for diagnosing a particular student's level of knowledge of the concept; (2) as a blueprint for the sequence of steps in a curriculum relating to the concept. [. . .] The teacher's awareness that concrete operational thought is confined to discrete situations and is not easily generalised would lead her or him to employ teaching techniques that used actual objects that could be physically organised in space (e.g. checkers on a board) and that the student could readily manipulate. Thus, the concrete operational student's acquisition of knowledge about the slope of the line would be facilitated through direct experience and observation of how the slope of a line changed as a function of the relative movement of objects in space. In contrast, the teacher's awareness that formal operational thought is propositional and abstract might lead to use of a more didactic approach which emphasised the formulation of rules and formulas that are embodied in the mathematical calculation of the slope of a line.

This brief description of a Piagetian approach to teaching the slope of a line can only provide a sketch of what would in the end be a very detailed curriculum sequence and set of teaching techniques that were geared to the different levels of cognitive development of students. However, the starting points must be a teacher who is well versed in Piagetian theory, and a programme of research that describes the developmental changes which occur in the student's knowledge about the slope of a line.

An information-processing approach to teaching about slopes: *Jill Larkin*

[. . .] Information-processing psychology views the human mind as an entity capable of taking in information, processing and storing it in a wide variety of ways, and occasionally reporting some of that information.

This branch of cognitive psychology has made extensive use of computer models that can describe mechanisms through which the human mind might process information. One should bear in mind that these computer implemented models are *not* like structured FORTRAN or ALGOL programmes. They are flexible systems that do not 'execute' like a structured flow-chart or pattern, but instead are capable of bringing to bear a large amount of knowledge to respond to new situations. Computer 'programs' of this type are capable of a variety of activities (e.g. playing chess and backgammon, solving physics problems, planning a shopping expedition). Such activities are ordinarily associated with intelligence.

The use of computer models provides us with a useful working definition of the kind of understanding that is central to many instructional tasks. When a problem-solver, human or machine, works to solve a problem, he/she/it must construct some internal representation of the problem that can be manipulated in efforts to develop a solution. This internal representation corresponds to the solver's understanding of the problem. There are clearly different kinds and levels of problem representation (or different kinds of understanding) that may vary in effectiveness for finding solutions. In both physics and in elementary arithmetic word problems, I have found it useful to roughly distinguish three kinds of understanding.

The first kind of representation I call *naive*. The entities included in such representations are familiar everyday objects, for example, cats, coffee cups, and steepness. Rules used to infer new information in naive representations also correspond to everyday experience. For example, cats can move independently across the table while coffee cups can not. Our capacity to reason about naive problem representations is very strong because it is supported by a life-time collection of knowledge.

Many problems can be solved on the basis of a naive representation. [. . .] All one needs to know to solve the following problem is that slope means steepness. Then one's naive knowledge about steepness of hills can take over. Certainly this is not the only way this question can be answered, but it is one effective way, and it serves to illustrate dramatically the power of tapping naive knowledge.

Problem 1:   The student is expected to understand that the slope of X with respect to Y does not equal the slope of Y with respect to X, i.e.,

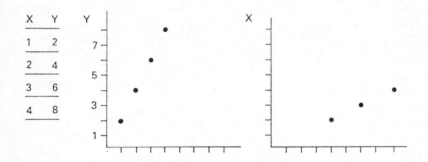

Thus my approach to developing an understanding of problem 1 would be to begin by simply telling students that (among other things) slope means steepness, and that steeper graphs have larger slopes. Of course, this would have to be supported by some active use of this knowledge, for example, in saying whether two graphs had the same slope or in saying which of two graphs had a larger slope.[1]

The second level of representation, I refer to as mathematical representation. These representations are composed of entities that have special meaning in the discipline of mathematics. Examples include lines, sets, and irrational numbers. The rules used to infer new information about these entities are also mathematically based, and involve knowledge not available to individuals without special training. For clarity, I find it useful to exclude from mathematical representations the straightforward algorithmic knowledge needed simply to compute an answer (e.g. the arithmetic 'facts', the long division algorithm).

For mathematics problems, mathematical representations are particularly rich structures essential to creative insightful problem-solving. Problem 2 (below) provides a good example of a problem that (beyond a trivial analysis) requires a mathematical representation.

Problem 2:   The student is expected to understand that changing the size of the units of X will not change the slope of Y, even though the scatter diagram appears changed, i.e.,

What knowledge would be required for a computer-implemented model to address the situation in problem 2? First, the machine would need knowledge about the ratios of sides of similar triangles. Knowledge of similar triangles must be connected to the specific knowledge structure describing the definition of the slope of a line. Otherwise there would be no way of accessing the similar triangles' information from the context of finding the slope.[2]

Finally, there must be a large number of connections between these various structures. This helps to insure that the knowledge can be accessed when it is needed. There should, in particular, be some connections to the individual's original naive understanding of slope as steepness. Indeed, the simple question of whether the two graphs in problem 2 have different slopes could be answered (without much understanding) on the basis of this naive knowledge alone. For an individual with a more sophisticated mathematical understanding of the situation, this naive inference serves as useful confirmation. This process of developing a rich set of associative links among many knowledge structures is a process that never ends. We are all capable of acquiring more understanding about even elementary aspects of our disciplines.

Thus, in designing instruction relevant to problem 2, I would spend a large amount of time developing a rich set of connections for inferring knowledge about the ratios of sides of similar triangles in the context of finding the slope of lines. Developing these inference rules would probably best be done by active processing (i.e., working a number of examples). This development is definitely different from being able to implement a computational algorithm for finding slope.

The third representation is what I call computational representation. Included in this are mathematical symbols, in this case algebraic symbols and operators, and numerals. The rules for inferring new information in this kind of representation are the algorithmic rules of computation, in this case rules of algebra.

Problem 3: A teacher wishes to teach students the meaning of slope in the equation for a straight line. At the end of instruction and as a result of it, the student will be expected to understand that:

$$\text{slope} = \frac{Y_1 - Y_2}{X_1 - X_2}$$

for any two points (X_1, Y_1) and (X_2, Y_2)

Problem 3 provides a good example of one that might be solved largely in a computational representation. The student needs explicitly to be told and to practice that the equation in problem 3 relates five elements (the slope, and four coordinate values). If any four of these numbers are known, the fifth can be found by substituting the appropriate values and solving for it.

However, such computational knowledge, stored in isolation, is tremendously vulnerable to forgetting. Indeed, all knowledge may be vulnerable to forgetting, but computational knowledge may pose special problems. The implication is that since knowledge is vulnerable to forgetting, one cannot safely learn isolated algorithms without strongly connecting them to the mathematical thinking on which they are based. Without the constraints these connections provide, reconstructing pieces of the algorithm that have been forgotten is almost impossible.

Thus, in teaching knowledge relevant to problem 3, the student should definitely be taught a computational algorithm and should practice it until it can be implemented reliably in a variety of situations. However, this algorithm cannot simply be a rote mechanism if it is to persist reliably in memory in its correct form. It must be connected to the mathematical knowledge discussed earlier, specifically in this case to the knowledge about ratios of length of sides of similar triangles.

Summary and conclusions

In this chapter, I have suggested some instructional implications of an approach based on information-processing psychology, a branch of psychology that views the human mind as a processor of information, and analyses tasks in terms of the kind of information that must be brought to bear to achieve the task. It is further concerned with how this information is stored and how it can be accessed.

My first suggestion is that for instruction in technical domains it is often useful to separate knowledge being used in the following three areas: (1) *Naive knowledge* represents knowledge of the everyday world. Many problems can be solved or checked using this knowledge, and students too often neglect it for a mistaken idea that mathematics problems must be solved 'mathematically'. (2) *Mathematical knowledge* is the rich conceptual knowledge of mathematical entities and of the rules for inferring information about them. Although it is only loosely linked to computation, I think this knowledge is the heart of even elementary mathematics. It requires extensive emphasis in teaching, and the student must be actively working with it to learn it. The reason is that many more links among items of knowledge are built when a learner is actively generating his own inferences. (3) *Computational knowledge* is the knowledge of how to implement computational algorithms. Because this knowledge, like other kinds, is vulnerable to forgetting, forgetting a portion of an algorithm means it will probably be implemented incorrectly unless the forgotten part can be regenerated. It is crucial that algorithmic knowledge be tightly connected to a well developed structure of mathematical knowledge. [. . .]

Three approaches to teaching slopes: Discussion and conclusions: *Fred Danner*

Should teachers be concerned with theories of learning? What practical difference do they make? [. . .] The theoretical perspective one takes regarding learners and tasks does make a practical difference for instruction. I will briefly describe how the theoretical perspectives differ in primary focus, how each views the task and the learner, and what these differences imply for instruction.

Primary focus

To solve any instructional problem, one must at least attend to both the task and the learner and each of the articles did so. However, there were sharp differences between the three approaches in their primary focus. Cegelka and Lewis, representing the behavioural approach, focused on the specific task and the observable behaviours required to complete it; Henry, representing the Piagetian approach, focused on the learner and the schemes which he/she brings to bear on a broad range of similar problems; and Larkin, representing the information processing approach, focused on how the task is represented by the learner. Each of these approaches, then, addresses the instructional problem from a different perspective – a perspective which strongly implies where one ought to direct one's attention in order to teach the material. Perhaps these perspectives can best be seen by considering what each of the participants wanted to know (or assume) about the task and the learner.

The task and the learner

Behavioural approach:
Cegelka and Lewis found it necessary to redefine the problem before they could proceed with their behavioural analysis. Their major focus was to determine specific component behaviours of the task and how to sequence them for efficient instruction. They placed much less emphasis on the learner, asking themselves only what prerequisite skills the learners might already possess and what would serve as effective reinforcers as they proceed through the task sequence.

Piagetian approach:
Henry reversed the order of importance, placing her emphasis on the learner. While she too analysed the task, it was not to determine the subskills necessary for its solution but rather to judge how learners at different cognitive levels would likely understand it. The specific task itself was not nearly as important to her as it was to Cegelka and Lewis since she viewed it as but one example of a larger class of problems involving the coordination of two dimensions. Therefore, she argued that the learner's underlying competence in this coordination of dimensions is critical for understanding his/her performance and is the key to promoting further progress.

Information-processing approach:
Larkin's position is a bit more difficult to characterise because it emphasises both the task and the learner in a way which is different from either the behavioural or Piagetian approaches. For her, the key to solving an instructional problem is understanding how it is represented by the learner. Therefore, she used the tasks to demonstrate how different kinds of problem representations could be manipulated to solve them and she emphasised the importance of determining what information the learner has stored in memory and how it is represented.

Implications for instruction

What does it mean? Do these approaches simply consist of three different sets of jargon with no practical consequences? I do not think so and the proof of this is in the very different proposals each has for instruction.

Cegelka and Lewis, with their behavioural focus on the task and component behaviours, indicate exactly how they would proceed. They would establish clearly observable desired behaviours, set up a sequence of progressively more difficult slope subtasks, and have the students practice at each level in the sequence until they reached some designated level of mastery. They also advocate the use of individually tailored reinforcement schedules to help move the students through the sequence. In their model, the teacher is the manager of instruction – the one who 'can effectively control the conditions necessary for learning' by eliciting and reinforcing correct responses.

The Piagetian approach, with its focus on the learner, provides a very different guide for action. If, as Henry states, 'the individual is the source of action and knowledge', then the teacher's job is not to reinforce correct answers but to strengthen the learner's own process of reasoning. To do so requires a teacher who is willing to accept and encourage 'incorrect' responses. Incorrect is placed in quotation marks to capture the Piagetian view that there are predictable developmental sequences of knowing each step of which is seen as correct by the knower (Duckworth, 1973, 1979). The Piagetian teacher, therefore, must begin by respecting the learner's view, understanding where it comes from, and creating opportunities for appropriate challenges to it.

Appropriate challenges are those which actively engage the learner on tasks which are just slightly ahead of him/her in a developmental progression. To choose such tasks for each child, the teacher would need a firm understanding of both the general features of children's thought and the specific cognitive levels of individual children. [. . .]

In Henry's model, the teacher is a perceptive guide who encourages and challenges learners to construct their own knowledge by providing them with ample opportunities to seek connections between related domains of knowledge.

The information-processing approach, with its focus on mental representation, implies a third model of instruction. Larkin views the human mind as a sophisticated processor of information which solves problems (and learns) by creating and manipulating mental representations. Since there are many ways problems can be represented and some are more broadly applicable than others, the teacher's job is to help children create effective representations, call them up when appropriate, and connect them to their previous knowledge of the world.

In effect, the teacher is a creative problem solver who analyses instructional problems in terms of how they might be represented, encourages students to apply their naive understandings, and then presents more powerful representations. [. . .]

Conclusion

Each of the three theoretical views presented here indicates a role for the teacher. I have called these roles: *effective manager*, *perceptive guide*, and *creative problem-solver*. The perspectives and assumptions that are the foundations of each theory chosen might reflect the differences between these roles more clearly but the point is that they are different and thus lead to very different teaching styles. This [. . .] demonstrates that a teacher's perspective – his or her theory of learning – has a very strong impact on what he or she might do as a teacher.

Notes

1 Of course, this trivialises this problem. A full understanding of the relation between reciprocal rates involves more mathematical understanding of the kind to be discussed.
2 I realise belatedly that, in fact, similar triangles must ordinarily follow slopes in a normal curriculum. However, I think the point of the example still stands.

References

Brown, M. (1979) 'Cognitive Development and Learning of Mathematics', in Floid, A. (ed.), *Cognitive Development in the School Years*. New York: Wiley.

Copeland, R. W. (1979) *How Children Learn Mathematics*. New York: Macmillan.

Duckworth, E. (1973) 'The Having of Wonderful Ideas', in Ralph, J. and Schwebel, M. (eds), *Piaget in the Classroom*. New York: Basic Books.

Duckworth, E. (1979) 'Either We're Too Early and They Can't Learn it or We're Too Late and They Know it Already: The Dilemma of Applying Piaget', *Harvard Educational Review*, 49, pp. 297–312.

Flavell, J. H. and Wohlwill, J. F. (1969) 'Formal and functional aspects of cognitive development', in Elkind, D. and Flavell, J. H. (eds), *Studies in Cognitive Development: Essays in Honor of Jean Piaget*. New York: Oxford University Press.

Inhelder, B. and Piaget, J. (1958) *The Growth of Logical Thinking from Childhood to Adolescence*. New York: Basic Books.

Kail, R. (1979) *The Development of Memory in Children*. San Francisco: W. H. Freeman.

Kamii, C. and De Vries, R. (1976) *Piaget, Children, and Number*. Washington, D.C.: National Association for the Education of Young Children.

Loftus, C. R. and Loftus, E. F. (1976) *Human Memory: The Processing of Information*. New York: Halstead.

Murray, F. B. (1980) 'The generation of educational practice from developmental theory', in Mogil, S. and Mogil, C. (eds), *Toward a Theory of Psychological Developmental*. Windsor: NFER.

Newell, A. and Simon, H. (1972) *Human Problem Solving*. Englewood Cliffs, NJ: Prentice-Hall.

Overton, W. F. and Newman, J. L. (1982) 'Cognitive development: A competence activation utilisation approach', in Field, T. *et al.* (eds), *Review of Developmental Psychology*. New York: John Wiley and Sons.

Reese, H. W. and Overton, W. F. (1970) 'Models of Development and Theories of Development', in Goulet, R. and Baltes, P. (eds) *Lifespan Developmental Psychology: Research and Theory*. New York: Academic Press.

Shavelson, R. J. (1981) 'Teaching Mathematics: Contributions of Cognitive Research', *Educational Psychologist*, 16, pp. 23–44.

Skinner, B. F. (1968) *The Technology of Teaching*. New York: Appleton-Century-Croft.

Snelbecker, G. E. (1974) *Learning Theory, Instructional Theory, and Psychoeducational Design*. New York: McGraw-Hill.

Trabasso, T., Isen, A. H., Dolecki, P., McLanahan, A. C., Riley, C. A. and Tucker, T. (1978) 'How do children solve class-inclusion problems?', in Siegler, R. S. (ed.), *Children's Thinking: What Develops?* Hilldendale, NJ: Erlbaum.

3.3

Developmental Psychology and the Child-Centred Pedagogy: The Insertion of Piaget into Early Education*

Valerie Walkerdine

Introduction

The British primary school is taken to be a paradigm of practice for a considerable proportion of the Western World. Here, children are to be enabled to develop at their own pace, to work individually, to be free and to grow up into rational adults. Such at least is the ambition of the pedagogy. In her book *Children's Minds* (1978) Margaret Donaldson begins by painting for us a picture of such a school, with children full of wonderment at the joy of learning. What, she asks, goes wrong? Why, in this model, do so many children apparently fail to learn and why does such a promising start end in failure for so many of them? The dream of the pedagogy which will set children free, which will serve as the motor of liberation, is not a new one: it is present in the early progressive movement of the 1920s and 1930s and is a familiar feature of the progressivism central to radical approaches to education in the 1970s. Is it a pipe-dream, this dream of the pedagogy to aid the liberation of children and thus promote some transformation in the social domain? Is it that the conditions for such a pedagogy are not possible? Why do so many children fail and what part does developmental psychology play in all this?
[. . .] I shall argue that one of the major problems with the notion of developmental psychology as implicated in a pedagogy of libera-

---

* The Walkerdine chapter considers the nature of the child-centred pedagogy and examines in-depth the 'historical conditions which produced the possibility of the developmental psychology/child-centred pedagogy couple'. An overview of the relevant history, rather than the detailed chapter examples, are included in this edited version of the chapter.

tion is in the way the terms of the argument are posed. Margaret Donaldson's (1978) answer lies in a *more effective psychology* which can be more accurate in telling us how children 'really learn' and therefore how to produce better, lasting learning. This seems an unproblematic enough goal. But is it as simple as it looks? What I aim to demonstrate is that the very lynchpin of developmental psychology, the 'developing child', is an object premised on the location of certain capacities within 'the child' and therefore within the domain of psychology. Other features are thereby externalised as aspects of a social domain which influence or affect the pattern of development and, consequently, the conditions of educability. It is axiomatic to developmental psychology that there exist a set of empirically demonstrable foundations for its claims to truth about the psychological development of children. My aim [. . .] is to demonstrate the problem in assuming that the way out of dilemmas about the possibility of both a liberatory pedagogy and a 'social' developmental psychology is in the limit-conditions of the project of a developmental psychology itself. [. . .] My task [. . .] is twofold: it is to demonstrate that developmental psychology is premised on a set of claims to truth which are historically specific, and which are not the only or necessary way to understand children. In addition I seek to establish that those practices, such as particular pedagogies and forms of schooling, are not mere applications of a scientific apparatus, but should be understood as centrally and strategically implicated in the possibility of a developmental psychology itself.

These are shock tactics, and they are intended to go beyond epistemological critiques. For example, epistemological critiques of Piaget [. . .] certainly examine the claims to truth upon which Piaget's enterprise is founded. However, they rely on treating the claims as valid or invalid in a way which fails to locate them in a historically specific regime of truth. Locating the work of Piaget within the constitution of the developmental psychology/child-centred pedagogy couple allows me to examine the very formation of the objects upon which Piaget's enterprise was founded and the practices in which his work was utilised.

Particular disciplines, regimes of truth, bodies of knowledge, make possible both *what can be said* and *what can be done*: both the object of science and the object of pedagogic practices. Pedagogic practices then are totally saturated with the notion of a normalised sequence of child development. [. . .] The apparatuses and mechanisms of schooling which do this range from the architecture of the school and the seating arrangements of the classroom to the curriculum materials and techniques of assessment. [. . .] If we examine particular apparatuses, it is possible to display the intimate connection between the practices and the set of assumptions about learning and teaching premised on child development.

The child-centred pedagogy in operation

I hear and I forget
I see and I remember
I do and I understand

The above quotation forms the frontispiece to the first teachers' guide to the Nuffield Mathematics project, *I Do and I Understand*. This was the first and most influential curriculum intervention into primary school mathematics in the 1960s. This quotation juxtaposes hearing and forgetting on the one hand and doing and understanding on the other. The polarisation of passive remembering and active learning produced the most important theoretical tenet in the recent history of the primary school. That children did not learn by 'hearing and forgetting' but rather by doing, itself leading to understanding, became embodied not only in assumptions about children but the conditions of their learning. 'I Do and I Understand' sets out two classroom plans, the old and the new. The new plan is radically re-arranged to make better provision for active learning. [. . .]

What is it that produced such a radical reorganisation of the pedagogical space? This reorganisation clearly cannot be understood outside the terms which make it possible: doing, activity, development, experiences, individual concepts, mental structures, to name some of the terms which are significant. If the pedagogic space and the terms of the discourse are so intertwined, it becomes important to understand how it happens that learning and teaching come to be expressed in the terms of individual cognitive development.

Let us take this a stage further by examining another apparatus of the pedagogy, this time in the form of a record card, of the type commonly filled in by nursery school teachers. [. . .] Certain features of an individual child's 'development' are recorded on the card, ranging from language development, physical and motor development, hearing, emotional/social, 'responses to the learning situation' and 'medical'. What does this tell us? Why are these categories chosen as salient to record? Every category requires an observation of behaviour which is stated as a developmental accomplishment: a capacity, itself produced through 'activity and experience'. There are no facts, no knowledge stated outside the terms of a developmental accomplishment.

One category, for example, is emotional/social and the following question is posed: 'Is his play: isolated, parallel, associative, cooperative, group?' Let us deconstruct the assumptions which are contained in the formulation of the question. Here are listed five types of play. First of all then, we can assume that a category, play, can both be differentiated from other aspects of classroom behaviour and performance and is pedagogically important; that is play is something which is expected as a classroom activity – it is part of the pedagogy. Secondly, the list exists as a framework of classification of *types* of play. This in turn assumes that each teacher is (1) familiar with the terms, (2) recognises the types of play when s/he sees them and (3) can discriminate good and normal from abnormal play. The teacher, therefore, must both recognise play as a significant category and have been *trained* to recognise and classify it along the lines set out in the record card. A whole apparatus of teacher-training is thereby implicated. [. . .]

It is possible to disentangle a complex web of related practices and apparatuses which together produce the possibility and effectivity of the child-centred pedagogy. Central to these is a system for the classification, observation monitoring, promotion and facilitation of the development of a variety of aspects of individual psychological capacities. In apparatuses and practices such as these it is axiomatic that there must exist a set of observational and empirically verifiable facts of child development. Central to the practice therefore is the *production* of development as pedagogy. By this I mean that development is produced as an object of classification, of schooling, within these practices themselves, made possible by the apparatuses which (among many others) I have singled out: record cards, teacher-training, classroom layout and so forth. Others would include teaching notes, work-cards, school and classroom organisation, architecture. It is in this sense that developmental psychology and the child-centred pedagogy form a couple: the apparatuses of the pedagogy are no mere application but a site of production in their own right. [. . .] It has been put to me that many teachers are not child-centred, so that my presentation does not reflect the 'reality' of many classrooms. [. . .] Classrooms are indeed many and varied, however the parameters of the practice are given by the common sense of child development which is everywhere, in apparatuses from teacher-training, to work-cards, to classroom layout. The apparatuses themselves provide a norm, a standard of good and possible pedagogy. [. . .]

I now examine the historical conditions which produced the possibility of the developmental psychology/child-centred pedagogy couple and ensured its sedimentation in the set of taken-for-granted practices that exist today. It will end with a tentative examination of how subject-positions are produced within existing practices, suggesting a way forward for the analysis of the production of subjectivity.

Science, psychology and the possibility of a 'scientific' pedagogy

In order to understand the conditions which make possible the modern developmental psychology/pedagogy couple we have to examine several issues: first, the school as an apparatus of regulation and classification and second the relation of that to specific forms of regulation and classification founded in *science*. [. . .] The belief in science and the concomitant struggle to find forms of legitimation and guarantee in science rather than religion forms a significant backdrop to the genesis not only of modern forms of rationality, but for the idea of rationality as natural and therefore to the search for a pedagogy which could produce the desired forms of individuality by means of natural development. [. . .]

The claims for a science of the rational were from the first intimately bound up with the possibilities of a scientifically validated and rational pedagogy. In *Discipline and Punish* (1977) Foucault documents the emergence of techniques of administration which were founded in the sciences. This body of apparatuses was made possible by changes associated with the rise of capitalist manufacture in which forms of power emerged wherein scientific knowledges allowed for the possibility of certain techniques of producing knowledge and in knowing about human beings, of classifying, normalising and regulating. These techniques of social regulation were taken up in many ways. But it is not the case that they were produced by some monolithic superpower for the domination of the emergent working class. On the contrary, while the effect might well have been to produce 'docile bodies', it was often liberals and radicals who proposed the new forms of scientific administration and pushed for them as preferable to the forces of religion. This tendency was certainly one which characterised the work of Marx among others. [. . .] The point here is to understand how it came to be the case that certain tendencies often inaugurated by individuals and groups outside public education and administration introduced ideas and practices which came to dominate public education. The particular moments of struggle in the public take-up of forms of education are very important because they reveal the way in which science envisaged as a tool of liberation was by its naturalisation the very basis of the production of normalisation.

Compulsory schooling was established in England around 1880. In order to understand how compulsory schooling became a site for political struggle it is important to understand the form of the arguments used for it. Jones and Williamson (1979) argue that all popular texts of that time note two problems in particular for which schooling (at first popular and later compulsory) was offered as a solution. These were crime and pauperism,[1] understood in terms of principles and habits of the population. It was this understanding of bad habits as the cause of crime and pauperism which led to the possibility of seeing popular education as the answer to the nation's ills, that is by the inculcation of good habits, notably of reading, in order, especially, to read the Bible. In this way, the problems of poverty, of pauperism and of poor relief were presented as moral issues concerning the habits and life of the poor. [. . .]

What was proposed as a form of popular pedagogy was the monitorial school, based [. . .] on a model of constant surveillance. Moral regulation of the habits of the population would be produced by constant monitoring and ceaseless activity. To understand all the conditions for the introduction of monitorialism and its transposition to a pedagogy based on covert normative regulation [. . .] we would need to examine who supported monitorialism, and what the terms and conditions in which it was opposed and therefore transformed. It certainly never commanded universal support.[2]

However, one of the conditions for the transformation appears to have been monitorialism's relative failure as regulatory device. [. . .] At the same time there were significant new discourses and practices of population-management being produced. [. . .] The term 'class' first emerges in the demographic sense in this discourse, particularly in the isolation of the 'dangerous classes' as the object of study. What we have here is the change in the object of study and therefore the consequent discussion and operation of the mode of instruction. [. . .]

A central feature of the production of scientific forms of regulation of the population was the development of population statistics. It is these which provided the basis of classifications of the normal in the many domains relating to the social regulation of the population, scientific rationalism: regulation according to the nature of the individual was covert, liberal, forward looking and sought greater effectivity through the promotion not of habits, but of understanding.

'Rational powers of mind' were put forward by some as the solution to a social problem which coercion had failed to remedy. As time progressed the anti-coercion lobby was thus to turn a moral into a scientific imperative.

[. . .] Robert Owen, a Scottish philanthropist who provided schools for the children of the workers in his New Lanark mills, was an important figure in the development of forms of pedagogy which were seen as left-wing and progressive. Like other radicals particularly in Scotland, he was a supporter of the French Revolution. While Robert Owen had at first admired the monitorial system he later denounced it as 'this mockery of learning' which could render a child 'irrational for life' (Owen, 1813). [. . .] In Robert Owen's schools teaching took the form of 'object lessons' based on the study of natural phenomena. This represents a considerable break with the study of Biblical texts, and also relates to contemporaneous shifts from classics to sciences in the education of the upper classes.

Owen, among others, was suggesting that the introduction of such techniques in the education of the poor would produce better citizens. [. . .] The form of the pedagogy was also subject to transformation. The proposed replacement for the schoolroom of the monitorial system was the classroom: the site of simultaneous instruction of children of the same age. This division of children into classes is consonant with the emerging practice of dividing the population into classes.[3] Simultaneous instruction was designed to render it suitable to the individual: hence grouping by age and the necessity of fitting the lesson to the age, through the mechanism of love. [. . .]

It is important to point out that there was no easy and simple flow from the one form of pedagogy to the other. There were struggles and political battles which took place in conjunction with other conditions. However, for our purposes, it is important that the transformation in the form of pedagogic regulation was simultaneously a discursive transformation and a transformation of apparatuses and practices: a new regime of truth included a field of administration. And it is in relation to the new form of scientifically produced regulation that psychology first enters the pedagogic stage.

Scientific psychology and the study and education of children

At the beginning of the twentieth century there were two parallel developments which related to the scientific classification of children: the first was child study, the second mental measurement.[4] [. . .] As part of the study of the population, children, as we have seen, were singled out as a class, to be classified in their own right. Characteristics, including those specific to children, were charted with a view to establishing what environmental conditions might produce physical illness, immoral and criminal behaviour. This survey work included histories of family 'pathologies'. It is important that at this moment developments in evolutionary biology, particularly the work of Darwin, were advancing in ways which were absolutely related. Consider, for example, the now well-known concept of the 'survival of the fittest'. It corresponds precisely to the relation between suitable 'stock' and environmental conditions. Indeed, Social Darwinism[5] utilised these concepts with direct reference to forms of social control and engineering, and it is not coincidental that eugenics was offered as a solution to the problems of the poor and 'degenerate' by a considerable number of those associated with the rise of psychology, population statistics and scientific education, such as Galton, Spearman, Cattell, Terman and Montessori (see Kamin, 1974; Rose, 1979). The shift of emphasis in control of the population from habits to degeneracy carries with it a central and strategic production of the *norm(al)*. [. . .]

Having established the individual as the proper object of the scientific gaze, [. . .] the new psychology linked and implicated the twin poles of heredity and environment from the very beginning. [. . .] The movement which produces the possibility of the individual as an object of science defined in terms of the twin poles of heredity and environment produces simultaneously the need for the development of scientific and empirical apparatuses and techniques of detection and some form of institutional provision which help produce and normalise such individuals.[6]

Certain fundamental issues and concerns provide some of the conditions of possibility for the emergence of Piaget's theory and empirical work in the form that it took. These are the issues of heredity and environment, the 'naturalness' of the development of rationality and the concern for a solution to the problems of the social order in a science of the individual. There is one more very important aspect. This is the development of the idea of 'the child' as an object both of science in its own right and of apparatuses of normalisation. These provided the possibility for a science and a pedagogy based on a model of naturally occurring development which could be observed, normalised and regulated. Thus, as it were, they permitted the idea that degeneracy could be nipped in the bud, by regulating the development of children in order to ensure their fitness as adults. [. . .]

It must by now be apparent that those twin techniques of mental measurement and child development were not formulated in the opposition in which they have been placed both pedagogically and psychologically, in the liberal and radical discourses and pedagogies of the 1960s and 1970s. Here, individualism and progressivism were posed as the liberatory alternative to reactionary forms of classification based on intelligence testing. In this sense, child development was not understood as a system of classification, an elision made possible by its interdiscursive relation to the humanistic moment of individual liberation.[7]

While it is indeed the case that theories such as Piaget's were set up in opposition to a view of inherited or pregiven intelligence, the general project within which his work is sited and the terms of its construction do not fall outside those already described. These psychological movements were always associated with techniques for classification such as the development of tests and with administrative apparatuses such as forms of schooling. Binet, in whose Paris laboratory the young Piaget worked, was one of the first to begin to devise such tests. It is commonly asserted (for example by Gruber and Voneche, 1977) that Piaget was more interested in the reasoning behind the responses which the children gave to the test items than in their normative performance on them. Piaget simply developed in one direction work in a tradition which was already firmly rooted in the scientific community.

The emergence of Piaget's genetic epistemology

In sketching out developments in psychology and education I have outlined some of the conditions which laid out the foundations for Piaget's enterprise. [. . .] Piaget began his career as a biologist and therefore it is consistent for him to express his concerns by reference both to contemporary biological discourses and to the political debates about war into which those discourses were inserted. These concerns emerge and re-emerge in Piaget's later work in a variety of different ways. His interest in the view that ontogeny recapitulates phylogeny meshes with other current discourses about play.

When later in Paris Piaget came into contact with both the work of Binet and psychoanalysis, he asserted the importance of the power of reason, the concern about 'what makes us human'. Using arguments recruited from psychoanalysis he suggested that the best course for mankind was to channel children's development away from the dominance of the emotions towards that rationality which alone would be the guarantor of progress. It is perhaps here that his search began for an analysis of spontaneous development which would chart the 'naturally occurring' progress of childhood towards scientific rationality.

Piaget's early work has to be understood in terms of a set of conditions which made it possible within a particular body of scientific discourses and regulatory practices. It is these regimes of truth and these administrative apparatuses which help to explain how Piaget's work came to be taken up in a particular way within early education. [. . .]

Scientific experiments in pedagogy

1912 saw the English translation of *The Montessori Method*, while already in 1911 the then Chief Inspector of Schools, Edmond Holmes, had published a book sharply critical of what was by then traditional class teaching. This book was based on a discussion of a country school in which children were offered 'free and joyful learning'. [...] Several points may be drawn from Holmes's approach: they are the references to the country, freedom, individuality, nature and love. In certain of the terms we can ascertain continuities from the class-based pedagogy which some had hoped would form the rational education only a few years earlier. Certainly, love and nature were already present, but the stress on individual freedom is a new departure. It is at this point that the first ideas of an individualised pedagogy emerged. Empirical work, including that of Piaget's natural normalised stages of development towards scientific rationality, provided a set of apparatuses making possible the monitoring of individual development and therefore the naturalisation of pedagogy itself. Indeed, what followed was a series of experiments in pedagogy which were also taken to be psychological experiments. That is, the observation and monitoring of child development became a pedagogy in its own right because those understandings taken to underlie the acquisition of knowledge were presumed to be based on a 'natural' foundation. The new notion of an individualised pedagogy depended absolutely on the possibility of the observation and classification of normal development and the idea of spontaneous learning. [...]

Hamilton observes that this new view of pedagogy 'took shape as a reaction against the claimed mechanisation of simultaneous instruction, just as the work of Stow and Kay-Shuttleworth represented a reaction against the arbitrary nature of pre-nineteenth century individualised instruction' (1981, p. 11). It is in this sense then that the term 'class teaching' began to take on the pejorative and reactionary connotations which it has in British primary schools today. [...]

Class-teaching could take on pejorative connotations because although it stressed understanding, it was an understanding which was based on 'facts'. It was the advances in mental measurement and child development which permitted the possibility of a pedagogy of the individual in which understanding as a goal was transformed into a normalised and regulated stage-wise progression. Teaching a class, therefore, while representing a break with monitorialism, was outmoded in view of the possibility of going beyond class to individual regulation. Class-teaching, then, came to stand for the old order – modernism and progress lay with the individual. [...] There began to appear several books which established individualised pedagogies as the way forward, for example, Caldwell Cook's *The Play Way* appeared in 1915. [...]

In the 1920s perhaps the most famous pedagogic experiment was Susan Isaac's Malting House School in Cambridge, set up explicitly as a scientific experiment. [...] The central figures of Isaac's method lay in the focus on certain basic problems and patterns of development. The function of the pedagogy, therefore, was to classify, observe and monitor the developmental sequences. Moni-toring was crucial in order to ensure the normalisation of develop-ment. [. . .] In intellectual terms activity, experience and playing were placed together: the child's spontaneous creation of scientific rationality grew out of play-like (because spontaneous) exploration of objects. It is the work of Piaget more than any other which provides the grounds for such a move. All that is required then is for the child to be provided with the conditions for spontaneous activity. [. . .] The questions we have to ask ourselves next are why these issues assumed an importance at that particular historical moment and how they got taken up in ways which moved them from being marginal, private experiments to becoming the basis of state primary schooling.

In 1918 the post-war Liberal government introduced an Educa-tion Act which established a national system of education. As part of this package nurseries were to be nationally organised. Post-war reconstruction depended heavily on notions drawn from the new psychology and education: regimentation, a term associated with the characteristics of the enemy (as militarism, Prussianism) became the enemy. Individualism, then, was the key term in opposition to regimentation. The natural individual was the hope for the future.

The Hadow Consultative Committee was first set up under Conservative government but took off in the months of the short-lived Labour Government. The first report published in 1928 dealt with the education of adolescents. In essence the report introduced the tripartite system of secondary education, controlled by the 11-plus examination, with streaming at the upper end of the junior school, according to arguments based on the concept of capacity. [. . .] It is often a mystery to students and teachers why nursery and infant education is so much more child-centred and progressive than junior, with secondary as the most 'reactionary' of all. Infant education is often held up as the model of good practice towards which teachers of older children should aspire. It is, however, not usually recognised that there are specific historical reasons why the practices at different phases in the education system should have different emphases. The introduction of 11-plus selection with its emphasis on capacity profoundly touched the junior and secondary schools in ways which left the earlier ages unaffected. The dis-courses of mental measurement and development were not under-stood as being in opposition until the attacks on selection and streaming of the 1960s,[8] the Plowden era. At this and only this point was the difference marked, the discourse split, the discontinui-ty produced.

The second and third Hadow reports (*The Primary School*, 1931; *Infant and Nursery Schools*, 1933) take up the simultaneity of the two discourses. Both reports basically legitimate, in the form of state recommendation, everything I have spoken about in terms of the child-centred pedagogy. Individual freedom 'is essential: and freedom only becomes dangerous when there is nothing to absorb the child's restless activity and provide an outlet for his experimental spirit'. Innate tendencies relate to biologised natural development. Pedagogy becomes the observation and recording of naturalised development. Physical, emotional and mental development are presented side by side in the same terms: the facts of child development. [. . .] The positive reception of Hadow was helped by the rise of totalitarianism and the impending Second World War. [. . .]

It is, however, pertinent to note how the features of post-war constructivism; the 1944 Education Act and the setting up of state-funded apparatuses helped ensure the dissemination and sedimentation of the new pedagogy. Importantly also, Piaget's work which developed the empirical apparatuses and refined the tools of classification concerning the stages of development was not published until after the Hadow report. It is, therefore, significant that transformations in the pedagogy, particularly in relation to mathematics and sciences, should take place after the Second World War. It is in this sense, then, that the apparatus of concepts and discoveries produced some noteworthy transformations in the pedagogy of observation.

In the 1960s and 1970s Piaget's work was part of the legitimation and production of practices aimed at liberating children. [. . .] It is perhaps the supreme irony that the concern for individual freedom and the hope of a naturalised rationality that could save mankind should have provided the conditions for the production of a set of apparatuses which would aid in the production of the normalised child. It is the empirical apparatus of stages of development which of all Piaget's work has been most utilised in education. It is precisely this, and its insertion into a framework of biologised capacities, which ensures that the child is produced as an object of the scientific and pedagogical gaze by means of the very mechanisms which were intended to produce its liberation.

In this sense then we can understand why Piaget's work appears in educational practices in such an apparently pragmatic way. If, for example, Piaget had not provided such an extensive and coherent set of empirical evidence and monitoring procedures one might speculate about his insertion into educational practices. It is those procedures which form part of the day-to-day running of classrooms, providing the taken-for-granted forms of a pedagogy which teachers frequently do not associate with the name of Piaget. Finally, since there neither is, nor ever has been, a Piagetian pedagogy, the relation of Piaget's work to pedagogy should be considered neither as application nor as distortion.

Classroom practice and the acquisition of concepts

Apparatuses of classification are central to the possibility and effectivity of practices of a particular form and content. In relation to the parameters of these practices it is possible to specify the production of the schemes and forms of teaching and learning and the process of acquisition of knowledge. The system of regulation and normalisation produces what counts as 'good pedagogy'. It produces, therefore, what counts as a 'good teacher'. We can [. . .] deconstruct the relations of the discourses and the practices which constitute the pedagogy to examine how children and teachers are subjectively produced, but more than that, we can actually analyse the activities and sequences which comprise learning itself. [. . .]

The example comes from the practice of an infant teacher engaged in teaching mathematics to a group of 6 to 7 year olds (top infants). She has been doing some work on place value (the nearest equivalent in old mathematics is 'tens and units'). Her view is that children discover number relationships by physically grouping and carrying out operations on concrete objects. She wants the children to discover aspects of grouping in tens from activities with objects which require that grouping. Her view is consonant with that expressed in the most popular textbook for teachers, Williams and Shuard's *Primary Mathematics Today* (1974). Williams and Shuard entitle their introduction to place value as 'The emergence of the place-value concept'. Such a terminology immediately locates place value as arising out of and in relation to the properties of the mind of the child – something which 'emerges' spontaneously. By implication, therefore, it is not taught and cannot be located within anything to do with the system of representation or notation or existing practices of discourses. This reading is further supported by the authors themselves:

> From the variety of forms in which children *experience* our number system – the cubes and rods, recordings of sums of money and measuring, graphs, the abacus and symbols for numerals – *there develops a capacity* to read and write numbers with a confident recognition of their meaning (Williams and Shuard, 1974, p. 163; my italics).

As part of her various practices the teacher in this example asks the children to bundle together groups of ten matchsticks, putting elastic bands around them. The children then work in pairs, each child putting out a number of bundles of ten and a number of single matchsticks in separate piles. These are to be put together, counted and an addition sum 'recorded' on paper. The teacher maximises the importance of the operations with the objects and minimises the importance of the written work by treating it as 'recording', which is to be understood as subsequent to and consequent upon, the mastery of relevant concepts, which takes place through discovery based on action. In the sequence which I have taken for analysis, one pair of children, Michael and Tony, does not engage in the task which the teacher has set up. Michael, in particular, wrote down the sum first never bothering to count the matchsticks. He worked out the answer by adding the columns starting with the tens – a procedure which he had not been taught. Indeed, such procedures were antithetical to the teacher's practice, smacking as they did of rote-learning rather than proper conceptualisation or real discovery. We know Michael's rationale because he conveniently explained it to his partner and to the teacher. His explanation to Tony is reproduced below:

M. Shall I tell you how I do it?
T. How?
M. Well, look you see when you get to a sum like this, right, look, you write the two numbers down, don't you – they're the tens and they're the ones. You put three tens down and I put two tens. We didn't put any ones down any of us, did we?
T. No.
M. So, we've got this sum thirty and twenty, haven't we? And altogether I add up this and that's three and two and that's what?
T. Five.
M. Three, that's five so you write down five and there's no there [sic] so you put five and that's how you make it. It's easy, innit see?

(During this explanation Michael points to the sum on paper as an example.)

Now, several things are important. First, Michael's technique succeeded for some time – until he had more than ten in the ones column and did not know what to do. Second, the teacher would not have known about this unless she had seen my videotape. On doing so, she became very upset, saying, 'I'll have to take him back. He obviously hasn't got it. I'll have to take him back and give him more experience . . . He shouldn't really be trying to do that yet.' So we have the failure of Michael's procedure understood in certain terms which have consequences for practice. The teacher understood his failure to get the correct answer as caused by conceptual failure, the remedy for which was to give him more concrete experience – he had gone too far too fast. Thus the remedy was more practice. His failure was also understood as *her* failure – that she had 'pushed' him – the worst sin of the child-centred pedagogy; she had not allowed him to go 'at his own pace'.

In this way we can note the complex interplay of relations between the objects and techniques of the discursive practice, the provision of teaching of a particular kind, the reading of the child's performance and the construction of the teacher's identity. I have shown this videotaped sequence to several groups of primary teachers. Although I had been at pains to select this teacher because she was well-known to be extremely competent, the teachers watching the videotape always tended to find fault with her, saying that she was not progressive enough: they never challenged the pedagogy itself. My reading of this response on the part of the teachers was that they actually recognised only too well teaching which was consonant with their own practice and actually felt threatened. So when I next showed the videotape to a group of teachers, I asked them to imagine that *they* were the class teacher in question and to tell me at the end of the tape how they would feel if Michael was in their class. Every time that I have used this method with a group of teachers the same thing has happened. The first things which were blurted out were: 'I'd feel I'd failed,' 'I'd feel guilty.' Then the teachers would go on to say what Michael's teacher had said: too far too fast, etc. The normative production of 'good teaching' means that the teacher must experience herself as inadequate, feel guilty, anxious and insecure. If the child has failed, by implication the teacher's gaze has not been total enough, she has not provided enough experience, has committed the 'sin' of 'pushing' the child. After all, within the parameters of the discursive practice, all children would and could develop correctly if only the teacher were good enough.

But, given a different discursive framework, it is quite possible to identify Michael's failure as *success*. Certainly a different set of assumptions about mathematics as knowledge would implicate a whole other further set of practices, producing different norms and readings of learning. Even given these practices, however, it is possible to argue that place-value is not produced through action but is an example of what Kline (1953) has called 'notation-directed change': that is one produced through changes in mathematical notation. Hence learning would not be about the internalisation of action but the recognition of the relation between the written signifiers and their combination on paper, since place-value is about that system of signification and not about action. In this sense we would read Michael's methods as very sophisticated and we would argue that he was but one small step from success, a step which could have been remedied by his starting by adding the ones column instead of the tens! In this very important sense, then, neither children's nor teachers' actions stand outside their insertion within a particular framework of practice, which provides both a reading and a 'solution'. To bring this point home let me elaborate it a little further. Let us consider an 'arithmetic fact' such as $2 + 2 = 4$. In one sense we can say that it appears to be a timeless mathematical truth. However, it depends not only on a binary system of notation, but, as I have argued elsewhere, relates to the system of signification which is mathematical discourse (see Walkerdine, 1982; also Rotman, n.d.). In a sense of $2 + 2 = 4$ as a statement incorporated into the discursive practices which make up primary school mathematics teaching, it is not timeless either. If we consider the shift from 'hearing and forgetting' to 'doing and understanding', what the statement $2+2=4$ means changes radically as do the practices for its production.

For example, it becomes viewed as the outcome of an understanding produced on the basis of internalised action leading to the development of number concept. The mathematical statement is therefore not a number fact, but the articulation of an underlying conceptual apparatus. The writing of the statement itself is minimised as 'recording', seen as the icing on the cake of real understanding: it is secondary and relatively insignificant. The practices for producing it, therefore, also shift dramatically. Since it is the product of individual cognitive development it requires, for its production, a whole set of apparatuses to facilitate individual learning.

The mastery of $2+2=4$ is at worst taken as evidence of parroting and therefore not proper learning, or at best as an indication of the child's having reached the requisite conceptual level: it is therefore an indication of a mental capacity. In this sense then what it means changes drastically at every possible practical level.

This brings me up against the most important point of trying to set out what kind of position I am advocating in relation to developmental psychology. I have shown that it is important not to dismiss developmental psychology as biased and thereby avoid engaging with its positivity in producing practices and therefore processes of learning. I hope that I have also identified the necessity of deconstructing the taken-for-granted basis of developmental psychology itself. [. . .] Laying bare the historical constitution of psychology's objects of study is the first step, but it is only the first. We still have to explain the constitution of children as learners; in this case we are interested in how children come to 'know'. How can we approach these issues in a way which does not reduce to that very psychology of which I have been critical? [. . .] I am not advocating disposing of all we know about children. Rather, my point is that developmental psychology's object is constituted in such a way as to reduce all problems to 'the child's acquisition of . . .', 'the development of . . .' It is precisely such formulations which I have sought to deconstruct. [. . .]

Conclusion: changing the present?

Throughout this chapter I have stressed that the production of the truth of developmental psychology is specific to a particular set of educational practices whose object is the developing child. I have argued that such psychology and such practices are normalising in that they constitute a mode of observation and surveillance and production of children. Given this, it is difficult to conceive of these practices as being the basis of any kind of pedagogy which could potentially 'liberate' children. Indeed the notion of liberation which underpins such political calculations assumes precisely that 'natural' child development which has been the focus of criticism in this chapter. However, the role of educational practice within some notion of radical transformation remains an important and unresolved question. In order to address it I will begin by reiterating some important conclusions. There is no psychology which exists outside the framework of a particular set of historical conditions of possibility, and, in the case of developmental psychology, those conditions which make possible this body of discourse and practice also produce the possibility of the child-centred pedagogy. The fixing and sedimentation of those discourses and practices is assured by the administrative apparatuses which produce particular forms of organisation and of sociality. Thus, empirical critiques within developmental psychology which argue about ages and stages or even about the importance of context will never be able to get outside the limits of the transcendental unitary subject.

Neither the child nor the individual can be liberated by a radical stripping away of the layers of the social. Such a model assumes a psychological subject laid bare to be re-formed in the new order. This was the aim of the liberatory pedagogy – to lay bare the psychological bones. But if social practices are central to the very formation of subjectivity the laying bare is an impossibility. In this analysis there is no pre-existent subject to liberate.

It is important to point out that the processes of normalisation are not the product of some repressive superpower hell-bent on keeping people in their place. That is, disciplinary power does not function through overt repression but through the covert reproduction of ourselves. Thus, liberals, radicals, feminists alike will advocate the child-centred pedagogy and will teach and learn within its orbit. Education is therefore more contradictory than suggested by those theories of 'reproduction' which assume a determinate or linear relation between the economy and schooling, which underplay it as a site of productivity in its own right.

In attempting to explain the production of the developmental psychology/child-centred pedagogy couple I have argued that psychology's status as science with particular practices for producing evidences and claims to truth is crucial in understanding the historical construction of the present form of schooling. This is in marked contrast to some other treatments of education in which ideology is taken to be the central component. For example, Sharp and Green (1975) in their study of progressive primary schooling use a model of false consciousness to explain the production of teacher identity. Because they understand child-centredness as ideology they have no way of understanding the centrality of its claims to truth and therefore its effectivity in producing practices. For instance:

> There is no direct logical relationship between the child centred vocabulary and the teacher's actions in all their complexity. The vocabulary does not immediately inform or motivate all their actions. Rather the teachers' actions are directly informed in an *ad hoc* manner by routines, habits and motivations, many of which in the immediacy of the classroom work will either be unconscious or only minimally reflexive. (Sharp and Green, 1975, p. 175).

They are forced into the above position because they do not have the theoretical apparatus to examine the complex relationship between teachers' statements and practices.

Using a different model of ideology, the Centre for Contemporary Cultural Studies Education Group (CCCS, 1982) in their historical analysis of the rise and demise of social democratic education place their faith almost exclusively in culture, representations and ideology. [. . .] However, it is crucial to point out that they simply fail to mention science. That scientific knowledges cannot be reduced to ideologies or cultural representations is supported by the power-knowledge position exemplified by Foucault, which the CCCS group reject because it cannot explain change. I would argue that by leaving out science they are attributing no importance in understanding change to the modern form of sociality founded in science's claims and guarantees to truth. [. . .] While statements from the human sciences do not cause change in educational practices, they are centrally implicated not only because of the forms of legitimation they offer and, therefore, the grounding in fact; but because they also offer the terms in which the scientific pedagogies are to operate. These terms, as we have seen, cannot be understood without access to the debates within, and the production of the science of, psychology.[9]

Change cannot be understood simply in terms of transformations in the representation of the same object, the same problem. Rather, transformations in the production of knowledges shift what the object is taken to be. Certainly there are continuities which are often minimised in the discursive shifts, but the very productive nature of those shifts assures us that they are not shifts in the representation of an underlying object. If we were talking about the shifts in representation we would have to operate as though psychological statements were ideological: an ideology that essentially distorts real relations. But psychology operates with a system of practices for producing evidences; it has claims to truth and to the production of fact. [. . .] In so far as it constitutes individuals, in this case children, as objects of its gaze it produces them as subjects. In so far as it creates a regime of truth premised upon a psychological individual then it prohibits other formulations which do not repeat individual–society dualism.

Acknowledgments

This chapter would not have been possible without the considerable help and support which I received from the co-authors of the book. In addition I would like to thank the following people for invaluable comments following readings of various draft versions: James Donald, Keith Hoskin and Bill Schwarz. Previous versions of this chapter have been presented to the Social and Political Sciences Committee, University of Cambridge, 1980, and the British Psychological Society Developmental Section Conference, 1982. The members of the Department of the Sociology of Education, Institute of Education, have been an important source of support and stability which helped to provide the conditions of possibility for production of this work. I am especially grateful for pertinent discussions with Basil Bernstein.

Notes

1 The term pauperism is used rather than poverty because of the way in which, as Jones and Williamson make clear, poverty was taken to be the result of the habits of the poor themselves.

2 See for example, R. Johnson, 'Really useful knowledge', in Clarke, Critcher and Johnson (1977), pp. 77–9.

3 'The new domain was defined at the point of intersection of two new ways of making statements about the population which were themselves formed during the early nineteenth century, as the result of the constitution of town police forces and town health boards, on the one hand, and as a result of the reform of prison administrations and those of Poor Law institutions on the others. These two new ways of making statements about the population formed a topographical analysis and a historical analysis respectively: and by their intersection defined a new field of objects of analysis, that is to say, the classes of the population. A class was accordingly defined by a web of topographical connections, which also characterised conditions whereby children were trained up as members of a class, and it was this that formed the moral topography of the class' (Jones and Williamson, 1979, p. 96).

4 The emergence of techniques of mental measurement is described in detail by Rose (1979).

5 See Greta Jones (1980) for more detail.

6 One aspect of this documented by Rose (1979) is the beginning of educational apparatuses which distinguished between those of normal and 'subnormal' intelligence and educated accordingly.

7 Such elision is present in many of the liberal and radical pedagogies from free-school movements to the stress on individual discovery in, for example, Barnes, Britton and Rosen (1971). The focus on 'the child' as a person, an individual in its own right, an autonomous agent was what allowed it to be counterposed to the grinding norms of the oppressive pedagogic classificatory

machines of selection and grading. I am at pains, therefore, to establish that the child-centred pedagogy and developmental psychology rely equally on systems of classification and regulation – though, because, as we shall see, it was, being linked to 'freedom', more covert than overt. It was not 'sorting and grading'. This stress on 'developing potential' has led many primary school teachers to understand their pedagogy as, at the very least, liberal. This helps to explain the significant lack of radicalism on the part of primary school teachers compared with those in secondary education. It is additionally important to note Basil Bernstein's (1971) use of the concept *invisible pedagogy* to designate a similar relation.

8 It is important in this respect to understand the recent singling out and vilification of Cyril Burt as a perpetrator of reaction. It is clear that while Cyril Burt did, indeed, provide evidence for the Hadow Committee his views were not expressly opposed by exponents of child development. It is also important that while the Plowden Report is similar to Hadow in many respects it does not contain any reference to mental measurement.

9 The kind of analysis undertaken here elides the problem of the competing claims to truth *within* a discourse, since there are claims, evidences and counterclaims. This is certainly important but cannot be understood outside the issue of the limit-conditions of the discipline itself. Also, importantly for this analysis, it is not always *all* of one theory which is taken up, as in the example of Piaget's stages of development. The stages were, as it were, prised apart from other aspects of the theoretical edifice and rearticulated with other, sometimes theoretically quite distinct, approaches. This process is very important in so far as it helps to explain how and in what circumstances particular pieces of work are taken up and utilised. So a particular pedagogy may be adopted because it satisfies a variety of people holding different interests and positions. For example the individualised child-centred pedagogy satisfied those concerned with juvenile crime, with psychoanalysis, with freedom, with 'keeping the masses in their place' and more, all at the same time and in different and contradictory ways. Thus the discourses informing the practice are not all of one piece, without seams or ruptures, but we can say that they get taken up in this popular way precisely because there are many discourses and interests which appear to be solved by the introduction of the new practice.

References

Barnes, D., Britton, J. and Rosen, H. (1971) *Language, the Learner and the School*. Harmondsworth: Penguin.

Bernstein, B. (1971) *Class, Codes and Control, Vol. 1*. London: Routledge and Kegan Paul.

CCCS (Centre for Contemporary Cultural Studies Race and Politics Group) (1982) *The Empire Strikes Back*. London: Hutchinson.

Clarke, C., Critcher, C. and Johnson, R. (eds) (1977) *Working Class Culture*. London: Hutchinson.

Donaldson, M. (1978) *Children's Minds*. London: Fontana.

Foucault, M. (1977) *Discipline and Punish*. London: Allen Lane.

Gruber, H. and Voneche, J. J. (1977) *The Essential Piaget*. London: Routledge and Kegan Paul.

Hamilton, D. (1981) 'On Simultaneous Instruction and the Early Evolution of Class Teaching'. mimeo, University of Glasgow.

Jones, G. (1980) *Social Darwinism and English Thought*. Brighton: Harvester Press.

Jones, K. and Williamson, J. (1979) 'Birth of the Schoolroom', *Ideology and Consciousness*, 6, pp. 59–110.

Kamin, L. (1974) *The Science and Politics of I.Q.*. New York: Erlbaum.

Kline, M. (1953) *Mathematics in Western Culture*. London: George Allen and Unwin.

Owen, R. (1813) *A New View of Society: Or Essays on the Principles of the Formation of the Human Character*.

Rose, N. (1979) 'The Psychological Complex: Mental Measurement and Social Administration', *Ideology and Consciousness*, 5, pp. 5–68.

Rotman, B. (n.d.) 'Mathematics: an Essay in Semiotics', unpublished manuscript, Department of Mathematics, University of Bristol.

Sharp, R. and Green, A. G. (1975) *Education and Social Control*. London: Routledge and Kegan Paul.

Walkerdine, V. (1982) 'From Context to Text: a Psychosemiotic Approach to Abstract Thought', in Beveridge, M. (ed.) *Children Thinking Through Language*. London: Arnold.

Williams, S. and Shuard, H. (1974) *Primary Mathematics Today*. London: Longmans.

3.4

Vygotsky's Contribution to Pedagogical Theory

James Britton

In his introduction to the original Russian edition of *Thought and Language*, Vygotsky had written, 'we fully realise the inevitable imperfections of this study, which is no more than a first step in a new direction'. In which direction? Vygotsky has this answer: 'Our findings point the way to a new theory of consciousness' – and he goes on to indicate four aspects of the work that are *novel*, and – consequently – 'in need of further careful checking'. I have the sense here of someone embarking on an idea he knows he cannot himself carry through to a conclusion. His four discoveries, to state them as briefly as I can, are these:

1 Word meanings *evolve* during childhood: it cannot be assumed that when a child uses a word he means by it what we as adult speakers would mean.
2 While accepting Piaget's theory of the growth of *spontaneous concepts* – ideas arrived at by inference from (or evidenced by) our own experiences, Vygotsky adds the notion of *non-spontaneous concepts* – ideas taken over from other people (notably teachers) – taken over as problems needing solution, or as 'empty categories', so to speak, which need time to find embodiment in our own experience and ground themselves in our own knowledge base. Vygotsky sees this as a two-way movement, 'upward' of spontaneous concepts, 'downward' of non-spontaneous concepts, each mode facilitating the other – and the joint operation being characteristic of human learning.
3 Vygotsky believed that mastery of the written language – learning to read and write – had a profound effect upon the achievement of abstract thinking. The *constancy* of the written language, grafted, so to speak, upon the *immediacy* of the spoken language, enables a speaker to *reflect* upon meanings and by doing so acquire a new level of control, a critical awareness of his/her own thought processes.
4 Speech in infancy, Vygotsky claimed, is the direct antecedent of

thinking at a later stage. When children discover that it is helpful to speak aloud about what they are doing, they begin to employ what Vygotsky termed 'speech for oneself'; and thereafter speech takes on a dual function and, in due course, develops differentially; conversation becomes more effective *as communication*, while monologue or 'running commentary' (speech for oneself) changes in what is virtually the opposite direction. That is to say, in conversation children extend their control of the grammatical structures of the spoken language and increase their resources of conventional word-meanings. In their monologues, on the contrary, they exploit the fact that they are talking to themselves by using as it were 'note form' – skeletal or abbreviated structures that would mean little to one who did not already share the speaker's thoughts – and *personal, idiosyncratic* word meanings – pet words, inventions, portmanteau terms, rich in meaning for the originator but minimally endorsed by convention.

Vygotsky observed these changes in the speech of children from about 3 years old to about 7 – changes that set up a marked difference between their conversational mode and their use of 'speech for oneself'. On the strength of these observations he speculated that, rather than 'withering away' as Piaget had suggested, speech for oneself became internalised and continued to operate as the genesis of thought, perhaps moving through the stages of *inner speech* to *verbal thinking* and thence to the most elusive stage of all – thought itself.

By this account, then, we *think* by handling 'post-language symbols' – forms that began as speech but which have been successively freed from the constraints of the grammar of the spoken language and from the constraints of conventional, public word meanings. It is this freedom that characterises the fluidity of thought – and accounts for the necessity of *imposing organisation* upon our thoughts when we want to communicate them.

It was a brilliant insight on Vygotsky's part to realise that when speech for oneself becomes internalised it is in large part because the child, in handling the freer forms of speech that constitute that mode, begins to be capable of carrying out mental operations more subtle than anything he or she can put into words. I think we can become aware of the reciprocal process when as we listen to discussion we engender some response – a question to be asked or a comment we want to make – and have a clear sense that the process of moving from the fluid operation of thought units to the utterance of rule-governed 'public' speech using conventional word meanings is one that may demand strenuous mental effort on our part.

When *Mind in Society* appeared in 1978, a review by Stephen Toulmin in the *New York Review of Books* underlined Vygotsky's concern with consciousness. He saw Vygotsky as denying on the one hand that human consciousness can be regarded as simply an effect of the genes, of *nature*, or on the other hand as an effect of environment – of *nurture* – claiming that both influences must interact in the creation of mind in the individual. He gave his review the title, *The Mozart of Psychology* [...] and suggested that Western psychology urgently needed to take on the broader perspective that Vygotsky had initiated.

It is in this work that Vygotsky's central contention becomes clear – the claim that *human consciousness is achieved by the internalisation of shared social behaviour.* A series of 'temporary connections' is made by the individual within the individual life-span; each link makes possible further links, each operation begins with external *observable social behaviour* – an exposed segment, as it were, of what is to become inner behaviour. Thus is indicated, surely, a new emphasis upon the observation and study of childhood activities for the light they throw upon later behaviours not open to observation.

But social behaviour implies interaction within a group whose activities have been shaped to cultural patterns. The relationship between individual development and the evolution of society is a complex one, not a matter of mere recapitulation or parallelism. The familiar story of the psychologist Kellogg and his chimpanzee comes to mind: the chimpanzee had acted as companion to Kellogg's infant son and for a period of years both creatures developed, so to speak, in tandem – able to share each other's activities – but only up to the point where the boy learned to speak: the young Kellogg is today, I believe, himself a scientist: the chimpanzee remains – a chimpanzee! In the historical development from animal to man, the acquisition of language is a watershed: in the development of the individual child from birth to 3 or 4 years, the acquisition of language is a watershed.

Speech, that begins as a shared social activity on the part of the child and becomes a principal means of the mental regulation and refinement of his individual behaviour – this is the prime example of Vygotsky's theory of internalisation to achieve consciousness. He gives us a further striking example when he claims that make-believe play in early childhood constitutes the earliest, and at that time only available form of *imagination*. It is nearer the truth, he says, to claim that imagination in adolescence and later is 'make-believe play without action' than it is to claim that make-believe play in young children is 'imagination in action'.

The implications of these ideas for pedagogy are, of course, enormous. If speech in childhood lays the foundations for a life-time of thinking, how can we continue to prize a silent classroom? And if shared social behaviour (of many kinds, verbal and non-verbal) is seen as the source of learning, we must revise the traditional view of the teacher's role. The teacher can no longer act as the 'middle-man' in all learning – as it becomes clear that education is *an effect of community*. Bruner, in a recent book, devoted a chapter to Vygotsky's ideas, and in a later chapter makes this comment:

'Some years ago I wrote some very insistent articles about the importance of discovery learning . . . what I am proposing here is an extension of that idea, or better, a completion. My model of the child in those days was very much in the tradition of the solo child mastering the world by representing it to himself in his own terms. In the intervening years I have come increasingly to recognise that most learning in most settings is a communal activity, a sharing of the culture. It is not just that the child must make his knowledge his own, but that he must make it his own in a community of those who share his sense of belonging to a culture. It is this that leads me to emphasise not only discovery and invention but the importance of negotiating and sharing – in a word, of joint culture creating as an object of schooling and as an appropriate step en route to becoming a member of the adult society in which one lives out one's life.' (Bruner, 1986, p. 127).

The notion that shared social behaviour is the beginning stage of learning throws responsibility upon those who interact socially with the growing child. By interacting in such a way that their awareness of approaches to skilled behaviour, their awareness of snags and obstacles to such behaviour are made available to learners, they are in fact (in Vygotsky's terms) *lending consciousness* to those learners and enabling them to perform in this relationship tasks they could not achieve if left to themselves. Again in Vygotsky's terms, this is to open up for the learner 'the zone of proximal development' – an area of ability for which one's previous achievements have prepared one, but which awaits assisted performance for its realisation. That assistance may take the form of teacher/student interaction, or peer tutoring, or group activity – as well, of course, as in the give and take of social cooperation in and out of school.

Viewed thus broadly, we might add that a learner by taking part in rule-governed social behaviour may pick up the rules by means hardly distinguishable from the processes by which they were first socially derived – and by which they continue to be amended. On the other hand, along may come the traditional teacher and, with the best intentions, trying to be helpful, set out to observe the behaviour, analyse to codify the rules and teach the outcome as a recipe. Yes, this may sometimes be helpful, but as consistent pedagogy it is manifestly counter-productive.

Taking 'community' in a micro sense, it is likely that we all live in a number of communities. As teachers we are responsible for one of those – the classroom. It is clear we have a choice: we can operate so as to make that as rich an interactive learning community as we can, or we may continue to treat it as a captive audience for whatever instruction we choose to offer.

Wherever Vygotsky's voice can be heard, perhaps that choice constitutes a Zone of Proximal Development for many of us.

References

Bruner, J. (1986) *Actual Minds, Possible Worlds*. Harvard University Press: Cambridge, Massachusetts.

Kellogg, W. N. and Louise, A. (1933) *The Ape and the Child*. McGraw-Hill: New York.

Piaget, J. (1926) *Language and Thought of the Child*. Routledge and Kegan Paul: London.

Toulmin, S. (1978) 'The Mozart of Psychology', *New York Review of Books*, XXV, 14, 28 September, New York.

Vygotsky, L. S. (1978) *Mind in Society*. Harvard University Press: Cambridge, Massachusetts.

Vygotsky, L. S. (1987) *Thought and Language*. Newly revised and edited: MIT Press: Cambridge, Massachusetts.

3.5

The Enterprise We are Part of: Learning to Teach

Arthur Applebee

[...] As educators concerned with language and learning we study how young people learn to read, write and speak, but rarely how our teacher-education students can best learn to teach.

In this chapter I argue that this lack of attention to the process of learning to teach has left the field of teacher education open to theories and approaches that do not blend well with our own beliefs about language learning. Further, that we already have some very powerful models of learning that apply very well to learning to teach if we only take the time to apply these models to teacher education in a systematic and intellectually rigorous way. If we do so, we can better protect the gains we have made in the teaching of English in recent years, and can give our teacher-education students a more powerful and consistent framework for approaching their classrooms.

Teacher education today

In the United States today teacher-education programmes are caught in the midst of a variety of conflicting directions and goals. Teacher education as a field of study has concerned itself primarily with the generic skills of teaching: classroom management, lesson planning, discipline and the setting of goals and objectives. Given the history of educational research in general in the USA, and of research on teacher education in particular, this work is often framed in a behaviourist tradition, focusing on the development of particular 'skills' and 'competencies', which must often be 'certified' before a teacher is allowed to teach. At the same time there has been in the past few years a growing emphasis on subject-matter preparation. [...] That a teacher should be, first, an expert in a particular discipline and, second, a teacher. In the field of English the practical result of such a recommendation is that teachers train first in traditional literary criticism and then come to a school of education for a year of additional training in classroom skills.

These two traditions, coming together in the training of teachers of English, are at heart antithetical. The classical, humanistic, elitist tradition of the college literature curriculum has little in common with the behaviouristic, reductionist, management-oriented tradition of teacher education. [. . .]

But our reliance on these two traditions to shape teacher education reflects our failure to think carefully about what a teacher must know and do, and to base our teacher-education programmes on the conceptualisation that results. Both traditions foster dangerous misconceptions about the nature of teaching, misconceptions that our beginning teachers will take with them into their classrooms.

Teaching as management

The misconceptions fostered by the teacher-education programme itself usually have to do with a view of teaching as a variety of skills and behaviours that can be 'trained' and 'improved'. In this image of teaching the skilled teacher is a technocrat, possessed of a variety of teaching technologies that can be deployed to control the classroom and to stimulate learning. In different versions, this image of teaching has led to management-by-objectives, to teacher-proof curricula, to mastery learning programmes, and to teacher-training programmes that emphasise such skills as 'redirecting questions', 'wait time' and 'asking higher-order questions'.

The problem with such approaches is that they are overly simplistic. They emphasise isolated components of a good teacher's behaviour and lose sight of the fact that what distinguishes a good from a poor teacher is the ability to utilize those skills effectively, as part of a larger conceptualisation of the teaching process. Good and poor teachers alike already 'redirect questions', 'ask higher-order questions' and 'wait for student responses', and simply increasing the frequency of such practices without providing an understanding of the contexts within which they are effective will not produce a better teacher.

As teachers of language, we should recognise the problems immediately. They are directly analogous to those we have long recognised in language programmes that focus on the subskills of reading, writing or speaking without providing real contexts for use. The examples from our field are many, ranging from the long tradition of unsuccessful teaching of the rules of formal grammar, to reading programmes that have been preoccupied with phonics, to spelling and vocabulary drills conducted in isolation from our students' own uses of language. We know that such skills-orientated programmes are easy to construct and easy to monitor; we know too that any improvements they generate in our students' reading and writing ability are minor and short-lived. Why then do we not react more quickly to similar problems in teacher-education programmes?

Teaching as scholarship

The other image of the necessary preparation for teaching stresses the importance of knowledge of the content field, in our case usually literature. On the face of it, arguments for the importance of such knowledge are unassailable: we can hardly teach a subject we do not know something about. The problem here is of a different nature; it concerns the role of such knowledge in school teaching.

When we start to teach a new subject, one of the most powerful influences on what we do is our memory of how we were taught. [. . .] Thus the teacher's role that is shaped by a conception of scholarship in an academic field, rather than by an understanding of the teacher–student relationship. As long as we leave our beginning teachers to rely upon the content of their college curriculum for their understanding of the content of [. . .] instruction, we are reinforcing a tradition of what Barnes (1976) has called 'transmission' rather than 'interpretation'. We are inviting teachers to tell students what they should know, rather than giving students an active role in making sense of new material.

An alternative view

But if there are serious problems in the two major conceptions shaping teacher-education programmes, where can we turn for an alternative view? The best source is in contemporary scholarship on language and learning, a rich body of scholarship which we have used to examine how schoolchildren learn but which we have yet to exploit fully to help us think about the problems of teacher education.

The past twenty years have been a particularly fruitful time for language studies, as indeed they have been for the study of child development in general. The theories of Piaget, Vygotsky, Bruner and others have become widely known, and with them has emerged an image of the child as an active participant in the process of the construction of knowledge. Approaches to reading instruction and to writing instruction have been transformed as teachers and scholars have become aware of the complex processes of comprehension and understanding that go into a reader's or writer's approach to a text. Rather than focusing on the accuracy of the final product, process-oriented approaches to instruction have sought to provide support for the young learner still in the process of solving the problems posed by a particular reading or writing task. 'Prereading' and 'prewriting' activities have become part of the conventional wisdom about effective instruction, as have multiple drafts, peer response groups, small-group discussion and other techniques designed to give students a more active role in the negotiation of meaning within their classrooms. [. . .]

As we have learned more about the processes of language and learning, we have also been developing a third body of knowledge to compete with generic teaching skills and traditional subject scholarship for a place in the teacher-education curriculum. This body of knowledge might best be thought of as *subject-specific knowledge of teaching*. In the field of English teaching this subject-specific knowledge is based on scholarship in a variety of fields, but the form it takes is rather different. In its most useful form subject-specific knowledge of English teaching is practical knowledge of the nature of children's English skills, the directions of growth these skills will follow, and the contexts that foster such growth. It is knowledge, for example, of the kinds of literature 12 year olds are likely to find difficult, how they make sense of specific works when they read them, and how teachers can structure classroom activities to develop new skills and strategies that may make initially difficult works easier.

In this form subject-specific knowledge of teaching looks very different from knowledge of traditional subject matter. The concerns of the scholar – whether those concerns focus on theories of literary criticism or structures of language – are different from the concerns of the classroom teacher. The universe of scholarship is not irrelevant to the universe of teaching, for the scholar and the teacher are likely to draw on the same texts and have, ultimately, shared goals of understanding those texts better. But the concerns of scholarship must be fundamentally reconstrued before they become relevant to the classroom. It is this reconstrual that should be at the heart of teacher-education programmes.

Principled practice

What should such a construal look like? One typical approach to defining content for teacher training has been to focus on the performance of expert practitioners or model programmes. Such a concern with identifying and promulgating examples of good practice underlies many popular movements in education. [. . .]

These attempts exemplify one seemingly very sensible approach to the specification of good practice. Each relies upon the provision of model approaches, validated against some external criteria. [. . .]

Though seemingly sensible, each of these attempts has failed to have a widespread impact on educational practice. Such failure may be due to the entrenched nature of current approaches to schooling, to the inability to reach a wide enough audience or to some fundamental flaw in the newly advocated approaches themselves. But I want to suggest another and more far-reaching reason for the failure of these reform movements: we have allowed our understanding of teaching and learning to focus on *what* we do when we teach – the activities and curriculum – rather than on *why* we do it – the principles underlying instruction in general and our subject in particular. We need the kind of shift in our thinking that we made in our understanding of reading and writing processes during the past two decades: from a focus on the skills that students need to a focus on the general process of making meaning, from *what* to *why*.

What difference would it make? Current attempts to promulgate 'good practice' give us careful, often enthusiastic, descriptions of new or reborn activities, activities that work beautifully in their original contexts, and that often continue to work well when transported by first-generation disciples. In the enthusiasm for defining good practice, these approaches are often codified in elaborate detail – a detail that describes very accurately exactly what goes on in the successful model classrooms. In turn, these codifications make their way into our methods course, either in encyclopedic methods texts or in collections of readings designed to introduce our students to a variety of successful techniques.

The trouble comes when the approach must be transferred to other schools and teachers, facing a different combination of student needs and experiences. In such a circumstance no set of materials and approaches can successfully be introduced 'as is'; they must be adapted and modified to fit each new context in which they are used. Teachers will take from the new materials what they need for their own classes. This process of 'taking from the new' approach often – perhaps even usually – preserves the form of the approach, but is equally likely to subvert the original purpose, *unless the original purpose is well understood*. If we truly understand *why* a particular approach is working, on the other hand, it is quite possible it will be successfully implemented in new contexts without incorporating any of the 'model' activities at all – if the functions of the original activities can be better served by other activities in the teachers' repertoire.

Where does this leave my concern with the content of teacher education? It suggests that our approaches to teacher training should focus on the development of *principled practice*. Rather than the teacher-proof models of good instruction, models of principled practice would rely on developing the novice teacher's understanding of *why* a particular approach was chosen, and on developing his/her expertise in creating his/her own solutions to the unique problems that a teacher faces in every classroom. Rather than focusing on particular activities that teachers should use, such an approach would focus on principles for orchestrating activities, for choosing what should happen next and why.

[. . .]

The process of learning to teach

So far I have focused primarily on the content of teacher-education programmes, on the question of what beginning teachers should know. But issues of content are not really separate from issues of the process of teaching: what we know is conditioned by how we have learned it.

Here again, our approaches to teacher education have lagged far behind our understanding of children's learning. Our studies of learning have increasingly emphasised the importance of learning in context, of allowing children to take ownership for what they do, of engaging them in an active process of problem definition and problem solving. Our approaches to teacher education, on the other hand, have continued to emphasise knowledge *about* teaching, gained primarily through reading about what others have done.

[. . .] What teachers choose to do in the classroom is shaped by a variety of complex factors, ranging from the demands of a particular curriculum to the needs of particular classes to the time of day and state of the weather. The art of teaching involves the ability to respond to these complex and interacting forces, selecting an approach that will provide the best balance at a given point in time, an approach that will look different on another day or in a different classroom. If we have taught our teacher-education students that the world looks otherwise – that there is a solution they can rely on day in and day out – they are in for a rude and usually painful awakening to the realities of classroom life.

What is our alternative? To use our teacher-education classes as places to introduce students to a range of real problems that they must face as teachers, clarifying principles of good practice as they struggle to find appropriate responses to the problems that we have introduced. If the problems are real, they will have no answers – only a range of alternative approaches that may be valid under different circumstances [. . .].

Principles of effective instruction

Much of my argument so far has been based on the assumption that much that we have already learned about language teaching can be applied, in turn, to the problems of learning to teach. I want to carry that argument one step further now, and to claim that the most effective teacher-education programmes will be governed by the same principles that govern effective teaching of oral and written language. The principles of practice that we teach our beginning teachers, in other words, should also govern how we go about that teaching.

Judith Langer and I, in a series of articles and reports, have argued that many problems in instruction can be traced directly to conceptualisations of teaching that reduce it essentially to a process of diagnosing what students know, teaching the missing information, testing to see what they have learned and reteaching – in a never-ending cycle (Applebee, 1986; Applebee and Langer, 1983; Langer, 1984; Langer and Applebee, 1986, 1987). This model of teaching fits well with 'transmission' views of instruction, but is fundamentally incompatible with process-oriented approaches in which error is expected as part of the process of learning, and in which constructive response and final evaluation are very separate (and necessarily separated) processes.

To provide teachers with an alternative way of viewing their teaching, we have developed the metaphor of *instructional scaffolding* as a way to think about the teacher's role in effective instruction. In this metaphor the teacher's role is one of providing appropriate support as students engage in new and more difficult tasks. This support should be structured to help students internalise new and more sophisticated problem-solving strategies which they will eventually be able to use on their own; at that point the scaffolding will no longer be needed and the teacher's attention can move on to new tasks.

We originally developed the notion of instructional scaffolding to describe effective teaching of reading and writing (Langer and Applebee, 1986), drawing for our arguments on earlier studies of the developments of young children's language skills in interaction with adults (who provided appropriate scaffolding to support early language activities). But the model can be generalised, and provides a good way to think about our work with beginning teachers. The model's five criteria follow:

1 *Ownership*   Activities that we ask students to undertake must provide room for them to make their own contribution to the task; activities will be less effective if students complete them simply by reciting the teacher or text. In our methods courses this

means that the problems we pose must be open-ended, not simply contexts for testing whether students have learned a technique or approach that we may favour.

2 *Appropriateness*   Activities should be too difficult for students to complete on their own, but not so difficult that they cannot complete them with help. Vygotsky put this best when he noted that 'instruction should be aimed not so much at the ripe, but at the ripening functions'. This implies a careful staging of the problems we introduce, beginning with activities which teachers-in-training can engage in by drawing upon their own experiences as students, and gradually introducing tasks which also require them to reflect upon their new experiences as teachers.

3 *Structure*   Instructional activities should model an appropriate sequence of thought and language. This will ensure that in carrying out the task students will also be given strategies and approaches which they can eventually use on their own. A corollary point is that the techniques that are introduced need to be highlighted as the strategies they are, making students aware of the tools that are available and the ways in which those tools can be used. Put another way, as we introduce students to new approaches, it also helps to cultivate the metacognitive skills necessary for them to use the approaches most effectively.

4 *Collaboration*   The teacher's role in the process of learning should be collaborative rather than evaluative. Evaluation also has a place in instruction, but the process of assessment needs to be separated from the process of teaching and learning. When the two are confounded, we test but do not teach.

5 *Transfer of control*   As students learn what we are teaching, the scaffolding we have provided needs to be removed so that they can take full control of the activity for themselves. Our attention as teachers can then move on to help them develop approaches to other, more difficult, problems which they cannot yet cope with on their own.

Reflective teaching

If we approach teacher education in the ways I have been suggesting, we will transform not only the teacher-training programme but also the vision of the teacher as professional. Teachers who emerge from such a programme will be teachers who have a way of thinking about and reflecting upon their experiences that will help them continue to grow, improving their own teaching and, ultimately, helping them contribute to a continuing professional dialogue about the principles of effective practice.

References

Applebee, A. N. (1986) 'Problems in Process Approaches: Toward a Reconcep-
   tualisation of Process Instruction', in A. Petrovsky and D. Bartholomew (eds),
   The Teaching of Writing. Eighty-fifth Yearbook of the National Society for the
   Study of Education. Chicago: NSSE.

Applebee, A. N. and Langer, J. A. (1983) 'Instructional Scaffolding: Reading and
   Writing as Natural Language Activities', *Language Arts*, 60, pp. 168–75.

Barnes, D. (1976) *From Communication to Curriculum*. London: Penguin.

Langer, J. A. (1984) 'Literacy Instruction in American Schools: Problems and
   Perspectives', *American Journal of Education*, 93, 1, pp. 107–32.

Langer, J. A. and Applebee, A. (1986) 'Reading and Writing Instruction: Toward
   a Theory of Teaching and Learning', in E. Rothkopf (ed.), *Review of Research in
   Education*, 13, pp. 171–94.

Langer, J. A. and Applebee, A. N. (1987) 'Language Learning and Interaction: a
   Framework for the Teaching of Writing', in A. N. Applebee (ed.), *Contexts for
   Learning to Write*. Norwood, NJ: Ablex.

3.6

Changing Perspectives on Teaching-Learning Processes in the Post-Plowden Era

Neville Bennett

Introduction

Reports, like theories, are products of their time, and at the time the Plowden Committee were considering their evidence few attempts had been made to develop empirical theories of teaching-learning processes in classrooms. Thus Gage (1963), for example, made a plea in the *Handbook of Research on Teaching* for researchers to take classroom phenomena seriously and design studies which related classroom processes to educational outcomes. There was little to guide them, however. There was a burgeoning literature of learning, little of which had any clear implications for pedagogy, and a few fairly crude theories of teaching, based not on the observation of practice, but loosely on American conceptions of democracy, manifested in such dichotomies as integrative versus dominative teaching. The theoretical cupboard was bare and the Plowden Committee responded by seeking refuge in ideology, by dipping eclectically into what Cremin (1961) called the pluralistic, often self-contradictory field of progressive education.

Simon, writing in Galton *et al.* (1980), argued that although the report was ambiguous in parts, it clearly and definitely espoused child-centred approaches in general, and concepts of informal education in particular. The classroom and curriculum processes categorising informal education are set out in Bennett (1976) and elaborated by Simon to present a sketch of the ideal Plowden-type teacher and her class:

> The children are active, engaged in exploration or discovery, interacting both with the teacher and each other. Each child operates as an individual, although groups are formed and re-formed related to these activities, which are not normally subject differentiated. The teacher moves around the classroom, consulting, guiding, stimulating individual children or occasionally, for convenience, the groups of children which are brought together for some specific

activity, or are 'at the same stage'. She knows each child individually, and how best to stimulate or intervene with each. In this activity she bears in mind the child's intellectual, social and physical levels of development and monitors these. On occasions the whole class is brought together, for instance, for a story or music, or to spark off or finalise a class project, otherwise class teaching is seldom used, the pupils' work and the teacher's attention being individualised or grouped.

What Plowden proposed, then, was a package deal. This, and the thin theoretical and empirical veneer used to justify such conclusions as ' "finding out" has proved to be better than "being told" ', stimulated the inevitable responses. Peters (1969) detected a yearning for some overall recipe for teaching and questioned why such an either/or view of teaching should be subscribed to. What has happened, he continued, 'is that a method for learning some things has become puffed up into the method for learning almost everything'. Bernstein and Davis, in the same volume, argued that sin and virtue appeared to have changed sides in the teaching transaction, and complained of a curious jumble of fact and prescription. Dearden (1973) rightly pointed out that the psychological doctrines used as justification of the approach prescribed could just as easily be used to justify opposing approaches. Bruner (1976) complained of a means-ends muddle, and Naish et al. (1976) argued sceptically that the evidence indicated that decisions about what teaching methods to recommend were taken prior to any survey of relevant research, and then various bits of psychological research were surveyed simply in the hope of finding support for the decisions already taken.

The aim of this article is not to present yet another analytic critique of the quality of Plowden's conceptualisations, but to provide an appropriate empirical perspective from which to consider the utility of the model of teaching prescribed. To this end changing trends in research on teaching-learning processes in primary schools during the last 20 years will be delineated. Theoretical and empirical perspectives will be emphasised more than actual findings in order to explicate the progress made in understanding and explaining classroom phenomena and their effects.

Teaching styles

Studies which adopted a teaching styles approach began in the late 1960s and continued for over a decade. They were characterised by the collection of data on teacher behaviours on which were based classifications or typologies of teachers. The resultant teacher types or styles identified teachers who were teaching in similar ways. These styles were then related to changes in pupil achievement and attitudes.

One strand of this body of research was influenced, at a theoretical level, by the Plowden Report. Data were gathered on behaviours identified in the report as being characteristic of progressive or informal teaching, and such studies resulted in dichotomies or continua of teacher styles variously labelled progressive-traditional, informal-formal and exploratory-didactic (cf. Barker-Lunn, 1970; Cane and Smithers, 1972; Bennett, 1976; HMI, 1978). In the United States the so-called open education movement, grounded in Plowden ideology, also stimulated a plethora of studies.

A second strand of research on teaching styles was influenced theoretically by interaction models. Here data were acquired on specific aspects of teacher-pupil interactions on which were based classifications of styles. The labels attached to these styles, however, tend to be based on predominant teacher roles such as 'actor-manager' (Eggleston et al., 1976) and 'classroom enquirer' (Galton et al., 1980).

It is not the purpose here to provide a review of the outcomes of such studies. Suffice it to say that contemporary reviewers in Britain and the United States are agreed that formal or traditional teaching does appear related to slightly increased learning gains in mathematics and language but that there may be gains in the affective domain from informal approaches (Gray and Satterly, 1981; Anthony, 1982; Giaconia and Hedges, 1983). Nevertheless, it has to be said that the ideological basis of Plowden's theory, aligned as it was to a particular set of political beliefs about the nature of man and society, has meant that the results of studies of teaching styles have tended to generate more political heat than pedagogical light.

What then is the status of research on teaching styles? Despite the fact that such studies were based on differing theoretical perspectives they shared common conceptions and assumptions about the nature of teaching and learning, and also shared difficulties of a technical and substantive nature.

Since teaching styles are composed of groups or bundles of teacher behaviours, the differential impact of individual teacher behaviours is impossible to ascertain. Thus, for example, it is not possible to identify a specific behaviour or behaviours within a formal or a classroom enquiring style which maximises achievement, or those within an informal style which appear to engender improved motivation. As such the findings are of little value in seeking improvements in teaching or teacher training. Secondly, examination of the research literature indicates that within-style differences in achievement are often as large as between-style differences. As such style is, in itself, insufficient to explain differences in outcomes. This could, in part at least, be due to technical limitations in statistical analyses of pupil change. Finally, teaching style studies assume a direct relationship between teaching behaviours and pupil learning which, paradoxically, carries with it an implicit denial of the influence of pupils in their own learning.

The inability of gross classifications of teachers to inform improvements in practice, doubts about style as a useful explanatory variable, and the myopic focus on the teacher were all powerful drawbacks to the approach. It had outlived its usefulness. New perspectives were needed which allowed specific delineation of teacher and pupil behaviours in relation to stated outcomes.

Opportunity to learn

An alternative theoretical perspective on teaching-learning processes, which overcame some of the drawbacks of the styles approach, emerged in the mid-1970s from a re-working and refining of a model of school learning first published a decade earlier (Carroll, 1963). This model, since elaborated by a number of theorists (Bloom, 1976; Harnischfeger and Wiley, 1976) utilises aspects of time and opportunity to learn as central concepts. The basic assumption is that there is no direct relationship between teacher behaviours and pupil achievement since all effects of teaching on learning are mediated by pupil activities, i.e. pupil learning activities are central to their learning. In particular the amount of time a pupil spends actively engaged on a particular topic is seen as the most important determinant of achievement on that topic. In this model the pupil, therefore, becomes the central focus with the teacher seen as the manager of the attention and time of pupils in relation to the educational ends of the classroom. In other words the teacher manages the scarce resources of attention and time.

These models have been very influential in research on teaching both in providing the theory to drive research studies and in interpreting past research which has utilised similar concepts. The body of research literature is now extremely large and only a brief account can be presented here [. . .]

The broadest definition of opportunity to learn is the amount of interaction children have with school – the extent to which they are exposed to schooling. Quantity of schooling relates to the total amount of time the school is open for its stated purpose and is defined by the length of school day and school year. Length of school day has, for example, been found to vary as much as six hours per week in Britain even in the same geographical locality. At the level of the individual pupil exposure to schooling varies in relation to the extent of pupil absence, and to school-based policies regarding the amount of homework. There are indications that length of school day, absence and homework are all related to pupil achievement. [. . .]

If curriculum allocation is conceived as the opportunity provided for pupils to interact with given curriculum content, then pupil involvement or engagement can be conceived as the use that pupils make of that opportunity. Many studies have provided descriptions of the extent of pupil involvement across all school ages and although the working definitions of pupil involvement are not always completely compatible there appears to be a law of two-thirds emerging. On average pupils appear to be involved about two-thirds of the time, but this varies markedly from class to class, and from pupil to pupil in the same class.

The extent of pupil involvement has also been studied within the context of classroom groups. The practice of grouping was encouraged by the Plowden Report where it was perceived to provide the best compromise in achieving individualisation of learning and teaching within the time available. 'Teachers therefore have to economise by teaching together a small group of children who are roughly at the same stage'. Among the benefits assumed of group work were that children would learn to get along together, to help one another and realise their own, and others', strengths and weaknesses. Advantages were seen in children having to teach and explain to others, and in stretching the more able children through the thrust and counter-thrust of conversation.

Unfortunately, research on classroom groups portrays a very different picture. At Junior school level both Boydell (1975) and Galton *et al.* (1980) report that group interaction is clearly differentiated by sex, conversations are not sustained and a high proportion of group talk is not related to the tasks set. The picture at infant school level is rosier with a higher level of talk devoted to the task and little sign of sex bias (Bennett *et al.*, 1984). Nevertheless, much of the talk appears to be about the task rather than its enhancement, i.e. talk which furthers task performance such as informing and explaining is very low, comprising some 8 per cent of all talk.

This, in part, is a function of how teachers manage groups. Plowden envisaged that teaching would be to groups, and that they would be involved in cooperative endeavours. However, although it is typical for children to be sat in groups, they actually work as individuals on their own tasks for the great majority of the time. Pupils sit in groups but do not work as groups.

Research relating pupil involvement to achievement has generally reported positive relationships but of widely varying strength. In general, however, the data would seem to lend some support to William James's argument of 1902, that 'whether the attention comes by grace of genius or by dint of will the longer one does attend to a topic the more mastery of it one has'.

Nevertheless the amount of time pupils interact with their task is by no means a complete explanation of achievement. Time has been likened to an empty box (Gage, 1978) which requires filling with comprehensible and worthwhile content. [. . .] The cluster of variables which have been of concern here include the presentation of the task; the sequence, level and pacing of content; teachers' levels of expectation of their pupils, and types of feedback from teacher to child, including those with behavioural and academic intentions.

The outcomes of research studies within the opportunity to learn paradigm have been relatively consistent and have been used as the basis for hortatory pleas for teachers to increase time on task (Denham and Lieberman, 1980); to develop experimental intervention programmes with the purpose of improving pupil achievement and/or classroom management (Emmer *et al.*, 1981; Gage and Colardarci, 1980; Good and Grouws, 1979); and for the development of prescriptive models of teaching such as the Direct Instructional Model [. . .] which shares many features with the characteristics of effective teaching recently stated in the ILEA Junior School Project (1986) e.g. the structured school day where pupils' work is organised by the teacher, a high level of pupil industry, low noise level, movement low and work related, single subject teaching, etc. (cf. Brophy and Good, 1985 for a comprehensive overview of this research). [. . .]

There is little to be gained from high pupil involvement on tasks that are either not comprehensible or worthwhile. Time is thus a necessary, but not sufficient condition for learning. As was argued earlier, time is an empty vessel but the research within the opportunity to learn approach has generally restricted itself to delineating and quantifying the dimensions of the vessel rather than attending to the quality of its content. Exhortations to increase curriculum allocation or to improve levels of pupil involvement are of no avail if the quality of the task is poor or not related to pupils' intellectual capabilities. The teaching styles and opportunity to learn approaches have provided abundant evidence on the relationship between teacher and pupil behaviours and long-term, norm-referenced, achievement measures, but what they have neglected are the mediation processes by which teaching and learning influence each other, together with an almost total neglect of the learning process itself. Such limitations throw into sharp relief issues central to the explanation of teaching and learning. Activities of the learner on assigned classroom tasks may be seen as crucial mediators in converting teacher behaviours into learning behaviours, but the models so far considered offer little comment on how these processes operate in practice. There is little description, analysis or explanation of how classroom tasks are assigned or worked under normal classroom conditions and constraints, despite the fact that most intended school learning is embedded in the tasks teachers assign to pupils.

Classroom tasks

Most recently therefore there has been a move from a process-product to a mediating-process paradigm (Doyle, 1979; Evertson, 1980), representing a shift in focus from time to task, utilising insights provided by cognitive psychology. From this perspective the tasks which pupils engage in structure to a large extent what information is selected from the environment and how it is processed. Tasks organise experience and thus an understanding of that experience, and the process of acquisition first requires an understanding of the tasks which pupils work.

An acceptance of this perspective requires a change in the conceptions of the learner from a behaviourist to a constructivist position, i.e. from a portrayal of the learner as an objective, passive recipient of sensory experience who can learn anything if provided enough practice, to a learner actively making use of cognitive strategies and previous knowledge to deal with cognitive limitations. In this conception learners are active, constructivist and interpretive, and learning is a covert, intellectual process providing the development and re-structuring of existing conceptual schemes.

However, reliance on a cognitive psychological perspective is insufficient to explain classroom phenomena. Constructivist models of the child contain no serious treatment of the nature of the social environment in which learning takes place. Thus any study which seeks to explain the dynamics between teaching and learning also requires a model of classrooms as complex social settings. Such models are rare. Doyle's (1979, 1983) ecological model of mediating processes is the most fully specified, viewing classrooms as enduring complex environments and information systems to which teachers and pupils must adapt.

Constructivist models of learning and mediating process models of classrooms point clearly to classroom tasks as the crucial mediators linking teachers and pupils. The only British classroom-based study to adopt this perspective collected data on teacher intentions, task specifications, pupil performance on their tasks, their understanding or misconceptions of these, and teacher diagnoses of completed tasks, to characterise the intellectual demands of the tasks set and whether these demands were appropriate to pupils' capabilities (Bennett et al., 1984).

From these data it was apparent that the tasks teachers set do not always embody their intentions, e.g. over one fifth of all tasks observed failed to meet their intended aim. The actual intellectual demand apparent in the majority of tasks in language and mathematics was limited to increments of knowledge or skill, and practice. There was thus little opportunity for the application of knowledge in new contexts or for the active discovery of new knowledge and skills. Approximately 40 per cent of tasks matched pupils' capabilities but there was a strong trend toward the overestimation of low attaining pupils and the underestimation of high attainers. In other words, low attainers were given work that was too hard and high attainers work that was too easy, a finding supported by HMI Surveys (1978, 1983, 1985; Bennett *et al.*, 1987). Teachers tended to stress the procedural aspects of tasks and mechanical progress through a scheme of work rather than pupil understanding. Neither were pupil understandings or misconceptions diagnosed by teachers, who generally limited themselves to judgements of whether things were right or wrong.

Although limited in number, studies utilising the task perspective have pointed to the significant influence of teacher knowledge systems on classroom practice, raising such questions as, how can teachers teach well knowledge that they themselves do not thoroughly understand? How can teachers make clear decisions regarding what counts as development in content areas with which they are not thoroughly conversant? How can teachers accurately and adequately diagnose the nature of pupil misconceptions or misunderstandings without an adequate knowledge base? These are important considerations in primary schools where teachers tend to be generalists and where worries are being expressed about the considerable proportion of teachers who have difficulty in selecting and utilising subject matter in some part of the curriculum. Similar sets of questions can also be raised about the teachers' knowledge base and actions regarding the management of learning in terms of setting the scene and the organisation of resources, both material and human, to provide optimal learning environments.

Current work is addressing some of these issues. Research on subject matter knowledge of teachers is virtually non-existent but a start has been made in detailing the characteristics of knowledge which constitutes skill in teaching in expert and novice teachers (Leinhardt and Smith, 1985). The characterisation of knowledge is difficult methodologically and attempts currently rely on representation by semantic and planning networks and flow charts. With such tools the ability to display teacher knowledge systems could, for example, determine whether teachers have conceptual understanding, and if, and how, this understanding is transmitted in teacher explanations.

The heavy demands made on teachers' knowledge structures to select and set tasks, diagnose pupil conceptions, teach cognitive processes, and manipulate complex learning environments for classes of children requires the routinisation of many teachers' actions. These simplify the complexity of the teaching task and reduce the cognitive load and ensure that diversion of cognitive resources from substantive activities and goals of teaching is less necessary. Not surprisingly, therefore, teacher routines are of increasing research interest (Leinhardt and Greeno, 1984; Lowyck, 1984; Olson, 1984) both in investigating the role they play in skilled teacher performances and the extent to which they are appropriate to the development of pupil understanding.

Conclusion

In viewing the last two decades of research on teaching-learning processes and their effects it is evident that three distinct trends are discernible, each characterised by a unique set of theoretical premises, assumptions, variables and methods. Research on teaching styles has shown that the package of teacher behaviours classified as progressive, informal or exploratory provides no particular advantages, particularly in the basic skills areas. The most recent British studies by HMI (1978); Galton *et al.*, (1980) and the ILEA Research Unit (1986) together with most other international studies, all present data on effective teaching practices which bear little relationship to Plowden's ideal type. Nevertheless it should be noted that this body of research has been descriptive, i.e. based on observations of current practice. But this practice rarely conforms to Plowden's prescriptions. The data gathered cannot therefore be considered a test of the theory itself.

The management of classroom groups is a good example of partial implementation. Teachers certainly organise their class into groups, but these are no more than physical juxtapositions of children engaged in individual work. Plowden, on the other hand, envisaged that groups would be the focus of teaching, and would be involved in collaborative activities. This latter practice would appear to be successful (cf. Bennett, 1985) whereas the former is not.

[. . .]

Research on teaching styles could only chart contemporary practice rather than provide a direct test of the prescriptions. It was also hindered by its inability to seek improvements in practice since the only option available was to embrace, or otherwise, a particular style comprising a particular set of behaviours. But complex instructional problems cannot be solved with such simple prescriptions. As Brophy and Good (1985) argue: 'in the past when detailed information describing classroom processes and linking them to outcomes did not exist, educational change efforts were typically based on simple theoretical models and associated rhetoric calling for solutions that were both over-simplified and overly rigid. No such solution can be effective'. Models of teaching were thus needed which were more powerful in their explanatory potential, which could direct attention to specific processes that could be improved, and which allowed greater understanding of the effects of process on outcomes. The opportunity to learn model directed attention to time allocations in schooling, curriculum and task, highlighting the importance of hitherto neglected variables, such as curriculum balance and pupil involvement. As Jackson noted as early as 1968 'in education courses and in the professional literature involvement, and its opposite, some form of detachment, are largely ignored. Yet, from a logical point of view, few topics would seem to have greater relevance for the teacher's work. Certainly no educational goals are more immediate than those that concern the establishment and maintenance of the students' absorption in the task at hand. Almost all other objectives are dependent for their accomplishment upon the attainment of this basic condition'. Yet this fact, he argued, quoting Morrison's work on the practice of teaching in 1927, 'seems to have been more appreciated in the past than it is today'.

Nevertheless research on opportunity to learn, in emphasising the quantification of time, neglected to characterise the nature and quality of classroom tasks. And, in common with the teaching styles approach, it neglected the process of learning itself. Until recently research on learning has tended to ignore the processes of teaching, and research on teaching has largely ignored the processes of learning. However, the recent focus on task structures has heralded an attempted reconciliation whereby concepts and models developed in the laboratories of cognitive psychologists are being brought to bear on problems specified with increasing precision by researchers on teaching. Thus time, or involvement, is now viewed as a necessary but not sufficient condition for learning, and the focus has shifted to study the interactions of teacher, pupil and task within complex social settings.

More specifically the focus of research is now on the quality of the classroom tasks which pupils engage, the accuracy of diagnosis of children's understandings and misconceptions of concepts and content, and the quality of teacher explanations to this end. This approach takes due account of the role of the pupil in mediating and structuring knowledge and places even greater stress on teacher competence in subject matter, pedagogical and curriculum knowledge. On the basis of the evidence of this approach, and its implications for teacher competences, Shulman and Carey (1984) note that

> one . . . develops a more modest image of the capacity of teachers . . . to discern the understanding or misconceptions of each pupil in the class, to monitor the variety of events occurring simultaneously in a particular classroom or to portray the subject matters in representations adequate for all pupils. The limitations of teachers are not a product of their low aptitude scores, they are a product of their humanity!

It is of interest to note in this regard that for much of his career Dewey never fully communicated to some who thought themselves to be his disciples the qualities demanded of teachers. A teacher, he argued, cannot know which opportunities to use, which impulses to encourage or which social attitudes to cultivate without a clear sense of what is to come later. With respect to character, this implies a conception of the kind of individual who is to issue from the school; and with respect to intellect, this implies a thorough acquaintance with organised knowledge as represented in the disciplines. To recognise opportunities for early mathematical learning, one must know mathematics: to recognise opportunities for elementary scientific learning, one must know physics, chemistry, biology and geology: and so on down the list of fields of knowledge. In short, he contended that the demand on the teachers is two-fold, a thorough knowledge of the disciplines and an awareness of those common experiences of childhood that can be utilised to lead children towards the understandings represented by this knowledge. However, he recognised that the demand of this was indeed weighty and easily side-stepped, arguing that simple as it is to discard traditional curricula in response to cries for reform, it is even simpler to substitute for them a succession of chaotic activities that not only fail to facilitate growth but actually end up miseducative in quality and character (cf. Cremin, 1961).

Unlike some of the Plowden recommendations which still have contemporary relevance, such as the role of parents and nursery education, the model of teaching prescribed has not stood the test of time. Theories of teaching-learning processes have since been developed which are more powerful in their explanatory potential, and have led to a more sophisticated understanding of the impact of classroom processes on intended outcomes. Thus, whether teachers teach in a so-called progressive or traditional mode is largely irrelevant. Teachers need a repertoire of teaching styles, the effectiveness of which can be judged against criteria delineated by recent research, i.e. the extent to which tasks are appropriate to pupil capabilities, the degree to which pupils are motivated and involved in their work, the quality of their understandings of content and concepts and the adequacy of teacher diagnosis and explanation. A similar report written today would no doubt reflect such findings, but as important, would contain a clear explication of their implications for training and practice, and consideration of the structures appropriate for successful implementation.

References

Anthony, W. S. (1982) 'Research on Progressive Teaching', *British Journal of Educational Psychology*, 52, pp. 381–5.

Barker Lunn, J. (1970) *Streaming in the Primary School*. Slough: NFER.

Bennett, S. N. (1976) *Teaching Styles and Pupil Progress*. London: Open Books.

Bennett, S. N., Desforges, C. W., Cockburn, A. and Wilkinson, B. (1984) *The Quality of Pupil Learning Experiences*. London: Erlbaum.

Bennett, S. N. (1985) 'Interaction and Achievement in Classroom Groups', in S. N. Bennett and C. Desforges (eds), *Recent Advances in Classroom Research*. Edinburgh: Scottish Academic Press.

Bennett, S. N., Roth, E. and Dunne, R. (1987) 'Task Processes in Mixed and Single Age Classes', *Education*, 3–13, 15, (1), pp. 67–79.

Bernstein, B. and Davies, B. (1969) 'Some Sociological Comments on Plowden', in R. S. Peters (ed.), *Perspectives on Plowden*. London: Routledge and Kegan Paul.

Bloom, B. S. (1976) *Human Characteristics and School Learning*. New York: McGraw-Hill.

Boydell, D. (1975) 'Pupil Behaviour in Junior Classrooms', *British Journal of Educational Psychology*, 45, pp. 122–9.

Brophy, J. E. and Good, T. L. (1985) 'Teacher Behaviour and Student Achievement', in M. C. Wittrock (ed.), *Handbook of Research on Teaching*, 3rd edn. New York: Macmillan.

Bruner, J. (1976) Foreword to *Teaching Styles and Pupil Progress*. Cambridge, Mass.: Harvard University Press.

Cane, B. and Smithers, A. G. (1972) *The Roots of Reading*. Slough: NFER.

Carroll, J. B. (1963) 'A Model of School Learning', *Teachers College Record*, 64, pp. 723–33.

Cremin, L. A. (1961) *The Transformation of the School: Progressivism in American Education, 1876–1957*. New York: Knopf.

Dearden, R. F. (1973) What is Discovery Learning? *Education*, 3–13, 1, p. 13.

Denham, G. and Lieberman, A. (eds) (1980) *Time to Learn*. Washington: NIE.

Doyle, W. (1979) 'Classroom Tasks and Student Abilities', in P. L. Peterson and H. L. Walberg (eds), *Research on Teaching: Concepts, findings and implications*. Berkeley: McCutchaw.

Doyle, W. (1983) 'Academic Work', *Review of Educational Research*, 53, pp. 159–200.

Eggleston, J. F., Galton, M. and Jones, M. E. (1976) *Processes and Products of Science Teaching*. London: Macmillan/Schools Council.

Emmer, E. T., Sanford, J. P., Evertson, C. M., Clements, B. S. and Martin, J. (1981) *The Classroom Management Improvement Study: an experiment in elementary school classrooms*, Research and Development Centre for Teacher Education. Austin: University of Texas.

Evertson, C. M. (1980) 'In Search of What Outcomes Mean for an Ecological Theory', in *Schooling Outcomes: five multidisciplinary perspectives*. San Francisco: Far West Lab, pp. 31–46.

Fisher, C. W., Filby, N. N., Marliave, R., Cahen, L. S., Dishaw, M. M., Moore, J. E. and Berliner, D. C. (1978) *Teaching Behaviours, Academic Learning Time, and Student Achievement*, Final Report, Phase IIIB, BTES. San Francisco: Far West Lab.

Gage, N. L. (1963) 'Paradigms for Research on Teaching', in Gage, N. L. (ed.) *Handbook of Research on Teaching*, Chicago: Rand McNally and Co., pp. 94–141.

Gage, N. L. (1978) *The Scientific Basis of the Art of Teaching*. Columbia, New York: Teachers College Press.

Gage, N. L. and Coladarci, T. (1980) *Replication of an Experiment with a Research Based In-service Teacher Education Programme*, Programme on teacher effectiveness. School of Education, Stanford University.

Galton, M., Simon, B. and Croll, P. (1980) *Inside the Primary School*. London: Routledge and Kegan Paul.

Giaconia, R. M. and Hedges, L. V. (1983) 'Identifying Features of Effective Open Education', *Review of Educational Research*, 52, pp. 579–602.

Good, T. L. and Grouws, D. A. (1979) 'The Missouri Mathematics Effectiveness Project: an Experimental Study of Fourth Grade Classrooms', *Journal of Educational Psychology*, 71, pp. 355–362.

Gray, J. and Satterley, D. (1981) 'Formal or informal? A Reassessment of the British Evidence', *British Journal of Educational Psychology*, 51, pp. 187–96.

Harnischfeger, A. and Wiley, D. E. (1976) 'Teaching-Learning Processes in the Elementary School: a Synoptic View', *Studies of Education Processes*, No. 9. Chicago: University of Chicago Press.

HMI (1978) *Primary Education in England*. London: HMSO.

HMI (1983) *9–13 Middle Schools: an illustrative survey*. London: HMSO.

HMI (1985) *Education 8–12 in Combined and Middle Schools*. London: HMSO.

ILEA (1986) *The Junior School Project*. London: ILEA Research and Statistics Branch.

Jackson, P. W. (1968) *Life in Classrooms*. New York: Holt, Rinehart and Winston.

Leinhardt, G. and Greeno, J. G. (1984) *The Cognitive Skill of Teaching*. LRDC University of Pittsburgh.

Leinhardt, G. and Smith, D. A. (1985) 'Expertise in Mathematics Instructions: Subject Matter Knowledge', *Journal of Educational Psychology*, 77, pp. 247–71.

Lowyck, J. (1984) 'Teacher Thinking and Teacher Routines: a Bifurcation?' in R. Halkes and J. K. Olson (eds) *Teacher Thinking* (Lisse, Swets and Zeitlinger).

Morrison, H. C. (1927) *The Practice of Teaching in the Secondary School*. Chicago: University of Chicago Press.

Naish, M., Hartnell, A. and Finlayson, D. (1976) 'Ideological Documents in Education: Some Suggestions Towards a Definition', in A. Hartnell and M. Naish (eds), *Theory and the Practice of Education*, Vol. II. London: Heinemann.

Olson, J. (1984) 'What Makes Teachers Tick? Considering the Routines of Teaching', in R. Halkes and J. K. Olson, *Teacher Thinking*. Lisse: Swets and Zeitlinger.

Peters, R. S. (1969) 'A Recognisable Philosophy of Education: a Constructive Critique', in R. S. Peters (ed.) *Perspectives on Plowden*. London: Routledge and Kegan Paul.

Plowden Report (1967) *Children and their Primary Schools*, Report of the Central Advisory Council for Education (England). London: HMSO.

Shulman, L. S. and Carey, N. B. (1984) 'Psychology and the Limitations of Individual Rationality: Implications for the Study of Reasoning and Civility', *Review of Education Research*, 54, pp. 501–24.

SECTION 4

Assessing Learning

Introduction

A major aim of assessment research in the 1980s was to make assessment an integral part of the teaching and learning process. Assessment was to be seen as a tool of the curriculum. To function in this way, assessment practice must validly and reliably represent those aspects of learners and their achievements that are educationally significant.

The readings in this section look critically at factors which affect the achievement of these aims. The implications for assessment practice of alternative views of learners and their achievements are also explored.

The subjective judgement of intelligence is considered in the extract from Robert Sternberg's chapter. He demonstrates the changes in emphasis in the subjective selections of intelligent behaviours as students progress through the education system. He is critical of the limits that this imposes on certain students and argues that schools must make explicit to students their view of intelligent functioning. Graham Richards revisits the debate on heredity versus environment and points to crucial incoherencies in the current controversy. He sees the treatment of heredity and environment as 'separable mutually independent variables' as unacceptable, particularly when there is no apparent limit to what constitutes 'environment'. As the concept of intelligence includes an ability to respond to, and learn from, environmental experiences he considers any attempt to quantify the contribution of environment to intelligence as misguided.

To achieve curriculum changes, Tolley argues, one must change the methods of assessment and learning. He questions the validity of external examinations and whether a 16+ examination is justified. His main concern is the inadequate range of learning experiences available to pupils and recommends broadening the curriculum into the work environment. This move he suggests needs to be accompanied by the development of assessment of work-based learning.

Futcher in his response to Tolley's paper reflects on the problematic balance between assessment validity and reliability and the interrelatedness of the two concepts. He sees cause for concern in the interchangeable use of 'measurement' and 'assessment' when it is assessment that is practised. He looks critically at Tolley's suggestions for reform and points to the need to research exactly what skills are needed to achieve proficiency in tasks. The validity of assessment is explored more generally in Desmond Nuttall's article. He offers a definition of the concept and ways of assessing it. In Nuttall's view educational achievement should aim 'to permit those assessed to show their best performance'. He describes features of tasks and assessment situations which foster this aim. He suggests that historically reliability and utility have prevailed in assessment but that the balance is now being redressed in favour of validity.

The way in which the selected purpose of assessment and the methods used to achieve it reflect assumptions about education and the nature of learning is the central theme in Brenda Denvir's paper. In assessment for teaching she describes how a constructivist view of learning shifts the assessment concerns from a search for 'right answers' to documenting children's strategies. Like Nuttall she describes features of assessments which affect pupils' perception of tasks. However, arguing from a constructivist position, she suggests that it is the child's perception of the task and not the teacher's which should be assessed.

In assessment for selection she confronts the additional problems of the lack of consensus about mathematical attainment (particularly given its cultural derivation) and the mismatch between selection aims and learner needs. Assessment for evaluation purposes should, according to Denvir, be about progress yet she questions whether this is true of the National assessment system. The notion of satisfactory and unsatisfactory performance in evaluative assessment suggests a norm-referenced approach which contradicts a constructivist perspective.

The extract from the report of Records of Achievement is included to highlight diverse and changing views on educational achievement. Two perspectives are significant when looking at achievement, conceptions of the curriculum, and conceptions of the person. Depending on which stance is adopted the view of achievement is altered. The report provides examples of these differences in recorded achievements but as yet their significance has not been a matter for research.

The Graded Assessment projects provide Margaret Brown with interesting comparisons of assessment practice. In looking at the views of learning that informed the assessment developments she notes the consequences of the explicit constructivist view present in the mathematics project and the conflicting, implicit models of transmission and constructivism underlying the science assessment criteria. She identifies the fundamental notion of 'level' of achievement as one of the common structural features of the projects. Like Denvir she looks critically at the validity of this assessment construct and presents an empirical rather than a theoretical justification for it.

Janet White's article looks at the view of language which informs the Assessment of Performance Units language assessment. She describes the view as functionally orientated, concerned with the creation and interpretation of meaningful texts. She contrasts this with the view of language concerned solely with parts of speech. She goes on to show how characteristics of this view of language learning are translated into assessment instruments to produce a valid interpretation of pupils' language achievements.

Within the context of science assessment Patricia Murphy addresses the problem of gender bias in assessment. She draws attention to factors outside the curriculum which affect boys' and girls' views of their own competence. These views are shown to alter pupils' perceptions of tasks and their achievements on them. Murphy argues that these effects constitute a major source of invalidity in assessment practice if performance is interpreted in terms of criterion-referenced achievement. Yet such effects need to be documented for a formative assessment purposes.

4.1

Second Game: A School's-Eye View of Intelligence*

Robert J. Sternberg

[. . .]
The main thesis of this chapter is that in the world of intelligence, we need to understand the rules of two games, that almost all of the scientists choosing to study intelligence have studied the rules of the first game, and that this exclusive preoccupation with the first game has been a mistake. The rules of the first game are set by nature: the investigator needs to discover the latent mental structures and processes that underlie intelligence in an objective sense. [. . .] The rules of the second game are set by society: the investigator needs to discover the manifest behaviours that the society labels as intelligent in various situations and that underlie intelligence in a subjective sense. It will be argued that the rules of the first game are universal, whereas the rules of the second game are socio-culturally specific.

Some might ask: why study the rules of the second game at all? They might argue that it does not matter what people think intelligence is; what matters is what it actually is. To the extent that there is a difference between what intelligence actually is and what it is thought to be, they would say that such a difference merely represents human error. [. . .] But this point of view is wrong scientifically, and it is not only wrong but also pernicious educationally.

It is important to understand intelligence in both its objective and subjective aspects. Each aspect addresses a different question with relation to the individual. The objective aspect addresses the question of the relation between intelligence and the internal world

---

* In his chapter Sternberg looks at different group's perceptions of intelligence. The three student vignettes he presents have been extracted to demonstrate how the objective manifestation of intelligence can affect both the way a student is perceived by others and the way the student perceives herself or himself.

of the individual. What goes on 'inside a person's head' that renders the mental functioning of that person more or less intelligent? The subjective aspect addresses the question of the relation between intelligence and the external world of the individual: what goes on in the society that renders the behaviour of an individual to be judged as more or less intelligent? To the extent that intelligence is defined in terms of adaptation to one's environment, both aspects of intelligence are important. [. . .] A person who is thought by society and the schools to be intelligent – or unintelligent – will be treated in certain ways, regardless of their 'actual' intelligence. [. . .]

To the extent one is interested in education, the subjective aspect of intelligence is of paramount importance, because the conceptions of intelligence held and inculcated by the school – the school's-eye view of intelligence – will determine what is rewarded and what is punished, and ultimately, who garners society's rewards and who does not. People have long recognised the differences between the objective and subjective aspects of intelligence, and their importance for schooling. [. . .]

There is not, truly, any one school's-eye view of intelligence. The view can vary depending upon the age of the children involved, the point of view (e.g. children, parents of school children, teachers, administrators), and the time and place of the school under consideration. [. . .]

Three profiles of intelligence: Alice, Barbara, and Celia

Consider three students – Alice, Barbara, and Celia – who are or have been genuine students in our psychology graduate programme at Yale. [. . .] In analysing the profiles of these students, two questions need to be addressed: which students, if any, are intelligent in the objective sense, and which are intelligent in the subjective sense?

Alice was the admissions officer's dream. She was an easy admit to our graduate programme at Yale. She came with stellar aptitude test scores, outstanding college grades, excellent letters of recommendation, and overall, pretty close to a perfect record. Alice proved to be, more or less, what her record promised. She had excellent critical, analytical abilities, and these abilities helped her earn outstanding grades in her course work during her first two years at Yale. When it came to taking tests and writing course term papers, she had no peer among her classmates. During her first couple of years in the graduate programme, she was an outstanding success. But after the first two years, Alice no longer looked quite so outstanding. In our graduate programme, as well as in other programmes, there is a shift in emphasis after the first couple of years. This shift reflects a change in emphasis in many endeavours in human lives. In standard course work, the emphasis is upon critical, analytical ability, just the kinds of things that standard intelligence tests measure fairly well. But after the first two years, there is a shift in emphasis toward more creative, synthetic aspects of intelligence. It is not enough just to be able to criticise other people's ideas, or to learn and understand concepts that other people have proposed. One must start coming up with one's own ideas, and figuring out ways of implementing these ideas. Alice's synthetic abilities were far inferior to her analytic ones, but there would have been no good way of knowing this fact from the kinds of evidence available in the admissions folder. For although conventional measures can give us a fairly good reading on analytic abilities, they give virtually no reading on synthetic abilities. Thus, Alice was 'IQ-test' smart, but she was not equally intelligent in all senses of the word, and in particular, in the synthetic side of intelligence.

Barbara was the admissions officer's nightmare. When she applied to Yale, she had good grades, but abysmal aptitude test scores, at least by Yale standards. Despite these low scores, she had superlative letters of recommendation. Her recommenders described her as an exceptionally creative young woman, someone who had designed and implemented creative research with only the most minimal guidance. Moreover, her resume showed her to have been actively involved in important and publishable research. Her referees assured us that this research was a sign of her own ability to generate and to follow through on creative ideas, and that it was not merely a sign of the ability of her advisors. The first time Barbara applied to Yale, her case was discussed at length, but she was rejected. The long discussions she received in the admissions committee meeting seemed almost an attempt by the committee members to salve their collective conscience, with their knowing that ultimately they would reject her. The vote was five to one against her admission. Unfortunately, most people like Barbara are rejected not only from our programme, but from other competitive programmes as well. As a result, they either have to enter a programme that is much less competitive or else enter a different field altogether.

This pattern of events is not limited to graduate school. There are thousands of people like Barbara who are rejected in a similar way from law schools, business schools, education schools, medical schools, and the like. But in Barbara's case, an unusual thing happened. The one person who voted for her admission (myself, of course) was so convinced of her talents that he hired her as a full-time research associate. At the same time that she was a research associate, she also took two courses, two-thirds of the standard load of regular first-year graduate students. Her accomplishments during her initial year at Yale should have been an embarrassment to the admissions committee. She was one of the best students in both her classes, despite her working full time. She was not as good in classes as was Alice, but was certainly way above the average. Moreover, she showed herself to have the outstanding research abilities that her referees had promised: she independently involved herself in creative, enterprising research. The next year, Barbara reapplied to Yale, as well as to other graduate programmes. This time around, the vote for her admission was unanimous, and she was also admitted to other equally competitive programmes. [. . .]

Although Barbara was never quite so excellent as Alice in her course performance, she was ready for the change in demands of the graduate programme. When these demands shifted from an emphasis on analytic abilities to an emphasis on synthetic abilities, Barbara was ready: indeed, she was in her element. Barbara did not have Alice's analytic abilities, but she greatly surpassed Alice in synthetic abilities.

Celia, on paper, appeared to be somewhere between Alice and Barbara in terms of her suitability for admission to the graduate programme. She was very good on almost every measure of ability to succeed in graduate school, but not truly outstanding on any of them. We admitted her, expecting her to come out near the middle of the class. This did not happen. Rather, Celia proved to be outstanding, although in a way that is quite different from Alice or Barbara. Celia's expertise proved to be in figuring out and in adapting to the demands of a complex environment in which what is required for success is not always what would seem to be required, on paper. Placed in a new kind of setting, Celia can figure out what is required of her, and then go ahead and do it just right. She knows exactly how to get ahead. In conventional parlance, Celia is 'street-smart'. She excels in practical intelligence. It is not that Celia never made mistakes. But she made relatively few of them, and corrected them quickly. Moreover, she put herself in a position in which everyone was convinced that she had exactly the abilities it would take to obtain a good academic job and then do well in it. Although she had neither Alice's analytic abilities nor Barbara's synthetic ones, she was better able to take what abilities she had and apply them to the everyday environment of academia than practically anyone else who had come along within the recent past. For example, she made sure that she would have three excellent letters of recommendation (the number customarily required for job applications), whereas neither Alice nor Barbara, despite their outstanding accomplishments, had quite assured themselves that three recommenders were so well aware of their work that they could be counted on for strong letters.

The vignettes of Alice, Barbara, and Celia, informal though they may be, tell us something about intelligence, both as it is objectively defined and as it is subjectively defined.

First, the perceived nature of intelligence can change with level of schooling. Through college, analytic abilities weigh heavily in teachers' evaluations of intelligence. These abilities are important in standardised ability and achievement tests, in some teacher-made tests, in classroom discussions, and the like. Later on, whether in school or on the job, synthetic abilities become more important – the ability to come up with one's own new ideas and ways of implementing these ideas. There is a transition from particular valuing of Alices to particular valuing of Barbaras that, although not complete, is nevertheless quite noticeable.

Secondly, conventional standardised tests measure analytic abilities fairly well, but scarcely measure synthetic abilities at all. Nor is it clear, at the present time, how synthetic abilities can be measured in a nontrivial way. But, for lack of adequate predictor measures, teachers and administrators use measures of analytic ability to predict success, even when they are inappropriate. Alices almost always have the edge on prediction.

Thirdly, conventional standardised tests do not measure very well the student's ability both to make the most of his or her latent abilities, and to implement these abilities in everyday settings, whether inside or outside the school. This ability to make the most of one's abilities in practical and social settings is important to intelligence as it is manifested in behaviour, and can itself be a kind of practical intelligence, or 'street-smarts'. Without at least some of Celia's skills, one's intelligence can simply get lost and have little or no impact upon the world.

Fourthly, schools may be rewarding ability patterns that pay off a great deal in the short-run, especially in early schooling, but not ability patterns that pay off in the long-run, especially in later schooling and in adulthood. The great contributions to the arts, sciences, and other fields are probably made by the Barbaras of the world, not by the Alices. There are many Alices who do extremely well in school then disappear into the woodwork, never to be heard from again.

Fifthly, this pattern of rewards may ultimately have pernicious effects on society and the contributions that can be made to it. The reason for this derives from reinforcement theory. Through the early years of advanced graduate education (in whatever field), students like Alice tend to be continually reinforced for their analytic abilities, because these are the abilities the school values. As a result, such individuals develop a pattern of use and capitalisation upon these abilities. When the reward system changes, as it eventually does, the Alices come to be intermittently, rather than continually, reinforced for their analytic abilities. After all, such abilities continue to matter – they just do not matter quite so much. But reinforcement theory predicts that intermittent reinforcement will sustain a given pattern of functioning more, rather than less, than continual reinforcement. As a result, the Alices of the world may well not seek other abilities in themselves that would lead to greater success in later life, even if they have these abilities within them to develop. The Barbaras and Celias, on the other hand, will be only modestly reinforced for their abstract analytic abilities early in their schooling. As a result, they may realise that they need to find other abilities within themselves upon which to capitalise. When the reinforcement pattern changes later in life, therefore, they may be more prepared than the Alices to capitalise upon their synthetic or practical abilities. The sad part of this story is that Alice might potentially have the synthetic or practical abilities of Barbara and Celia, but never find, develop, and capitalise upon these abilities because of the pattern of reinforcement she has received in her schooling.

Finally, there is a danger that students such as Barbara and Celia may come to perceive themselves as not particularly intelligent because of their lesser test scores and the lesser reinforcement they receive in school. When, later on, they do start to succeed, they are potentially at risk for perceiving themselves as imposters, that is, people who succeed despite the fact that they are not very capable. They may view themselves as 'putting one over' on the world rather than as capable people in their own right.

In sum, the vignettes show that the subjective side of intelligence *does* matter, having substantial effects upon the way in which rewards are distributed by the schools and, ultimately, by the students, both to themselves and to others. [. . .]

Conclusions

In recounting the above vignettes, I have argued that intelligence in the objective sense can manifest itself in different forms, and that the form in which it manifests can have substantial effects both upon the way a student is perceived by others and upon the way the student perceives himself or herself. [. . .]

Students of intelligence have focused the lion's share of their efforts upon discovering the nature of intelligence as it exists, somehow, within the head, independent of the context in which it is manifested. I have argued in this chapter that these efforts need to be complemented by efforts to understand how intelligence is perceived. Our efforts to understand and predict school success will always be limited if we fail to take into account the complex interaction between intelligence, as an objective construct *inside* the head, and intelligence as a subjective, social construct *outside* the head.

The ways in which people define intelligence are important in all aspects of living, and particularly in schools. We need to understand how the view of intelligence held by the school interacts with the view of intelligence held by both parents and children. To the extent that these views match, both teachers and students will be playing the 'second game' of understanding intelligent behaviour in the same way. To the extent that these views mismatch, however, teachers and students will be playing the same game with different rules, and will encounter mutual frustration, and potentially, mutual disrespect. Evidence from a variety of sources suggest that there are multiple conceptions of intelligence, that people use these conceptions in their evaluations of themselves and of each other, and that to the extent that their conceptions are discrepant from each others', they will undervalue the intelligence of the others from whom their views differ. All of our efforts to understand, measure, and even train intelligence will be of limited value unless we take into account the subjective as well as the objective side of intelligence. [. . .] There is a need for schools to make explicit what is often now implicit – their conception of what constitutes intelligent functioning on the part of the student. It is clear that their conception may well not match up to the conceptions of many of their students. [. . .]

4.2

Getting the Intelligence Controversy Knotted

Graham Richards

The 'intelligence' controversy clearly knows no bounds. With the recent contributions from H. J. Eysenck (1982) and Stephen Furner (1983) the most fundamental problems of contemporary philosophy of science are being invoked, while Howard F. Taylor (1980), James Flynn (1982) and S. H. Irvine (1983) reveal methodological problems of increasingly baroque complexity. By this stage I am feeling rather punch-drunk, reeling from nearly two decades of trying dutifully to monitor the debate while maintaining some autonomy of perspective. During this time two or three conceptual muddles have been nagging away at me which initially seemed so elementary that I felt it was my own understanding which was amiss. Perhaps somewhere in the mountain of literature they have been unravelled, but if so, none of those I have spoken to can enlighten me as to where. It is true that they sometimes nearly break the surface in e.g. D. W. Pyle (1979), P. E. Vernon (1979) and Howard F. Taylor, but they are never clearly confronted. In what follows I will strive to place these conceptual riddles before you in the hope that someone somewhere can resolve them for me.

First, *if* genetic determinants operate, they must do so by setting an upper limit on attainable intelligence, a ceiling above which the individual cannot go. This point is often obscured by the eagerness of writers (on both sides) to get into the technical depths of how heritability is to be defined and so forth, but is clearer in popular works such as H. J. Eysenck (1962) and implicit in the hereditarian case that increasingly good education will reduce the environmental contribution to IQ score variance. It is hard, in any case, to see how else they could operate. This limit we can term GI (genetic intelligence, D. O. Hebb's (1949) Type A intelligence). Clearly then, what environmental factors do is determine how near to this limit the individual actually comes, how close their measured intelligence (MI) comes to GI. *An individual with a very high GI will obviously be potentially prone to far greater environment-induced shortfall than one with very low GI.* Environmental factors can never augment GI, only serve to lower MI from it to a greater or less degree. Since MI can never be higher than GI we cannot, even at this stage, view heredity and environment as separable variables. It makes no sense to talk in a general way about the proportion of MI determined by either source since the degree of possible environment-induced variance increases the higher GI is. (This is not the same as Taylor's 'gene – environment co-variance' notion.) While Hebb long ago differentiated 'fluid' and 'crystallised' intelligence, this has ever since been interpreted fairly routinely as expressing a bland 'interactionist' position. My first puzzle then is why this *a priori* necessity of postulating *differential* effects of environment depending on GI is never mentioned, and why heredity and environment are treated as separable, mutually independent, variables.

The second puzzle is really the first one in new guise. Whatever we mean by intelligence, beyond extreme operational definitions, it presumably has something to do with the individual's ability to respond to and learn from their environmental experiences. This is explicit, for example, in the definitions by Piaget, Helm and Wechsler cited in Pyle. Although not exactly synonymous, the concept 'intelligence' certainly incorporates then the notion of susceptibility to environmental influence. This further undermines the orthodox structuring of the problem, for how can 'environment' be considered as an independent variable affecting a dependent variable called 'intelligence' when we already implicitly accept that, in some sense at least, being influencable by the environment is a part of what we mean by being intelligent, and being immune to such influence a hallmark of stupidity? At this point an infinite regress looms. If we translate 'intelligence' into 'the capacity to be influenced by one's environment', the great controversy becomes 'To what extent is the capacity to be influencable by one's environment due to heredity or the influence of one's environment?', which can in turn be bracketted: 'To what extent is "the extent to which one's capacity to be influenced by the environment is determined by heredity or the influence of one's environment", due to heredity or the influence of one's environment?' Of this there is, patently, no end. The upshot though is to reinforce my first point, that susceptibility to environment-induced variance in MI will itself be a function of GI. The born genius might under some circumstances become an idiot, the born idiot cannot be transformed into a genius. *Again therefore it is thoroughly muddled to imagine that a general statement is possible about relative weights of environment and heredity in determining intelligence, since the very concept of intelligence is compounded with that of degree of susceptibility to environmental influence.* This problem could only be eliminated if someone were able to come up with an acceptable definition of intelligence that did not refer explicitly, or implicitly, to the quality of the transactions, between the individual and their environment.

In practice we cannot of course know the degree to which MI reflects GI in any given case, though we may be able to make shrewd guesses on occasion, and the extremely high MI person might be plausibly assumed to be operating near their GI ceiling. But consider the situation described by Eldridge Cleaver (1968) where bright black prisoners deliberately underperformed on IQ tests in order that the guards underestimate their abilities. This is clearly a strategy devised by high GI individuals as a result of their responsiveness to their environment, resulting in a gross GI and MI mismatch. Paradoxically, lower GI prisoners with less insight and responsiveness might perform in such a way that there is far less mismatch, perhaps even scoring higher than the first group. One is not dealing here simply with administration problems, or subject deception, but with a direct demonstration of the differential effect of 'environment' on high and less high GI individual's MI.

As a more artificial conundrum, let us imagine that two sets of monozygotic twins are participating in a study on heredity and intelligence. One set have MIs of 150, the other set MIs of 70. At least they have when first measured. But alas, in each pair one of the members is hit on the head by a falling brick, and when measured again the first pair have MIs of 150 and 70, the second pair MIs of 70 and 55. Presumably a brick on the head is an 'environmental factor'. How can we now make a *general* estimate of the relative contributions of nature and nurture to this final set of scores? Note though that there would be a tendency, if this situation recurred often enough, for the threatened members of high GI pairs of twins to escape the brick more frequently than their low GI counterparts due to quicker RTs, and more awareness of danger leading to their wearing hard-hats, while skill of unhit twin in reacting in such a way to minimise the injury could lessen the effects on MI even if they did not escape. We might conclude then that overall there is a greater chance of the low GI twin suffering environmental damage, but the effect of that damage, if incurred, would be greater on a high GI twin. But presumably a hard-hat is as much 'environmental' as the brick the impact of which it averts. At least it is not hereditary. So the twin who retains an MI of 150 due to wearing of a hard-hat owes this score, on the second occasion of measurement, as much to the 'environmental' factor as the one who got hit owes its drop to 70 to the same source! It is genuinely unclear to me how the implicit notion of genotypic potential articulates with the current methodology of looking at heredity and environment as alternative sources of variance (to be parcelled out between them).

All this leads onto my third major source of conceptual difficulty, the notion of 'environment' itself. While a fairly specific meaning can perhaps be given to 'heredity' (though I baulk at trying to do so), 'environment' remains a totally open concept. In a way the current status of the term is comparable to that of 'space' in physics prior to Machian positivism – 'The Environment' is some absolute factor of semi-metaphysical status. Does it in fact mean anything more than 'not-hereditary'? If not then the conceptual problem becomes even more acute, for it would mean that far from being separate sources of variance, heredity and environment are really two poles of a single bipolar construct 'heredity-environment', or 'heredity vs. non-heredity'. 'Environment' includes everything from perinatal anoxia to sympathetic teaching, from one's native language to one's clothes, from diet to Daddy. Can these really be all lumped together as a single supposed independent variable which can be given constant weighting as a general determinant of something called 'intelligence' which is itself conceived as the extent to which one is affectable by it?

The present writer's sympathies are basically with those who wish to see the debate transcended rather than see a victory for either camp. It is clearly not true, as Herrnstein claims (1983), that 'In the technical literature, virtual unanimity reigns: most of the variation among individual IQs is due to variation in genes', but his complaints of extreme media bias against the pro-hereditary case need attending to there can be little doubt that Heber's delinquencies probably offset Burt's. Freeden (1979) convincingly shows how the ideological line-up between right-wing political ideologies and pro-heredity positions *vis-à-vis* intelligence only emerged after the rise of Nazism. Early 20th century radicals such as the Webbs and Laski were keen Eugenicists. Since both the Soviet Union and the United States have ideologies which believe in social perfectibility via large-scale industrial technology, it is not surprising that both are concerned with the kind of formal assessment techniques which IQ tests represent. Whether or not the source of intelligence is environmental or hereditary is of subsidiary importance, a matter for academic debate, the important thing from such a system's point of view is that techniques for assessing it be available, that psychology be constructed in part as a discipline producing evaluation technology.

What I have tried to do here is to raise the question of the face validity of the controversy given our 'common-sense' understanding of the meanings of the terms 'intelligence' and 'environment'. What really determines the extent to which individuals 'fulfil their potential' is not 'the environment' in some abstract sense but a host of specific and often uncontrollable factors which can only be studied ideographically – encounters with inspirational teacher figures, family attitudes, 'chance' reading, 'peak experiences', etc. The demand that we try to ensure the maximisation of the probability of such circumstances arising via 'environmental' control over education, health and so forth, is surely justifiable on basic humanistic grounds and does not rest on any particular outcome of the nature – nurture controversy.

In the end of course it is 'environment' which, via natural selection, determines heredity, and were it ever possible to conclusively demonstrate that the US black population had a lower mean GI than US whites it would be nothing but further evidence as to the extent of their oppression over two centuries, for who is to say that the differential did not result from such factors as selective breeding for low intelligence by plantation owners, greater likelihood of lynching and imprisonment among the more intelligent affecting their reproduction rate, and influx of genes from white rapists, whose intelligence is also significantly below average, in Florida at any rate (Vera *et al.*, 1979)?

Summary

Attention is drawn to a number of conceptual issues: (1) If heredity sets the ceiling for attainable intelligence then non-hereditary factors ('environment') will have a potentially greater range of effects on those with high genetically determined intelligence (GI) than on those with low GI. (2) 'Intelligence' actually means, among other things, 'susceptibility to environmental influence' and this thoroughly tangles the controversy since the extent to which 'environment' determines the degree to which one is susceptible to it will depend on one's prior susceptibility to it, again implying that the situation is different for high and low GI cases. (3) The concept of 'environment' is itself rather difficult to comprehend however, since it is hardly definable except negatively as 'that which is not hereditary' and can thus hardly be treated as a coherent independent variable in determining anything. (The first two points represent difficulties within the current frame of discourse, the third is a problem for this frame itself). (4) The current ideological linkages are themselves socio-historically constructed rather than logically necessary. (5) 'Heredity' is itself determined by 'environment' in the long run and thus, even if gene pools differ in current mean MI, there is nothing immutable about this and historical 'environmental' explanations for it might be found.

These points are not presented as constituting a coherent position on the writer's part, rather as pointing to crucial incoherencies in the current controversy. If the parties centrally involved in this controversy wish the rest of us in the discipline to continue attending, perhaps they could unravel these knots for us?

References

Cleaver, E. (1968) *Soul on Ice*. New York: McGraw-Hill.

Eysenck, H. J. (1962) *Know your own IQ*. London: Penguin.

Eysenck, H. J. (1982) The sociology of psychological knowledge, the genetic interpretation of IQ, and the Marxist-Leninist ideology. *Bulletin of The British Psychological Society*, 35, pp. 449–51.

Flynn, J. R. (1982) Lynn, the Japanese, and environmentalism. *Bulletin of The British Psychological Society*, 35, pp. 409–13.

Freeden, M. (1979) Eugenics and progressive thought: A study in ideological affinity. *The History Journal*, 22, 3, pp. 645–71.

Furner, S. M. (1983) A contribution to Eysenck's debate upon the relationship between IQ and a Marxist interpretation of ideology. *Bulletin of The British Psychological Society*, 36, pp. 179–80.

Hebb, D. O. (1949) *The Organisation of Behavior*. ch. 11. Chichester: Wiley.

Herrnstein, R. J. (1983) IQ encounters with the press. *New Scientist*, 98, pp. 230–2.

Irvine, S. H. (1983) Lynn, the Japanese and environmentalism: A response. *Bulletin of The British Psychological Society*, 36, pp. 55–6.

Pyle, D. W. (1979) *Intelligence*, ch. 1. London: Routledge and Kegan Paul.

Taylor, H. F. (1980) *The IQ Game*. Brighton: Harvester.

Vera, H., Barnard, G. W. and Holzer, C. (1979) The intelligence of rapists: New data. *Archives of Sexual Behavior*, 8, 4, pp. 375–7.

Vernon, P. E. (1979) *Intelligence – Heredity and Environment*. San Francisco: W. H. Freeman.

4.3

Learning and Assessment

George Tolley

[. . .]

The curriculum

[. . .] By curriculum I mean what is taught, how it is taught and how outcomes are assessed. Bringing in assessment means that one is concerned with what is learned and how it is learned. Content, process, outcomes – these are the three battlegrounds of the curriculum, the scenes of constant skirmish and currently of much more than that. Looking back over the last forty years or so in education I have to conclude that where change is desired, there is an implicit belief that what matters most are structures, and the next most important thing is content.

My own belief, however, is that if significant change is desired and if objectives are to be met then they are much more likely to be achieved by starting first by changing methods of assessment and by ensuring that methods of learning are changed. I am not concerned here with the precise direction or objectives of change that are required, but with the instruments for achieving change. The dominance of education by examinations worries me immensely and the massive inertia of the examinations system appals me. My thesis is that in the initial training and subsequent development of the teacher, teaching (especially at secondary level, teaching of the subject) has been given undue and unfortunate priority over learning and assessment. I wish to make some observations, therefore, upon both the context of learning and upon assessment.

In *Better Schools*[1] there is the bland understatement: 'Examinations exert a strong influence on the secondary school curriculum', followed by an implication that examinations should be displaced from a dominant position to one of service of the curriculum. It is worth repeating what the White Paper says about the purpose of examinations.

The Government believes that the examinations taken at school should serve the following objectives:

1 to raise standards across the whole ability range,
2 to support improvements in the curriculum and in the way in which it is taught,
3 to provide clear aims for teachers and pupils, to the benefit of both and of higher education and employers,
4 to record proven achievement,
5 to promote the measurement of achievement based on what candidates know, understand and can do, and
6 to broaden the studies of pupils in the fourth and fifth secondary years and of sixth form students.

Examination

[. . .] The major purposes of examinations as currently perceived and expected by the great bulk of people inside and outside education are, I believe, to provide a basis of selection (for further education, employment or training) and to provide some indicator of future potential. The present examination system, by and large, is all about grading. Teachers know, and are trained to know, a good deal about grading. They are not trained to know much about assessment. But teachers also have perceptions and expectations of educational objectives overall – about assisting personal development intellectually, physically, morally, about encouraging the realisation of personal potential, about helping young people to understand the world in which they live, to be able to live a full life in that world and to appreciate the views and the needs of others. The divorce between the objectives of education, as shared by so many teachers and parents and the reality of the system as it is bent to satisfy the needs of examinations has been commented upon so much that one must assume that there is no will to insist upon the primacy of educational objectives over the secondary, distorting values of examinations as currently operated. Now there might be some redeeming virtue in examinations if they were reliable in what is expected of them. But are they? Of what use are examinations? Examinations in schools and in higher education are, for the most part, exercises in grading people into some sort of rank order, the order expressing a level of performance within narrow criteria, in the ability to reproduce knowledge under artificial conditions. As to the predictive value of these examinations, such research as has been done indicates that it is not very good. [. . .] We know that results in school examinations are widely used as selection (or rather, as rejection) instruments in selecting for employment, but there is no evidence to support a view that they predict performance on the job. Neither do the (largely) paper-and-pen tests give much indication of personal qualities that are often more important than knowledge or skills.

To be of value, assessments must satisfy requirements of validity, reliability and convenience. Now school examinations, upon which the edifice of selection for higher education and many occupations is built, which dominate the curriculum, have reliability (that is, assessments are repeatable), they are convenient (in that they are simple and relatively inexpensive to administer) but they do not meet what should be the central, essential requirement of assessment, that of validity, I mean that the test shall achieve what it is designed to do. Examinations must usually satisfy more than one criterion of validity, so that there is room for argument about the extent of the validity of forms of assessment. If one asked how far public examinations are valid in the terms of the objectives of examinations set out in *Better Schools*, one could expect a good deal of argument but few could agree that examinations have significant validity in the context of those objectives. Public examinations have especially poor validity in measuring or indicating competence. By competence, I mean the ability to perform a task satisfactorily. They have some validity in measuring performance on a particular occasion and in particular, and narrowly constraining, circumstances. They do not indicate or measure the basic ability to perform. Moves towards criterion-references (and away from norm-referencing) and towards the adoption of some form of record of achievement should be helpful in improving the validity of examinations and school records, but may well do this at the expense of convenience. Whether these will achieve any significance by way of overcoming the totally disproportionate importance attached to examinations is doubtful. We have a vast industry of public examinations in schools, the effectiveness of which is dubious, the influence of which is distorting and which, although repeatedly questioned, continues in its dominant role, swathed in tradition, mystique and esteem.

I suggest that reforms are necessary in three areas, aimed at improving the validity and the usefulness of examinations. First, as part of a process of reducing the number and extent of public examinations, to question seriously the necessity for 16+ examinations. If these examinations are intended to provide a basis of selection for either employment or for continuation in full-time education then they have to be questioned on grounds both of need and of effectiveness. The job market at 16 is rapidly disappearing. Increasingly the trend is towards entry into employment at 17+ or 18+. [. . .] If a 16+ examination were needed to assist selection for employment, then we do not have it, but is it required for such a purpose? If a 16+ examination is needed to assist selection for education and training over the 16–18 period, then does it have to be in its present form as a national system? I believe the answer to both questions is 'No'. The burden of proof as to the effectiveness of the 16+ examinations for purposes of selection for employment or for further education must be upon those who maintain and operate the present system. But progress is not likely beyond the process of argument and counter-argument unless a second area riddled with mystique and obfuscation is tackled.

The second area is that of the objectives of selection – both for employment and for education and training. [. . .] Subjective criteria are important in any serious process of selection, whether for employment or for further study, but one must question whether objective criteria are stated at all adequately by those who are selecting, especially when giving pride of place to performance in examinations. What competencies are looked for? That is a question that requires clearer answers than are generally apparent at the moment, and those answers must be reflected in what assessment processes in schools are seeking to express.

This leads on to the third area in which change and reform are necessary. Teachers need to secure much better knowledge and understanding of assessment processes. [. . .] Teachers are not trained adequately or effectively so to assess. [. . .]

Learning experiences and the world of work

The central purpose of examinations is to assess what has been learned. If the main thrust of the assessment process is to measure the extent to which an individual can reproduce knowledge transmitted to him, then we must presume the adoption of a certain view of the learning process. It is not my purpose here to attempt to analyse factors that relate to the learning process. I wish to comment upon one aspect only and that is the trend towards (the fashion almost of) work-based learning of one sort or another. [. . .]

An adequate range of learning experiences cannot be provided within the environment of a school. Neither can such be provided, I believe, within the constraints imposed by traditional subject disciplines. Forms of work experience, or awareness of the work environment, are attempts to broaden learning experiences and to place subjects in real situations. The growth of interest in work experience and work-based learning has coincided with the decline in opportunities for employment of young people, with growing difficulties in the job market and with the virtual collapse of apprenticeship. At a time when entry of the 16-year-old school leaver into employment has become a possibility for only a minority of leavers, there has been a burgeoning of schemes that give prominence to work experience as an essential, or highly desirable aspect of learning. Technical Vocational Education Initiative (TVEI), CPVE (Certificate of Pre-Vocational Education), the many forms of schools-industry links, the list is a long one and the demand for work experience places of one sort and another is growing to such an extent that employers are seriously concerned at the pressures they face to provide both volume and quality. [. . .]

Work-based learning

My thesis is that [. . .] emphasising and extending work-based learning, [. . .] has far-reaching implications for schools. For work-based learning is not confined to, or constrained by, specific objectives of narrowly conceived job training. It goes well beyond training for skills relevant to a job or an occupation into the area of transferrable skills and the development of personal effectiveness. What is being claimed, to put it bluntly and crudely, is that many young people who leave school with little to demonstrate in the way of transferrable skills and personal effectiveness (and there are some who would claim that it is the job of education to provide these things) learn these things in a learning environment that is vastly different from that of school. If this claim can be sustained then the boundaries between education and training, that have been maintained tenaciously for one reason and another for generations, begin to disappear, processes of assessment in school will have to change and the school curriculum will have to respond to the spur of achievement in a very different learning environment.

Some of the differences between work-based learning and class-room learning are obvious and considerable: work-based learning is more participative; it is more directly related to immediate outcomes of performance; it has in it much more of self assessment; it is not dependent upon a time-table that is structured according to blocks of knowledge based upon subjects; what is learned has to be demonstrated; many would say that, for them, it is 'more real'. Now I am not saying that schools must give way to work experience as providers of education, nor am I pressing for a lowering of the school leaving age to 14, or whatever. Part of the difficulty is that one runs the risk, when trying to get a serious debate on work-based learning, of being accused of seeking to denigrate education and the education system. I am not trying to do either. What I am saying is that since the clear trend is towards later entry into the job market proper we need to be clearer than we seem at the moment on the respective and complementary roles of full-time education and work-based learning. It seems clear enough to me that TVEI, CPVE (and various combinations of these) are blurring the bound-aries, are creating exciting combinations of learning environments, posing significant challenges to cherished notions both of the purity of education and of job or occupational skills. Assessment of work-based learning is not well developed. I have tried to say earlier in this paper that I do not believe that assessment of competence is well developed either. Attention to improving both could well improve the understanding of the learning process and could lead to improvement in the learning environment. [. . .]

Note

1 HMSO (1984), *Better Schools*, Cmnd 9469. London.

4.4

Measurement or Assessment: A Fundamental Dichotomy and its Educational Implications*

Glenn Futcher

Introduction

In his article 'Learning and Assessment' George Tolley seems to be essentially concerned that assessment techniques are developed to match the current growth in work-experienced based learning. In his very thought provoking and undoubtedly well thought through arguments, he presents the view that the central purpose of any method of assessment is to assess what has been learned, and equally correctly points out that the method of assessment used must be reliable, valid and convenient. Whatever system is developed must fulfill these three basic conditions, and that the assessment assesses what has been learned is in fact a part of the notion of validity: content validity. It is a perennial problem in testing to have an adequate balance between reliability and validity, and this is the starting point for this discussion.

Reliability and validity as criteria

Reliability is essentially concerned with the stability of scores from any test.[1] If a student can gain significantly different marks on two administrations of a test, then the test is not reliable. If two or more judges assess one candidate and their ratings differ substantially,

---

* This chapter was a paper written in response to the article 'Learning and Assessment' by George Tolley in *Education Today*, 35, 3, pp. 16–23. It deals with choices in educational measurement and assessment and their implications for educational method as raised by Dr Tolley, presenting some of the work in recent testing theory which is of relevance in the current discussion. The chapter draws mainly on work in language testing which seems, so often, to be at the frontiers of testing theory.

then the assessment is not reliable. Reliability can be calculated as a figure in numerous ways: in traditional pencil and paper tests the Kuder-Richardson reliability coefficient is often used[2] and in the rating of judges the tetrachoric correlation is used.[3] The problem with the latter method is that one has to assume that either the judges or the activity judged is a reliable measure of ability. If both are unreliable, then agreement in unreliability will show up in results as a reliable rating.

Validity encompasses a variety of concepts. The one which is of most concern to Tolley is content validity, where the content of the testing situation adequately samples the content of the learning situation. Tolley also mentions another crucial aspect of validity: we must define precisely what we are looking for in the assessment, and be sure that we assess it. This aspect, construct validity, is concerned with the study of the theoretical basis of the test: if a test is based upon inaccurate analysis of the task to be measured then the test will not be a valid measure of that task.

Finally, reliability and validity are closely related. If a test is not reliable then it is not measuring anything; if it is not measuring anything then it is not valid. One could reliably measure something, but it may not be what one intends to measure. Validity is concerned with proving that what a test is measuring is indeed what the test claims to measure.[4]

The dichotomy

Theoretically, this brings us to a major problem: measurement or assessment? So far, the terms have been used interchangeably, but it is clear that they are not in fact interchangeable. Measurement entail that the method employed be reliable and have both content and construct validity. Assessment, on the other hand, lacks at least one of these three features. At some stage the subjective opinion of the assessor comes into play.

Another feature, which may or may not be present in either measurement or assessment, is predictive validity. This is the extent to which a given test (which is used now to mean any method of measurement *or* assessment) can predict future success in either an academic course or employment. For a test to possess predictive validity it must be reliable, but need not possess content or construct validity.

At present, both national and institutional examinations seem to be assessing student abilities rather than measuring them, but they often *claim* to be measuring them. This is surely at the heart of Tolley's criticism, as he does in fact call for reliable and valid tests, that is, true measurement. In this, he is correct. Very few examining bodies provide information concerning reliability, validity, construct criteria, or scoring procedures. The mystique of the system is thereby perpetuated, and many teachers who know little about testing have a blind faith in the system. Hence Tolley's comment that teachers should be better informed.

Solutions

When it comes to solving the problems inherent in the English testing systems Tolley is less helpful. He points to two areas which need attention, which will be dealt with below, criterion-referencing and profile systems.

Criterion-referencing or norm-referencing

During the era of development of scientific measurement norm-referencing became popular,[5] and it is still the most widely used method of measurement. In short, it rests on traditional statistical analysis of tests and test results. Its theoretical foundation is one simple assumption: various skills which are measured are equally distributed throughout the population. In each skill it is inevitable that some will be excellent, some will be poor, and the majority will be 'roughly average'. I make no judgement as to whether this is true or not, but if an educator believes this to be true, then there is no reason to abandon norm-referenced tests.

Secondly, norm-referencing allows an educator to place *every* student on a scale and state, within a given range of error, in what percentage of the population (e.g. top 10 per cent, bottom 5 per cent etc.) the student is with regard to the defined skill.[6] Such precision demands large sample populations upon which to standardise tests, and demands that tests possess reliability, validity and practicality.

The recent development of criterion-referenced tests has been prompted by a dissatisfaction with the assumption that half the population must be below average, together with the awareness that many norm-referenced tests had ignored content validity at the expense of reliability which is essentially a statistical criterion.[7] [. . .]

Whereas a norm-referenced test spreads students over a curve of normal distribution, a criterion-referenced test is only interested in pass or fail: it divides students into two groups, those who can and those who cannot, those who meet the criterion and those who do not. It is not concerned with differences among the very good or very poor, or among those who just meet the criterion and those who just fail on the criterion. It divides the testees into two neat groups.

The question which springs to mind is how the criteria are set. Criterion-referenced tests have been over concerned with content validity since their inception, so that their content more accurately represents the ultimate performance they are meant to predict, and construct validity has been by-passed, so the criteria have been set in the following way: successful students in various academic courses or vocational fields have been tested, and their average scores used as the criteria for the new testees. In other words, norms for restricted population samples form the criteria. So far, therefore, criterion-referenced tests are norm-referenced tests in disguise, and will remain so until theorists can state that for (A) vocation or course, (b) (c) and (d) skills are essential at (x) (y) and (z) levels. We are still a long way from this.

Profile systems

Profiles of student achievement can be drawn up on either a norm-referenced or a criterion-referenced system of testing. However, at least one assumption underlies the whole process. This is that whatever proficiency is being measured (for it *has* to be measured), it is possible to break it up into sub-skills. That is, proficiency (A) consists of (x) (y) and (z) skills. Student (S) meets criteria set for (x) and (y), but needs further tuition or practice in skill (z) before (s)he can carry out task (A) proficiently. This, in turn, demands that we provide empirical evidence to show that skills (x) (y) and (z) are indeed independent skills and not merely a construct of educators. [. . .]

One thing is certain, however, and this is that a profiling system offers diagnostic power, given that the ranges of error in measurement between isolated skills is limited.

Conclusions

1. When Tolley highlights 'transferrable skills' it is necessary to agree with him that these are indeed important, but need much more careful definition and research. He is thus perfectly correct to state that the development of new techniques is essential, but these should be measurement techniques as defined in this paper.
2. While profiling is essentially neutral to the criterion/norm-referenced debate, this would certainly be a step in the right direction, although the problems involved in developing such a system mean that it is not as yet practical. Equally, the call to criterion-referenced tests is presently unwise, not only because they are still based on norm-referencing, but also because the national examining boards have tried to introduce criterion-referencing in

current examinations, and this is what has caused much of the present confusion.

3. The way forward lies with those in education concerned with accurate and fair measurement, who are prepared to conduct the necessary research to discover exactly what skills (and in what proportion) are needed to achieve proficiency in various tasks. To discover if these are equally distributed among students or whether they are basic common human abilities. The washback effect on the curriculum will then be enormous, rather than leaving the skills we must teach at the mercy of those who may randomly decide what should be tested.

Notes

1 E. Ingram, 'Basic Concepts in Testing', in J. P. B. Allen and A. Davies (eds) (1977) *Testing and Experimental Methods*. Edinburgh Course in Applied Linguistics, Vol. 4. London: OUP.
2 A. Harrison (1983) *A Language Testing Handbook*. London: Macmillan.
3 B. J. Carroll (1985) *Make Your Own Language Tests: A Practical Guide to Writing Language Performance Tests*. Oxford: Pergamon Press.
4 A. S. Palmer and L. F. Bachman (1981) 'Basic Concepts in Test Validation', in J. C. Alderson and A. Hughes (eds) *Issues in Language Testing* (ELT Documents 111). London: The British Council.
5 R. Lado (1961) *Language Testing*. London: Longman. The National Criteria (1985), HMSO, Department of Education and Science.
6 P. D. Pumfrey (1977) *Measurement Reading Abilities: Concepts, Sources and Applications*. London: Hodder and Stoughton.
7 J. Oller (1979) *Language Tests at School*. London: Longman.

4.5

The Validity of Assessments

Desmond L. Nuttall

[. . .]

The concept of validity

Every assessment is based upon a *sample* of the behaviour in which we are interested; we intend to generalise from the particular sample of behaviour we observe to the universe of that behaviour. To take an example: when a classroom test of mental arithmetic is given, the teacher is not simply interested in the answers to her questions, she is interested in what the answers tells her about the children's grasp of particular knowledge and processes (e.g. the multiplication tables) and what she therefore needs to do in the way of further teaching. Occasionally it is possible to be comprehensive (for example, one could test every one of the tables up to 12) but much more often it is impossible: one cannot test a child on every possible addition sum, let alone on every possible reading passage. So to say that a child has mastered addition or can read fluently, one is bound to be making a generalisation from limited evidence.

But the generalisation is not necessarily only to the domain of the behaviour defined in an abstract way. Having tested a child on the two times table, to conclude from a flawless performance that he therefore knows all his tables is obviously a faulty inference. But equally if the child had been tested by an unknown adult visitor to his classroom and found incapable of reciting his tables, it might be inappropriate to conclude that he did not know his tables; if his mother or his teacher had asked him, he might have recited them confidently. The universe of the behaviour of interest has therefore to be carefully defined and will embrace the conditions and occasions of assessment as well as the content.

The fidelity of the inference drawn from the responses to the assessment is what is usually called the *validity* of the assessment. In practice, an assessment does not have a single validity; it can have many according to its different uses and the different kinds of inference made, in other words according to the universe of generalisation. This is a slightly different formulation of the term 'validity' from the one offered in many textbooks of which the definition given by Nuttall and Willmott (1972) is typical: 'The extent to which a test or examination does what it was designed to do.' The formulation is, however, consistent with it and accords with modern views, such as those of Messick (1984):

> Elsewhere I have maintained that test validity is an overall evaluative judgement of the adequacy and appropriateness of inferences and actions based on test scores (Messick, 1980). As such, validity is an inductive summary of both the existing evidence for and the potential consequences of test interpretation and use (p. 231).

As Rogoff (1981) points out, it is not clear where we should draw the boundaries of our generalisations. He gives the example of the conclusions that might be drawn from successful performance on a syllogism problem: the individual (a) will do well on the next syllogism; (b) will do well on other kinds of logic problems; (c) will be logical in many situations; or (d) is smart. The specification of the domain of the behaviour in which we are interested is thus critically important; I return to this issue later.

The formulation of validity put forward here tends to embrace another desirable characteristic of good assessment, namely reliability. Only if the assessment if repeatable, using another assessor or on another occasion, is it of any value. This is another aspect of generalisation – across assessors or occasions – as the formulation of generalisability theory by Cronbach and his colleagues (1972) recognises.

Different aspects of generalisability are sometimes in tension, since the pressure for standardisation and uniformity arising from the need for generalising across assessors and occasions can conflict with establishing conditions that will allow a faithful sampling of the behaviour of interest. A third desirable quality of good assessment, namely utility, can also be in conflict with validity and reliability. Utility embraces the convenience, flexibility and inexpensiveness of the assessment, inevitably considerations of some importance. It was mainly lack of utility that lead to the demise of specially mounted practical science tests in examinations taken by 16 year-old students in the UK; no one felt that experimental investigation was unimportant. The National Criteria for science in the examinations introduced in 1988 require the assessment of the skills involved in experimental investigation, and the examination boards are already pointing to the cost implications, while accepting that science examinations will become more valid.

Ways of assessing validity

If we accept validity as meaning the degree to which the responses to the assessment can be generalised, the way to explore it is through the relationship of these responses to other assessments of the same behaviour (and of different behaviours as well to check that our assessment is not unduly contaminated). In the textbooks this type of validation would be known as construct validation, and in the minds of many psychometricians it subsumes or replaces all the other kinds of validation that textbooks list, e.g. face, instructional, content and so forth (see, for example, Angoff, 1986).

In an applied setting, we may have a very clear idea of what it is we are trying to assess (the construct). For example, in selecting applicants for university places, we are interested in predicting how well they will 'do', which is usually interpreted to mean how they will fare in their final examinations. It is relatively straightforward to examine the statistical relationship between tests and examinations taken by university applicants and the first-year or final results of those admitted. Research in Europe and North America (Mitter, 1979) has shown that attainment at the end of schooling is the best predictor of university examination performance, better than aptitude tests and ratings from interviews but not particularly good (in the sense that some who do well at 18 will not do very well in their finals, and vice versa). But many would argue that success at university should not be measured just in terms of final examination performance, but in other ways (e.g. student politics, journalism, drama and sport). To decide upon the criterion of success is often difficult in occupational settings as well; should salespersons be judged in terms of volume of sales or customer satisfaction, or by some global rating by supervisors (which may be contaminated by 'halo effect')? Often, then, there is no single criterion or, in other words, the universe of the behaviour in which we are interested is difficult to describe. This is particularly true in education or non-specific training. The variety of circumstances in which we hope that the education or training may be valuable is almost impossible to describe. If we cannot define the universe, we can hardly be expected to judge how representative the sample of behaviour we assess actually is. So validation is a difficult process in all but the most straightforward selection procedures, and is impossible if we do not have a clear idea of what it is we are trying to assess.

Evidence about the validity of assessments

Assessments (through tests, interviews, examinations, performance appraisals, simulations and so forth) are in daily use for educational and occupational selection, and there have been many studies of their predictive validity. (It might be argued that there have not been enough studies: in the UK, school examination results are widely used in selection for employment without any evidence that they do predict performance on the job. In the USA, validation of selection procedures has been done much more rigorously to establish that they do not have adverse impact, i.e. that they do not discriminate unfairly between groups such as ethnic groups, the sexes or different age groups.)

Ghiselli (1966) conducted a very comprehensive review of the validity of occupational aptitude tests, almost all paper-and-pencil tests, some general such as reasoning or intelligence tests, others rather more specific like clerical aptitude or mechanical reasoning tests. The validity of these predictors were modest with a median correlation coefficient of .19 when criteria of job proficiency were used. When criteria obtained during the training phase were used (often tests and examinations more similar in type to the selection tests than were the job proficiency measures), the median correlation coefficient rose to about .30. This resembles the value often achieved in educational selection (e.g. attainment at 18+ against university performance, see Mitter, 1979, and examinations at 16+ against performance in technical education, see Williams and Boreham, 1971).

Another comprehensive review was carried out by Samson, Graue, Weinstein and Walberg (1984). They summarised studies relating academic performance to subsequent occupational performance (using criteria such as income, job satisfaction and effectiveness ratings) in professional fields. The mean validity coefficient of the educational predictors was only .155. The highest coefficients were found in the fields of business and nursing, middle values in engineering and teaching, with negligible values among medical doctors and PhDs.

It is fair to conclude that paper-and-pencil tests and examinations have very modest predictive validity against criteria of occupational performance. When the criteria are themselves paper-and-pencil tests or examinations, the validity is somewhat higher, but the experience of organisations that allow open entry and self-selection is that much talent is wasted by relying on conventional selection devices (see various contributions in Mitter (1979) and also Nuttall (1983) for a summary of the experiences of the Open University).

Less is known about the predictive validity of other kinds of assessment used in selection, but the validity of more job-specific assessments tends to be higher. For example, Jones (1984) reports:

'The types of [selection] tests used [in the USA] have tended to become more specifically job-related. The general tests of reasoning have proved much more difficult to validate' (Appendix L, p. 8).

The general consensus is that performance assessments and simulation (e.g. work samples and trainability tests) have higher predictive validity than paper-and-pencil tests (Hecht, 1979; McClelland, 1973; Monjan and Gassner, 1979; Priestley, 1982; Robertson and Downs, 1979; Spencer, 1983).

Priestley (1982) concludes that practice has shown that the more closely the sample of behaviour assessed resembles behaviour on the job and the more the criteria of occupational success are justified (for example, by job analysis and job relevance), the stronger is the basis for validity, though it must of course be demonstrated in any particular application. Analysis of the job and the skills it requires allows the devising of appropriate assessments so that there is a point-to-point correspondence between the assessment and the criterion (Robertson and Downs, 1979), but sometimes, once a skill is present in sufficient amount to allow the job to be done, improvements in that skill do not necessarily lead to enhanced job performance. In such circumstances, Spencer (1983) argues that one should attempt to identify the factors or skills that differentiate the person who is good at the job from the person who is exceptional. Not all the skills that appear in the job analysis will necessarily differentiate the excellent from the good.

Factors influencing performance

Examples given below show how in some circumstances an individual may be able to demonstrate his or her mastery of a mathematical operation, for example, while in other circumstances he or she cannot. The notion of a distinction between *competence* (the basic ability to perform) and *performance* (the demonstration of the competence on a particular occasion or under particular circumstances) has become increasingly important in examining the factors that influence performance especially when that performance is being assessed. A fuller statement of the distinction between competence and performance comes from Messick (1984):

> Competence refers to what a person knows and can do under ideal circumstances, whereas performance refers to what is actually done under existing circumstances. Competence embraces the structure of knowledge and abilities, whereas performance subsumes as well the processes of accessing and utilising those structures and a host of affective, motivational, attentional and stylistic factors that influence the ultimate responses (Flavell and Wohlwill, 1969; Overton and Newman, 1982). Thus, a student's competence might be validly revealed in either classroom performance or test performance because of personal or circumstantial factors that affect behaviour (p. 227).

It should be noted that this definition of competence, widely accepted in the psychological literature, differs from that used in the world of occupational training. One current definition from that world is 'the ability to perform a particular activity to a prescribed standard' (see FEU, 1986).

The psychological construct is a very slippery notion, of course (see Wood and Power, 1984) and we have to find a way of operationalising it. Dillon and Stevenson-Hicks (1983) propose that the operational definition of competence should be the level of performance obtained under elaborative procedures beyond the performance level obtained under standard conditions. There have been many attempts to develop elaborative procedures particularly among the retarded, often using training procedures (e.g. Feuer-stein, 1980). Another approach is collaboration between tester and student to help the student to produce his or her best performance. This has affinities with Vygotsky's (1978) concept of the zone of next development, which represents the gap between the present level of development and the potential level of development, identified on the basis of what he or she can already do provided that he or she receives the best possible help from an adult.

It is not clear, however, that the operational definition proposed by Dillon and Stevenson-Hicks is particularly helpful. They are, in effect, simply proposing a different universe of generalisation, albeit one that reminds us of our responsibility to attend to the influences upon performance. Research on the conditions that facilitate or hamper performance has not always been very systematic but it is growing in importance, as two examples from the work of Hudson (1966, 1968) show. He worked with 17 year-old students using tests of divergent thinking (e.g. How many uses can you think of for a brick?) One example is anecdotal: Hudson entered a class and was rather angry and aggressive with the group of students who were about to take the test. Their performance was significantly higher than on a previous occasion (unlike other groups who were re-tested). The second example arose from more systematic work. Hudson found that 17 year-olds specialising in the study of science offered fewer responses to divergent thinking tests than arts special-ists. Yet, when he invited science specialists to imagine that they were a bohemian artist called McMinn (for whom a character sketch was supplied) and to answer the test in the role of McMinn, he found that the science specialists then gave as many (and as bizarre) responses as the art specialists. In other words they were capable of producing more responses than they chose to under standard conditions.

A study of cross-cultural research (e.g. Laboratory of Compara-tive Human Cognition, 1982; Cole and Means, 1981), research among the retarded or the socially deprived (e.g. Wallace, 1980; Zigler and Seitz, 1982) and more general work on task presentation (e.g. Donaldson, 1978; Bell, Costello and Kuchemann, 1983) suggests that the following interrelated factors are particularly significant in affecting performance under conditions of assessment:

1 motivation to do the task and interest in it (influenced by the personal experience and the instrumental value of performing it);
2 the relationship between the assessor and the individual being assessed and the conditions under which the assessment is made;
3 the way in which the task is presented, the language used to describe it, and the degree to which it is within the personal experience of the individual being assessed.

The first, motivation, is so obvious that it merits little discussion, though that is not to dismiss its importance. Performance will never be as good as if the individual sees no point in performing, and it is a real challenge to the teachers of many alienated young people to convince them that there is a point in studying subjects like history and geography. The enhanced motivation of young people in post-compulsory education and training schemes to which many educators and supervisors testify is generally attributed to the obvious relevance of the activities to employment and wage-earning. Other motivating factors are the enthusiasm of the teacher for the subject ('infectious enthusiasm') and tangible and accessible rewards (e.g. certificates) to which the success of the graded test movement is often, but still rather uncertainly, attributed (Nuttall and Goldstein, 1984).

The relationship between assessor and student is important in many ways. Among the first to elaborate the competence-performance distinction were the socio-linguists who found that minority groups and deprived young people would show very limited vocabulary and speech forms with middle-class white investigators while having very rich conversation among themselves. Many characteristics of the assessor (e.g. ethnic origin, sex, status) can affect the students' performance, as can the degree to which the assessor provides support, encouragement and help, and the quality of such support and feedback. An assessor known to the student can often elicit a higher level of performance (provided that the relationship between them is good), but there are qualifications to this generalisation. Hudson's anedoctal finding has already been mentioned and can be seen as an example of how challenge and competition can fire enhanced performance in conformity with the Yerkes-Dodson Law: too little or too much anxiety leads to lower performance than if one is moderately anxious. More generally, the conditions of testing can be influential: Seitz, Abelson, Levine and Zigler (1975) found that young children tested in the home performed worse than another group tested in a classroom, contrary to expectation. Observations suggested that maternal anxiety about the child's performance inhibited that performance. Moreover, it is a common finding that performance during a course of study (assessed continuously by the teacher) is better than performance in the examination (see, for example, Cohen and Deale, 1977). It is often concluded that teachers are overgenerous in their assessments; an alternative conclusion is that the conditions under which course work was conducted and assessed elicited or facilitated genuinely better performance.

The effect of the way in which the task is presented has been studied extensively. In reviewing the findings of the first Assessment of Performance Unit surveys of mathematical performance, Eggleston (1983) concluded; 'The significance of differences in presentation seems to be unquestionable (p. 6). This may be as simple as presenting the same numbers for addition vertically or horizontally; in the latter case 20 per cent fewer 11 year-olds could give the correct answer. But the task is not identical; an extra step (lining up the columns appropriately) is needed when the numbers are presented horizontally. Yet both tasks are on the topic of addition. This small example reinforces the point made at the beginning: a careful specification of the domain of behaviour of interest is necessary. Not only does one have to specify the addition of three numbers (containing up to three digits) but also how those are to be presented physically; alternatively, if the physical presentation is not specified, the assessor must vary it to ensure that the sampling of behaviour is representative of the whole domain of addition. And should the presentation be in mathematical (i.e. abstract) form or as a problem in words? Again, Eggleston (1983) gives examples of how the same mathematical task presented in different forms leads to different levels of performance, concluding that 'the success rate is, in general, diminished when the mathematical performance is embedded in an everyday "problem" formulation' (p. 9). The format of the question can also have an effect; for example, the fact that the answer to a multiple-choice question can be guessed correctly can lead to an incorrect inference about competence (Wood and Power, 1984). And simply changing the position of a question in a test can make the question appear easier or harder (Leary and Dorans, 1982).

Bell, Costello, and Kuchemann (1983) summarise the results of a wide range of studies in mathematics under five categories of factors influencing performance:

1 context (especially familiar or unfamiliar)
2 readability (including all sorts of linguistic factors)
3 size and complexity of numbers (mentioning the striking feature that complicated numbers appear to make it more difficult to *recognise* which operation is needed)
4 number and type of operations and stages (of which vertical and horizontal addition provide a simple example)

5 distractions (including superfluous information).

There is similar work in the field of Piagetian psychology which shows how children's capacities have often been underestimated because of the way in which the problem has been presented (e.g. Brown and Desforges, 1979; Bryant, 1974; Donaldson, 1978). For example, Greenfield (1966) found that her African subjects showed conservation-of-liquids when they were allowed to pour the liquids themselves, but not when she did all the manipulations.

The conclusion is inescapable: the way in which the task is presented, the presenter, and the perceived significance of the task to the student – factors which might be termed the 'context' of the task in a broader sense than that used by Bell *et al.* (1983) – can all have a major effect on the performance of the person presented with the task. Assessment (like learning) is highly context-specific and one generalises at one's peril.

Conclusions

It seems appropriate to sidestep the psychological construct of competence and to think simply in terms of the conditions that elicit the individual's best performance. Modern educational assessment is beginning to strive to permit those assessed to show their best performance, and to take account of the factors that might prevent the best performance from being demonstrated (Messick, 1984; Wood, 1986). Research, as usual, has no unambiguous answers about how this can be achieved but features of the task and the conditions of assessment that seem to be elaborative are:

1 tasks that are concrete and within the experience of the individual
2 tasks that are presented clearly
3 tasks that are perceived as relevant to the current concerns of the student
4 conditions that are not unduly threatening, something that is helped by a good relationship between the assessor and the student.

The goal of releasing the best performance from people being assessed seems highly desirable in human terms as well as psychologically illuminating, but does it contribute to improving the validity of the assessment? One hypothesis about why performance assessments are better predictors of occupational competence than paper-and-pencil tests is that paper-and-pencil tests have fewer elaborative features than performance assessments. But a more plausible hypothesis is that it is due to the lack of match between the nature of the tasks in a paper-and-pencil test and on the job, and between the context of testing and normal occupational performance. A paper-

and-pencil test taken under very formal standardised conditions is about as unlike real life as you can get. The magnitude of the generalisation from the performance assessment to occupational performance is very much more limited.

Consequently it does not automatically follow that eliciting best performance improves validity. One is most likely to improve validity by improving the sampling of tasks and contexts from the universe of interest – and that means defining the universe very much more carefully than we have done in the past. If the successful employee needs arithmetical skills, then the nature of the skills and the conditions under which they have to be deployed need to be spelt out so that appropriate tasks and appropriate conditions can be devised. If it is difficult to specify the universe (because, for example, the trainee might be employed in so many different circumstances), a wide range of tasks should be administered under a wide range of conditions. If the job requires the task to be done under pressure, then the assessment should put the trainee under similar pressure, even if that means that best performance is not elicited. (In the longer run it might be more fruitful to change the job so that best performance can be utilised.)

With the benefit of hindsight, it seems strange that so much effort should have been put into the development and validation of general paper-and-pencil tests, when everything points to their artificiality, their remoteness from the nature of any normal job and their unelaborative conditions of administration. It seems likely that considerations of utility and reliability have prevailed over considerations of validity. The signs are now that validity is claiming its rightful pre-eminent position, and that the careful specification of the universe of generalisation is helping to stimulate improved conditions of assessment and more thought about evoking an individual's best performance.

References

Angoff, W. H. (1986) *Validity: an Evolving Concept*. Princeton, NJ: Educational Testing Service (mimeo).

Bell, A. W., Costello, J. and Kuchemann, D. (1983) *A Review of Research in Mathematical Education*, (Part A: Research on Learning and Teaching). Windsor: NFER-Nelson.

Brown, G. and Desforges, C. (1979) *Piaget's Theory: a Psychological Critique*. London: Routledge and Kegan Paul.

Bryant, P. E. (1974) *Perception and Understanding in Young Children*. London: Methuen.

Cohen, L. and Deale, R. N. (1977) *Assessment by Teachers in Examinations at 16+*. Schools Council Examinations Bulletin 37. London: Evans/Methuen Educational.

Cole, M. and Means, B. (1981) *Comparative Studies of How People Think*. Cambridge, MA: Harvard University Press.

Cronbach, L. J., Gleser, G. C., Nanda, H. and Rajaratnam, H. (1972) *The Dependability of Behavioural Measurements*. New York: Wiley.

Dillon, R. F. and Stevenson-Hicks, R. (1983) 'Competence vs. performance and recent approaches to cognitive assessment'. *Psychology in the Schools*, 20, pp. 142–5.

Donaldson, M. (1978) *Children's Minds*. London: Fontana.

Eggleston, S. J. (1983) *Learning Mathematics*. APU Occasional Paper. London: Department of Education and Science.

FEU (1986) *Assessment, Quality and Competence*. London: Further Education Unit.

Feuerstein, R. (1980) *Instrumental Enrichment*. Baltimore: University Park Press.

Flavell, J. H. and Wohlwill, J. F. (1969) 'Formal and functional aspects of cognitive development', in D. Elkind and J. H. Flavell (eds) *Studies in Cognitive Development*. New York: Oxford University Press.

Ghiselli, E. E. (1966) *The Validity of Occupational Aptitude Tests*. New York: Wiley.

Greenfield, P. M. (1966) 'On Culture and Conservation', in J. S. Bruner, R. P. Oliver and P. M. Greenfield (eds), *Studies in Cognitive Growth*. New York: Wiley.

Hecht, K. A. (1979) 'Current Status and Methodological Problems of Validating Professional Licensing and Certification Exams', in M. A. Bunda and J. R. Sanders (eds), *Practices and Problems in Competency-based Education*. Washington, DC: NCME.

Hudson, L. (1966) *Contrary Imaginations*. London: Methuen.

Hudson, L. (1968) *Frames of Mind*. London: Methuen.

Jones, J. E. M. (1984) *The Uses Employers Make of Examination Results and Other Tests for the Selection of 16–19 year olds for Employment*. Reading: University of Reading (unpublished M. Phil. thesis).

Laboratory of Comparative Human Cognition (1982) 'Culture and Intelligence', in R. J. Sternberg (ed.), *Handbook of Human Intelligence*. Cambridge: Cambridge University Press.

Leary, L. F. and Dorans, N. J. (1982) *The Effects of Item Rearrangement on Test Performance: a review of the literature*. Research Report Rr–82–30. Princeton, NJ: Educational Testing Service.

McClelland, D. C. (1973) 'Testing for Competence Rather Than for Intelligence', *American Psychologist*, 28, pp. 1–14.

Messick, S. (1980) 'Test Validity and the Ethics of Assessment', *American Psychologist*, 35, pp. 1012–27.

Messick, S. (1984) 'The Psychology of Educational Assessment', *Journal of Educational Measurement*, 21, pp. 215–37.

Mitter, W. (ed.) (1979) *The Use of Tests and Interviews for Admission to Higher Education*. Windsor: NFER.

Monjan, S. V. and Gassner, S. M. (1979) *Critical Issues in Competency-based Education*. New York: Pergamon.

Nuttall, D. L. (1983) 'Unnatural Selection', *Times Educational Supplement*, 18 November, p. 19.

Nuttall, D. L. and Goldstein, H. (1984) 'Profiles and Graded Tests: the Technical Issues', in *Profiles in Action*. London: Further Education Unit.

Nuttall, D. L. and Willmott, A. S. (1972) *British Examinations: Techniques of Analysis*. Slough: NFER.

Overton, W. F. and Newman, J. L. (1982) 'Cognitive development: a competence/utilisation approach', in T. Field *et al.* (eds), *Review of Human Development*. New York: Wiley.

Priestley, M. (1982) *Performance assessment in Education and Training: alternative techniques*. Englewood Cliffs, NJ: Educational Technology Publications.

Robertson, I. and Downs, S. (1979) 'Learning and the Prediction of Performance: Development of Trainability Testing in the United Kingdom', *Journal of Applied Psychology*, 64, pp. 42–50.

Rogoff, B. (1981) 'Schooling and the Development of Cognitive Skills', in H. Triandis and A. Heron (eds), *Handbook of Cross-cultural Psychology*, Vol. 4. Boston, MA: Allyn and Bacon.

Samson, G. E., Graue, M. E., Weinstein, T. and Walberg, H. J. (1984) 'Academic and occupational performance: a quantitative synthesis'. *American Educational Research Journal*, 21, pp. 311–21.

Seitz, V., Abelson, W. D., Levine, E. and Zigler, E. (1975) 'Effects of place of testing on the Peabody Picture Vocabulary Test scores of disadvantaged Head Start and non-Head Start children'. *Child Development*, 46, pp. 481–6.

Spencer, L. M. (1983) *Soft Skill Competencies*. Edinburgh: Scottish Council for Research in Education.

Vygotsky, L. S. (1978) *Mind in Society*. Cambridge, MA: Harvard University Press (first published in Russian in 1934).

Wallace, J. G. (1980) 'The Nature of Educational Competence', in J. Sants (ed.), *Developmental Psychology and Society*. London: Macmillan.

Williams, I. C. and Boreham, N. C. (1971) *The Predictive Value of CSE Grades in Further Education* (Schools Council Examinations Bulletin 24). London: Evans/Methuen Educational.

Wolf, A. and Silver, R. (1986) *Work-Based Learning: Trainee Assessment by Supervisors*. Sheffield: Manpower Services Commission.

Wood, R. (1986), 'The Agenda for Educational Measurement', in D. L. Nuttall (ed.), *Assessing Educational Achievement*. Lewes: Falmer Press.

Wood, R. and Power, C. (1984) *An Enquiry into the Competence-Performance Distinction as it Relates to Assessment in Secondary and Further Education*. South Australia: Flinders University (unpublished report).

Zigler, E. and Seitz, V. (1982) 'Social Policy and Intelligence', in R. J. Sternberg (ed.), *Handbook of Human Intelligence*. Cambridge: Cambridge University Press.

4.6

Assessment Purposes and Learning in Mathematics Education

Brenda Denvir

Assessment, in one form or another, has always been an integral part of any resourced educational system, indeed of any self-conscious teaching/learning scenario in which both learners and teachers ask 'how are we doing?' The forms of assessment are many and what is chosen and implemented affects fundamentally the learning experiences of the pupils. The choice will be determined by the particular purposes which it is intended to fulfil. In turn both the purposes which are chosen and the methods which are used to achieve the required ends reflect assumptions about the purpose of education and the nature of learning. Moreover the chosen assessment system is the mechanism whereby the whole society affirms what is valued within education. Assessment, then, is a basic issue in education, because it both reflects and communicates deeply held convictions about how children learn, what children should learn and why. Given this awareness of the fundamental integration of assessment within the educational endeavour, contemporary efforts to devise and carry out assessment need to consider the questions:

1 who is being assessed?
2 what is being assessed?
3 who is devising/carrying out the assessment?
4 how is the assessment carried out?
5 what is the purpose of the assessment?

in order to ensure that the assessment practice does reflect what is known about learning and what is held to be true about educational worth.

In answer to the last question, four purposes of assessment will be considered under their respective headings: *assessment for teaching*, *assessment for selection*, *assessment for evaluation* and *assessment for curriculum control*. The discussion within these sections will also consider the importance of the first four questions and how the issues are related to a theory of learning.

Assessment for teaching

Assessment for teaching is termed 'formative'. It involves collecting sufficiently detailed information about the children which helps the teacher plan and teach effectively in order to maximise childrens' future learning. In contrast 'summative' assessment sets out to describe what children have already achieved, usually for the purpose of either selection or evaluation Formative assessment may involve one or more of a range of assessment activities from informal observation to oral, practical or written procedures. In some instances it may be impossible for the teacher to select appropriate learning activities for a particular student without collecting specific and detailed information. This deliberate gathering of information for teaching is termed *diagnostic assessment*. It is a type of formative assessment in so far as it looks ahead to future learning activities, but usually it involves the use of specific procedures or protocols. There is, however, no clear cut distinction, but a continuum between formative and diagnostic assessment. Towards one end of this lies, for example brief verbal questioning of the whole class about their ideas in a particular topic; towards the other lie perceptual discrimination tasks designed by psychologists. Diagnostic assessment will not be necessary for all students, at all times, but will be needed when more general formative assessments fail to indicate activities from which children can learn.

Recently, the importance of assessment for teaching, both formative and diagnostic, was emphasised in the National Curriculum report of the Task Group on Assessment and Testing (DES, 1988) which recommended that:

> the basis of the national assessment system be essentially formative, but designed also to indicate where there is a need for more detailed diagnostic assessment. At age 16, however, it should incorporate assessment with summative functions (para 27).

'Diagnostic assessment' is a metaphor from the medical world, originally referring to special treatment for 'remedial' students. The remedy was seen as more practice in identified areas of weakness. It was based on several beliefs: mathematics as a collection of arbitrary, fixed procedures; teaching accomplished by telling and learning by repetition; the learner as a passive container, waiting to be filled with knowledge, but possibly not receiving the knowledge because of a 'block'. This transmission of learning fails to take into account research which indicates that children are active in their learning and logical in solving tasks. In von Glasersfeld's (1987) words: 'Children . . . are not repositories for adult 'knowledge' but organisms that, like all of us, are constantly trying to make sense of, to understand their experience' (p. 12).

For example, pre-school children (Carpenter *et al.*, 1983) were able in interview, to solve simple word problems in number, despite the absence of any formal teaching, whereas a subsequent study, after some weeks of teaching, indicated a decline in the logic of their reasoning in relation to these tasks and a greater tendency to use a method which they had learned but which was inappropriate. Not only does a 'transmission model' of beliefs about the learning of mathematics fail to account for what is observed, but it promotes rote learning of rules, a form of learning which is not helpful to children who will be expected to be flexible, adaptive and able to change in response to our rapidly developing and complex technological society.

By contrast, a constructivist view of learning, rooted in the work of Piaget, and currently explored in depth by von Glasersfeld (1984) sees children as agents in their own learning. What they have come to know arises through active construction of concepts in making sense of their experiences. For many teachers and educators the cognitive shift from an assumed 'transmission' model to constructivism begins when they themselves begin to notice what has been documented in research, namely that children use strategies which they have not been taught (cf. Groen and Resnick, 1977). These invented strategies are intelligently based on the child's own understanding of the world, which is often different from the way that it is seen by the adult. For example, (Denvir, 1984), when Theo was asked the question 'Peter has nine sweets, Mark has five; how many more does Peter have than Mark?' she replied 'four', but when asked to write down how she had worked this out, she wrote '$6 + 7 + 8 + 9 = 4$'.

Students responses in individual interviews (quoted, e.g. in Dickson, 1984, p. 262–3) support this perception of learners actively and logically seeking solutions. There are a number of projects which have been based, more or less strongly, within a general constructivist framework, accepting that children do develop their own strategies. They vary in their perceptions of how the teacher might best respond to this knowledge. Some take the view that the strategies which children develop are 'wrong' so that the teacher's job is to prevent them, or, if this proves impossible, root them out. Others make a point of accepting that, for any child, *all* the strategies which are developed and *all* the concepts that are constructed are logical and intelligent to that child and that, as a consequence, they provide both a valuable means of gaining insight to the child's understanding and also a starting point from which learning must progress. Different research projects have taken different stances, some characterised by the importance of avoiding or correcting misconceptions, others by the necessity of working from the conceptions that children have already formed.

In a programme of research based at King's (formerly Chelsea)

College extensive interviewing was carried out in a range of mathematical topics as part of the secondary mathematics project 'CSMS' (Hart, 1981). The strategies which children used were identified; in many instances, the same 'incomplete' or 'inappropriate' strategy was used by many students, producing the same incorrect answer. Frequently these strategies were invented by the students rather than taught by the teacher. In the subsequent study, 'Strategies and Errors in Secondary Mathematics' (e.g. Booth, 1984) these strategies are referred to as 'child methods' and give correct answers for easy questions, but not for more complex items. The 'Chelsea Diagnostic Mathematics Tests' (Hart et al., 1984) which are based on this research, were designed to measure students' levels of understanding and identify particular errors which each of them make. 'Levels' are described for each test and these refer both to the mathematical ideas and the strategies which students use. In this way, the work assumes that children's strategies indicate the quality of their mathematical understanding. In this sense it takes a constructivist stance. However it does not consider the whole context in which the children are doing mathematics and in this sense it fails to take into account children's perceptions of what they are doing, namely their goal or intention in tackling the problem.

Using only a small sample of children, we (Denvir and Brown, 1986a), developed an oral and practical diagnostic assessment to assess 'low attaining' 7–9 year-olds' understanding of number. Again the technique was to attempt to identify children's strategies, but this assessment was based on a framework which described the orders of acquisition of number concepts. We identified 'hierarchical strands', in which, for the children interviewed, the acquisition of one ability depended on the development of an earlier ability, allowing assessment of each child's 'understanding' of number concepts. Within this research study, all the data were gathered from interviews, consequently it was possible to determine, to some extent, whether or not the child's perception of the task was similar to that of the researcher. Thus it takes a slightly more strongly constructivist stance than that of the CSMS work. One finding of the teaching study carried out as part of this research (Denvir and Brown, 1986b) has considerable implications for the teaching of mathematics and, in particular, for the use of a diagnostic assessment as part of a teaching programme. While the order in which children acquired particular concepts, strategies and ways of perceiving aspects of number fitted the hierarchical framework which we had developed, it did not give a clear indication of what children would *learn next*. Rather it indicated a whole range of possible ideas that children might soon grasp. Therefore it did not support a step-by-step approach to teaching the next skill in the hierarchy, but instead suggested possible areas of development which were useful in planning the teaching. In this work it was possible to mark children's progress through several broad 'stages' which were characterised by the development of various strategies. The description of these stages differed, then, from the levels in the national curriculum mathematics guidelines, which describe, instead, the types of problems that can be solved at the various levels. There is considerable difficulty about how to phrase attainment targets for the national curriculum. If they include some reference to strategy they will encourage the rote teaching of procedures, yet if there is no pointer to the significance of the strategy which is used, the validity of the assessment and its implications for the teaching are likely to be lost. There are two substantial caveats about the support which the Denvir and Brown study gives to perceiving mathematical development progressing through fixed stages. First, this work was carried out in a small number of London primary schools which followed roughly similar curricula. There is no guarantee that the mathematical development of children who are given very different learning experiences will proceed in a similar way. Secondly, this study was undertaken in a narrow domain of number and provides no evidence that children's development in other aspects of the mathematics curriculum, such as spatial awareness, would parallel their grasp of number.

These, and other studies, indicate that assessment of students' understanding of concepts is more validly based on their use of strategies than totalling the number of items answered correctly or incorrectly in a written test. However there are difficulties in using childrens' strategies to measure mathematical attainment. These arise because children are active agents in their own learning: as they are presented with a task, they explore and think about it, and their strategies change and develop. How the child tackles the problem is frequently more a function of the context, mode of presentation, and individual interpretation than of the child's cognitive or intellectual ability.

First, the mathematical thinking that is prompted in an individual depends on context as well as underlying mathematical structure. For example, a highly motivating task, or a familiar and easily recognised context might prompt a 'common sense', pragmatic solution (Murphy, 1988a), a mathematical context might stimulate the recall of a standard procedure and an unfamiliar context may be avoided, generating no response. Thus a child's performance on any mathematical task may not provide a valid description of that child's *mathematical* knowledge. Individuals will be affected in a different way by different contexts. For example, as Murphy points out (1988b) girls' or boys' performances may be artificially lowered by the choice of a gender specific activity. In a similar way individuals have preferences, or specific knowledge, of some contexts and not others. To minimise this difficulty, children need to be assessed in a range of contexts and the contexts in which they are most likely to succeed should be sought, in order to accurately reflect mathematical understanding. Here, however, lies a further danger, of artificially boosting children's performance by presenting an assessment in a context with which the child is familiar and which prompts a particular strategy, but as a rote learned rather than a reasoned response.

Secondly, the mode of presentation and response is likely to influence students' thinking. One reason for the widespread use of written tests is the ease of administration and collection of data. Oral and practical assessments take more time yet yield richer information, which will often need thoughtful interpretation. In order to examine the feasibility of assessing children's understanding of number in a class, rather than an individual setting, we (Denvir and Brown, 1987) carried out a small-scale study with 8–11 year-olds. Individual responses in a class test were compared with responses to the same items presented in an individual interview: many were found to differ. For example in an item requiring interpolation on a 'decimal' number line where only the points 10 and 20 were numbered, but the line was marked in intervals of 0.1, one of the children marked the point 9.8 to represent 8 in the class assessment, whereas in the interview, she was able to work out and mark the correct point. In the study about one quarter of the children performed markedly less well in the class test than they did in the interview.

The third difficulty is related to both of those already outlined. In order to reflect accurately the child's mathematical thinking, it is necessary to assess the response in terms of the problem which the child perceives. There is, in most assessment activities, an assumption that once a question has been posed then the problem as perceived by the teacher becomes the child's problem. Yet von Glasersfeld writes (1989)

> language is not a means of transporting conceptual structures from teacher to student, but rather a means of interacting that allows the teacher here and there to constrain and thus to guide the cognitive construction of the student ... the problem situations themselves, given that they do not exist independently in an objective environment, are seen, articulated and approached differently by different cognizing subjects

In fact inability to 'see' what the teacher 'sees' is likely to result in what is, to the teacher, an 'inappropriate' response, which is unlikely to be credited for what it truly represents.

Teachers carry out *formative assessment*, sometimes deliberately, but often unconsciously, selecting activities intuitively. While these judgements are frequently based on sound experience, they are often not clearly articulated and thus underrated, labelled as subjective and accorded less status than numerically quantifiable results of standard written tests, although they usually reflect children's performance with greater sublety.

To avoid the difficulties outlined, a current curriculum development project uses assessment only in so far as it assists the teaching and learning process. In order to establish a common meaning for the activities, these are embedded within a theme in which children have 'expert' knowledge and the meaning of the tasks is negotiated through discussion. The work aims to help teachers provide challenging learning tasks, at an appropriate level, which are rich in mathematical and scientific concepts and procedures, will motivate children and will thus enhance learning. In this work, formative assessment is seen to involve collecting a range of different types of information about the children, including an awareness of:

1 the mathematical and scientific concepts and procedures which they have grasped
2 the contexts in which these have been experienced and understood
3 the children's interests, knowledge and expertise in their everyday world, as well as in their school work.

For example, in a sequence of activities to determine which of a selection of metals was the most suitable for the clip on the top of a pen, children suggested that they should decide which metal was 'the bendiest'. In a discussion of the word 'bend', one child was thinking only in terms of a bend in the road and was, therefore, before adequate discussion linked with handling the metals, unable to begin to investigate 'bendiness'. The subsequent sequence of activities also revealed a great deal about children's difficulties with measurement: they neither saw a 'need' for it, for it was self-evident which one bent most easily, nor, when they had realised a need for measure, were they able to decide what to measure. Within this work, children's discussion and the way that the activities were tackled gave considerable evidence about their understanding of the ideas: much was revealed about children's thinking in small incidents as well as in the general strategies that were used.

While this type of assessment is demanding for teachers and involves careful observation and interpretation of children's responses, it provides a much more valid basis for the analysis of their understanding than do the results of items in a written test. In terms of usefulness for planning the teaching, it will invariably provide the teacher with far greater insight into the children's understanding and the nature of their learning difficulties. Moreover, it enables the teacher to become more skilled, professionally, in understanding how learning proceeds, in analysing what skills and understandings

284 DEVELOPMENTS IN LEARNING AND ASSESSMENT

are implicit in particular tasks and, consequently, in developing greater formative assessment skills. Thus formative assessment seeks to serve students interests by helping teachers teach more effectively.

Assessment for selection

While assessment for teaching is termed 'formative', assessment for selection and evaluation is 'summative'. Within school, students may be selected for a teaching group according to particular aspects of their school performance. This may be done in a rigid way, as in setting or streaming or there may be *ad hoc* groupings for particular activities within the classroom. Selection also takes place for purposes which go beyond the school. Some Local Education Authorities assess children before transfer in order to make allocations to secondary schools. Public examinations, schools and colleges own assessments and profiles are frequently used to decide whether or not a student will be accepted for a job, educational training or higher education.

Selectors need good predictive information in order to determine which people will benefit from the opportunities they are empowered to grant, who will make valuable contributions in employment and who will excel in the given area. They need information about what constitutes and causes success or failure within a particular domain, as well as strategies for detecting this at the time of the selection. There are, however, numerous difficulties associated with assessment for selection. First, the state of knowledge about what, precisely, we mean by mathematical attainment and what particular aspects are needed for certain jobs or courses of study are unclear. Knowledge is culturally defined and what we mean by 'doing mathematics' varies: one aspect of mathematical knowledge is not a 'given', equally accessible to all. As society changes, so does the knowledge that children pick up incidentally and so does the learning which takes place in school. This cultural shift varies in timing and emphasis from one situation to another and assessments may vary considerably in the account they take of the differing experiences of different students.

The second difficulty has already been discussed in the section on formative assessment. Even when there is clarity about the required attributes there is still difficulty in measuring who has or who has not acquired them. Thirdly, there are insurmountable difficulties in ensuring equal opportunities for all, regardless of gender, socioeconomic or cultural background, because all assessment tasks are located in a culture and context which will benefit some students and handicap others. Finally, when assessment for selection is emphasised within a educational establishment, it has a detrimental effect on those who judge themselves unlikely to be selected for anything which is highly valued.

Assessment for selection primarily serves the interests, not of the learners, but of the selectors, or those whom they represent, that is those concerned with industrial or economic achievement or academic excellence. Nevertheless, these assessments for selection, concerned primarily with what happens beyond the school, have considerable effect on what happens within the establishment. Curriculum choices for *all* may be affected by the interests of a minority who wish to pursue university courses, resulting in inappropriate courses for the majority.

In a similar way, selection for teaching groups within the school may serve the interests of the teachers or the organisation of the school, rather than the learning needs of the pupils. Such organisation of teaching groups encourages the belief that learners' attainment is at one of a number of discrete levels, rather than along a complex continuum. While students are grouped according to similarity of attainment for organisational convenience, the allocation of students to groups has, at best, arbitrary cut-off points. Moreover there is little evidence to support the notion of psychologically meaningful levels across different topics in the mathematics curriculum. Levels may be defined, normatively, by examining distributions of the population, but these are likely to vary, depending on the curriculum which is followed. The oversimplifications which are made for organisational purposes are likely to lead to inappropriate curricula for many and also will affect adversely the attitudes of many, through the labelling associated with allocation to a bottom set or a stream.

The effects of assessment for selection may be unfair in allowing equality of opportunity, or ineffective in selecting appropriately. Above all, such assessments may have a large and negative influence on those who are not selected for whatever benefits are offered.

Assessment for evaluation

As noted in the opening paragraph, it is natural for evaluation to take place within the educational system. However there needs to be some notion of what is of value and for this to be agreed between those who carry out, devise, interpret and benefit, or fail to benefit from the assessment. Here, difficulty is likely to arise, because of the considerable differences between what is valued by those who espouse a constructivist view of learning and those who hold a 'transmission' model. Further disagreement is likely to arise between different views of what is meant by 'doing mathematics', for the subject itself develops, but, more importantly, what is useful and therefore of interest is not a fixed body of knowledge but varies according to society's perceived needs in a particular place at a particular time.

It is important to be clear about what is to be evaluated and whether the assessments which are used have the required capability. For example, if it is the intention to represent what has been achieved and decide whether a particular child, class, or school is making satisfactory *progress* it is important to assess the progress and not simply the present attainment. It is not clear at the time of writing that the current proposals for the statutory national assessment system envisage any measure of progress, rather they seem set to measure achievement. Furthermore, there is little purpose in deeming any performance or progress 'unsatisfactory', unless there are also means for affecting improvement. Again, it is not clear what resources will be available to teachers, schools or Local Education Authorities who find that their performance or progress is unsatisfactory. While evaluation sets out to assess outcomes such as progress or performance, inevitably it is persons who are labelled. Such labelling readily leads to poor motivation and disengagement from the tasks of teaching and learning.

There are difficulties with the notion of 'satisfactory'. It implies some sort of norm. But a norm is difficult to define and contrary to a constructivist view of learning, which envisages, rather than a sequence of mathematical ideas which are neatly and fully grasped each in turn, a constantly developing elaboration of mathematical ideas. Children's rates of progress are erratic: the transition from one idea to another may be accomplished quickly by one learner, slowly by another. It calls into question the notion of 'unit of progress', how this might be defined and what constitutes such a 'unit of progress' in relation to a profile. Again, background variables, affecting performance and progress, such as socio-economic group have proved difficult to quantify, making the idea of a 'fair' comparison yet more elusive.

What is required for individual learners is some notion of progress in relation to past performance, some norm-referenced data, that is progress in relation to other learners and also a measure of progress in relation to mathematical objectives. This information can, like the Records of Achievement (1988), help individuals to be aware of their own strengths and weaknesses. This is best done by students and teacher agreeing together what has been achieved and determining what should be the subsequent focus.

Assessment for evaluation needs to ascertain that it adequately and accurately reflects what progress has been made. It also needs to ensure that adequate resources are available to remedy any deficiencies which are exposed.

Assessment for curriculum control

Since pupils, teachers, schools and Local Education Authorities will be judged by students' performances in assessment tasks, teachers will prepare their pupils well, in order to achieve a satisfactory performance. Therefore, imposed assessments will have a controlling effect on the curriculum, whatever the reason for determining what assessments are carried out and why. Consequently, now that assessments are to be imposed by statute, politicians have considerable powers of curriculum control. The important issues here relate to 'whose interests are served?' and 'are the needs of both the individual and the whole community adequately safeguarded?'

Summary and discussion

Different views about mathematics and theories of learning have been considered and, overarching the different purposes of assessment two types, formative and summative, have been distinguished. The question of whether formative and summative assessment involves the same or different activities depends on what theory of learning is espoused. In particular, it depends on the view that is taken of children as learners. Where they are seen as empty vessels to be filled, passive recipients of knowledge in a 'transmission' model of learning, teaching is equated with instruction and practice. Since this model essentially holds that children learn what they are told, summative and formative assessment are identical activities in which children know what they have been told, while what they have not been told they do not know. Assessment, both summative and formative involves finding out what is known and not known. In contrast, where children are seen to be agents in their own learning, actively constructing knowledge, summative assessment will provide a resume of what is firmly established 'robust' knowledge, while formative assessment will focus, in considerably greater detail on the areas in which the child is currently learning: Vygotsky's 'zone of proximal development'. Thus the content of formative assessment, as well as the level of detail will be markedly different from the summative.

   A more serious distinction yet remains to be made, for different stances will lead to very different teaching approaches. Those who accept the 'transmission model' of learning will, in any case adopt a strongly didactic, instructional, teaching approach. Yet it is not so clear that those who hold a constructivist view of learning, a view now widely held within epistemology, philosophy and psychology, will be free to adopt a pedagogy which maximises the implicit learning potential of this view. For the constructivist teacher, the two purposes of assessment are in direct conflict. An emphasis on summative assessment demands that children be prepared to perform well in assessment tasks, whether or not they have grasped the underlying ideas. Thus teaching would aim to cover up any lack of understanding of concepts by learning set rules and procedures. In contrast, an emphasis on formative assessment demands a teaching approach in which children's conceptions are clearly exposed, enabling the teacher to plan activities which address the real issues which confront the learner.

Hope for improvement in children's mathematical education lies essentially in the planning of better teaching, which addresses more directly the problems and issues in learning. Essentially better teaching will come about through greater understanding, on the part of teachers, of the interaction between children and the tasks that they are given. Good formative assessment linked to stimulating learning tasks could be a major factor in effecting this improvement. Given the stated emphasis of the Report of the Task Group on Assessment and Testing on formative and diagnostic assessment, how is this to be safeguarded? Will the effect of national assessment realise the potential which now exists for improved pedagogy, or will it bring about a return to the learning of rote procedures? Will the presence of a national curriculum allow exploration of new and improved teaching strategies? Will it encourage greater professionalism among teachers and greater sharing of new ideas for stimulating children to be more active as learners? Or will it instead result in a stranglehold on what must be done and said within the classroom?

References

Booth, L. R. (1984) *Algebra: Children's Strategies and Errors. A Report on Strategies and Errors in Secondary Mathematics Project.* Windsor: NFER/ Nelson.

Broadfoot, P., James, M., McMeeking, S., Nuttall, D. and Stierer, B. (1988) 'Records of Achievement: Report of the National Evaluation of Pilot Schemes.' Report submitted to the Department of Education and Science and the Welsh Office, HMSO, London.

Carpenter, T. P., Hiebert, J. and Moser, J. M. (1983) 'The Effect of Instruction on Children's Solution of Addition and Subtraction Word Problems', *Educational Studies in Mathematics*, 14, 1, pp. 55–72.

Denvir, B. (1984) 'The Development of Number Concepts in Low Attaining 7–9 year olds'. Unpublished PhD thesis, University of London.

Denvir, B. and Brown, M. (1986a) 'Understanding of Number Concepts in Low Attaining 7–9 Year Olds: Part I', *Educational Studies in Mathematics*, 17, 1, pp. 15–36.

Denvir, B. and Brown, M. (1986b) 'Understanding of Number Concepts in Low Attaining 7–9 Year Olds, Part II.' *Educational Studies in Mathematics*, 17, 1, pp. 143–64.

Denvir, B. and Brown, M. (1987) 'The Feasibility of Class Administered Diagnostic Assessment in Primary Mathematics', *Educational Research*, 29, pp. 95–107.
DES (1988) Report of the National Curriculum Task Group on Assessment and Testing. London.
Dickson, L., Brown, M. and Gibson, O. (1984) *Children Learning Mathematics*. London: Holt, Rinehart and Winston.
Groen, C. J. and Resnick, L. B. (1977) 'Can Pre-school Children Invent Addition Algorithms?' *Journal of Educational Psychology*, 69, pp. 645–52.
Hart, K. M. (ed.) (1981) *Children's Understanding of Mathematics 11–16*. London: John Murray.
Hart, K. M., Brown, M., Kerslake, D., Kuchemann, D. and Ruddock, G. (1984) *Chelsea Diagnostic Mathematics Tests*. Windsor: NFER/Nelson.
Murphy, P. (1988a) 'Insights Into Pupils' Responses to Practical Investigations from the APU', *Physics Education*, 23, 6, pp. 330–36.
Murphy, P. (1988b) 'Gender and Assessment', *Curriculum*, Winter, Vol. 3, pp. 165–71.
von Glasersfeld, E. (1984) An introduction to radical constructivism in P. Watzlawick (ed.) *The Invented Reality*. New York: Norton.
von Glasersfeld, E. (1987) Learning as a Constructive Activity in C. Janvier (ed.) *Problems of Representation in the Teaching and Learning of Mathematics*. Hillsdale, NJ: Erlbaum.
von Glasersfeld, E. (1989) 'Environment and Communication', in L. Steffe (ed.) [Proceedings of the International Conference of Mathematical Education, Hungary, 1988]. New York: Lawrence Erlbaum Associates (pubs.).

4.7

Records of Achievement: Report of the National Evaluation of Pilot Schemes*

PRAISE team:
Patricia Broadfoot, Mary James, Susan McMeeking, Desmond Nuttall and Barry Stierer

Introduction

Background

Since the passing of the 1944 Education Act which heralded the provision of secondary education for all children, there has been a steadily increasing expectation that achievements during this phase of schooling should be marked by some form of certification. In the words of chapter 10 of the 1963 Newsom Report.[1] 'Boys and girls who stay at school until they are 16 may reasonably look for some record of achievement when they leave.' For many young people this expectation has been met by the award of examination certificates by external examining bodies. However, public examinations were never intended to cater for all young people, and some boys and girls still leave school with no record of their experiences and achievements during their years of compulsory schooling. When in 1973 the school-leaving age was eventually raised to 16, the acknowledged problem was further highlighted by the fact that those for

* The Department of Education and Science, in partnership with local education authorities, provided support for nine pilot schemes of records of achievement. PRAISE (Pilot Records of Achievement in Schools Evaluation) was the national evaluation of these pilot schemes. In the report of the evaluation one section describes the specific aspects of educational achievement which featured in the pilot records. These included: (a) extra-curricular and out-of-school activities; (b) subject-specific achievement; (c) cross-curricular achievement and (d) personal and social qualities and skills. This description (without the report examples) is reproduced below.

whom public examinations were not designed would have to remain in school for an additional year. In this context it became especially important to work towards the creation of worthwhile goals which would give all young people a sense of achievement which might be appropriately recognised. This aspiration came to be widely shared and has resulted in a number of explicit attempts to provide youngsters with records of achievement, sometimes known as profiles.

During the 1970s and early 1980s, therefore, a number of independent initiatives were undertaken in this respect. Although they varied widely in approach, they had the common aim of seeking to provide school leavers of all levels of attainment with a positive statement of achievement across a range of activities. An increasingly coherent philosophy also emerged. This emphasised assessment as part of the educational process and made pupils equal partners with teachers by giving them a prominent and active role. It also emphasised a need for positive, constructive, detailed and useful records which would support learning in school and help the school leaver to provide employers, trainers and other potential 'users' with the kind of information they required. Above all, it emphasised that the processes of recording should develop the self-concept, self-confidence, self-esteem and motivation of young people in such a way that they could gain the maximum benefit from their education.

Statement of policy

In November 1983 the Government demonstrated that it was aware of this trend by issuing a draft policy on 'records of achievement for all school leavers'. Comments received included suggestions and criticisms but indicated almost unanimous support for such records. In the autumn of 1984, therefore, the Department of Education and Science and the Welsh Office published *Records of Achievement: A Statement of Policy* which incorporated many of the suggestions on the draft and presented the case for records of achievement based on the philosophy outlined above. As such it was widely welcomed by education professionals and became a key reference point for those involved in developing recording systems.

According to the 1984 policy statement the purposes of records of achievement were seen to be:

1 To recognise, acknowledge and give credit for what pupils have achieved and experienced, not just in terms of results in public examinations but in other ways as well.
2 To contribute to pupils' personal development and progress by improving their motivation, providing encouragement and in-

creasing their awareness of strengths, weaknesses and opportunities.

3 To help schools identify the all round potential of their pupils and to consider how well their curriculum, teaching and organisation enable pupils to develop the general, practical and social skills which are to be recorded.

Aspects of achievement

Extra-curricular and out-of-school interests and activities

All case study schools have aimed to cover extra-curricular and out-of-school interests and activities in their recording systems. At first view there seems much value in this since choice of leisure time activities and work experience often says much about an individual which is of potential interest to employers and can provide interesting material for discussion at interview (e.g. the Hawthorn RC school girl who runs a pig and rabbit breeding business and wants to make a career in agriculture). It also appears to have value as a way of strengthening pupil-tutor relationships by providing an opportunity for tutors to discover a different side of their pupils and by giving in-school achievement a new perspective. [...]

In relation to this aspect of achievement we would wish to make four points. First, placing extra-curricular and out-of-school achievement on the recording agenda may imply an increased responsibility on the part of the school to provide extra-curricular activities. Secondly, teachers need to be acutely aware of the possibilities for social divisiveness and personal intrusion inherent in such an aspect of recording. Thirdly, pupils need to be made aware of the possible uses to which their records might be put to enable them to be both wide-ranging and judicious in their choice of evidence to record. Fourthly, pupil autonomy is an important principle to protect in the context of this aspect of recording.

Subject-specific achievement

With the exception of two schools whose RoA (Record of Achievement) was confined to personal achievement, all of the schools we have studied have, at some point during the pilot period, attempted to include pupils' achievement in their academic subjects within the RoA system. Hence we are able to report an emerging consensus in this area, as we were in the area of extra-curricular and out-of-school activities in the previous subsection.

However, the scale and nature of such recording varied enormously according to the vantage points from which the recording of subject-specific achievement was carried out, and according to the notions of subject-specific achievement which underpinned it.

This diversity can be represented by describing *three broad types of recording of subject-specific achievement*. These are not 'ideal' types in any pure sense, and aspects of more than one type may be found within a single school. Nevertheless, we have found them to be a helpful way to understand the range of practices and definitions which abound in this area.

Within the *first type*, pupils' achievement in their subjects was recorded from a 'tutorial' vantage point. This type was generally built upon the responsibilities of form tutors for keeping an overall 'watching brief' on pupils' academic progress. Hence, whilst this vantage point held the potential for a comprehensive view of a child's experience of the academic curriculum, in the cases we studied it tended to be generalised and partial, lacking the specificity of assessment concepts relevant to each subject or course area. Often such records had the familiar character of the form tutor's overview found in conventional reports to parents or school leavers' testimonials. Certainly this type did not in itself require changes in the way that individual subject departments conceptualised achievement in their areas or in the way they organised teaching, learning, assessment and recording. [. . .]

Within the *second type*, pupils' achievement in their subjects was recorded by subject teachers, but the emphasis of the RoA system was on *summarising* achievement and *reporting* that portrayal to particular outside audiences at certain times in a pupil's school career (we are not referring here exclusively to summative RoAs). Reporting frameworks were generally devised to reflect and incorporate existing methods of teaching, learning and assessment, and internal recording. For example, course work would be taught and marked by teachers in a traditional way, often using marks or grades, but achievement over a given period would be expressed in the form of positive prose comments, and discussed with pupils, at the point when summary reports were required. [. . .]

Within the *third type*, recording grew out of a reappraisal by subject staff of notions of subject-specific achievement and a restructuring of teaching, assessment and record-keeping. The emphasis here was on such formative processes as the explication of learning objectives, the development of modules or units of work, continuous criterion-referenced assessment, the grounding of records in evidence of pupils' work, teacher–pupil dialogue and a systematic approach to the diagnosis of strengths and weaknesses. [. . .]

It would not be appropriate for us to advocate the universal adoption of one of these types, because to do so would not only be to judge one kind of RoA system as superior to another but to say that one form of curricular organisation is to be preferred. [. . .]

None of these types, for example, necessarily precludes the adoption of a wide definition of achievement which goes beyond the knowledge of subject content to include conceptual, practical, process, personal, social and attitudinal achievement. Neither does any type necessarily preclude a central role for formative processes of self-assessment, review and target-setting, although these are more clearly formalised in the last. [. . .]

We now turn our attention to the different *conceptions of subject-specific achievement* which have underpinned recording systems in our case study schools. In this respect, our evidence suggests that systems developed to record subject achievement, within any of the types outlined above, pay attention to one or more of the familiar trilogy of knowledge, skills and attitudes. By *knowledge* we mean propositional knowledge specific to the subject which is assessed by requiring pupils to demonstrate recall and understanding. Traditionally this has had a prominent role in education and, according to our evidence, is still an important focus for assessment, recording and reporting. *Attitudes* constitute another aspect which has always been a prominent focus for recording in relation to subject achievement, in particular the interest in, and disposition towards, work within the subject as demonstrated by effort, commitment and motivation. Assessment of a pupil's 'effort' has had a long history in education in England and Wales although the assessment of attitudes *deliberately fostered within the curriculum* (such as those promoted within, for example, health education) is a different matter.

Skills constitute a third aspect and it is this area which has received particular attention in some schools and schemes, in keeping with the current prominence of skills-based approaches to curriculum and course design and development. Indeed 'skills' has become something of an educational buzz-word, the meaning of which has been obscured by possible over use. This observation applies equally to the term 'processes' to which it is closely allied, sometimes to the extent of being used synonymously. For the purposes of clarification, variations in the meanings attached to the term 'skills' can be conceptualised according to definitions on three dimensions. On the first dimension, narrow definitions of achievement in terms of skills often focus on performance of some generalised operation (or process) devoid of reference to specific content and context (e.g. problem-solving) although more comprehensive definitions acknowledge that skill also involves knowledge of ends and the means to achieve them (propositional knowledge) and a disposition to use means to achieve ends (attitudes). On the second dimension, the concept of a skill developed in subject contexts can be restricted to what might be termed practical or craft skills (e.g. ball control in PE; manipulation in CDT) or it can be broadened to take in intellectual skills (e.g. critical analysis, investigation) and personal and social skills (e.g. empathy, collaboration). On the third dimension, skills can be singular and discrete (e.g. asking questions, hypothesising, collecting data, categorising) or they can be composite (e.g. investigating, researching) indicating different orders of skills in which higher order skills subsume lower order skills. [. . .]

Our evidence suggests that, at least for summary purposes, a broad definition on all of these dimensions is to be preferred, i.e. that the skills of most interest are higher order, inclusive skills defined as practical knowledge in personal, social and intellectual areas as well as craft skills.

Although most of the schools which we studied implemented RoA systems which incorporated subject-specific knowledge, attitudes and skills, to a greater or lesser degree, a few chose to make skills (or processes) a principal focus for recording. In these contexts what was identified, assessed and recorded as skill or process achievement varied widely both between and within institutions, along the lines described above. A number of issues of special interest emerged but the greatest problems were experienced when skills were recorded as atomistic, general competencies devoid of reference to the content and context of demonstration. [. . .]

On the basis of this evidence, our judgement is that subject achievement which is recorded in terms of skills will need to include reference to the content and context of performance if it is to have validity and meaning. Whilst skills may have similarities in different contexts they are also distinguished by their content, it cannot be assumed therefore that they are entirely transferable.

Similarly, although it may be helpful to record the performance of numerous discrete skills (e.g. in comment banks) at the formative stage, the indications are that these need to be summarised in more holistic ways when there is a summative intention to report to other audiences. Thus ways need to be found to order achievements in some kind of hierarchy such that atomistic skills, if it is felt that there is value in recording them, are subsumed within more holistic categories at the stage of reporting. This is important because the constraints on space in any summary document create a need for selection, but limited selections of atomistic skills tend to trivialise and misrepresent achievement. [. . .]

Our evidence also points to a growing recognition that a wide range of skills is brought into play in learning within subject contexts. This range is likely to include intellectual, social and personal skills as well as manipulative skills. Indeed, the experience of teachers in some schools suggests that curricular opportunities for demonstrating social and personal skills are best provided within the formal academic curriculum where they arise naturally and are often an essential element (e.g. skills of collaboration).

On the basis of our evidence, our judgement is that a broad definition of skills appropriate for development and recording in subject areas should be encouraged, and that this should include skills of a personal and social kind which have an important bearing on subject-specific achievement. Indeed we feel that this is an important and valid way of approaching the recording of cross-curricular achievement and personal qualities, which is more specifically discussed in the next two sections.

Cross-curricular achievement

In our case study work we encountered two basic approaches to understanding the term 'cross-curricular' and we feel that these need to be taken into account in the continuing debate on recording pupil achievement. First, there was the approach to cross-curricular which centred on the *pupil*. This approach was grounded on the assumption that general processes, concepts and skills can be identified which do not appear exclusively related to the substantive content of subjects. They are recognised to have a level of generality although they do not require some common agreed attempt across subject areas to foster the same skills in different contexts. Thus cognitive skills of investigation, social, personal and psycho-motor skills, and attitudes to learning, have all been referred to at one time or another as cross-curricular achievements. Such achievements may be developed, demonstrated and recorded in subject-specific contexts without reference to other subject areas. In some cases, as mentioned in the previous section, they may be considered *essential* to achievement in those contexts, in which case aspects of subject and cross-curricular achievement become indistinguishable and the term 'cross-curricular' becomes simply a way of indicating a level of generality beyond the particular. The substitution of terms such as 'general competencies' for 'cross-curricular skills' is significant in this respect. [. . .]

The second approach appeared to centre on a notion of cross-curricular which related to *school organisation*, and suggested skills which could be fostered, assessed and recorded in two or more departments and which were therefore identified as a shared objective. [. . .] In practice, there was sometimes movement from one approach to the other and the skills framing both kinds of approaches were often roughly similar.

The strength of the first approach was that it allowed for the possibility that no two departments could foster precisely the same skill because skills have a knowledge content which is to some degree context specific, even though they may have much in common at a general level of analysis e.g. drawing conclusions from evidence. On the other hand, the second approach had the advantage of encouraging fruitful discussion and collaboration between departments. Ideally, some combination of these two approaches should be possible – they are not mutually exclusive. However, in the light of the evidence from our case studies that cross-departmental agreement is difficult to achieve and that transferability is a questionable assumption, our judgement is that the first approach has the greater potential in this area. [. . .]

Personal achievement

From what has been said already readers will be aware that, in addition to extra-curricular and out-of-school interests, RoA systems in case study schools often included reference to personal and social achievements within subject-specific and cross-curricular recording. Indeed, as our analysis progressed, what had at first seemed to be clear conceptual categories became increasingly blurred. However, in keeping with their interest in portraying the whole person, all schools consciously developed a 'personal' element as part of their recording procedures, either as a separate record or within the curricular elements of the RoA. Although one can argue that all recording is personal because it focuses on individuals, schools in pilot schemes appeared to use the term in a more restricted sense to refer to achievements, experiences and qualities which were assumed to be pupil-specific rather than curriculum-related. Sometimes the reference was to personal qualities or attributes and sometimes it was to personal skills. The distinction is an important theoretical one but need not concern us here because in no case was there any interest in recording immutable individual characteristics which could not be fostered, developed or influenced by educational experiences. It is interesting that what in one place was labelled a personal quality (initiative, reliability, punctuality) was elsewhere described as a skill. On the whole any lists of such qualities or skills developed by schools or schemes to guide recording exhibited a remarkable degree of similarity. The proscription of comments on a pupil's honesty was widely advised; and the need to include some comment on attendance was also usual, although this was neither a quality or a skill.
[. . .]

Our evidence suggests that schools regard personal qualities and/or skills as an important aspect of achievement which deserves recognition within the RoA because personal and social development is held to be an important purpose of education. However it does not seem to us that universal agreement over what counts as personal achievement should be considered a pre-condition for objectivity, any more than it is in any other area (language, mathematics or science, etc.). Criteria are, of course, implicit in the public form of discourse that teachers participate in for assessing such development. In other words the kinds of categories and criteria which have emerged through trial and review in the DES pilot phase are likely to have value in a record of achievement. As long as they are publicly accessible they are also likely to be used as starting points for discussion in other schools wishing to develop recording systems appropriate for their own special contexts. If criteria emerge and evolve in this way it is unlikely to be necessary to prescribe a list of qualities or skills to be recorded.

However, experience in pilot schools strongly suggests that, in order to be fair, personal qualities or skills should be recorded with sufficient detail of the content and context of demonstration to indicate what is recorded is bounded achievement rather than fixed and immutable personality traits. There was also a considerable degree of agreement within pilot schools that comments should only be made on those personal qualities and skills which can be demonstrated in relation to the school's educational programme. This of course has implications for curriculum planning and demands that opportunities for fostering personal qualities and skills should be part of curricular and/or extra-curricular provision. [. . .]

Overview

In our discussion of aspects of achievement we adopted a categorisation which often framed professional discourse in case study schools. However, the terms 'extra-curricular', 'subject-specific', 'cross-curricular' and 'personal' have strong associations with the way the curriculum is *organised* in secondary schools and this may be misleading. At various points we have said that these categories are not distinct or mutually exclusive in terms of what constitutes achievement. For example, personal qualities are not distinct from social skills since they may only be demonstrable in social contexts; what are called cross-curricular skills, such as co-operation and taking responsibility, are often indistinguishable from formulations of personal achievement; and both so-called cross-curricular and personal achievements are integral, even essential, to subject-specific achievement.

We are impressed therefore by the way in which the Hargreaves Report, which influenced the development of the London Record of Achievement, avoided tying the discussion of aspects of achievement to the organisational structures of schools. Instead it created categories of analysis labelled simply aspects of achievement I, II, III and IV. Aspect I related to propositional knowledge as assessed by examinations with an emphasis on an individual's ability to memorise and organise content; aspect II related to practical processes and skills involved in applying knowledge e.g. problem-solving, investigative skills or manual skills; aspect III related to personal and social skills such as communication, co-operation, initiative, self-reliance and leadership; and aspect IV related to positive attitudes associated with motivation and commitment.

According to this analysis it is possible to see what we have referred to as subject-specific, cross-curricular and personal achievement can incorporate more than one of aspects I to IV. Indeed the authors of the Hargreaves Report argued that subject-specific achievement properly encompasses all four. The fostering of all these aspects of achievement therefore transcends organisational boundaries; recording in relation to most aspects can, and perhaps should, take place in relation to all elements of the educational programme of schools. Although the practice may fall short of the theory, as indeed our evidence suggests, this was the thinking underlying the development of units and unit credits in ILEA. In so far as units and unit credits can in principle be developed to cover all aspects of achievement in relation to any curriculum unit – academic or pastoral – we feel the approach has much to recommend it. Of course, if Hargreaves' four aspects were to be used as straitjackets for the development of skills in every curriculum unit, classified under four reporting headings, rather than simply as categories for analysis, then their effects could be deleterious. The advantage of the Hargreaves approach, as we see it, is that it provides a reminder of the comprehensiveness and multi-dimensionality of subject achievement, and has some potential to erode the hard-and-fast academic and pastoral divide which has been erected and sustained by essentially organisational boundaries. The implications for curriculum planning, for teaching and learning, for assessment and recording and for in-service and other forms of support are of course substantial. However, our evidence leads us to the conclusion that this broadening of the scope of recording across the whole curriculum is the only valid way to portray the educational experience of the whole child within the existing organisational structures of schools.

Note

1 Ministry of Education (1963) *Half Our Future*. Central Advisory Council for Education. London: HMSO.

4.8

Graded Assessment Projects: Similarities and Differences

Margaret Brown

Background

The development of 'graded tests', which more recently have evolved into 'graded assessments', constitutes a significant innovation in classroom assessment. It has taken place in England during the last decade, starting in the mid-1970s in the area of modern languages (Harrison, 1982; Pennycuick and Murphy, 1988).

In response to proposals perpetuating the traditional nature of 16+ examinations, which was held responsible for dissuading all but a minority of pupils from continuing the subject to examination level, teachers of modern languages formed into local groups to develop alternative models for curriculum and assessment based on a 'functional' approach to language. They produced sets of objectives graded by level of competence, with corresponding tests, following the model of examinations for professional interpreters.

The characteristics of graded tests as used by the GOML (Graded Objectives in Modern Languages) movement were:

– progressive, with short-term objectives leading on from one to the next;
– task-oriented, relating to the use of language for practical purposes;
– closely linked into the learning process, with pupils or students taking the tests when they are ready to pass' (Harrison, 1982, p. 13).

In fact, both these early graded test systems and others set up later generally shared two other common features. First, they were generally organised into a set of successive levels, designed in most cases so that average students might expect to pass level 1 at the end of year 1 in the secondary school, level 2 at the end of the second year, and so on. Secondly, they were not only task-oriented, but also incorporated at each level a set of objectives (grade criteria). Thus most graded test systems were criterion-referenced, with criteria which often included both active and practical aspects.

The first evaluation of a graded test system was extremely positive in terms of attitudes of students, teachers and parents (Buckby *et al.*, 1981). Rises of the order of 20 per cent in the numbers of pupils continuing with the study of modern languages were reported fairly consistently across different schools.

Not surprisingly, evidence of improvement in student motivation on this scale attracted attention. For example, the Cockcroft Committee of Inquiry into the Teaching of Mathematics (DES, 1982) tentatively recommended graded tests for low attaining 14–16 year olds, which resulted in two studies being funded (Close and Brown, 1988; Foxman *et al.*, 1988).

On a wider front, in 1983 two major local education authorities, Oxfordshire and Inner London, each decided to form a consortia with examination boards in order to develop graded test systems in the major subjects.

The *graded assessment* projects which are the subject of this paper are the product of the London consortium, in which the main partners are the Inner London Education Authority, King's College London, and the London East Anglia Group for GCSE. In the case of the mathematics project, the Nuffield Foundation has also provided generous support. Within the consortium, graded assessment schemes are being developed in science (GASP – Graded Assessment in Science Project), mathematics (GAIM – Graded Assessment in Mathematics), modern and community languages (GAML – Graded Assessment in Modern Languages), craft, design and technology (GACDT), and English.

By 1983, approaches to assessment had become much broader, incorporating, for instance, observation by teachers during class-work and assessment negotiated between pupil and teacher. The term 'graded tests' was therefore superseded by 'graded assessment' so as to allow, and indeed encourage, such non-test methods where appropriate.

Aims

The Graded Assessment projects each have as their major aim the production of a continuous assessment scheme which will record the progress between the ages of 11 and 16 of students across the whole range of attainment.

The schemes have each been designed to be implemented alongside a variety of existing teaching schemes and teaching organisations. They share commitments to:

1 assessing practical and oral work
2 assessing group work
3 assessing processes, especially problem-solving processes, as well as content
4 assessing extended activities over which students have a considerable degree of control

5 enabling students to become actively involved in their own assessment and learning
6 encouraging assessment in conditions which allows *all* students to best demonstrate their understanding and skills.

Thus in common with the earlier GOML schemes there is an emphasis on functional competence, experiential learning and student autonomy, and to these is added a commitment to equal opportunities.

In addition to these educational aims it was necessary to have the more pragmatic intentions of providing:

1 the facility to convert the continuous record into a summative GCSE grade which is accepted as valid without any supplementary final examination;
2 graded assessment certificates from a national examination group (LEAG) issued at intervals during the 11–16 period;
3 formative profile records which will feed into Record of Achievement schemes, in particular the London Record of Achievement, which have been trialled as part of government policy (DES 1984, 1989).

Structure: levels

The graded assessment projects share common structural features. Nevertheless, since each has been developed independently by a group of teachers, or teachers and researchers, they differ considerably in detail according to the perceived views and needs of teachers in that subject.

Each of the schemes is built on a structure of levels, with the highest seven levels designed to be equivalent to the seven GCSE grades, A–G. However the total number of levels in each scheme varies according to the number of levels below GCSE grade G the team felt it was both useful and possible to differentiate. In all schemes except science, the levels are designed to be roughly equivalent to a year's progress.

The number of levels depends partly on when teaching is likely to start in that subject. For example French and CDT are subjects which generally start at 11, and thus have added only a few preliminary levels below the seven GCSE levels, resulting in a total of 8 levels in French and ten in CDT. The science scheme has more levels than this only because they are expected to be completed at a faster rate.

In mathematics, where teaching starts at age 5 and learning much earlier, there is already a wide spread of achievement at age 11, documented in the Cockcroft Report as being equivalent to at least seven years' progress. Thus the GAIM scheme has a total of 15 levels with levels 9–15 designed to be equivalent to the GCSE grades.

The expected progress of different students through the mathematics levels is shown in Figure 7 which is based on data from Hart (1981).

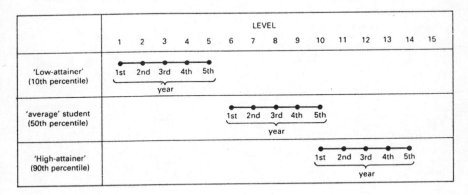

Figure 7   The expected progress in the GAIM project of students at the 10th, 50th and 90th percentiles respectively

The English scheme was originally presented as an unlevelled profile, for reasons which are discussed later. However it is now being modified to correspond to the form of the other schemes.

Structure: content

Each of the graded assessment schemes incorporates both *criteria* and *activities*. The *criteria* enable a clear definition of what is required to be given to students, teachers, parents, and others. They also allow flexibility in the exact assessment methods used, which is especially important if the schemes are to be used alongside a variety of teaching materials. The criteria are similar in nature to the statements of attainment at each level within the National Curriculum targets. For example:

Science (GASP), process skills criterion in the area of 'planning', level 7 (out of 15):
   P7 Able to identify ONE variable in an activity and suggest a strategy for keeping it constant.
Mathematics (GAIM), topic criterion in the area of 'number', level 7 (out of 15):

N 7.5 Consistently uses division to solve problems of sharing or grouping using a calculator where necessary.

Activities of an open nature, to encourage exploration and problem solving, often in groups, are included within each of the graded assessment schemes. These serve to counteract the analytical nature of the criteria and ensure that students are able to apply their skills in open situations. These are often of a cross-curricular nature; for example:

Design a bookcase that will hold 100 paperback books.

Although this is a GAIM practical problem-solving activity, it could equally well be a GACDT design brief, and could profitably be carried out in a cross-curricular context.

Activities are normally appropriate for a wide attainment range and assessment is 'by outcome' according to the level of the work produced.

Two issues which relate to the underlying psychological assumptions of the graded assessment projects are discussed in the next two sections.

Validity of levels

The notion of 'levels' was clearly both integral to the graded test movement and a virtual prerequisite for establishing a correspondence between graded assessment and GCSE grades. However the subject of levels is one which has given rise to considerable controversy in education, more recently in respect of the recommended structure for the National Curriculum (e.g. Howson, 1989; Noss, Goldstein and Hoyles, 1989; Brown, 1988, 1989).

The question as to whether 'valid' levels can be defined can be interpreted in different ways; for example it might include consideration of:

1 whether there is any psychological basis for the definition of levels;
2 whether consistent and progressive levels of attainment can be empirically identified, either across a whole subject area or in different domains within a subject;
3 whether a useful description of a student's attainment in a subject can be provided by one of a set of levels defined somewhat arbitrarily, but on a basis of 'experienced' judgement.

Noss *et al.* (1989) reiterate an argument often made against graded assessment, that since evidence indicates that students learn in different sequences, it is impossible to define 'meaningful' levels of attainment. This argument had, for example, been made strongly by teachers of English, in the London consortium as elsewhere, with the result that the initial team charged with developing graded assessment instead elected to produce a level-free profile of skills in English.

In fact it is not clear that the learning of English proceeds any differently from learning in other subjects.

Much school knowledge, clearly, can be learned in any order; for example the order of acquisition of specific vocabulary, techniques and generalisations depends very much on the learning context, whether in language, science, geography or mathematics. Nevertheless all subjects would recognise some dimension of increased complexity or abstraction which differentiates between the competences of novices and experts. Indeed psychologists, including Piagetians (e.g. Peel, 1971) and neo-Piagetians (e.g. Biggs and Collis, 1982), have attempted to provide a basis for this and to illustrate its application to different subjects.

Although some of the graded assessment projects would claim to be informed by such theory, it is unlikely that any would go so far as to assert that their levels represented psychologically differentiated, let alone innate, learning stages.

Nevertheless most would claim that despite individual differences in the order of learning, there is enough broad consistency within the population, whether for psychological or pedagogical reasons, to render levels a useful simplified model to describe students' learning, at least in separate domains. They would also claim that their levels were founded on some empirical evidence of difficulty gradient.

In mathematics, for example, research such as that by the Concepts in Secondary Mathematics and Science project (Hart, 1981) and Brenda Denvir (Denvir and Brown, 1986) showed that although individual conceptually based skills and strategies were learned in different orders, 'levels' within each topic area could be obtained by grouping together items of a similar difficulty. If students were then judged to have attained a level provided that they had succeeded on two-thirds of the items on that level, then less than 5 per cent of students behaved inconsistently, in that they attained a level without having attained all easier levels.

The work of these projects, and that of other projects based at King's College (previously Chelsea College) (e.g. Dickson, Brown and Gibson, 1984), was used to define the levels within the Graded Assessment in Mathematics project. Further survey data was available from the Assessment of Performance Unit (DES, 1986) and from the examination boards.

Although there was probably more research data available in mathematics than in other subjects, there was also survey data in science, in particular from research teams based at King's College such as the Concepts in Secondary Mathematics and Science project (Shayer and Adey, 1981) and the APU science team (e.g. DES, 1984b). In the former case the research indicated that Piagetian levels could be used to analyse levels of performance in science.

Despite the scepticism of English teachers, including the initial graded assessment team, the APU language team had also succeeded in differentiating valid levels of competence in different aspects of English language (e.g. DES, 1984a).

Thus on balance existing research seems to support the fact that consistent levels of performance can be differentiated empirically, at least in separate aspects (e.g. written narrative in English) or domains (e.g. processes in Science) or conceptual areas (e.g. algebra in Mathematics) within a subject.

The extent to which a single overall level in a subject is 'meaningful' depends to some extent on the method of aggregation of levels across different domains. To maintain the criterion-referenced nature of the assessment the graded assessment subjects have generally employed a 'trailing edge' aggregation process e.g. to obtain an overall level 5 a student must reach at least level 5 in all domains. This has been preferred to the more usual averaging because it conveys a clearer meaning.

Whether a single level can provide a useful description of competence across a whole subject area depends on the purposes for which assessment is used and what alternatives are available.

For example in the disputed area of language, a recent graded assessment project, Staged Assessment in Literacy, a joint development between the Northern Examining Association and Manchester University, has used overall levels for assessment with apparent success in terms of acceptability to teachers, pupils and users.

A further example is provided by the School Mathematics Project, which, having decided to follow the recommendations of the Cockcroft Report, designed a graded assessment scheme for low attaining 14–16 year olds on the basis of its newly written textbooks. Thus the content of level one was defined by the contents of books 1–4, level two by the contents of books 5 and 6, and level three by the contents of books 7 and 8.

In comparison with the considerable trialling that has occurred relating to the definition of levels within the London graded assessment schemes, this seems rather arbitrary, yet a recent evaluation (Close and Brown, 1988) has shown that teachers and students have found the scheme very valuable both for detailed diagnostic purposes and for providing a broad indication of progress. This was in spite of the fact that it was clear that some of the concepts and skills had been assigned to inappropriate levels when judged by their relative difficulty.

Thus evidence suggests that the use of levels in graded assessment schemes at the very least can provide explicit information which is useful and readily interpreted by students and teachers provided they understand its limitations. Within separate domains it aspires to provide a simplified description of student conceptual development which is accurate enough for most diagnostic purposes, although differentiation between levels is generally justified empirically rather than theoretically.

The nature of learning

The example of the School Mathematics Project scheme given above highlights the contrast between two possible extreme views of what is being assessed. While the SMP scheme indicates primarily what progress is being made through a particular teaching scheme, the Graded Assessment in Mathematics (GAIM) scheme endeavours to provide a record of a child's mathematical development theoretically independent of any teaching materials followed. The London graded assessment schemes in other subjects take intermediate positions on this continuum, as will be demonstrated below.

The two extremes reflect two different models of learning – the *transmission model* and the *constructivist model*. The *transmission model* assumes that learning is mainly dependent on the teacher and that the purpose of assessment therefore is to determine the effectiveness with which a body of knowledge has been communicated by the teacher to the student. The *constructivist model*, in contrast, assumes that knowledge is built up by the student in the form of connected schemas, and that what is taught is only one, and not necessarily the most important one, of many factors which influence this process. In this case the purpose of assessment is to represent as closely as possible the current state of a student's conceptual development in a subject, without being confined to the implemented curriculum.

The relative appropriateness of the two models depends on the nature of the subject. At one extreme is mother-tongue learning, in which progress is clearly affected strongly by home and other influences, and for which models of learning have been extensively researched. At the other extreme is probably the learning of a foreign language, in which students' experience is mainly, but not necessarily, confined to the classroom. It may well be this difference that has accounted for the early development of graded assessment with modern languages, often in close relationship to teaching schemes, and the comparatively late extension to English, for reasons of the perceived complexity of the learning process.

A further influence on the relative acceptability of the two learning models may be teachers' experience of 'failure'. In English and mathematics, for example, it is most clear that some students have attained very limited competence even after years of careful teaching, and hence the constructivist model is attractive in terms of its power to explain this failure.

The relative factual content of a subject may also be of significance. It is of interest that history and geography, subjects with a broad factual content but only more recently attempting to develop a progressive structure of processes, have remained outside the graded assessment camp while being occasionally modularised to match with segmentation of teaching syllabuses. In fact it is possible to make the argument that modular or unit-based assessment schemes assume a transmission model of teaching and for this reason have found little favour among teachers of mathematics or languages. It will be interesting to see how this affects the use of levels in the National Curriculum in geography and history.

The way that levels have been defined by the various graded assessment schemes reflects the views of the development teams, and probably the traditions of the wider subject culture, with respect to the two models of learning.

Thus working within mathematics, the GAIM scheme takes an unashamedly constructivist view. For example:

1 It assumes that on entry at age 11, and at any point thereafter, students will be distributed over almost the full range of 15 levels, and be at different levels in different topic strands.
2 It defines each level as one year's average development for a student at that level, recognising that the amount of mathematics in level two will therefore be considerably less than that in level fourteen.
3 It has a unique definition of each level with no variation in content for different teaching schemes.
4 It insists on a gap of at least two weeks between teaching and assessment to try and ensure that only internalised and relatively permanent knowledge is assessed.
5 It encourages assessment of content-based criteria in open-ended situations, during informal discussion or by self-assessment, again to try to ensure that knowledge is internalised rather than context-bound.

The reason for this extreme constructivist stance derives from the background of the team members, some of whom had been involved extensively in research programmes, and others whose teaching experience had been with SMILE, a London based individualised scheme allowing a high degree of curricular differentiation in mixed ability classes.

In contrast, the Graded Assessment in Science Project (GASP) takes a more transmission-oriented view, in particular with respect to its content dimension. For example:

1 It assumes that all students will start on level one at age 11 but that increasing differentiation will occur throughout the 11–16 period as students either fail tests or take longer over acquiring skills.
2 Although the GASP process skills and explorations dimensions are defined in a similar way to their counterparts in GAIM, the content dimension of each level is defined in terms of two or three content units, each content unit being defined as approximately 560 minutes of teaching time.
3 In many cases neighbouring levels are differentiated in terms of content only by the addition of extra units of similar difficulty, the particular units being determined according to the scheme of work in the school.
4 The testing in the content dimension is on the basis of written tests which take place at the end of each unit of work and for which students are encouraged to revise – content is not assessed in the course of explorations, although process skills may be.
5 The written test items are classified in relation to their difficulty, using the broad categories of 'easy', 'medium' and 'hard'; there is no clear attempt to identify strands of conceptual development within the content dimension.

Thus the GASP assessment assumes a constructivist model in the dimensions of process skills and explorations, but a transmission model in the content dimension, probably because of the greater factual contribution in this dimension, and also perhaps because the style of teaching within science classrooms tends more towards whole class teaching and less towards individualisation than in mathematics.

However it should be noted that there is less difference in classroom practice than might appear in theory, since mathematics teachers often decide to assess the GAIM part of their own teaching schemes. In effect there is probably a trade-off between assessment based on the transmission model, which is easier for the teacher to operate, and that based on the constructivist model, which gives a more accurate representation of student learning.

Future development

The current situation is that the graded assessment schemes become publicly available for the full range of pupils from September, 1989, when the first phase of development comes to an end. At present more than 60,000 pupils, in over 150 pilot schools in 20 local education authorities, are using one or more of the schemes. The first GCSE awards through graded assessment will be in 1989, and although for mathematics a pilot scheme only has been approved because of the need to waive part of the national criteria, the science and CDT schemes have full GCSE approval. The English scheme is behind the others for reasons which have already been explained.

Thus the graded assessment schemes are in the process of achieving a significant change in secondary school assessment, with grades in the final examination at 16+ being achieved on the basis of continuous teacher assessment over the 11–16 period. Unfortunately this is taking place just as the national curriculum and its assessment machinery are being put in place.

Although it is a compliment to the graded assessment movement that the structure chosen for the national curriculum follows that of the graded assessment schemes, the details of the targets and the levels do not match. In particular the targets and levels of the graded assessment schemes have been determined by recourse to research and long-term trialling, rather than by political negotiation. Moreover the summative external assessment 'at or near the end of each key stage' which forms part of the 1988 Education Reform Act is at odds with the wholly internal and continuous nature of graded assessment.

If the teacher assessment component recommended by the Task Group on Assessment and Testing (DES, 1988) survives, clearly the graded assessment schemes could provide that element, although not without some reluctant adjustment. Otherwise it is an ironic fact that the present Government will have strangled at birth a movement which shared its aims of achieving higher educational standards by means of more highly motivated students and teachers and better informed parents, but which could claim rather more evidence of 'proven success' than can be assembled to support the national curriculum plans.

References

Biggs, J. and Collis, K. (1982) *Evaluating the Quality of Learning: the SOLO Taxonomy*. New York: Academic Press.

Brown, M. (1988) 'Issues in Formulating and Organising Attainment Targets in Relation to Their Assessment', in H. Torrance (ed.) *National Assessment and Testing: A Research Response*. British Educational Research Association.

Brown, M. (1989) 'Graded Assessment and Learning Hierarchies in Mathematics: an Alternative View', *British Educational Research Journal*, 15, 2.

Buckby, M., *et al.* (1981) *Graded Objectives and Tests for Modern Languages: An Evaluation*. London: Schools Council Publications.

Close, G. and Brown, M. (1988) *Graduated Assessment in Mathematics: Report of the SSCC Study*. London: Department of Education and Science.

Denvir, B. and Brown, M. (1986) 'Understanding of Number Concepts in Low Attaining 7–9 Year Olds: Part 1. Development of descriptive framework and diagnostic instrument', *Educational Studies in Mathematics*, 17, pp. 15–36.

Department of Education and Science, Committee of Inquiry into the Teaching of Mathematics in Schools (1982) *Mathematics Counts ('The Cockcroft Report')*. London: Her Majesty's Stationery Office.

Department of Education and Science, Assessment of Performance Unit (1984a) *Language Performance in Schools: 1982 Secondary Survey Report*. London: Department of Education and Science.

Department of Education and Science, Assessment of Performance Unit (1984b) *Science in Schools: Age 13 report no. 4*. London: Department of Education and Science.

Department of Education and Science (1984c) *Records of Achievement: A Statement of Policy*. London: Her Majesty's Stationery Office.

Department of Education and Science, Assessment of Performance Unit (1986) *Mathematical Development: A Review of Monitoring in Mathematics, 1978 to 1982*. London: Department of Education and Science.

Department of Education and Science (1989) *Records of Achievement: Report of the Records of Achievement National Steering Committee*. London: Department of Education and Science.

Dickson, L., Brown, M. and Gibson, O. (1984) *Children Learning Mathematics: A Teacher's Guide to Recent Research*. London: Cassell, for the Schools Council.

Foxman, D., Ruddock, G. and Thorpe, J. (1988) *Graduated Tests in Mathematics: A Study of Lower Attaining Pupils in Secondary Schools*. Windsor: NFER-Nelson.

GAIM (Graded Assessment in Mathematics) Team (1988) *GAIM Development Pack*. London: Macmillan.

Harrison, A. (1982) *Review of Graded Tests: Schools Council Examination Bulletin 41*. London: Methuen Educational.

Hart, K. (ed.) (1981) *Children's Understanding of Mathematics: 11–16*. London: John Murray.

Howson, G. (1989) *Maths Problem: Can More Students Reach Higher Standards?* London: Centre for Policy Studies.

Noss, R., Goldstein, H. and Hoyles, C. (1989) 'Graded Assessment and Learning Hierarchies in Mathematics', *British Educational Research Journal*, 15, 2.

Peel, E. A. (1971) *The Nature of Adolescent Judgement*. London: Staples Press.

Pennycuick, D. and Murphy, R. (1988) *The Impact of Graded Tests*. Basingstoke, UK: Falmer Press.

Shayer, M. and Adey, P. (1981) *Towards a Science of Science Teaching*. London: Heinemann.

4.9

APU Language Assessment: Some Practical Consequences of a Functionally Oriented Approach

Janet White and Tom Gorman

The theoretical underpinning of the APU language surveys

The APU language surveys are based on a functional view of language derived largely from the work of M. A. K. Halliday (Halliday, 1978; 1985). In brief, this theory holds that language is shaped according to its contexts of use: as reflective language users we recognise not only the broad set of options available to us in the choices between speaking and writing, but within these modes, many other generic patterns which serve distinct purposes in the expression or negotiation of meaning (Thornton, 1987; Gorman *et al.*, 1988).

The significance of such a view of language for teaching and assessment is that it prompts us to identify educational outcomes in terms of the functions of language which pupils need to understand and achieve competence in, across the whole range of subjects studied. For the purposes of teaching and testing alike, the focus is on the creation and interpretation of meaningful texts. Obviously such a view differs from one which sees language as a set of rules fixed in exemplar sentences, which provide for practice in parsing, copywriting or slotfilling exercises in the name of vocabulary development. This latter view has been well satirised as pertaining to 'the linguistic flat-earthers' (Thornton, 1986) – i.e. those who believe that language revolves round the parts of speech, and who also subscribe to other superstitious beliefs as well:

1 the notion that meaning resides wholly in words
2 the idea that speech is a debased form of writing
3 the idea that grammar may be good or bad.

The linguistic flat-earthers are a hardy species none the less. They are well represented among journalists and media folk, but schools too play a part in their reproduction. Despite the writing of language policies which seem to privilege 'personal growth' or 'our literary heritage' or even 'communication skills', a great deal of what gets transmitted in the way of language education can be summed up in the inseparable triad of grammar, punctuation and spelling, with large tracts of the writing produced in English lessons falling into the category of story/description (Britton *et al.*, 1975; HMI, 1978, 1979; Christie, 1985; Brook, 1987). The survey framework devised for national monitoring purposes explicitly rejects the label 'English' in order to resist compartmentalisation within a subject-specific boundary. The elements within the current (last) surveys are generally applicable to all parts of the school curriculum. Key assumptions underlying the assessment framework are as follows:

Using language is a co-operative activity

When messages are exchanged, the 'units' of exchange are not normally single words or sentences but longer stretches of talk or writing produced in a context which the listener or reader takes into account when interpreting what is said. Assessment programmes should reflect this.

Language is purposeful

Assessment activities should reflect the purposes for which pupils use language in daily life, recognising that language serves to express both the speaker's or writer's experience of the world and the inner world of consciousness. The tests therefore include tasks in which pupils are asked to hypothesise, speculate, reason and think imaginatively – activities which have a conceptual as well as a communicative function.

Using language in school involves the association of different language modes

Where appropriate, assessment should involve pupils in using different modes of language (reading, writing, listening and speaking) in an interrelated way, reflecting language use in the classroom.

Different varieties of language are used in different circumstances

Pupils are using language effectively when they use it in a way that is appropriate to the purposes they have in mind, the subject matter or topic under discussion, and the audience or readership envisaged.

The context in which the communication takes place is also relevant.

There are conventions governing what it is thought appropriate to say and how it should be said or written. Some genres of writing, in particular, are highly conventionalised in style of address and layout. Experienced speakers and writers learn both to observe conventions and to depart from them when it suits their purpose.

Communicative acts, spoken or written, have common features or components

Verbal communication, spoken or written, can be analysed with reference to a number of criteria. Assessors might focus on the content of what is said and on how what is said is organised or sequenced. They might also take note of the forms of expression used as the speaker or writer selects from the different options available in *vocabulary and syntax*. They will also need to take into account how such expression varies *stylistically* in relation to such factors as audience, genre, topic and context.

Communication in different modes involves different demands

The criteria used in assessing talk and writing *differ* in that writers and readers have to learn to use and interpret a range of *orthographic conventions* by which spoken language is represented in writing. These include features relating to the formation of letters, and conventions governing word division, punctuation and spelling. They also need to become familiar with different types of graphic presentation.

Speakers, on the other hand, have to learn to make effective use of the many verbal and non-verbal features that are exploited by fluent talkers to communicate audibly with appropriate emphasis and pacing. In the analytic marking schemes used in APU assessment a number of these *verbal performance features* are taken into account, and are referred to as a pupil's *orientation to listener*.

Performance is affected by the type and mode of response required

Pupils' performances will vary in some cases according to whether they are asked to give written or oral responses. The mode in which material to be interpreted is presented, whether in writing or recorded on tape, also affects performance.

Performance and attitudes are interrelated

It should be possible on the basis of a monitoring programme to establish not simply whether pupils can read and write or speak for specified purposes but whether they do so, voluntarily. It is also relevant to assessment and teaching to investigate what language activities they regard as enjoyable, useful or especially difficult.

Performance is task-related

Tasks differ in their linguistic, cognitive and communicative demands. Such differences need to be taken into account in assessing pupils' performance.

Components of APU language surveys

The assessment framework used for both age 11 and age 15 pupils in 1988, comprises seven main components:
1 reading
2 writing
3 listening and speaking
4 attitudes to language
5 work sampling
6 cross modal study
7 interpretation of video

Within these main divisions, a variety of interacting language uses are assessed, as described briefly below:

Reading

Six reading booklets or workpacks are used in the survey, two of which are repeated from the previous years. The reading materials incorporate texts drawn from children's literature, works of reference and everyday reading material. A variety of formats are used, including looseleaf packs of expository material. The selection is intended to mirror the cross-curricular functions of language in learning.

Pupils are required to use different reading strategies according to the scope (amount of text needed to be read) and focus (semantic orientation) of the questions asked. Pupils give written responses of varying length, as well as completing/constructing tabular or diagrammatic representations of what they have read.

Based on the experience of previous surveys, materials have been designed to explore certain notable areas of difficulty for pupils:

1 the interpretation of different written styles and registers
2 the understanding of metaphorical uses of language
3 selective reading, reinterpretation and synthesis of expository material.

By contrast with previous surveys, each pupil completes at least two reading booklets, thus providing more intensive data on both task difficulty and individual pupil performance. Approximately 2700 pupils take part in the reading survey.

Writing

Six writing tasks are used, two of which are repeated. As with the reading materials, new tasks have been designed to provide more information about areas of difficulty especially in relation to other 'subject' areas.

Thus, in the category of expository writing, the writing to be done is either based on, or developed as a reponse to accompanying reference material; we link with the work of APU science by using a task from the practical investigations category or asking for an account of recent learning with maths or science content. At the same time, thought has been given to ways of providing 'scaffolding' for pupils to use in organising their writing, so that the less able are not left to flounder, and the more able have something to adapt or build on.

A characteristic of the administration of the writing surveys is that all randomly selected groups of pupils work on the same task, following an introductory discussion with the teacher in charge of the session, guided by suggestions in the accompanying teachers' notes.

The genres of writing assessed relate both to patterns of work in the primary school and to the demands of secondary school. Although fewer writing tasks are employed in this survey than in previous years, the cross-curricular intent is preserved, as are variations in intended readership.

The new survey design entails each pupil completing two or three writing tasks in separate testing sessions. The stronger links thus secured between individual pupils' performance and specific task effects will yield richer pupil and task profile data than were available from previous surveys. Approximately 2700 pupils take part in the writing survey.

Work sampling

This component draws on a subsample of pupils in the writing survey and is used to gather pieces of work done under normal classroom conditions. The course-work collection provides evidence concerning the writing curriculum in schools, both in terms of the spread of work available to be collected, and by giving some indication of the conditions most typically associated with the day-to-day generation of written work.

In the current surveys, we sample some work which is comparable, in generic terms, to that done in the main survey. We retain the option for pupils to select an example of their 'best work', since this has proved illuminative of children's criteria for success in writing. Up to three pieces of work may be collected from any one pupil, thus providing a potential total of six samples of extended writing from those involved in work sampling and writing.

Information on the classroom context of writing will be sought with respect to:

1 questions of revision or drafting practices
2 teacher or group input to writing
3 use of source material or models for writing
4 writing for readers other than the teacher and
5 the rationale for particular writing assignments in the curriculum as a whole.

Oracy

In the framework used for language assessment, speaking and listening are not separated: the tasks involve both the interpretation and production of sustained talk. All tasks entail a sequence of language activities which vary in terms of the function of the activity, and also vary in terms of mode (for example, discussion based on reading material, leading to a written outcome). A principle behind the design of the tasks is the purposeful application of talk in learning.

Throughout the activities the teacher/assessor's role is to establish a context for talk and to record it: not to direct or control it. For the oracy component, randomly selected pupils choose a partner to work with, and these pairs may combine into groups for collaborative activities. Grouping arrangements among pupils lead to flexibility in pair/individual/group work typical of good classroom practice, and serve to minimise task reluctance factors sometimes associated with testing. Approximately 2100 pupils take part in the oracy survey.

Eight oracy tasks were used in the primary survey and nine at secondary, including two from the previous round. Each assessed pupil participates in three tasks. Pupils' oral performance are assessed in a range of contexts with reference to these genres or functions of talk:

1 narration
2 problem solving
3 persuasion and argumentation
4 speculation
5 reporting
6 instructing
7 explaining
8 planning.

The tasks are designed to have a cross-curricular emphasis. They include, for example, a number of scientific experiments and, at secondary level, the collaborative development of strategies for playing a mathematical game, which pupils subsequently teach a second pair of students to play.

Attitudes to language

In previous surveys, we used separate questionnaires relating to pupils' attitudes to reading and writing. The information gained has shown the extent to which pupils' achievements in literacy are associated with their perceptions of themselves as readers and writers, in terms of what they find easy/difficult, enjoyable/not enjoyable, useful/dispensable about reading and writing. These data have been particularly illuminating as to gender difference in orientation to literacy, and also as to pupils' range of experience with different types of language.

For the 1988 surveys, composite questionnaires were devised. These include questions to do with television viewing and perceptions of oral language usage. The questionnaires are completed by subsamples of pupils in both the reading and the writing surveys.

Cross-modal study

From the above description of the survey framework, it will be seen that although we have included tasks which depend on integrated uses of language (for example, reading → talk → writing), the existing scheme does not allow for the assessment of more than one mode in any detail. The cross modal study provides the means of making direct comparisons of pupils' performance in reading/ writing/oracy. Arrangements were made with schools, for example, for students to complete written work, involving the compilation of a booklet for use by younger pupils, on the basis of collaborative reading focused on different aspects of a topic, about which each pupil also gave an oral account.

Televised materials and teletext

A subsample of pupils, is selected from the oracy sample. These pupils watch video-ed excerpts from contemporary television. Their interpretation of the programmes is assessed with reference to aspects of form and content of the medium.

There are a number of reasons it was thought necessary to extend the surveys to include televised material – not the least significant factor being that students typically watch between twenty and twenty-five hours of television a week, and that through this medium they are introduced to a range of varieties of language in contexts other than those that they would normally encounter.

The 1988 secondary survey also incorporated an enquiry into (but not a survey of) student's interpretation of teletext and the strategies that they used in accessing this.

Outcomes from different modes of assessment

The type of assessment used depends on the nature of the linguistic product or interaction we have to deal with.

Four main types of assessment are used: impression marking, analytic marking, on the spot assessment of oral language, and discrete item assessment.

These forms of marking yield different types of information about the nature of pupil performance. From the impression marks awarded to written or spoken texts, we can gain some idea of relative task difficulty; these scores can also be studied to illuminate differences in performance of groups of pupils.

The advantage of impression marking is that it is easily carried out, and embodies the types of judgements which teachers commonly make of their pupils' language. The disadvantage is that it provides few diagnostic clues. For this, we use analytic marking. The systems devised for use in the writing and oracy surveys demand close attention to all linguistic features of a text, and ultimately contribute to our knowledge of what children need to know about language in order to be considered successful in any given written or spoken task.

Previous surveys were designed to give information on groups of pupils, rather than to develop 'profiles'. One consequence of the changed design 1988 surveys, is that rather than spreading analytic marking over a wide range of tasks, more scripts per task will be marked in this way. As a result, we will be better placed to answer questions such as:

1 What linguistic features are important in completing any task successfully?
2 What combination of features is characteristic of children's work at various levels of performance?

Generalisable information of this nature is currently lacking in the UK. While many teachers are starting to work with the idea of functional differences in language, these ideas tend to be held at a global level, and need more clarification with respect to what children actually say, write or are required to read.

Previous survey work in language

Prior to the monitoring programme, surveys of language performance were based on sentence-completion tests composed of decontextualised items (Gorman *et al.*, 1982). These tests gave no information about how well pupils could read the variety of materials representative of the demands of schooling or everyday life. A decade ago, there were no national data about pupils' ability to write extended prose, nor was there any procedure for assessing oral language which gave credence to the purposeful interaction of speaking and listening. There was considerable doubt in the minds of the English teaching profession as to whether reliable assessments could be made of something so intangible as oral language (MacLure and Hargreaves, 1986; Brooks, 1987). Views as to the ease or difficulty of certain language activities, or the demands of different types of reading or writing, were based largely on hearsay, and more likely to be influenced by psychological (Piagetian) or folk linguistic criteria, than on any principled study of children's actual performance in language (Williams, 1979). Extensive differences in performance outcomes and orientation toward literacy on the part of boys and girls were likewise uncharted (White, 1986; Gorman, 1986; White, 1987).

Sources of change and innovation

While it would be an exaggeration to think that, thanks to the work in APU language, rudimentary notions about language assessment had been swept away, it is the case that the work accomplished by a succession of monitoring surveys goes on providing reference points in the debate about changing standards of teaching and assessment in English. For example, the rationale behind the language surveys has been explicitly drawn attention to in HMI documents ('Bullock Revisited' and 'English 5–16'), and has been instrumental in mediating changes in examining procedures for GCSE, where for the first time oral language assessment appears as an obligatory component for all pupils. Two of the largest curriculum development projects in language – the National Writing Project and the National Oracy Project – have taken note of both the framework and the findings of the APU surveys in the context of developmental work in classrooms, and the most recent of the National Curriculum documents, 'English 5–11', highlights aspects of APU language work as good practice in recording and assessing children's achievements. Beyond this, the work has gained international recognition, and has had a direct influence on the IEA Study of Written Composition at the level of task type and method of assessment (Gubb, Gorman and Price, 1987; Gorman *et al.*, 1988).

There are promising signs that the curriculum implications of the work being taken up by teachers of other subjects, and this movement can only be enhanced by continuing collaboration between the monitoring teams; as recent publications testify, we are in a much more knowledgeable position as to the role of language in learning than was the case when the APU programme started (White, 1987 and 1988).

It is now commonplace for language teachers and curriculum writers to speak of a 'range of purposes for reading and writing', a 'range of readers for children's writing', the 'role of talk in learning', and to draw on the frameworks devised by the APU to assist in the definition of these purposeful uses of language.

Clarification of assessment procedures/pedagogical implications

Of course, the work of APU language has not been an isolated influence in bringing about changes in the educational context over the past decade. In many subject areas we have seen a paradigmatic shift away from a concentration on the products of learning to a preoccupation with the processes by which pupils learn. In the case of language, this is something of a false distinction, but it has had beneficial effects in raising the consciousness of teachers and pupils alike about what is involved in the production of a written or spoken text, how writing may be changed by collaborative revision, or best be edited to maximise its effect for others. Similarly, increased concentration on 'talk' has the potential to link it purposefully to learning, and to question the seeming inevitability of all classwork leading to *written* outcomes.

Where a number of new initiatives in language education continue to fall short is in the area of assessment of outcomes. For example, granted that red-pen corrections of surface features and copying out of 'corrections' is seen to be a minimal contribution to a pupil's understanding of the power of written language, what else can an enlightened teacher put in its place, that will simultaneously support and challenge the pupil, record development in a systematic way, and prove informative to other teachers, parents or employers?

It is in this area that the contribution of the work of the APU monitoring teams is still under-exploited. To date, the pedagogical implications taken from the work have been those to do with listing a range of genres that children need to know how to use in school. More difficult for teachers to assimilate (and for us to describe) are the linguistic features that are needed for the realisation of these different text-types, yet a worthwhile input to the language curriculum would presumably be a set of explicit criteria for evaluating different types of talk and writing, applicable to pupils of various ages.

References

Barnes, D. (1987) 'The Politics of Oracy', conference paper delivered at UEA

International Oracy Convention 1987. Published in MacLure, M. *et al.* (eds) 1988, *Oracy Matters: Teaching and Learning in the Spoken Language*. Milton Keynes: OUP.

Britton, J., Burgess, T., Martin, N., McLeod, A. and Rosen, H. (1975) *The Development of Writing Abilities (11–18)*, Schools Council Research Studies. London: Macmillan.

Brook, D. (1987) 'Some Lessons from Language Monitoring', in Jones, M. and West, A. (eds) (1987) *Learning Me Your Language*. London: Mary Glasgow Publications.

Brooks, G. (1987) *Speaking and Listening: Assessment at Age 15*. Windsor: NFER-Nelson.

Christie, F. (1985) *Language Education*. Victoria: Deakin University Press.

Department of Education and Science (1982) *Bullock Revisited: A discussion paper* by HMI.

Department of Education and Science (1986) *English from 5 to 16*. London.

Firth, J. R. (1957) Papers in Linguistics 1934–51. London: Oxford University Press.

Gorman, T. P., White, J., Orchard, L. and Tate, A. (1982) *APU Language Performance in Schools, Secondary Survey Report No. 1*. London: Department of Education and Science, HMSO.

Gorman, T. P. (1986) *Pupils Attitudes to Reading*. Windsor: NFER-Nelson.

Gorman, T. P., White, J., Brooks, G., MacLure, M. and Kispal, A. (1988) *Language Performance in Schools: A Review of APU Language Monitoring 1979–83*. London: HMSO.

Gubb, J., Gorman, T. P. and Price, E. (1987) *The Study of Written Composition in England and Wales*. Windsor: NFER/Nelson.

Halliday, M. A. K. (1978) *Language as Social Semiotic: The Social Interpretation of Language and Meaning*. London: Edward Arnold.

Halliday, M. A. K. (1985) *An Introduction to Functional Grammar*. London: Edward Arnold.

HMI (1978) *Primary Education in Schools*. A survey by HM Inspectors of Schools. London: HMSO.

HMI (1979) *Aspects of Secondary Education in England*. A survey by HM Inspectors of Schools. London: HMSO.

Holbrook, D. (1979) *English for Meaning*. Windsor: NFER-Nelson.

MacLure, M. and Hargreaves, M. (1986) *Speaking and Listening: assessment at age 11*. Windsor: NFER-Nelson.

SEC (1986) *Draft Grade Criteria in English: Report of the SEC Working Party*. London: Secondary Examinations Council.

Task Group on Assessment and Testing (1988) *National Curriculum: A Report*. DES and The Welsh Office.

Thornton, G. (1986) *Language, Ignorance and Education*. London: Edward Arnold.

Thornton, G. (1987) *APU Language Testing 1979–1983, An Independent Appraisal of the Findings*. London: Department of Education and Science, HMSO.

White, J. (1986) 'The Writing on the Wall: Beginning or End of a Girl's Career?' *Women's Studies International Forum*, 9, 5, pp. 561–74. Oxford: Pergamon Press.

White, J. (1987) 'The Role of Language in Design and Technology: Implications for Curricular Changes', in *Studies in Design, Education, Craft and Technology*, 19, 2, Spring 1987.

White, J. (1988) *Pupils' Attitudes to Writing*. Windsor: NFER-Nelson.

White, J. and Welford, G. (1988) *The Language of Science, Making and Interpreting Observations*. APU/ASE.

Williams, J. (1979) *Learning to Write or Writing to Learn?* Windsor: NFER-Nelson.

4.10

Gender and Assessment in Science

Patricia Murphy

Summary

Science education is in a state of flux. One continuing stimulus for change is the perceived lack of achievement of pupils. To consider how changes in the curriculum can address this problem some of the factors which limit pupils' achievements in science are explored with reference to the results of the APU science surveys and research in the area of women and science.

Introduction

There have been numerous attempts to alter science education, for diverse motives. What many initiatives share is a concern that only a small minority of pupils leave school with a positive achievement in science. A particular concern has been the low number of girls studying physical science after the age of thirteen. The change in the examination system in the UK has been followed by the introduction of a national curriculum with specified guidelines for science. Consequently science is no longer a subject that pupils can opt out of. The system of subject 'options' is often cited as a reason for girls' underachievement in science. The introduction of national curriculum guidelines in the form of statements of attainment, attainment targets and programmes of study should result in a much greater degree of consistency in the science education that pupils receive. Of course, much will depend on how the guidelines are translated into school practice and what account is taken of gender in the classroom experiences, and assessment practices provided for pupils.

The science guidelines (NCC, 1988) include several innovations: a greater emphasis on scientific skills; the fostering of certain attitudes, in pupils and, to the subject; and an appreciation of the nature of science. The primary outcome remains the same i.e. the attainment of scientific knowledge and understanding for generating and applying theories and explanations. The introduction of a national science curriculum raises many questions. One of which is whether such guidelines can ensure greater equality of *outcome* of science education for girls and boys alike and how this is to be achieved in practice?

There is a growing consensus that we have a limited understanding of the role the affective domain plays in learning. It is important to know how pupils' *feelings* affect their perception of, and engagement with, science activities and assessment tasks. These concerns are not addressed by consideration of general attitudes to learning, or to specific subjects. Rather, attention must be directed towards the *process* whereby pupils construct an experiential world and an image of themselves within it. Mechanisms which operate within the school and classroom have a crucial effect on this process. Both the mechanisms and the process are subject to the mediation of gender, class and race. The outcome of this mediation affects learning because our personal knowledge and self-image determine our future experiences. The process is clearly a very complex interaction of a range of structures and influences, some internal to the school and others external. Nevertheless, it is possible to identify some of the interactional features and their effects on pupils' science performance (as measured by the APU science surveys).

Background

The APU science project is part of a national monitoring exercise which has looked at the science performance of pupils at three ages (10/11 in primary schools and 13 and 15 in secondary schools). Between 12,000 and 16,000 pupils, of all abilities and all curriculum backgrounds, from 500 to 1000 schools, were surveyed at each age in each year from 1980–84. Up to 30 different test packages were administered (n = $\sim$450 − $\sim$1000) in a single survey at one age. The question banks are the most varied and extensive of their kind and incorporate many of the characteristics outlined in the science curriculum guidelines. The results are therefore particularly relevant (DES, 1988; DES, 1989a; DES, 1989b). The description of the results given is largely qualitative but refers only to significant and characteristic responses of pupils. Of course when overall differences between populations of girls and boys arise they reflect differences for only *some* of the girls and *some* of the boys in the sample. Research developments in the area of gender and science are used to inform the selection and interpretation of the results.

Earlier attempts to address the problem of girls' alienation from science viewed schools as 'transmitters' of sex-roles, with pupils acting as passive conformers. The pupils' conformity is expressed in girls' and boys' different interests, expectations of careers, and attitudes to learning and to school subjects. The school's transmission role is typified by the stereotyping of school texts and careers advice; and in teachers' different attitudes to, and subsequent treatment of girls and boys as learners.

These combined factors were held responsible for the channeling of girls away from science. Ameliorating strategies had limited success. The factors identified were important but many others were neglected and the view of a simple 'sex-role' dichotomy was inadequate. The strategies also assumed that the problem was largely one of attitudes.

The findings of research into gender differences has long since established that the measured cognitive abilities of populations of girls and boys differ little, if at all, in contrast to the differences within populations (Hyde, 1981; Rosenthal and Rubin, 1982). However, there is a whole array of processes in operation from earliest childhood onwards whereby a particular view of 'masculinity' and 'femininity' holds sway. Schools are actively involved in determining this dominant perspective. This arises in spite of a range of actual male and female relationships existing in schools and of known individual differences. There have been many simple, but none the less effective, pieces of research to demonstrate the effects of such a gender regime on pupils. A typical example which is pertinent in this context is the work of Goddard-Spear (1983). In her study teachers were given samples of written work in science to assess. The work was attributed at random to either a girl or a boy and then the attribution was swapped. The study showed that written work attributed to a girl was commonly given lower grades, than identical work attributed to a boy. The combination of 'boy's' work marked by a female teacher was most likely to produce a generous assessment and conversely the severest that of 'girl's' work marked by a male teacher. The findings also showed that the teachers' judgement of factors central to the marking exercise was more likely to be influenced by gender than their judgement of less relevant factors.

Whatever understanding exists of the concept of gender determines how the differences in the school achievement of boys and girls are perceived and whether indeed they are regarded as problematic. Similarly this understanding will determine the solutions judged to be appropriate. A misconception (as described in the earlier attempts to deal with girls' alienation from science) leads to misguided solutions which subsequently fail.

How we perceive gender differences arising has considerable implications for the proposed national assessment system (DES, 1988). The assessment model recommended is formative in nature but it is expected, in addition, to address summative and evaluative

purposes. Gender differences in performance will have very different implications depending on the assessment purpose at issue. For
summative assessment it may be advisable to remove biased questions if one can be sure that they do not represent differences in
scientific achievement. However, for formative assessment it is vital
to understand how gender differences arise and the consequences
they have for pupils' engagement with, and subsequent achievements in, science. The tension between the needs of these two forms
of assessment is heightened when the scope of the assessment is
limited as is the case for the national system. This tension is
considered in the discussion that follows of gender differences in
science performance.

Differences in experiences – performance effects

There is an increasing amount of evidence which links school
performance differences to the different experiences of girls and
boys, in school and out (Johnson and Murphy, 1986). One of the
APU science tests involves the use of apparatus and measuring
instruments. Pupils are also asked what experience they have, out of
school, of the various measuring instruments used. In this test girls'
and boys' overall scores are the same across the three ages. Yet if we
look at performance on individual instruments, we find no difference for the use of rulers, thermometers, measuring cylinders and
scales, but at age 11, boys are better able than girls to use stopclocks
and handlenses. At age 13 and 15 boys move ahead on stopclocks,
handlenses, microscopes, ammeters, voltmeters and forcemeters.
Apart from the ammeter and voltmeter boys' performance is better
than girls' precisely on those instruments that they claim to have
more experience of outside school.

Boys' greater facility at using an ammeter and a voltmeter may
well arise from them having more practical experience with electricity. This is evident in their reported greater familiarity with simple
circuits and electrical toys and gadgets, in school and out, which
allow boys to develop a 'feel' for the effects of electricity and how it
can be controlled and manipulated.

If the results of assessment are to be interpreted correctly it is
important that this additional background information is collected.
There are no recommendations in the national assessment guidelines to this effect. A failure to collect this information would mean
that the results could be interpreted as reflecting innate differences.
Consequently the decisions about where to go next in the curriculum and more importantly *how* would be misinformed. The different experiences that pupils have out of school do not lead only to
differences in their skills but more importantly to differences in their

understanding of the situations and problems in which their skills can be used appropriately. To overcome this pupils require experience of problems where the need for the skills is understood. In this way pupils will select instruments themselves and engage with them purposefully. This is a very different curriculum strategy to simply encouraging *practice* with instruments.

If the results for the whole assessment in science, at each stage, are scanned other effects due to experiential differences are apparent. Questions spanning the range of tests but involving such content as health, reproduction, nutrition and domestic situations are generally answered by more girls than boys. The girls also tend to achieve higher scores on these questions. In situations which are more 'masculine', e.g. building sites, racing cars, the converse is true. For example, when reading from graphs and tables pupils' performance is very similar. However, if the table to be read is concerned with traffic flow boys overall achieve a higher score than girls. For a similar question based on a day in the life of a secretary, girls achieve a higher score than boys. Generally, if a question involves an electrical content, irrespective of whether any specific knowledge of it is required, fewer girls respond to it and boys obtain higher scores. These performance effects arise from the combination of avoidance by some pupils and the heightened confidence of others. Similar context effects have been noted in maths, language and design and technology assessment. These results indicate the need for a broader data collection to that specified in the national guidelines. Moreover it suggests that other features of tasks, in this case the content, are being assessed rather than the criterion intended. Thus pupils' results interpreted in terms of criterion performance would be misleading and unhelpful.

The alienation of groups of pupils from areas of learning is not a new phenomenon. 'Science anxiety', Mallow (1987) is widespread and the 'science anxious' pupil is likely to become the scientifically illiterate adult. The most common response to anxiety is avoidance. Even if pupils persevere there may still be problems. Only one of the APU science tests – the application of physics concepts – shows a consistent difference in pupils' performance at the three ages with boys ahead of girls. Even when girls continue with physics to a first examination level the survey results indicate that they do not fully overcome their earlier knowledge disadvantage, nor indeed do many of them overcome their initial lack of confidence in practical work.

Evidence available from classroom interaction studies indicate that the differences in the nature of the feedback that girls and boys receive about their classwork leads girls to have lower expectations of success and affects the way pupils interpret future experiences, Dweck (1978). In one of the APU tests pupils have to tackle practical investigations in science. A sample of 13–14 year olds were asked how they felt about doing the investigations. About 20 per cent reacted to those that looked overtly scientific by saying they could not do them. They went on to explain that they were no good at science, their teacher 'knew' this. The majority of these pupils were girls. These same pupils competently tackled investigations set in a more everyday setting.

In the APU practical observation test, girls' performance is often better than boys at the three ages. The pupils express a similar positive liking for the questions yet they differ in their views about their performance. Girls generally rate their performance lower than boys do. This is quite a common finding even where the girls' performance is actually higher. When the pupils' estimated performance is compared with their actual performance the girls' predictions are found to be more accurate than the boys.

More girls than boys express uncertainty about being able to deal with a practical assessment context. This problem was overcome in the APU surveys because of the expressed interest in what the pupil 'chose' to do and not in a single 'right' method or answer. Girls and boys do appear to experience practical work differently. Randall's study (1987) concluded that this contributes to girls' science anxiety and reluctance to pursue practical subjects. Other studies have found that girls' and boys' behaviour and self-perceptions influence classroom interactions. The combination of girls' timidity and boys' bravado result in the assumption of boys' greater competence. This in turn leads to girls being marginalised in the laboratory, Whyte (1981), and in computer workshops, Culley (1988).

Alientation leads pupils to define areas of the curriculum where they expect to be successful or conversely unsuccessful. Any tasks set in these areas are subsequently avoided by many girls and boys. This has the effect of lowering their performance in assessment and ensuring that in class they miss vital learning opportunities. Alienation can also arise when there is a mismatch between pupils' learnt expectations of the subject and the presented task. Some boys, in the age 13 sample, reject the domestic-orientated investigations as 'not to do with science'. They have a restricted view of the purposes that their knowledge can, and should, serve. This 'view' is transmitted by the learning and assessment activities that are chosen in science. The effects of alienation must be distinguished from differences in ability in order to correctly interpret achievement for formative or summative purposes. In most instances the effects of alienation result in the assessment of factors unrelated to the criteria being scored. This is a particular difficulty in any assessment which assumes that the content of a task serves merely as a vehicle for the application of skills. Nor is the problem addressed by extending scoring schemes to include content criteria. Low performance arising from alienation is a consequence of pupils' beliefs about the content in relation to themselves rather than a representative measure of their knowledge of it.

Differences in 'ways' of experiencing

The current selection of knowledge, forms of expression and purposes to be served in science education reflect a particular consensus where right and wrong, relevant and irrelevant are clear cut and unambiguous. Little account is taken of alternative values and ways of knowing. Yet research into learning styles suggests that ways of thinking and notions of relevance are dependent on what the child has been encouraged to attend to. Thus different patterns of nurturing, Chodorow (1978), Harding (1985), produce different styles which themselves produce alternative world-views and values. Our values determine what problems we perceive and the solutions we find acceptable. Consequently pupils may not 'see' the same things or perceive the same problems in classroom or assessment settings. Children enter school with learning styles already developed. Some of which are not only different to that advocated in various subjects but incompatible with them, Cohen (1986).

Typically girls tend to value the circumstances that activities are presented in and consider that it gives meaning to the issues to be addressed. They do not, therefore, abstract the issues but consider them in relation to the content which then becomes part of the whole problem. Boys as a group, conversely, do consider the issues in isolation judging the context and the content of the activity to be idiosyncratic. Their approach allows them to distance themselves from the context which they judge to be irrelevant. Assessment practice assumes that cues will be understood in the same way by all pupils. To decide what is relevant, or not, to the 'task' is also regarded as unproblematic. Yet the common assessment strategy in science of focusing down from a novel, open situation to a specific theory, in which a narrow view of relevance dominates, reflects only one way of thinking. A way highly valued in a male-dominated subject. It is, therefore, unsurprising that the APU results show that boys at the three ages more readily accept the assessor's model of the task and function within it than girls who will more often perceive ambiguity or other issues of relevance. This is also true for the boys who feature in the lower science performance bands. These pupils, and many girls, will redefine or reject the set task.

Pupils will experience the 'same' event differently as a result of differences in what they have been encouraged to attend to. Looking across pupils' performance at age 11 and 13 on the bank of observation tasks more girls than boys note colour similarities, differences and changes. Boys observing the same resource are more likely to note differences in structure or composition. Girls tend to note smells, sound and texture more than boys. An assessment task to judge how well pupils can *interpret* observations assumes that the observations are equally accessible to all pupils. However, a resource could be selected which because of the differences in what pupils consider to be noteworthy would mean that pupils were interpreting different sets of sensory data. Hence an assessment of pupils' ability to interpret would be misinformed.

Another example demonstrates the different images pupils have and how these can be reflected in the problems they chose to pursue. In the assessment of practical investigations more girls in the age 13 sample appeared not to understand some of the problems. Their behaviour often appeared random and 'off task', for example if trying to find out which of two materials was the better insulator some girls were observed dipping the material in water, blowing air through it, and even making prototype jackets of it. To understand this behaviour it was necessary to first view it as thoughtful, then to consider the context of the problem and, most importantly, to ask the pupils what the problem was as far as they were concerned.

This problem concerned human survival when stranded up a mountainside. The material was for making a jacket. The actual investigation was heavily cued to be concerned only with thermal conduction and pupils were even recommended to use cans of hot water and to lag them with the materials provided. However for some of the girls the context overrode the cued investigation and they stayed with the broader problem presented, in this case, as a motivating context. Thus it mattered how porous the material was to wind, how waterproof, and whether indeed it was suitable for making a jacket. There are at least three issues arising from this small scenario. First, if we intend to locate science problems within everyday or social settings then a broader view of what is relevant and of the range of problems that can legitimately arise needs to be understood, particularly if we wish to foster a divergent and critical approach to problem-solving. Secondly, if we change the values that underpin assessment it is important to recognise the effects of changing them in a short time-scale. At the moment such a change would disadvantage some boys. Finally, while all teachers need to focus onto specific learning opportunities the route taken to this must take account of pupils' various and different values, experiences and expectations.

A final example to demonstrate the importance of pupils' different ways of experiencing comes from classwork in four primary and secondary schools with pupils aged from 8 to 15. Several tasks were given to the pupils including designing: a boat to go round the world; a new vehicle; a learning activity for children. The pupils' designs covered a wide range but there were striking differences between girls and boys. The majority of the boats designed by primary and lower secondary boys were power boats or battleships of some kind or another. The detail the boys included varied except that the majority had elaborate weaponry and next to no living facilities. Other features included detailed mechanisms for movement, navigation and waste disposal. The girls' boats were generally cruisers with a total absence of weaponry and a great deal of detail about living quarters and requirements, including food supplies and cleaning materials (notably absent in the boys' designs). Very few of the girls' designs included any mechanistic details.

The choice of vehicle design and purpose also varied for girls and boys. Many boys chose army-type vehicles, 'secret' agent transport or sports cars. The girls mainly chose family cars for travelling, agricultural machines or children's play vehicles. The detail the pupils focused on was generally the same as before. Where boys and girls chose the same type of vehicle they still differed in their main design function. For example, the girls' pram design dealt with improving efficiency and safety. The boys' pram was computerised to allow the child to be transported without an accompanying adult.

Fourth-year pupils considered the problem of developing learning activities for young children. Overwhelmingly boys' designs were of adventure or assault courses exclusively communicated in drawings. Other designs were largely for games about numbers and shapes, often computerised. The girls focused on games, generally letter games associated with animals and colours. The majority of girls communicated their ideas in writing or by producing a prototype. No girl referred to computer games.

These very different perceptions of the same problem reflect the way girls are encouraged generally to be concerned with everyday human needs. It was noteworthy that when the pupils had to *focus on an aspect* of their designs the boys had few difficulties. The girls however remained with the larger design. If a problem is perceived to be about human needs as is the case for many girls in the examples quoted then it is not a simple matter to reject that perception and to focus on a more artificial concern, i.e. the learning of a specific subject outcome or the assessment of the same. Furthermore an ability to do this may only reflect a limited and uncritical view of problems and problem-solving strategies. All pupils will benefit if some attempt is made to relate the focus to the larger problem and to discuss individual perspectives of relevance.

Investigative or design tasks are recommended for 'naturalistic' assessment (DES, 1987). Furthermore one out of two profile components in the science curriculum orders is devoted to exploration and investigation. Consequently pupils' investigative and problem-solving skills will be formally assessed. Yet how can the responses just described be scored? The boys' and girls' problems draw on, and reflect, different aspects of their science understanding. To deal with assessment outcomes of this type it is necessary to move away from notions of a scoring scheme reflecting a 'right' answer to consideration of pupils' strategies in the light of the problems they *perceive*. Assessment of this type will not, however, produce a simple coherent view of achievement to address a summative purpose. A further concern these responses highlight is the point at which an assessment snapshot is taken. If it is at the initial point of focusing down then girls' achievement in science will be considerably under represented.

Styles of expression and achievement

Because girls have learnt to attend to the circumstances that activities are presented in means that their style of expression is often different to that of boys. The APU language surveys showed that girls choose to communicate their feelings about phenomena in extended reflective composition. Boys on the other hand when responding to the same task will provide episodic, factual and commentative detail. Depending on which subject is being assessed and the modes of expression and learning style favoured in that subject girls' and boys' performance will either be judged as 'good' or 'bad'. Thus the boys' style may well disadvantage them in the humanities or in a language assessment yet advantage them in science. It is clear that in order to fully express their achievements girls and boys need to deploy a range of modes of expression. This means that the curriculum would have to plan for this outcome and provide learning opportunities to this effect. However, this cannot happen if a national assessment system continues to reflect traditional subject-based values. Nor should the scores on profile components represent differences in style as differences in achievement on criterion-referenced tasks.

It is likely that there will be elements of self-assessment in the assessment procedures used in schools in future. Gender differences may give rise to problems in the interpretation of these assessments. For example, an ability to consider a range of issues as reflected in a typical 'girl's' learning style will appear to indicate a greater sense of self-awareness and criticism (critical issues in self-assessment) yet this may not be the case. If the record requires pupils to describe and reflect on the task they have tackled the fact that girls see tasks in much broader terms will mean that they have difficulty in describing them succinctly. This could then be interpreted as an inability to understand the task as opposed to perceiving a different task. The PRAISE study (1988) has noted similar differences between girls and boys. The effect of different learning styles can, depending on circumstances, both elevate and depress pupils' performance.

Features of tasks

The effects of experiential differences and alternative learning styles influence pupils' performance across the curriculum. Their combined effects alter both the problems tackled and the solutions sought. The nature of their influence depends a great deal on features of tasks which often have little to do with the criterion being assessed. For example it has been established that multiple choice questions in traditional examinations disadvantage girls as a group (Harding, 1979; Murphy, 1981). The general process of abstracting and focusing down on a right answer demanded in multiple choice items does reflect a 'boy's' style of thinking. Girls are far more likely to see ambiguity in the items as they will also take into account the context and content of the item. This commonly leads them either to see no right answer or to see several.

The APU science tests included multiple-choice items but of a non-traditional type and here there were no overall differences in the performance of girls and boys. There were instances where girls achieved higher scores than boys on such items. This would happen if the context favoured the girls or if what had to be abstracted were variables that girls considered noteworthy but boys had learnt to discount as irrelevant. Yet a multiple-choice item set in a physics context concerned with structural variables would have the opposite effect.

Similarly it has commonly been noted that girls are disadvantaged by practical tests. The APU Science surveys include three practical tests and yet this same effect is not apparent. Indeed girls express an equal liking for the practical observation tasks and in general achieve higher scores than boys. Scrutinising the differences in the practical tests which produced these opposite effects shows that it matters what type of question is asked and what mode of response is allowed. Girls can, and will, perform competently, and more importantly with enjoyment, in tasks where they can use their knowledge in a practical context, in an open task which allows them to determine what is relevant to the solution.

Discussion

If assessment is to address a formative purpose, i.e. inform teachers of pupils' learning difficulties and successes so that their curriculum can be planned more effectively, then gender effects in performance must be understood. Furthermore summative assessment outcomes claiming to measure what pupils have 'learnt and mastered' (DES, 1988) must not reflect gender bias if such bias misrepresents pupils' achievements.

It is commonly believed that the results of large scale surveys such as the APU Science project demonstrate levels of gender differences which when extrapolated to the classroom are next to negligible. This belief is disputed by the research findings discussed here. Gender differences in performance arise because of a multitude of interactive effects related to features of tasks and of pupils. In any one task these effects work for and against groups of pupils. Thus a multiple-choice question set in a biological context of children and nutrition may show no overall difference in the performance of girls and boys. Yet the multiple choice demand to focus down on a single, decontextualised 'right' answer will have a negative effect on some girls. While the content and context will deter some boys.

The scale of the APU Science surveys allowed some gender related task characteristics to emerge. The task characteristics are like layers of an onion, each additional layer obscuring and confounding what the task is actually measuring about pupils. Given these findings it was decided to remove the effects of the layers by setting open situations to pupils which allowed them to define the task and the solution to it. In such classroom situations it is apparent, and consistent across ages, that many girls and many boys define similar gender-related tasks and solutions. These gender alternatives usually go undetected in classrooms and assessments as one can generally only 'see' what one is looking for.

The combination of the survey results and in-depth research confirmed that there were gender differences in pupils' self-images, values and concerns. Consequently when making sense of the world pupils accord significance to different issues, and aspects of sensory input and information generally. The overall effects can be summarised in the contextualised responses of girls and the decontextualised responses of boys.

The insights gained led to a reconsideration of some of the survey results. For example, there were no significant overall differences between girls and boys in the observation tests in terms of the criteria being assessed. Yet when tasks were selected which spanned the assessment criteria but which required pupils to observe particular variables such as colour, feel, smell and sound then significant gender differences in favour of the girls were apparent. Similar groups of tasks which favoured boys could also be detected. Revisiting the banks of questions in the light of hypothesised gender differences has allowed profiles of tasks to be posited which would disadvantage girls and boys. On the basis of these profiles of 'hostile' task characteristics it is possible to identify benign characteristics. Given present understanding a benign task would focus on use of knowledge rather than abstract explanations, would have a practical context but not be overtly scientific in terms of equipment and instrumentation, be open in as much as it allows pupils to determine relevance by testing out and rejecting their own hypotheses in the light of the data they collect. In such tasks the pupils can feel ownership of the problem. To be open in this way there must be potential for action in operation and response. Finally pupils need to talk about what they do and what they find out.

Clearly there is much more to be identified about the sources of gender differences in assessment tasks. One cannot assume that similar overall task performance for girls and boys means that gender effects are not in operation. For formative assessment it is crucial to continue to explore how gender effects operate so that in the same classroom, following the same curriculum groups of pupils' experiences are markedly different. The introduction of a national curriculum, accompanied by teacher assessment, provides a golden opportunity for putting the issue of gender high up on the agenda.

References

Chodorow, N. (1978) *The Reproduction of Mothering*. Berkley, CA: University of California Press.

Cohen, R. (1986) *A match or not a match: A study of intermediate science teaching materials in Forum 86*. The Science Curriculum NFSS.

Culley, L. (1988) 'Girls, Boys and Computers', *Educational Studies*, 14, 1, pp. 3–8.

DES (1988) *Task Groups on Assessment and Testing: a report*. London: DES.

DES (1988) *Science in Schools Age 15: Review Report*. London: DES.

DES (1989a) *Science in Schools Age 11: Review Report*. London: DES.

DES (1989b) *Science in Schools Age 13: Review Report*. London: DES.

Dweck, C. S., Davidson, W., Nelson, S. and Enna, B. (1978) 'Sex Differences in Learned Helplessness: The Contingencies of Evaluative Feedback in the Classroom', *Development Psychology*, 14, pp. 268–76.

Goddard-Spear, M. (1983) Sex Bias in Science Teachers' Ratings of Work and Pupil Characteristics in Contributions to the Second GASAT Conference, Oslo, Norway.

Harding, J. (1979) 'Sex Differences in Performance in Examinations at 16+', *Physics Education*, 14, pp. 280–84.

Harding, J. (1985) Values Cognitive Style and the Curriculum in Contributions to the Third GASAT Conference, A.S.E. Hatfield, England.

Hyde, J. (1981) 'How Large are Cognitive Gender Differences', *American Psychologist*, 36, 8, pp. 892–90.

Johnson, S. and Murphy, P. (1986) Girls and Physics: Reflection on APU Survey Findings. London: APU.

Mallow, J. V. (1987) 'Science Anxiety', *College Physics*. New York: Worth Publications.

Murphy, R. (1981) 'Sex differences in Objective Test Performance', *British Journal of Educational Psychology*, 51, pp. 1–9.

NCC (1988) National Curriculum Consultation Report, Science. London: DES.
PRAISE (The Pilot Records of Achievement in Schools Evaluation team) (1988) 'Records of Achievement: Report of the National Evaluation of Pilot Schemes', Report Submitted to the Department of Education and Science and the Welsh Office. London: HMSO.
Randall, G. J. (1987) 'Gender Differences in Pupil–Teacher Interacted in Workshops and Laboratories in Gender under Scrutiny: New Enquiries in Education'. London: Hutchinson Open University.
Rosenthal, R. and Rubin, D. (1982) 'Further Meta-analytic Procedures for Assessing Cognitive Gender Differences', *Journal of Educational Psychology*, 74, 5, pp. 708–12.
Whyte, J. (1981) 'Observing Sex Stereotypes and Interactions in the School Lab and Workshop', *Educational Review*, 36, pp. 75–86.

Index